Audience Response Systems in Higher Education:
Applications and Cases

David A. Banks
University of South Australia, Australia

 Information Science Publishing

Hershey • London • Melbourne • Singapore

Acquisitions Editor:	Michelle Potter
Development Editor:	Kristin Roth
Senior Managing Editor:	Amanda Appicello
Managing Editor:	Jennifer Neidig
Copy Editor:	Angela Thor
Typesetter:	Cindy Consonery
Cover Design:	Lisa Tosheff
Printed at:	Yurchak Printing Inc.

Published in the United States of America by
      Information Science Publishing (an imprint of Idea Group Inc.)
      701 E. Chocolate Avenue
      Hershey PA 17033
      Tel: 717-533-8845
      Fax: 717-533-8661
      E-mail: cust@idea-group.com
      Web site: http://www.idea-group.com

and in the United Kingdom by
      Information Science Publishing (an imprint of Idea Group Inc.)
      3 Henrietta Street
      Covent Garden
      London WC2E 8LU
      Tel: 44 20 7240 0856
      Fax: 44 20 7379 0609
      Web site: http://www.eurospanonline.com

Library of Congress Cataloging-in-Publication Data
Audience response systems in higher education : applications and cases / David A. Banks, editor.
   p. cm.
  Summary: "This book discusses the importance of creating Audience Response Systems (ARS) to facilitate greater interaction with participants engaged in a variety of group activities, particularly education"—Provided by publisher.
  Includes bibliographical references and index.
  ISBN 1-59140-947-0 — ISBN 1-59140-948-9 (softcover) — ISBN 1-59140-949-7 (ebook)
  1. Education, Higher—Computer-assisted instruction. 2. Teaching—Aids and devices. 3. Communication in education. I. Banks, David A., 1948-
  LB2395.7.B319 2006
  378.1'734—dc22
                                      2006002658

British Cataloguing in Publication Data
A Cataloguing in Publication record for this book is available from the British Library.

All work contributed to this book is new, previously-unpublished material. The views expressed in this book are those of the authors, but not necessarily of the publisher.

Audience Response Systems in Higher Education:
Applications and Cases

Table of Contents

Section II

Preface

Audience response systems (ARS) comprise hardware and software that is used in conjunction with face-to-face educational processes to support, deepen, and enhance learning by promoting greater interaction between all those engaged in a learning activity. The price of the systems has fallen dramatically over the past 10 years, and they offer a low-cost investment that has the potential to significantly improve face-to-face teaching and learning. They can be used with small or large groups, and can easily be set up for a single one-off session, or established as permanent installations.

The overt aspects of interaction are achieved by means of a feedback loop in which a question is asked, or an issue is raised (Figure 1). The question is typically displayed via PowerPoint slides. Each participant indicates their response from a set of options provided on the slide by using a personal data entry device to transmit one or more digits to a receiver attached to a computer. The input device may be a simple numeric keypad, sometimes referred to as a "clicker" or "zapper," or a full-text entry device such as a laptop computer, personal digital assistant (PDA), or mobile phone. The ARS software on the computer then processes the acquired data and displays the resulting transformed data on a public screen via a data projector. It is possible, and in many cases desirable, to insert a nontechnology-supported discussion activity between the raising of a question and the entry of responses.

The process can be used to encourage responses from all participants, and these responses can be anonymous. For students who are shy or from some cultures where "loss of face" is a significant issue, the anonymity afforded by an ARS can provide an opportunity for them to participate without fear of ridicule, should they volunteer an incorrect response. Students are also provided with the opportunity to see how other members of the group view the issue, and are thus able to gauge their own level of understanding relative to the whole group. In some cases there may be a single "right" answer, and this allows summative assessment to take place, if required. In many other cases there will be no single "right" answer, and in this situation, the collected data can be used as a trigger for discussion, that is, for a formative development process.

Figure 1. The ARS outline process

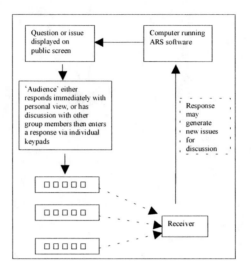

Figure 2. A typical keypad, slightly larger than a credit card (image courtesy of KEEpad Pty)[1]

Although it can be argued that the word "audience" may not be the best word that could be used to describe these systems in the context of education, it has been used in the title of this book for the pragmatic reason that this will obtain the greatest number of "hits" when an internet search is carried out by readers wishing to find more information. Five years ago, the systems would typically have been found under the headings of group decision support systems (GDSS) or group process support systems (GPSS), and these still provide rich and significant areas of literature to support the application of these systems. The nomenclature used to describe these systems is still evolving, and they can be found variously described as classroom response systems, electronic voting systems, or simply by their product name.

The word "audience," coupled with the use of this technology in such popular game shows as "Who Wants to be a Millionaire," can suggest a relatively passive, or at best, intermittently-involved group of participants, but the key aim of the technology in educational settings is to turn potential passivity into dynamic interaction. The technology itself cannot achieve this, of course. Only when such technology is carefully embedded within designed human processes can significant gains be made in the overall process. This suggests that the users of the technology need to have a clear idea of why they are using the technology, and how it can be used effectively within broader educational structures and processes. The technology, in itself, does not offer some wonderful new "magic bullet" that will offer learning gains simply by its adoption. It can certainly provide novelty and fun for all participants, but must be used within the context of the teaching and learning process for its full promise to be achieved.

In the context of education, the "systems" aspect of the phrase should be taken, as for all information systems, as meaning that the technology is simply part of an overall learning system that has as its actors the academic and support staff, and the learners, and is situated within an educational environment. The instant feedback provided by the technology allows the learning facilitator to identify problem areas, and immediately revisit areas where there is evidence of lack of understanding. Prior knowledge can be explored when a course first starts, so that the risk of boring students who may already have a grasp of the basic subject material can be avoided. The feedback can also allow adjustment of pacing as easily. In cases where the feedback indicates that some ideas are quickly assimilated, the pacing of the course can be adjusted so that more time can be spent on more problematic areas.

These systems have been, and still are, used in business, as well as at all levels of training and education. The words "higher education" appear in the title of the book to manage the scope of the publication. This does not mean that the approaches detailed by the authors of the chapters cannot be applied in other settings, and some authors have extended the boundary of "higher education" into K-12, and into conference and consultancy areas. Even though the cost of these systems has been constantly dropping in the past 5 years, there will still be a need to justify the purchase in an educational environment where competition for scarce resources is increasingly problematic. The possibility for extended use of these systems to support public relations' exercises, links to K-12 for recruitment support, and for consultancy opportunities with the business world may help build a stronger case for procurement.

From my own perspective, I found it frustrating that although there was a considerable body of literature relating to these systems, it was scattered throughout a wide range of journals, books, and collections of conference papers. My aim in editing this book was to bring together, into a single collection, the work of a number of authors who have been involved with the development of these systems, are currently using the systems, or who are extending the underlying theory or technology. Chapters range across articulation of the history and development of these systems, discussion of educational theories that appear to be appropriate for their use, and cases illustrating current examples of their use in practice. The subject areas illustrated in this book include law, engineering, computing, medicine, physics, mathematics, and psychology. There is no reason to prevent the systems from being used to support art, history, or philosophy, or any other subject area. This is an exciting area to work in, and there are important lessons to be learned by looking at the work of those people who have been involved in the development and application of these systems. Some of the authors in this book have a long history of involvement with these systems, while others are only just starting the journey. All adopters of these systems seem to go through a similar development process, and this means that considerable "reinvention of the wheel" has taken place. It is hoped that this book will not only prompt more educators to explore these systems, but also help reduce the need for reinvention and allow ideas to be shared so that both teaching and further research can be encouraged in this field.

The book is organized into three main parts, or themes, although there is some overlap between them. The first part (Chapters I to IV) provides some historical context from the perspective of individuals who have been involved with Audience Response Systems for a considerable period of time. The midsection of the book (Chapters V to XX) provides practical cases in a variety of subjects, interleaved with discussions of aspects of pedagogy associated with the application of these systems in educational settings. The final part of the book (Chapters XXI to XXIV) outlines some of the directions that the technological components of these systems may take in the future. I have used the final chapter to outline some of my own work, to draw together the key themes in the book, and to suggest possible directions for the future. A brief description of each chapter follows.

Section I

Chapter I: *A Brief History of Networked Classrooms: Effects, Cases, Pedagogy, and Implications*, by Louis Abrahamson of The Better Education Foundation. This chapter poses the question "for an idea apparently more than forty years old, why did it take this long to happen?" It provides a brief history of early response systems, and draws upon the author's experience to outline hardware development, and some of the pedagogic challenges and successes. It concludes with a positive and enthusiastic view of the future of these types of educational support systems.

Chapter II: *Audience Response Systems: Insipid Contrivances or Inspiring Tools?* by Eugene Judson of Arizona State University and Daiyo Sawada of the University of Alberta. This chapter also provides some historical material, and then goes on to take a critical view of the value of these systems in terms of their impact on student achievement, the overall benefits that may be obtained, and the impact on pedagogy for ARS to be used effectively. They suggest that one powerful way forward is to consider the deliberate formation of learning communities.

Chapter III: *The Use and Evolution of an Audience Response System*, by Ray A. Burnstein and Leon M. Lederman of Illinois Institute of Technology (IIS), Chicago, reports on 10 years of development of wireless ARS at IIS from the spring semester in 1994 with an elementary physics class. Approaches to developing ARS questions built on Bloom's Taxonomy are presented, and they explore a multiple-choice category identified as "partially-correct multiple choice" that supports the higher levels of the Taxonomy. Several limitations to the use of ARS are presented and some thought offered on ways that academics can be helped in their adoption of these systems.

Chapter IV: *ARS Evolution: Reflections and Recommendations*, by Harold M. Horowitz of Socratec, Inc. This chapter documents the more technical aspects of the development of ARS from work carried out by the author at the IBM Management Development Center in the mid-1980s through to several recent commercial systems. He notes that an infrared transmitter today costs less than 10% of a similar device a decade earlier. He finally offers 10 pragmatic tips, based on his many years of experience with these systems, for the effective use of these systems.

Section II

Chapter V: *Practical Lessons from Four Years of Using an ARS in Every Lecture of a Large Class*, by Quintin I. Cutts of the University of Glasgow in the UK, reports on the introduction and extensive use of an ARS in an introductory computing class. He stresses the need for, and great value of, the sharing of logistical and pedagogical ideas among the staff at his university. Unlike many adopters who introduce the use of an ARS in a rather piecemeal way, he outlines a much more sweeping introduction. The chapter shares many practical insights involved in the complex process of adapting existing courses for use with an ARS.

Chapter VI: *Using an Audience Response System to Enhance Student Engagement in Large Group Orientation: A Law Faculty Case Study*, by Sally Kift of the Faculty of Law at Queensland University of Technology, explores the application of an ARS to help a large and diverse cohort of students who are faced with transition between disciplines, or at their first entry point to the university. This is a stressful time for students and traditional orientation processes, and Kift puts forward a persuasive case that suggests that an ARS can offer significant benefits at this critical transition point.

Chapter VII: *Question Driven Instruction: Teaching Science (Well) with an Audience Response System*, by Ian D. Beatty, William J. Leonard, William J. Gerace, and Robert J. Dufresne of the Physics Education Research Group at the University of Massachusetts, explores Question Driven Instruction, a pedagogic approach that focuses specifically upon teaching that is supported by an ARS. The chapter is a blend of theory and practice, and illustrates how an ARS can be used to encourage and support deep learning. They advocate ARS-mediated activity as a primary course design goal, rather than an approach that uses an ARS as an occasional adjunct to traditional practice. They acknowledge that using new teaching techniques can be difficult or threatening, and offer their experiences in approaches to support new adopters.

Chapter VIII: *Anonymous Polling in an Engineering Tutorial Environment: A Case Study*, by Steven M. Durbin and Kristi A. Durbin of the University of Canterbury in New Zealand, provides a case study examining the introduction of an ARS to a second-year introductory-level engineering tutorial. The ARS was introduced in response to problems created by poor attendance at tutorials due to changes in the profile of the student population. It was felt that increasing student participation, and adopting both visual and verbal approaches, would help to alleviate this problem. The new approach was well received, and several other departments are exploring the technology.

Chapter IX: *Using Audience Response Aystems to Develop Critical Thinking Skills*, by Robert Webking of the Department of Political Science at the University of Texas and Felix Valenzuela of the Yale Law School, discusses the introduction of an ARS to political science classes at the University of Texas at El Paso. The chapter explores a number of issues related to active participation, and the place of anonymity in the process. They strongly feel that the introduction of an ARS has improved the level and quality of student engagement in a variety of class sizes, and has contributed positively to the development or enhancement of critical analysis skills.

Chapter X: *Using the Personal Response System to Enhance Student Learning: Some Evidence from Teaching Economics*, by Kevin Hinde and Andrew Hunt of the University of Durham, examines the extensive use of an ARS with introductory economics students to support the building of classroom communities, to promote deeper questioning, and as a feedback mechanism to inform the teaching process. The system was introduced partly in response to the need to improve face-to-face learning in the light of both increasing class sizes and shifts in the expectations of recent student cohorts. They provide discussion of data from a questionnaire administered to 219 students who had used the ARS.

Chapter XI: *Evaluating Electronic Voting Systems in Lectures: Two Innovative Methods*, by Gregor E. Kennedy of the Biomedical Multimedia Unit at the University of Melbourne, and Quintin I. Cutts and Stephen W. Draper of the University of Glasgow, departments of Computing Science and Psychology respectively, focuses upon observation and audit trails as tools for evaluating students' and teachers' perceptions of Electronic Voting Systems. They have developed an observational coding schema, and present the results of their observational work. Their second approach examines ways of dealing with the wealth of rather messy data that is generated during the use of these electronic systems, so that it can be used to support auditing to provide insights to the process under consideration.

Chapter XII: *Selected and Constructed Response Systems in Mathematics Classrooms,* by Leslee Francis Pelton and Timothy W. Pelton of the University of Victoria, Canada, discusses their use of audience response technologies to support the teaching of mathematics. They differentiate between the typical keypad systems that allow participants to choose from a menu of predetermined options (selected response) and systems which allow participants to construct their own responses, which are entered onto a handheld computer (constructed response). They provide details of their use of both types of systems in practical classroom settings.

Chapter XIII: *Theorizing the Transformed Classroom: Sociocultural Interpretation of the Effects of Audience Response Systems in Higher Education*, by William R. Penuel (SRI International, USA), Louis Abrahamson (Better Education Foundation, USA), and Jeremy Roschelle (SRI International, USA), develops a theoretical framework to support exploration of the use of ARS in classroom settings. They note the importance of helping students to identify misconceptions as a vital step in development of deeper learning. Such approaches can be challenging for staff and students alike, and the chapter considers how the idea of classroom communities based on mutual trust may help in providing an appropriate basis for improved ARS-mediated learning environments.

Chapter XIV: *Wireless Interactive Teaching by Using Keypad-Based ARS*, by Jiankun Hu, Peter Bertok, Margaret Hamilton, Graeme White, and Anita Duff of RMIT University in Melbourne and Quintin Cutts of the University of Glasgow, brings in their experiences in the use of ARS, particularly with students from a variety of cultural backgrounds. They present two cases, the first being a fairly concrete programming-oriented course with a rich mix of cultures; the second case being a broadcast network engineering course with more abstract concepts, again with a high percentage of students with a non-English speaking background. The chapter also considers practical implementation issues, and closes with some future plans.

Chapter XV: *The Audience Response System: A New Resource in Medical Education*, by Vivienne O'Connor, Michele Groves and Sandy Minck of the University of Queensland, shows how ARS have been adopted as part of the response to increases in various demands in medical education, as the educational mode shifts from a traditional teacher-centric model towards a learner-centred interactive model. Building from a problem-based learning model, they explain how an ARS can be used in conjunction with large-group clinical symposia to explore such issues as misinformation, clinical reasoning, and medical errors. The chapter presents data from a year-end survey, along with comments from students.

Chapter XVI: *Learning and Anxiety: Exploring Individual Judgement Processes in a Learning Environment with a Group Support System*, by Sam Groves, Tony Gear, Cath Jones, and Michael Connolly of the University of Glamorgan, and Martin Read of the University of Portsmouth, shows how an understanding of group support processes can coupled with appropriate use of an ARS to reduce the social influences that may inhibit a group from arriving at desired outcomes. They argue that the use of an ARS can help to provide a safe environment within which effective communication and shared meaning can be achieved. They provide a brief educational case, and then identify a range of other activities that an ARS can support.

Chapter XVII: *The Trial of an Audience Response System to Facilitate Problem-Based Learning in Legal Education*, by Kelley Burton of the School of Law at Queensland University of Technology in Brisbane, provides a case-based perspective on the trial of an ARS to support a core second-year undergraduate law subject. The trial involved 140 full-time and 40 part-time students, and was based around a case study involving a specific legal issue. A problem-based learning approach is used, and the task is of a formative nature. A survey of the students was undertaken using the ARS and the feedback was strongly positive, but the author acknowledges that this may be due to the novelty of the approach, and further studies are needed.

Chapter XVIII: *Live Assessment by Questioning in an Interactive Classroom*, by Michael McCabe of the Department of Mathematics at the University of Portsmouth, UK. This chapter builds on the analogy of popular TV quiz shows, and provides a wide range of interesting and practical ideas for the use of ARS in the classroom. He notes the problem of the unpredictability of students' responses, and stresses the need for a lecturer to develop the skill to utilise the technology effectively, and to be able to respond in flexible and "unscripted" ways to the flow of the process. He also stresses the importance of pedagogy driving the development of the technology rather than the other way round.

Chapter XIX: *Eight Years of Asking Questions*, by Jim Boyle of the University of Strathclyde, reflects on the experiences of the Department of Electrical Engineering in their attempts to remedy declining class attendance through the development of an interactive classroom. The technology was only one part of the project, considerable thought being given to the whole learning experience. In addition to the introduction of an ARS, attention has been paid to Peer Instruction, Problem-Based Learning, and Studio Teaching, along with revised curricula. The latter part of the chapter presents the lessons that have been learned from their experiences, and looks forward to future developments.

Chapter XX: *Interactive Response Systems in Higher Education*, by Mick Wood of the Learning Development Unit at the University of Central Lancashire, provides a view through the eyes of a multimedia development officer. He details the procurement process and some of the technical issues that needed to be addressed to implement the chosen system. The chapter indicates the type of support services that need to be provided for these systems to be brought into operation and maintained. The chapter provides details of how the system is being used to support e-marketing and physiology modules, and also a conference application.

Section III

Chapter XXI: *CommuniCubes: Intermediate Technology for Interaction with Student Groups*, by Stephen J. Bostock, Julie A. Hulme, and Mark A. Davys of Keele University, provides details of a nonelectronic approach that can be used in both large lecture theatres and small seminar rooms. The chapter makes the point that if the learning design is well thought through, it is possible to make use of quite simple "technology." This technology has the added benefit that a Braille version could be used with blind students, providing greater opportunities for disadvantaged students. Details of the use of CommuniCubes with 120 first-year psychology students in lecture,s and with smaller groups of law students are presented.

Chapter XXII: *Creating a Constructed Response System to Support Active Learning*, by Tim Pelton and Leslee Francis Pelton of the University of Victoria, Canada, outlines the development of a prototype classroom interaction system that utilises handheld computers that participants use to communicate with a laptop computer managed by the learning facilitator. The handheld computers enable students to produce images that can be shared via the central laptop computer. After a short training time, students became proficient and had a positive response to the system. The prototype is non-commercial, and the authors encourage broader participation in the ongoing development.

Chapter XXIII: *Instructor Mobile Audience Response System*, by Jay Dominick and Anne Bishop of Wake Forest University, USA, describes an ARS in which the instructor has a PocketPC wireless linked to the students, thus allowing freedom to roam and work with small student groups in a lecture theatre. The instructor device can access the lecture theatre computer and remotely manage data that appears on the public screen. The authors present the view that this freedom to roam allows instructors to operate in their natural classroom style without the need to return to a fixed computer. Pilot projects using the system with physics, chemistry, sociology, and mathematics are briefly presented.

Chapter XXIV: *Using Mobile Phones and PDAs in Ad-Hoc Audience Response Systems*, by Matt Jones of the University of Waikato, New Zealand, and Gary Marsden and Dominic Gruijters of the University of Cape Town, South Africa, explains their novel use of mobile phones as ad hoc audience response systems. Unlike many of us who ask for mobile phones to be turned off when we start sessions, these authors request that phones be turned on! The pilot study system is described, and applications to first-year programming and human-computer interaction classes are presented. The latter part of the chapter explores the use of PDAs and advanced mobile phones.

Chapter XXV: *Reflections on the Use of ARS with Small Groups*, by David A. Banks of the University of South Australia, focuses on the use of ARS with groups of between 5 and 50 students to support presentation feedback, peer review, course evaluation processes, as well as some group activities, to support a process-oriented Masters course. Three brands of ARS have been used to support this work, and the use of a larger electronic meeting system is also outlined to indicate the value of text entry systems: some comparisons being drawn between the various systems.

Endnotes

[1] http://www.keepad.com

*   All chapters in this book have been subjected to review by at least two reviewers. The authors were not advised of the names of the reviewers, and the reviewers were not advised of the names of the authors.

Acknowledgments

I wish to acknowledge the help of all involved in the process of bringing this book from a feeling that there was a need for a book in this field, through to a tangible product. The support and flexibility of the publishing team at Idea Group Inc. (IGI) has been invaluable in guiding, prompting, and dealing with problems in a very positive and timely manner. Particular thanks go to Medhi Khosrow-Pour, Jan Travers, Michele Rossi, Renée Davies, and Kristin Roth at IGI for their very professional and helpful approach.

My sincere thanks go to the many contributors who made this book possible. Not only did they write the chapters, but many of them also served as domain-specific reviewers for one or more chapters. I must also offer special thanks to those contributors whose supportive and encouraging e-mails and phone calls convinced me that this was a valuable project to work on.

Other constructive and insightful reviews were provided by "volunteers" who provided the perspective of educators who have not (yet!) been involved in ARS activity, but who are all very experienced in the higher education sector. My thanks go to the following individuals for taking on the role of reviewer of at least one chapter:

Judi Baron, University of Adelaide, Australia

Renay Buchanan, Central Queensland University

Stephen Burgess, University of Victoria, Australia

Allan Carrington, University of Adelaide, Australia

Bill Dempster, University of Strathclyde, UK

Don Falconer, University of South Australia

Brenton Fiedler, University of South Australia

Kay Fielden, UNITEC, New Zealand

Michael Gendron, Central Connecticut State University, USA

Jim Gotaas, University of Central Lancashire, UK

Tom Gray, University of Strathclyde, UK

Robert Hamilton, University of Strathclyde, UK

Jo Hanisch, University of South Australia

Chris Johnson, University of Arizona, USA

Ann Monday, University of South Australia

Chris Stewart, University of South Australia

Shirley Wheeler, University of South Australia

Graeme White, RMIT University, Melbourne, Australia

Trevor Wood-Harper, University of Manchester, UK

Not only did Jim Boyle contribute and review, he also managed to convince some of his colleagues to take part in the review process, so special thanks to him. Thanks also go to Kay Fielden for helping identify ARS users in New Zealand, and to Renay Buchanan for helping identify Australian contributors.

Thanks go to Fran Benson of IML UK for providing some leads to potential authors in the UK, and to Sally Bateman of KEEpad Australia for suggesting potential Australian contributors.

I must acknowledge the efforts of those individuals who worked hard to make a contribution to the book, but were unable to complete the process due to personal or work circumstances. I hope that we may be able to work together in the future, should the opportunity arise.

This process does not take place in a vacuum, and I must thank Maureen and Magnus, my ever helpful neighbours, for inviting me in for mind-saving cups of coffee and a change of subject when they saw me wandering around at those times when I could not face the screen any more.

And last, but certainly by no means least, I must thank my partner, Ann, for her patience and support, particularly at those (extensive) times when piles of papers threatened to swamp every available surface.

Section I

Chapter I

A Brief History of Networked Classrooms:
Effects, Cases, Pedagogy, and Implications

Louis Abrahamson, The Better Education Foundation, USA

Abstract

The objective of this chapter is to explain the huge, burgeoning sense of excitement surrounding response systems, and more generally, networked classrooms today. Also why, for an idea apparently more than 40 years old, it took this long to happen! Beginning with a brief history of early response systems, it takes up the story from the author's own experience, leading through hardware barriers, misconceptions about pedagogy, and classroom successes, to summarize the variety of uses, and how they lead to improved teaching and learning. It then discusses why this is such a potentially important area of study for improving education, and finally goes on to describe the emerging characteristics of, and rationale for, more powerful types of modern systems.

Introduction

Today, at almost every university in the USA, somewhere a faculty member in at least one discipline is using a response system in their teaching. This is a phenomenon that has mushroomed to its present stage, mainly within the past three years, from a mere handful of pioneering educators a decade ago. Also, the revolution appears not to be limited to higher education. A cursory Web search, conducted in early 2005, found names of over 3,000 school buildings at the primary and secondary levels in the USA also using response systems. On the technology front, a brief survey showed 12 manufacturers of networked classroom systems,[1] compared with one or two a little more than a decade ago.

Amazingly, these generally somewhat primitive tools are used in just about every discipline taught. An example from the author's own experience: in the process of inquiring about response system usage at the University of Texas at Austin[2] for a letter of recommendation, I was told that response systems were being used that semester in over 10 disciplines, including physics, chemistry, psychology, biology, mathematics, criminal justice, computer science, library science, pharmacy, and physical education.

In education, few things happen this fast or with such endemic impact. Arguably, not since the overhead projector, has a piece of technology received such widespread acceptance as an aid to classroom teaching. The purpose of this chapter is to give some of the history behind this apparently sudden success story, and also to introduce the work described in this volume by giving some of the practical and theoretical background upon which the success has been based.

Personal Background

It is a salutary exercise for me, because I have spent a good deal of the past 20 years working with some of the predecessors of today's response systems, as well as some more advanced networked classrooms, and have firsthand experience of the history and difficulties behind the current successes. I also believe there is an excellent case to be made that current response systems represent only the first, humble step in an exciting, but as yet little explored territory of pedagogical tools that have the power to transform teaching and learning in formal education.

My interest in networked classrooms began almost by accident. From an education in physics and applied mathematics, I was 18 years into a career in aerospace[3] and managing my own research company when, in 1985, we had a small amount of unbudgeted overhead money that needed to be spent during that year. Within certain limits, as specified on government CPFF[4] contracts, the choice on how to spend it was mine, so I decided to use it to pursue an old dream of improving teaching. With two colleagues (Fred Hartline & Milton Fabert) we built the first prototype of a series of systems known as Classtalk. Classtalk I was a response system constructed of surplus (i.e., junk) Atari keypads, each modified to include an additional communication circuit board, an LED display, and connected to the teacher's computer by a special-purpose digital multiplexer. Our main test system was installed in a large lecture hall (seating 200 students) at Christopher Newport University,[5] where it was used for teaching physics. After a couple of years of use, at the end of every semester, we took surveys of the students. Almost 90% of the students said they understood the subject better, came to class better prepared, paid more attention in classes, and enjoyed it more (Abrahamson, 1999, 2000). The professor (Dr. George Webb) said that the entire atmosphere in his class had changed; that it had become a much more lively, active, and friendly place. He found that weaker students, who would previously have dropped his course, would stay in to risk taking a "D" because they were enjoying it. He also found that the feedback he obtained from the system improved his teaching, and he could engage their interest and thinking in ways that were not possible before (Abrahamson, 1995).

An Early History of Response Systems and Learning Results

The idea of using an electronic system in a classroom for gathering and aggregating student answers to questions has been around for almost 40 years. But it is not a story of steady growth and success. Rather, it is one of pioneering efforts, followed by failure, with subsequent reinvention by others who (at least initially) had no knowledge of the prior work. The first systems actually built and used appear to be those installed in a lecture hall at Stanford University in 1966, and another at Cornell University about 1968 (Littauer, 1972). There are also descriptions of German and Japanese patents about this same period, but it is not known if working versions of these systems were ever built. Details of the construction of the Stanford and Cornell systems are not available today, but some idea of the technological difficulty of implementing such systems in the premicroprocessor prenetwork age can be inferred from verbal reports of early users of the Stanford system (Linn, 2004) who said that it either "never worked," or "was a total pain to use." Some insights into the limitations of the technology of the day can be gained from the patent descriptions, one of which details, for example, a maze of wiring, analogue electronics, and aggregation represented by four voltmeters on the teacher's podium, each voltmeter dial representing the number of students selecting a particular answer to a multiple choice question. The Cornell system seems to have been more successful, perhaps because it was the brainchild of the same physicist, Raphael Littauer, who actually taught with the system and who seems to be the first person reporting positive classroom experiences from response system use.

In their recent paper, Judson and Sawada (2002) give probably the best summary to date of early work on response systems, some of which they report stemmed from research by the military on training techniques. They state that in every one of these early test cases student attitudes towards use of response systems in university lectures was uniformly positive (Bapst, 1971; Brown, 1972; Casanova, 1971; Garg, 1975; Littauer, 1972). However, they also quote early results from Bapst (1971), Bessler (1969), Bessler and Nisbet (1971), Brown (1972), and Casanova (1971), showing no gains in student achievement from the use of response systems.

Two Lucky Accidents

Had my colleagues and I known of these results before starting our experiments, we would likely never have built a system at all, or gone to the trouble of wiring it into a lecture hall. But, perhaps fortunately, coming from a background outside of education research, we were unaware of them at the time of our work with Classtalk I. We were also the unwitting beneficiaries of two lucky accidents. The first was that (due to cost) we had only 64 keypads in a lecture hall that seated 200 students. So, we designed the software to accept answers from (up to) four students at each keypad, which could be passed between them. Because of the limited two-meter length of the hardwired cord, students formed natural groups, and began conversing with each other: something not usually natural in this commuter school where few students know each other.

The second accident was the pedagogical orientation of the professor. At the time he began using the system, George Webb was a Dean at the university, and had taught the same introductory physics course for over 15 years. He not only knew the material like the back of his hand, but despite his other duties, chose to continue teaching because he enjoyed it. The system gave him the opportunity to try out pedagogical ideas, and he was secure enough, both in his knowledge of the material and his professional circumstances, to risk failure. From our observations of early semiembarrassing lecture periods, and from his own reports, both were important, because even using the system every single lecture, he appeared to be still improving with his new teaching methods after three semesters.

Perhaps had George Webb known of other people's failures a decade and half before, there is a possibility he may not have stuck with it. However, in retrospect, I feel this possibility is remote because even after a couple of weeks, he expressed a sense a huge potential. It would also be naïve to think that he was unaware of the significant differences between his approach and underlying philosophy to that which commonly existed in education a decade before when the earlier tests had been conducted. For example, the idea of students speaking to each other carried little utility in an educational world governed by behaviorist dogma, but he encouraged it in his lectures, and it worked naturally because the short cords encouraged students to form groups. Interestingly, these groups tended to stay together lecture after lecture, even meeting to study together out of lectures. His questions, and those of his colleague (Professor Randy Caton) who taught a more advanced physics course using the system, covered a range of pedagogical purposes. For example, on introducing a new topic, he would often very carefully choose a question that had an obvious answer based on everyday nonphysicist thinking, but which was invalid. When over 90% of the class chose this answer and found out that they were all wrong, they suddenly became interested and were more than ready to listen to the first part of the lecture. Often, George would do an experiment in class, but ask a question before to have students predict the result. With the aid of unconventional props (on one occasion I recall a crash helmet & goggles) he would try to trick the class into making a wrong prediction. Such questions were intended to motivate and elicit exploratory initial thinking. Subsequent questions were designed to focus attention on specific processes, usually requiring solution of a problem. Next, larger conceptual issues would be addressed to test understanding of the necessary concepts, and the ability to generalize from a specific case to another area or general principle.

One of the missing elements in this early work was the comparative measurements of student achievement. Attempts to do comparisons with student achievement from prior years were confounded by the fact that fewer students than before now dropped the course. It is my belief, though, that even if we had been able to obtain such data, doubt and skepticism would still have been a common reaction.

Roots of Doubt and Skepticism

A few years ago, a celebrated set of sayings made the rounds on the Internet.[6] These were interesting because they revealed misconceptions about technologies which later became commonplace. These ideas were so thoroughly wrong, and often made by people who should obviously have known better, that today they provoke mirth. Yet, at the time when they were made, one can imagine newspaper reporters and informed readers nodded their heads seriously and accepting these supposedly wise opinions.

In the mid-1980s, when I first became involved in prototyping and testing the first version of Classtalk, I received many comments about the dangers of a computer network in classrooms. With 1984 and George Orwell in people's minds, "Big Brother" was a common appellation. This thinking came from the idea that teachers would use the power of a networked classroom system to constantly watch over, and perhaps to even intimidate and harass students. Although these comments were made by experienced educators, their predictions did not come true, and a few years on, after the classroom successes were becoming too obvious to refute, only one teacher to my knowledge had approached the Orwellian prediction. Before discussing this, it is appropriate to ask why the big brother prediction tends not to happen. Although it is an area where more research is needed, the answer appears to be that in most educational situations, aggressive surveillance poses penalties for the instructor in terms of student attitude, reduced student motivation, and unpleasant classroom atmosphere. These are strong disincentives and they seem to self-correct bad situations. The case of the early teacher — a psychology professor — probably explains it. For reasons best known to himself at the time, he forbad talking in his classes, and to enforce his rule, separated the 30 students out in all directions across the 200 seat lecture hall. Every class period, he asked a large number of factual recall questions and terminology definitions which the students were supposed to know. As a result, they hated the subject, the system, and him. For this unfortunate professor, the problem was self-correcting. Many students dropped his class early on, and those who remained gave him low evaluations at the end of the semester. The professor, whereupon, reported back that the system, "was not for him," and discontinued its use.

Much later, with coresearchers at the Ohio State University (Owens et al., 2004), in work with high school teachers and more advanced systems, we uncovered a more powerful explanation for the absence of Orwellian worlds in networked classrooms. That is, the data itself coming from the system appears to lead teachers to question their pedagogical strategies, and to discover better ways to teach. For example, a high school teacher reported:

... when I first started using Navigator I thought it was kind of a self-contained device that would give what I needed ... with myself in a bubble of just that technology. That's where I was when I first started. ... my perception was I could stand behind the desk, watch the answers coming in. Look at the teacher console and get what I needed and then look at the results of class and get what I need and give them what they need. Well, it didn't turn out that way! .... I had very strict rules about not talking. ... I didn't want the answers or the results skewed. ... That has come full circle and now I want them to communicate because I think through communication with other students they're going to get what they need or at least get closer to what they need. (Owens et al., 2004)

Need for a Workable System and Greater Visions

In 1992, we were at a turning point. Two years earlier, I had terminated involvement with my NASA business, founded a new, education research company, and quickly received a National Science Foundation (NSF) Small Business Innovation Research (SBIR) Phase I grant for $50,000. This money was quickly used up in early research, and we had languished for a year while NSF tried to make up its mind over a much bigger "Phase II" grant. A Russian biophysicist[7] (a recent émigré) was working full-time in my spare bedroom, a student programmer[8] with my colleague Fred[9] in his garage, and my other colleague, Milton,[10] was prototyping the electronics in his attic. What we were trying to do was to build a next generation system, one that employed networking in a robust way, with handheld computers for students, and a flexible, easy-to-use interface for the teacher. We were painfully aware (from lengthy repair trips every couple of weeks to repair our Classtalk I system — mending wiring, replacing connectors, or diagnosing failed electronics), that classrooms are hostile environments, and the necessity for even occasional maintenance was unacceptable. Today, our goal of a class-wide computer network sounds simple, but it is easy to forget that this was still pre-Web, and wireless networking was a dream for anything other than high-cost space or military hardware.

Some people said then, and others continued to say well into the '90s, "Well just use hands!" by which they meant, "Why is a response system needed at all?" After all, the reasoning went, raising hands has been used in classrooms for centuries: mainly what was needed now was simply new pedagogy. However, there are two very good reasons why raising hands just does not work very well. First, students lack anonymity, so they tend to look around to see what everyone else is doing, and it is only the very brave who take a low, minority position. In some of my own (unpublished) research teaching at the University of Zimbabwe in 1991, I had gone to significant lengths in preparing packs of six color-coded cards that I handed out to each group of three students in a 75-person software engineering lecture course. When I asked a multiple-choice question, I would write it on the board and color code each option with a color corresponding to one in the packs of cards.[11] At counting time, one student in each group would hold up a card, six students would count (one for each color), and from their totals, I could quickly draw a histogram on the board. All the backs of the cards were white so students could not see what others had chosen unless they turned around, but still I found that many would, and answers would coalesce around one or two options. With hand raising, the problem is much worse because hands are raised sequentially in groups for those favoring each option. The second reason arises from the fact that students are aware there is no record of their positions. So, either they do not respond at all to a question, or they respond without giving the issues much thought. This defeats the object of the process because from a cognitive science perspective, it is the thinking through the issues, establishing positions, and committing to them, that promotes learning. Although it took modern cognitive science to show why the process works, this profound insight into effective pedagogy goes back 2,400 years to Socrates and his teaching on the ancient Greek Agora. By the 1980s, two of the few places that this technique was used regularly in formal education were in the Oxford/Cambridge tutorial system in England, where a few students meet regularly with a professor in his or her study. The reason is obvious: it is extremely difficult to teach in a Socratic way in a classroom of 20 or more students and involve every student all the time.

In July 1992, I had a call from Dr. Beverly Hunter at NSF who told me that they were going to remove our project from the small business program as there were severe doubts about its future commercial viability. However, because they believed that the research was important, they intended to transfer our proposal to the research division that normally funded university grants, and would award us twice the amount we had requested — half a million dollars — a lot of money at that time! This early research was very important, although the results were not published till later (Abrahamson, 1998, 1999, 2000), and it is worth describing briefly what they were. First, they showed the enormous pedagogical depth of questioning. Second, that the process of providing answers is generalizable, beyond questioning, to a wide range of "tasks". The implications from the conjunction of these results were important to design of the networked software and hardware required to facilitate them. For example, if a task is as simply structured as answering a multiple choice question, then a handheld unit may be very basic, with only as many keys as there are options on the question. On the other hand, a more open-ended question, a set of questions, or inputting homework, probably requires a screen and a full set of alphanumeric keys (or pen input with character recognition). It also needs a more powerful network, and more complex management and aggregation software on the teacher's computer. It also assumes the ability for task activities to run asynchronously on the various student computers, so students can work through tasks at their own pace, instead of everyone in lockstep. If we take the concept of a task further, to say proving a theorem, executing a simulation, or participating in a learning game with all the students in the class, then local intelligence in a handheld is a necessity, as is the need for system programmability. Here, system programmability means the ability of a system to accept cooperating special-purpose programs that can execute simultaneously on the different computers in the system, but are designed to "know" how to communicate with each other, and be downloadable to handhelds with complimentary parts running on the teacher's computer. Or, further at the next stage in system capability, the class would be dividable into large groups, with each group performing totally different tasks specifically designed for their learning needs — like remediation of a prerequisite concept-while others who have understood are not held back. Or, small groups working together, to produce a joint consensus answer. Or, a group interaction model of "consensus with dissent" like the U.S. Supreme Court, where a consensus answer is required, but individuals can dissent. To implement these elements of the vision, the software system would need to be able to create different environments at different handhelds within the same classroom. The key elements that would make this system dissimilar from stand-alone computing were that (a) task assignments would be controllable by the teacher, (b) student responses would be transmittable and available on the teacher's computer, (c) these could be aggregated in pedagogically meaningful ways to permit quick assessment on a class-wide or group-wide basis, (d) private information and feedback would be kept private except at the discretion of the teacher, and (e) aggregated or anonymous collections of individual responses could be shown publicly. We also envisaged roles for two types of authoring: one by teachers taken from existing curricular materials, textbooks, and the like, that could with extreme ease be used with the system with or without the need to copy them into the system; and a raft of more complicated activities which could be programmed by curriculum specialists, companies, or other third-parties. In retrospect, the road ahead would have been much easier if this vision had never existed, but it did color choices for the next generations of systems that were collectively known as Classtalk II.

A Powerful Research Team and Technical Achievement

With the new NSF grant, and a powerful group of 14 "expert collaborators"[12] from around the USA, Classtalk II systems were developed and installed in lecture halls at five universities[13] and two high schools,[14] with small test systems at two additional universities.[15] It turned out to be an appropriate time. Not only did each member of the research team have their own existing NSF research grants, they were all ready to use the system in their pedagogical research. With two exceptions, they were all physicists. One nonphysicist, Professor Mary Budd Rowe, a Stanford Professor of Education, deserves special mention. Her research in the 1960s on teachers' questioning had produced interesting results (Rowe, 1974a, 1974b). She had found that while almost all teachers used questioning in their teaching, that this was sadly superficial from the cognitive point of view. In fact, her timing data showed that almost all teachers paused only long enough for students to access their short term memories. There was not even time for students to retrieve any information from their long-term memories, let alone process the information from a cognitive point of view. In other words, the questioning used by most teachers was useful only for short-term factual recall. Professor Rowe died in 1996, but we treasured her advice and support on this project. The other nonphysicist, Professor Jill Larkin, was a psychologist who had also worked in physics education, and performed widely quoted work on cognition and the differences between the learning of experts and novices (Larkin et al., 1980a, 1980b).

The first generation of Classtalk II, developed with the new NSF grant funding, was a modern system and ahead of its time in some respects. It was built around three hardware elements: a Macintosh computer for the teacher, HP palmtop "PC" computers for students, and a special purpose modern network connecting them. All the test site systems (as listed above) were installed and up and running between January and August 1993. The old system at Christopher Newport was replaced first and used as a debug site; UMASS, Harvard, Ohio State, and Carnegie Mellon were next in that order. To give some feeling for the technical difficulty in February 1993, I will describe first use of the Harvard system. Starting on a Saturday with snow thick outside, our team of four PhDs, led by a satellite systems engineer, ran wires and installed network boxes and outlet jacks in the mammoth 500 seat lecture hall, drilling out blocked cable ports and crawling on the ground under the suspended, elevated, concrete floor. After a 12-hour work night

Monday, the first class commenced on Tuesday morning with Eric Mazur teaching "RLC circuits" to 250 students. Most were pre-med, they were somewhat unenthusiastic about having to take two semesters of calculus-based physics, and being Harvard students, decidedly impatient with any experimentation using them as guinea pigs. I stood in the back of the hall as Fred Hartline ran the system and Eric lectured, quaking in my shoes at the thought of a bad system crash. But, the system worked flawlessly, the students loved it, and Eric's pedagogy, which he had already been practicing with Scantron sheets, was masterful. Only later did I find out that the system had, in fact, crashed, but that as we had designed, Fred was able to automatically restart it and relog in all the students on their palmtops via software, without anyone ever knowing.

As an interesting aside, during the system installation and first use, an elderly physicist on sabbatical from Cornell University came and encouraged us, telling of his success with a system he had built over 20 years before. It was Raphael Littauer!

Pedagogical Ferment, Research Results, and Further Barriers

In May 1993, and again at the same time in spring 1994, our full research team met in Williamsburg Virginia to discuss pedagogy and results from their use of networked classrooms. There were three main results from these meetings. First, early student survey results from four sites — Harvard, University of Massachusetts (UMass), Ohio State, and Christopher Newport University (CNU) — were uniformly positive, and confirmed the prior data from George Webb's work (Abrahamson, 1995, 1999, 2000). That is, the great majority of students believed they understood the subject better, came to class better prepared, paid more attention in classes, and enjoyed it more. They also thought that the professor had more insight into their points of difficulty with the subject matter. In addition, data at Harvard (Mazur, 1997) and Ohio State from pre/post-test data on the force concept inventory showed dramatic increases in student conceptual understanding over prior pedagogical techniques used by the same professors, and over standard lecturing by other professors in comparable courses (Hake, 1998). These results were complimented by qualitative research from the UMass group (Dufresne & Gerace, 1994; Dufresne, Gerace et al., 1996). Second, there were two, coherent, different pedagogical approaches described. One from Eric Mazur focused on "Peer Instruction" and formative assessment via "ConcepTests," which he laid out as a seven step process in a seminal work (Mazur, 1997). Probably one of the reasons Mazur's work has been so enormously influential in the field is because, in this publication, he spelled out in such detail what the pedagogy was, why it was designed as such, how he applied it, what the results were, and also crucially gave a library of all of his ConcepTests, so that it was easy for other physics teachers to begin using them. Also, as Mazur was an energetic, articulate, and charismatic spokesman for his work, he was invited to an untold number of speaking engagements at U.S. universities, conferences, and seminars around the world.[16] Because of Mazur's work, the term "ConcepTests" is now well known in education, and libraries of these have been developed for many additional physics courses, as well as numerous other disciplines, including chemistry, mathematics, biology, geology, astronomy, medicine, business, and economics, among others.

An alternate approach developed by the UMASS group of Bill Gerace, Jose Mestre, Bob Dufresne, Bill Leonard, Laura Wenk, and Ian Beatty, was based on constructivist ideas and elicitative questioning, along with formative assessment, resulting in numerous publications (Dufresne & Gerace, 1994; Dufresne et al., 1996; Dufresne et al., 1996; Dufresne et al., 2003; Mestre et al., 2003; Beatty, 2004). This work was more comprehensive in its theoretical underpinnings than any that had come before it, and we shall return to some of the implications later.

In the meantime, to return to 1994, at this point another more thoughtful objection was raised, namely that of "coverage." That is, teachers, particularly university professors in the scientific and engineering disciplines, traditionally feel that they have to "cover" every part of their curriculum in lectures. And, curricula are crammed because they have expanded to fill all the available time. So, professors would say, "If I use lecture time to stop, question, and then act upon the information I get back from the students, I'll never be able to cover the material." Mazur gave the answer to this problem. He said that one has to step back and think what lectures are really for. He relates a little story where in the beginning, students complained that he went "too fast" in lectures, and there was no time to follow and copy down his notes. So, he had all his notes printed out and distributed to students so they would not have to slavishly copy from the overhead in lectures. Then he was criticized for lecturing, "straight out of his notes!" Then Mazur had a brain wave: perhaps he really was on the track of a bigger idea. After all, students (especially Harvard students) did not need him to read notes to them. They could read the notes themselves and do it before coming to a lecture. Then lectures could become places where students would have time to think, discuss, and best of all, understand. So, initially with Classtalk, he had students answer questions on the readings (notes, textbook, etc.) immediately at the beginning of each class, before he began lecturing. Later he did this over the Web, with a time window for students to answer that terminated a short while before class began.

The final objection was perhaps the most honest and the most real. It was made by a professor at the University of Zimbabwe to whom I had given a system in 1987. My idea was that university faculty in a developing country would surely be under less pressure for research, publications, and career advancement, than their counterparts in developed countries. Thus, I reasoned, they might have more time to concentrate on teaching. A year after installing the system, I visited the university and was disappointed to learn that it had been used at one international conference, as well as for several presentations to various government officials and university administrators, but only two or three times for actual teaching. My friend, the professor, apologized, and being the honest, decent person he is (as well as being a great teacher), said, "Look, I tried, and I can't teach like that. I'm in my fifties, I'm isolated here, I'm teaching advanced electronics. When I was at university they taught vacuum tubes! I have trouble staying two chapters ahead of the students in the textbook, and I just don't have a broad enough overview of the material to teach like that!"

These three major pedagogical objections, Orwellian, coverage, and limited teacher knowledge, far from being daunting, were actually very exciting. The first was made by those with the least insight, the second by university faculty who regarded the status quo of passive regurgitative lectures as acceptable pedagogy, and the third showed that the use of a response system practically mandated more competent teaching, as shown by the need for greater subject and pedagogical content knowledge. Better teaching was the goal from the beginning, and it is a valid contention yet to be proved in research that use of a response system (for those who stick with it) ends up teaching teachers both. That is, teachers who are prepared to admit in front of a class that they might not know something have a significant incentive to find out — which process cannot but lead to better subject knowledge. Also, as numerous teachers have reported, it is one thing to find out, from asking a question, that the majority do not understand. It is quite another to then summon up one's best elucidation of the point in question, ask another question, and find the majority *still* do not understand. This process again cannot but help teachers from reflecting on their teaching, and motivating the seeking of better pedagogical content knowledge.

Crossing the Chasm

From an economic and developmental perspective, to anyone who has studied the adoption of new ideas, particularly ones that involve technology, it is obvious that there is a period, after initial successes, that ideas either succeed or fail. In his book, Moore (1999) refers to this period as, "crossing the chasm." In the sober times of 1994, well before the dot-com bubble, I had only to have experienced a single system installation like that described earlier at the Harvard Science Center, with its attendant wiring, to realize that the cost of such a process would severely limit the potential of this technology for changing the way that people teach. Also, in addition to the technological hurdles of going wireless, there were those of market understanding of the pedagogy, and the real problems of quantitative research validating the approach at different educational levels, class sizes, student populations, and subject matters, combined with a huge need for curricular materials, and teacher professional development. So, with all these risks, it is little wonder that my attempts to obtain venture capital to make an economically viable system failed, and that in early 1995, I had to lay off 8 of our 11 employees. However, with the help of UMass and NSF, under difficult circumstances, we were able to take the next step of a semiviable "calculator-based" system. This was necessary, as Hewlett Packard had discontinued the palmtop PC that we had used in initial Classtalk II research, and their new model cost close to U.S. $700 — far too expensive for students to purchase. We noticed, though, that math and science students did buy graphing calculators. I will not go into the technical issues of networking graphing calculators, save to say that these were significant, but that we were successful, and that over the next half-decade sold more than 100 systems. These systems were not as capable or as slick as the palmtop PC systems, but they worked, and provided a base for continuing pedagogical development and growth in the core of pioneers who made this development possible.

In December 1996, seeing little hope of obtaining the significant amount of technology development funding required, we sold exclusive rights for all our intellectual property (Abrahamson et al., 1989, 1990) to Texas Instruments (TI), the leading maker of graphing calculators in the US, and leading developer of digital signal processing chips for wireless communication worldwide. The catch was, though, that TI would not agree to promise to ever actually make a networked classroom system. So, the enterprise was stuck in a holding pattern with rapidly aging technology, but needing to support the pioneer teachers who were doing increasingly wonderful work with the systems in classrooms.

The way out of the impasse came from a very unlikely source. In 1996, we had sold four Classtalk systems to the brand new Hong Kong University of Science and Technology. The head of the physics department there, Professor Nelson Cue, formerly a physics professor in the USA, who purchased and used the systems, saw the power and the limitations. He went to the Hong Kong government with a request for funding a truly commercially viable form of the technology, and his request was granted. Professor Cue also had contacts in the powerful Hong Kong manufacturing sector via a Harvard PhD physics alumnus, who was managing director of an electronics company,[17] and a member of the university Board of Regents. Together they decided that Classtalk had been far too ambitious, and that the technology to support such an approach at that point in time, for an acceptable price, was simply not available. They reasoned that rather, if one was prepared to step back and use one-way pseudonetworking via mature and low-cost television remote control technology, then the goal *could* be accomplished. The key to their reasoning was the obvious problem of cost and maintenance associated with wires in lecture halls. Also, as we had found, hardwired systems were almost totally impractical in rooms with movable desks and chairs, which comprise almost all smaller classrooms.

Infrared wireless technology solved a multitude of problems associated at that time with RF[18] communication, such as interclassroom communication and battery life. Also, since the cost and power of computer projection technology had decreased rapidly by that time, the problem of one-way transmission, inherent in TV remote control technology, could be solved by making students check visually, on the overhead screen, to see if their response had been received by the teacher's computer. They decided further to cut the cost of student handheld units by eliminating the screen (which would have been required for login), and building in a unique identifier into each handheld. In this way, each student would automatically be uniquely identified no matter where she or he was located in any classroom. This approach also mandated limiting question types to multiple-choice only. This last decision, while somewhat restricting pedagogy, meant that a student need only press a single button to respond to a question in class. Thus, a student could buy, own, and carry his or her unit to any classroom where a system was in use and the system would recognize it, and by inference, the student him or herself. In 1998, I traveled to Hong Kong to meet Professor Cue, and we agreed to work together on the "PRS," as his system was called, which we did for the following two years.

The PRS was an instant success, and immediately provoked imitators. The impact of Eric Mazur's innovations and his increasing fame had spread, and produced a pent-up demand for cost-effective systems. Today, almost all response systems sold worldwide are based on Professor Cue's groundbreaking simplifications that produced the first, truly commercially viable response system that was also robust, reliable, and low-cost. There have also been notable other innovations. For example, the company eInstruction, based in Dallas, Texas, which sells a response system known as the CPS, has cut the price of a student response pad to barely a few dollars (apparently little above their cost), and also sells a Web-based service for which students pay an annual fee in the range of U.S. $12-15 that automatically provides class lists to professors, and updated class-partici-pation grades for that student, with past class response histograms to students, over the company's Web site.[19] These innovations, taken together, mean that a university professor could begin using classroom network-based pedagogy with almost zero initial equipment cost. The costs for the pedagogical changes are significant, however, and we take up this issue in the next section.

Creating Effective Learning Environments

In 1990, when, as a scientist, I decided to believe my own data, it seemed, even if it were only partially true, that we had stumbled onto something significant. However, my prior NASA work had done little to prepare me for understanding the true nature of what "it" was or how "it" worked. Thus, when I decided on a change of career, I did not know that the so-called "soft" sciences are actually harder than the "hard" sciences, and that the can-do attitude which flowered in NASA's earlier days, breeding popular heroes, was a very different world than education, where low wages, lower prestige, and often stupefying management, bred teachers who were unsung, but also true heroes. Also, at the university level, professors who paid too much attention to their teaching (especially if it was at the expense of research) often paid dearly in their career advancement.

The science behind what teachers do is really, really hard. It is hard to understand, hard to model from a scientific point of view, and hard to measure. Sometimes, as my wife recovered from breast cancer, or on trips, I would take a load of books, and return a month or two later with no more apparent understanding than when I had left. With one exception, however, I had, over the years, learned a lot from the UMass group, and Bill Gerace in particular, and when I confided to him my frustrations with the science of learning, he told me of a special blue ribbon committee that had been set up by the National Research Council (NRC) to review and summarize what was known about how people learn. His former student, an early Classtalk user, and now a well-known researcher, Professor Jose Mestre, happened to be serving on this committee. I contacted Jose, and he directed me to the just published book, authored by the committee, called, "How People Learn," (HPL) (National Research Council, 1999). One small chapter in the middle of this book[20] hit me like a lightening bolt. In it, the NRC Committee on the Science of Learning went well beyond their charter of summarizing what was known about learning, and put it all together, applying it to describing what it took to create effective learning environments. These, they said, should be *learner* centered, *knowledge* centered, *assessment* centered, and *community* centered.

Superficially, these terms may sound like jargon-filled platitudes, but when understanding the breadth and depth that the committee had covered in putting the ideas together, it was a remarkable achievement. Essentially, they had expressed 30 years of research in cognitive science, and synthesized it in the form of four overlapping ideas. For me, it put all the struggles I had had, to make sense of the field, neatly into perspective.

Rather than repeat here what the committee said, I will take an extract from a paper with two high school teachers to explain how the four centerednesses play out in networked classrooms (Abrahamson, Davidian, & Lippai, 2000). That is, a networked classroom can help teachers to:

1. understand the existing conceptions that students bring to a setting, and extend and make connections with students' prior knowledge;

2.   exert an appropriate amount of pressure on students to think through issues, establish positions, and commit to positions;

3.   focus on conceptual understanding, and reveal, diagnose, and remedy misconceptions.

Also, the technology can naturally facilitate formative assessment that:

4.   gives feedback to students, and opportunities for them to reverse and improve the quality of their thinking and learning;

5.   stimulates a sense of community where class discussion, peer interaction, lack of embarrassment, and knowledge of class positions, creates the realization that others have the same difficulties, and opens the way to nonconfrontational competition, enthusiastic pride in class achievement, and perception that students and teacher are on the same side.

Thus, as shown in Figure 1, networked classrooms can assist teachers in creating learning environments that raise the level of all the four HPL centerednesses, and do it for all students.

Figure 1. Aspects of the learning environment catalyzed by a networked classroom

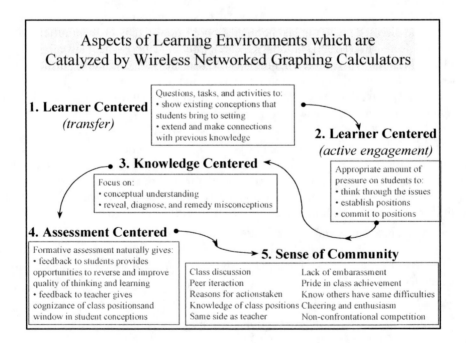

Brief Overview of the Evidence

It is highly tempting, at this point, given my new career status as quasi-neophyte educational researcher and cognitive scientist, for me to wish to plunge into summarizing past studies on response systems. And, to go wider and deeper, showing the links between the affordances of networked classrooms, and key results from the past 35 years of cognitive science research. But, the reviewers have restrained me, if only because such an exercise needs to be performed with due gravitas, which is not the nature of this chapter. Also, although much more work is needed, there are other papers in existence that partially cover this ground, and provide an entrée to relevant bodies of literature. For example, with respect to summarizing other work, Roschelle, Penuel, and Abrahamson (2004) identified 26 studies in mathematics, chemistry, and the humanities reporting positive outcomes. These range from promoting greater student engagement (16 studies), increasing understanding of complex subject matter (11 studies), increasing interest and enjoyment of class (7 studies), promoting discussion and interactivity (6 studies), helping students gauge their own level of understanding (5 studies), teachers having better awareness of student difficulties (4 studies), extending material to be covered beyond class time (2 studies), improving quality of questions asked (1 study), and overcoming shyness (1 study). Also, another chapter in this present volume (Penuel, Abrahamson, & Roschelle, 2005) is specifically aimed at developing a theoretical structure to describe the diverse experiences of students and teachers in networked classrooms.

There is a philosophical issue, in the nature of desirable future work, for which a comment may be appropriate. That is, from a human point of view, no matter the data or its source, if it is not what people expect, we tend to find reasons for dismissing it. Even in the hard sciences, unexpected results from another team's work are suspect,[21] and it is easy to see why it should be more so in sciences with more difficult experimental conditions. In education today, anything less than a randomized trial tends to be viewed as lacking definitive proof, and studies with this level of rigor clearly need to be done.[22] But, in the meantime, going back to aerospace, if one factor was present along with the unexpected results, I found that more often than not, that they *would* be believed. That crucial factor was a clear and valid explanation of the mechanisms behind the results. And if these made sense, then the disbelief would vanish. So, ways to explain the results also need to be researched.

For nonacademics, it may be simpler still! That is, for them, key indicators, such as the following quote, are already there, and tell it all. The quote comes from a high school math teacher,[23] whose students had routinely broken all records at her school in attaining "fives" in AP Calculus BC, widely thought to be the most difficult course it is possible to take in a US high school. But, at this school, with this teacher, students think it is "easy." The teacher, a prior Presidential Awardee, said, "… the data becomes addictive — after three years of using the system, it's still teaching me how to be a better teacher!" So, the reasoning goes, if feedback can help a champion teacher grow for three years, then the likelihood exists that it could help less celebrated teachers improve even more.

A Look to the Future

Most audience response systems currently on the market are, in a sense, single function, being designed to provide quick student responses to multiple-choice questioning, which are automatically aggregated and anonymously displayed. Networked classrooms are potentially capable of doing much more than this. I believe that the present genre of systems is, but the first technological and pedagogical stepping-stone towards a future that will encompass tools that are vastly more powerful and flexible. I indicated before, in this chapter, how visions for such advanced systems have existed since early research with Classtalk I. Finally, now, a decade and a half later, we are beginning to see commercially available production systems that embody this functionality.[24] Also, the research domain is vibrant with advanced systems under development at the following universities in the USA: Vanderbilt, the University of Illinois at Champagne-Urbanna, Harvard, University of Massachusetts, and the University of Texas at El Paso, as well as in Germany, Chile, and Taiwan.

Rather than describe the functionality of any particular system, I will describe some of my own favorite capabilities (bearing in mind that this list is far from exclusive).

1. Open ended questions and activities. Although multiple-choice is a powerful questioning tool capable of great subtlety and fine distinctions, it is limited by the preconceptions of the questioner or question preparer. These can tend to lead student thinking patterns, or worse, force a choice that does not represent what a student really thinks. Unless reasoning can be explored, the results may be less than meaningful. Aggregating answers in a pedagogically meaningful way is, of course, the central difficulty in open-ended questioning, and space here does not permit a complete discussion of the problem. However, one example from Roschelle, Penuel, and Abrahamson (2004b) shows that creative solutions are not only possible, but can work very well in classrooms.

   "A glimpse at an 8th grade algebra lesson that Hegedus and Kaput designed shows why these researchers are enthusiastic. After asking each student to 'count off' different numbers, the teacher poses a mathematical challenge that varies according to the count-off number. Students work on separate and slightly different challenges. This lesson's challenge is to create a function whose graph starts at the student's given number and goes through the point (6, 12). Using a calculator, each student specifies a mathematical function. Using the classroom network, the teacher rapidly "harvests" all the solutions to display on a projector. The students now see their work on a shared screen, which leads to passionate discussion about the functions they created. The teacher can guide the students in investigating new structures that appear in the aggregated set of lines, such as the varying slopes of the lines. The graphed functions can also control a motion animation on both the students' units and the classroom display. Each student's function thus becomes part of a mathematical model of a race, dance, or parade. Hegedus and Kaput (2003) reveal strong improvements for 7th, 8th, and 9th grade students on items found in state achievement tests. Jim Kaput and co-investigator Stephen Hegedus are excited about more than just the improvement in test scores: Classrooms that integrate dynamic software environments with connectivity can dramatically enhance students' engagement with core mathematics beyond what we thought possible."

Of course, the activity described above was used in a small classroom, and would obviously not work well in a lecture hall with 300 students. This brings up a crucial point. Twenty years ago, I thought that lecture hall use of a networked classroom system was bound to be more incrementally beneficial than a smaller classroom of say 20 to 30 students. In times before Classtalk II and the beginnings of research in smaller classrooms, almost everyone working in the field would have shared my opinion. Indeed, many would have said that the use of a system in a class of 5 to 10 students was unnecessary, if not inappropriate. I have since changed my opinion completely, and have come to believe that in spite of the enormous improvement possible in large lecture halls, the potential benefits are even greater in smaller classrooms, including those down at the latter range previously considered marginal. This is probably a topic for another volume, because most of the research in smaller classrooms has been conducted at the primary and secondary educational levels, and some of it has also been with more advanced systems. Nevertheless, one point causing pedagogical differences between small and large classrooms needs to be made here. That is, acoustics. In most lecture halls, the professor wears a cordless microphone, without which he or she would not be heard. Questions are usually not directed to students unless the professor has runners with second, third, or more microphones, something usually only seen at special events, invited lectures, or conferences. This inability to easily communicate by voice imposes severe restrictions on feasible pedagogical strategies, which is why Eric Mazur's innovation, "Please take a minute, turn to your neighbors, and convince them of your answer!" is such a powerful and popular stratagem for this environment.[25]

2. Sharing data. Particularly in the sciences and mathematics, introduction of real world data is an important pedagogical tool, as seen in the following example involving linear and exponential functions from Abrahamson et al. (2000).

    "In another pre-calculus class we (Davidian & Lippai) had students address an example of the 19th century Malthus Problem comparing exponential population growth with linearly increasing food supply. Students were asked to predict if and when food shortages would occur and how these predictions would change with increased rate (but still linear) of food supply. After seeing the histograms of class predictions, students performed the actual calculations and compared graphs on their calculators. The dramatic power of exponentially increasing quantities over linear was heightened because few had predicted the effect." These calculations were then used as the basis for discussing actual, real, population growth data downloaded to students over the classroom network from the Internet.

3. Homework. At the university level, Web-based homework systems have become widely used.[26] Time spent out of class, either alone or with other students working in groups, is important because it involves working through issues associated with knowledge currently being addressed in the course. From a cognitive science perspective, the process of thinking, testing, and applying processes and ideas is

valuable to learning (Cooper, & Lindsay, 1998). It is also a natural opportunity in which to exercise appropriate formative assessment. Web-based systems do enable such processes, and are certainly cost-effective for huge, introductory university courses when compared with manual grading, but they are also, perhaps, more automated than desirable, focusing almost exclusively on the "right" answer. They can also encourage students to share answers, although many systems now randomize input variables so that every student receives a unique problem. The idea is that students will then discuss processes and reasoning between themselves, rather than answers. Another approach is to use a classroom network and have students input answers to select questions at the beginning of class, as described, for example, in Abrahamson (1998).

"Jan Andrews is an 8th grade math teacher. Students push to get into her class to enter their homework on a networked calculator. Jan uses a free-form five-question skeleton set for collecting homework. Every day she identifies five of the previous night's homework problems on the board. She uses a free text binning because of its simplicity and manually checks exceptions as they come in. Five minutes after the start of class she knows who did their homework, who had problems, & what these are. She will deal with them before moving onto new material."

For effective, formative assessment, this approach is probably superior to an automated system, but is limited to smaller classes. Although at middle and high school levels, teachers may typically teach as many as 150 students spread over five classes, this method can easily be done at the beginning of every one.

4. Projects, labs, and extended activities. Projects are known to be an extremely effective way to teach (Norman & Schmidt, 1992; Polman & Pea, 1997; Thomas, 1998), but they are also difficult for a teacher to track. That is, some groups may progress rapidly while others languish in unproductive activity. Networks classrooms can be used to track activities and allow a teacher to spot problematic situations, in a timely fashion, through the simple device of an extended activity with responses, answers, conjectures, models, data, or other work products required to be "turned-in" over the network at predetermined stages.

5. Participatory simulations and games. These are very important categories of activities for experiential learning, and add excitement and motivational elements to a classroom. Leading examples of work in this area have been developed under NSF funding by Wilensky and Stroup (2000, 2002) and are known as "Participatory Simulations," where each member of the entire class participates actively in controlling some aspect of a simulation. For example, using a TI-Navigator in a participatory simulation such as "Disease," developed as part of the NetLogo project (Wilensky, 1999). The "Disease" model simulates the spread of a disease through a population that consists of on-screen icons (turtles) controlled by individual students using the arrow buttons on their calculator via the TI-Navigator network. Turtles move around a space represented on screen by a grid of patches, possibly catching an infection, with a probability determined by the teacher. Sick turtles make patches they land on infectious for a time, during which healthy turtles on the patch have a certain chance of becoming ill. A plot shows the number of infected turtles over time, and there is the option of sick turtles flashing to show that they are infected, or keeping turtles' state of health hidden

from public view. As Owens et al. (2004) note, no matter how the various parameters (chance of infection, initial number of infected turtles, sickness public or hidden) are changed, the same basic plot shape (a logistics curve) emerges. Among the benefits of this sort of activity are (a) an experiential learning experience for students, (b) a cooperative learning experience for students, (c) a physical and visual connection that students can make to mathematical objects such as graphs.

Another example from Wilensky and Stroup's work (2000, 2002) is known as "Gridlock." The activity relates to an inner-city traffic-light network in the "City of Gridlock." The Mayor of the city has a terrible problem with traffic flow, and the class has to try to solve it for him. Each student controls one traffic light shown on the computer projection of the inner-city roads, and the class, beginning with trial and error, has ultimately to figure out the algorithm that will get the simulated traffic flowing smoothly. Owens et al. (2004) report the following interview with a teacher that used this activity in her classroom. She began by explaining that she had seen roomfuls of PhDs having significant difficulty with this problem. But, her graduating AP calculus class was different, and exhibited a cohesion that solved the problem more easily than their elevated superiors.

Davidian: I said, after the AP [exam] we're gonna do another fun one, so we did "Gridlock," and it was just amazing. I've seen "Gridlock" done. ... I've participated in "Gridlock" at conferences with strangers and it was a disaster, with everybody crashing into everybody, etc. etc.. And, it was interesting in my class because it was all, ... they talked to each other, and they listened to each other, and that's come from having done this all year long, and Navigator has done that, in the way I explained it before, but it's followed through in even fun activities. So, the class has become a community and it's established itself and it's not dependent on anything other than now with, "That's just the way they are!"

According to this teacher's description, the key to her class's success in this type of competitive situation seems to have been due to their ability to work together as a team. She also states that, in her opinion, this ability was due to their experience, over the class year, with TI-Navigator. This model of class collaboration is an interesting result, given the fact that the nation's high schools are often divided many ways in exclusionary cliques and groups.

This example is important because it illustrates some of the less obvious benefits of networked classrooms, and how they help learning. For example, the teacher's perspective was that her class engaged in learning as a "community." In a later chapter in this volume, Penuel et al. (2005) discuss such effects from a sociocultural perspective, and provide a theoretical explanation as to why they occur.

Lastly, I would like to state my belief that an awareness of what is possible is now springing out of experience with today's simple systems. That is, new, advanced systems will not be created simply because technology continually marches forward. Rather, they will come from increasingly sophisticated pedagogical needs. These new systems will be more capable, and promise additional flexibility over current products, and will also be easier to use. Teaching requires a remarkable degree of multiprocessing. Not only does a teacher have to think of the subject matter and how to teach it, but it is also necessary to have an image of what is happening "in all those heads" out there in the classroom. Add to that working a computer, interpreting screens and data, keeping order, making frequent eye contact, and the workload is arguably akin to a pilot landing a large, passenger jet aircraft. But, computer technology has made even this easier than it used to be. A couple of years ago (before 9-11), I was privileged to be in the cockpit of a brand new, fully loaded Boeing 747-400 with "all glass" instrumentation displays. We were approaching New York's Kennedy Airport on autopilot, and it was a beautiful, clear winter morning, with the World Trade Towers rising to our left. A message came from the control tower at Kennedy, changing the runway on which we were to land. The pilot broke his conversation in midsentence, punched in the number "6," and resumed talking where he had left off, looking back to the rear of the cockpit. The huge plane banked, turned, and executed an S-maneuver. One which, I am sure, none of the passengers realized our pilot was not physically handling the controls to execute. Just before touching down, the pilot took the controls to land the giant plane.

I gave this example not because I think the classroom will become more automated, but rather because a teacher needs sophisticated tools, just as an airline pilot, so their precious cargo will arrive safely at the immediate academic destination on their various life journeys.

Conclusions

This chapter had four objectives: firstly, to explain the current excitement surrounding response systems and networked classrooms today; secondly, to set this description in historical context from the personal perspective of the author; thirdly, to delineate the tantalizing nature of the effects of these tools on teaching and learning, and how they augur for additional research; and fourthly, to describe the emerging characteristics of, and rationale for, more powerful types of modern systems.

The reader will judge if these goals have been satisfied, but at least it is hoped that the chapter will prove useful, as gaining an overview of this field is not easy. Publications are scattered through a variety of journals and across several disciplines. In many cases they exist only in the form of conference presentations or publications with limited accessibility.

Finally, it has been difficult to write this chapter without occasional reference to contemporaneous efforts at primary and secondary educational levels. For this the author apologizes. From another perspective, though, it is encouraging because it shows that far from being a "university only" or "lecture hall only" tool, response systems are being found useful at all segments of the educational spectrum. Thus, it is my personal hope that this edited book will not exist in isolation, but that it will be the first of a series of volumes that will deal with additional parts of the educational spectrum.

Acknowledgments

It can be seen from reading this chapter that many people have been mentioned as participating in the development of networked classrooms and associated pedagogical techniques. There are also a great many others who played crucial roles and contributed key ideas, but because of space limitations, as well as the focus of this volume, have not been mentioned. To all of you, I humbly offer my personal thanks, and take the liberty of also hereby thanking you on behalf of all those who have benefited, are benefiting, and will benefit, from better educational experiences associated with networked classrooms.

References

Abrahamson, A. L. (1995). *Classtalk: A 21ˢᵗ Century tool for teachers - An ancient concept in teaching* (videotape). Yorktown, VA, Better Education Inc.

Abrahamson, A. L. (1998, June 3-6). *An overview of teaching and learning research with classroom communication systems (CCSs)*. Paper presented at Samos International Conference on the Teaching of Mathematics, Village of Pythagorion, Samos, Greece. New York: John Wiley & Sons.

Abrahamson, A. L. (1999). *Teaching with a classroom communication system - What it involves and why it works.* Minicourse presented at VII Taller Internacional, Nuevas Tendencias en la Ensenanza de la Fisica, Benemerita Universidad Autonoma de Peubla, Puebla, Mexico.

Abrahamson, A. L. (2000). *A brief history of Classtalk.* Presented at Teachers Teaching with Teachnology (T-Cubed). International Conference, Dallas, Texas.

Abrahamson, L., Davidian, A., Lippai, A. (2000). *Wireless calculator networks - why they work, where they came from, and where they're going.* Paper presented at the 13ᵗʰ Annual International Conference on Technology in Collegiate Mathematics, Atlanta, Georgia.

Abrahamson, A. L., Hartline, F. F., Fabert, M. G., Robson, M. J., & Knapp, R. J. (1989). *An electronic classroom enabling self-paced interactive learning.* Washington, DC, United States Patent Number 5,002,491.

Abrahamson, A. L., Hartline, F. F., Fabert, M. G., Robson, M. J., Knapp, & R. J. (1990). *An electronic classroom enabling selfpaced interactive learning.* Brussles, Belgium, European Patent Number 90 304 587.0.

Bapst, J. J. (1971). *The effect of systematic student response upon teaching behavior.* Unpublished doctoral dissertation, University of Washington, Seattle. (ERIC Document Reproduction Service No. ED060651).

Beatty, I. D. (2004). Transforming student learning with classroom communication systems (ERB0403). *Educause Center for Applied Research (ECAR) Research Bulletin, Issue 3,* Boulder, Colorado.

Bessler, W. C. (1969). *The effectiveness of an electronic student response system in teaching biology to the non-major utilizing nine grouppaced, linear programs.* Muncie, IN, Ball State University.

Bessler, W. C., & Nisbet, J. J. (1971). The use of an electronic response system in teaching biology. *Science Education, 3,* 275-284.

Brown, J. D. (1972). An evaluation of the Spitz student response system in teaching a course in logical and mathematical concepts. *Journal of Experimental Education, 40*(3), 12-20.

Casanova, J. (1971). An instructional experiment in organic chemistry, the use of a student response system. *Journal of Chemical Education, 48*(7), 453-455.

Cooper, H., Lindsay, J. J., Greathouse, S., & Nye, B. (1998). Relationships among attitudes about howmework, amount of homework assigned and completed, and student achievement. *Journal of Educational Psychology, 90*(1).

Dufresne, B., & Gerace, B. (1994). *Using "extended scenario" to enhance learning during interactive lectures.* Retrieved March 25, 2003, from UMass Physics Education Research Group Web site.

Dufresne, R. J., Gerace, W. J., Leonard, W. J., Mestre, J. P., & Wenk, L. (1996). Classtalk: A classroom communication system for active learning. *Journal of Computing in Higher Education, 7*(2), 3-47.

Dufresne, B., Gerace, B., Leonard, B., Mestre, J., & Wenk, L. (1996). Using the Classtalk classroom communication system for promoting active learning in large lectures. *Journal of Computing in Higher Education, Edited volume - Student-active science: Models of innovation in college science teaching.*

Dufresne, B., Gerace, B., Leonard, B., Mestre, J., & Wenk, L. (2003). Using a classroom communication system for promoting active learning in large lectures. *Journal of Computing in Higher Education,* (March).

Garg, D.P. (1975). *Experiments with a computerized response system: A favorable experience.* Paper presented at the Conference on Computers in the Undergraduate Curricula, Fort Worth, TX. (ERIC Document Reproduction Service No. ED111355).

Hake, R. R. (1998). Interactive-engagement versus traditional methods. *American Journal of Physics 66,* 64-74.

Hegedus, S., & Kaput, J. (2003, July). *The effect of a Simcalc Connected Classrooms on students' algebraic thinking.* Paper presented at the the the 27th Conference of the International Group for the Psychology of Mathematics Education held jointly with the 25th Conference of the North American Chapter of the International Group for the Psychology of Mathematics EducationPsychology in Mathematics Education, Honolulu, Hawaii: College of Education, University of Hawaii.

Judson, E., & Sawada, D. (2002). Learning from past and present: Electronic response systems in college lecture halls. *Journal of Computers in Mathematics and Science Teaching, 21*(2), 167-181.

Larkin, J., McDermott, J., Simon, D. P., & Simon, H. A. (1980a). Expert and novice performance in solving physics problems. *Science, 208,* 1335-1342.

Larkin, J. H., McDermott, J., Simon, D. P., & Simon, H. A. (1980b). Models of competence in solving physics problems. *Cognitive Science, 4,* 317-349.

Linn, M. C. (2004). (Personal Communication).

Littauer, R. (1972). Instructional implications of a low-cost electronic student response system. *Educational Technology: Teacher and Technology Supplement, 12*(10), 69-71.

Mazur, E. (1997). *Peer instruction: A user's manual.* Upper Saddle River, NJ: Prentice Hall.

Meltzer, D. E., & Manivannan, K. (1996). *The Physics Teacher, 34,* 72.

Mestre, J. P., Gerace, W. J., Dufresne, R. J., & Leonard, W. J. (2003). *Promoting active learning in large classes using a classroom communication system.* Retrieved March 12, 2003, from http://www.psrc-online.org/classrooms/papers/mestre.html

Moore, G. A. (2002). *Crossing the chasm: Marketing and selling high-tech products to mainstream customers* (revised ed.). New York: HarperCollins Publishers.

National Research Council (1999). *How people learn: Brain, mind, experience.* Washington, D.C., National Academy Press.

Norman, G. & Schmidt, H. (1992). The psychological basis of problem-based learning: A review of the evidence. *Academic Medicine, 6,* 557-565.

Owens, D. T., Demana, F. A., Louis, A., Meagher, M., & Herman, M. (2004). *Developing edagogy for wireless handheld computer networks and researching teacher professional development* (ED479499). Washington, DC: ERIC, 137.

Penuel, W. R., Abrahamson, A. L., &Roschelle, J. (2005). Theorizing the transformed classroom: A sociocultural interpretation of the effects of audience response systems in higher education. *Audience response systems in higher education: Applications and cases.* D. A. Banks. This Volume.

Polman, J., & Pea, R. D. (1997). *Transformative communication in project science learning discourse* (ERIC ED407283). Paper presented at the Annual Meeting of the American Educational Research Association, Chicago.

Roschelle, J., Penuel, W. R., & Abrahamson, L. (2004). *Classroom response and communication systems: Research review and theory.* Paper presented at the American Educational Research Association 2004 Annual Meeting, San Diego, CA.

Roschelle, J., Penuel, W. R., & Abrahamson, L. (2004b). The networked classroom. *Educational Leadership, 61*(5), 50-54.

Rowe, M. B. (1974a). Wait-time and rewards as instructional variables, their influence on language, logic and fate control: Part I, Fate control. *Journal of Research in Science Teaching, 11,* 81-94.

Rowe, M. B. (1974b). Relation of wait-time and rewards to the development of language, logic, and fate control: Part II, Rewards. *Journal of Research in Science Teaching, 11,* 291-308.

Thomas, J. W. (1998). *An overview of project-based learning.* Novato, CA, Buck Institute for Education.

Wilensky, U. (1999). NetLogo. Evanston, IL: Center for Connected Learning and Computer-Based Modeling, Northwestern University. Retrieved from http://ccl.northwestern.edu/netlogo

Wilensky, U., & Stroup, W. M. (2002). *Participatory simulations: Envisioning the networked classroom as a way to support systems learning for all.* Annual Meeting of the American Educational Research Association, New Orleans, LA.

Endnotes

[1]   TI, ETS, Promethean, SiliconChalk, eInstruction, GTO-Calcomp, LearnStar, LearnTrac, Renaissance, SynchronEyes, Quizdom, H-ITT

[2]   The premier institution in the Texas university system

[3]   — which had included research work on Concorde, Space Shuttle, and Space Station in the fields of acoustics, structural dynamics, heat transfer, and psycho-physics —

[4]   CPFF – "Cost Plus Fixed Fee"

[5]   In Newport News, Virginia

[6]   "I think there is a world market for about five computers." — Thomas J Watson, founder of IBM speaking about the possible future needs of computers.

"Nothing can come along that will beat the horse and buggy." — Chauncey DePew, President of the New York Central Railroad, warning his nephew about investing in Henry Ford's new company.

"This 'telephone' has too many shortcomings to be seriously considered as a means of communication. The device is inherently of no value to us." — *Western Union memo, 1877*

"There is no reason anyone would want a computer in their home." — Ken Olson, president, chairman and founder of Digital Equipment Corp., 1977

"The wireless music box has no imaginable commercial value. Who would pay for a message sent to nobody in particular?" — David Sarnoff's associates in response to his urgings for investment in the radio in the 1920s.

"Who the hell wants to hear actors talk?" — H.M. Warner, Warner Brothers, 1927.

"Heavier-than-air flying machines are impossible." — Lord Kelvin, president, Royal Society, 1895.

"Mr. Bell, after careful consideration of your invention, while it is a very interesting novelty, we have come to the conclusion that it has no commercial possibilities." — J. P. Morgan's comments on behalf of the officials and engineers of Western Union after a demonstration of the telephone.

"That is the biggest fool thing we have ever done ... the [atom] bomb will never go off, and I speak as an expert in explosives." — Admiral William Leahy to President Truman (1945)

"Even if the propeller had the power of propelling a vessel, it would be found altogether useless in practice, because the power being applied in the stern, it would be absolutely impossible to make the vessel steer." — Sir William Symonds, Surveyor of the British Navy (1837)

[7]   Dr. Lev Tannen

[8]   Robert Knapp

[9]   Dr. Fred Hartline

[10] Milton Fabert

[11] Others trying a similar approach later included Mazur Mazur, E. (1997). Peer Instruction: A User's Manual. Upper Saddle River, NJ, Prentice Hall., and Meltzer (Meltzer, D. E. and K. Manivannan (1996). The Physics Teacher 34: 72.)

[12] George and Jane Webb (CNU); Bill Gerace, Jose Mestre, Bob Dufresne, and Bill Leonard (Univ. of Massachusetts); Eric Mazur (Harvard Univ.); Fred Reif and Jill Larkin (Carnegie Mellon Univ.); Allan VanHeuvelen (The Ohio State Univ.); Mary Budd Rowe (Stanford Univ.); Jim Minstrell (Mercer Island HS); David Hestenes, and Malcom Wells, (Arizona State Univ.), and Gregg Swackhamer (Glenbrook North HS);

[13] Harvard (250 students), Univ. of Mass. Amherst (100 students and 300 students), Christ. Newport Univ. (200 students), Ohio State (250 students), Carnegie Mellon (200 students)

[14] Mercer Island (Seattle), Glenbrook North (Chicago) both 30 student classrooms

[15] Stanford Univ. and Arizona State.

[16] Amazingly, at the same time as conducting groundbreaking pedagogical work, he also continued to head a large physics research team at Harvard with a number of doctoral students.

[17] Varitronics

[18] RF – radio frequency electromagnetic waves

[19] The concept of providing and charging for such a service was pioneered by Marty Abrahamson, my son, who works for eInstruction.

[20] Chapter XIII

[21] For example, in aerospace, perhaps *their* calibrations were off, instrumentation bad, sensors in wrong places, sloppy environmental control, and so forth.

[22] I am currently involved in just such a randomized assignment study of student achievement in algebra and physical science involving 130 teachers, funded by the U.S. Dept. of Education- Institute of Education Sciences, "Classroom Connectivity in Promoting Mathematics and Science Achievement," and begun June 1, 2005. Participants include The Ohio State University, The Better Education Foundation, CRESST — Univ. of California Los Angeles, and Texas Instruments.

[23] Ann Davidian, MacArthur High School, Levittown, N.Y.

[24] For example the just released TI-Navigator 2.0.

[25] Also, Eric does make use of voice feedback because he turns his microphone off and walks close to groups where he can overhear their discussions.

[26] For example, WebAssign, Blackboard, etc.

Chapter II

Audience Response Systems:
Insipid Contrivances or Inspiring Tools?

Eugene Judson, Arizona State University, USA

Daiyo Sawada, University of Alberta, Canada

"History is philosophy teaching by example and also by warning."
Lord Bolingbroke

Abstract

Surprising to many is the knowledge that audience response systems have been in use since the 1960s. Reviewing the history of their use from the early hardwired systems to today's computer-integrated systems provides the necessary scope to reflect on how they can best be used. Research shows that the systems have had consistent effects on motivation, and varying effects on student achievement over the years. The intent of this chapter is to consider lessons learned, consider the relation of technology and pedagogy, and to highlight elements of effective use. This chapter emphasizes the crucial role of pedagogy in determining whether audience response systems can lead to greater student achievement.

Background

New educational technology can hold grand promise. The ideas of motivated learners and effortless teaching grab the attention of even the most ardent Luddite. Who among us would not, at least, be intrigued after hearing about a tool which can rapidly move students toward deep understanding of content, and help instructors immediately realize the comprehension level of students? This is a compelling description, and it can be applied to audience response systems. Unfortunately, it is also a description that too often takes on the tone of a sales pitch, and it is important to realize that this sales pitch for audience response systems has reverberated on college campuses for nearly four decades.

Contrary to any vendor's claim that audience response systems are a new teaching tool, these devices have a history stemming from the 1950s, when United States Air Force personnel used electronic devices to respond to multiple choice questions integrated into training films (Froelich, 1963). By the 1960s, elaborate versions of audience response systems had taken a toehold in university lecture halls. Though less sophisticated than the wireless systems common today, the audience response systems of the 1960s and 1970s were far from crude. Designers developed hardwired systems that provided each student with their own transmitter station, while professors were kept informed of overall responses via a series of needled gauges. Supplementing the hardwired systems of yesterday with prepared multiple-choice questions (presented via slide projectors) made these systems remarkably similar in appearance and function to today's high-tech systems.

Early models, such as the commercially available Spitz Student Response System (Brown, 1972), and the Anonymous Audience Response System (Garg, 1975), were marketed as teaching tools that would improve education by providing instructors with immediate student feedback. With a jet-age name that held promise of being a true teaching machine, the Instructoscope went further by also providing individual feedback to students at their stations by lighting either green or red lights (Boardman, 1968). In response to high

Figure 1. Instructor's view of the electronic response room. Notice the two slide projectors in the background: one projector for questions, and one for displaying content material (Bessler, 1969).

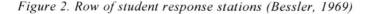

Figure 2. Row of student response stations (Bessler, 1969)

commercial costs, Littauer (1972) described in "Educational Technology" the construction and use of a homemade student response system he assembled at Cornell University.
All of these early systems were technically quite adequate; all had the ability to elicit
student responses to multiple-choice questions. Some systems provided students
individual feedback; some of the systems even recorded for the instructor the answers
from every student in the lecture room. Yet, despite the promise, by the mid 1970s there
was a sharp decline in the literature on the use of audience response systems. Despite
a hopeful beginning, no mention of any such system is found again in the literature until
the 1990s. In retrospect, it seems universities, at the very least, lost interest in what was
then a new and promising piece of educational technology.

The reemergence of interest in audience response systems in recent years is exemplified
by a comparison of two studies that highlight this cyclic curiosity. First, in 1972, Chu
reported a National Science Foundation project, funded at Skidmore College, where a
costly audience response system had been installed. The evaluation project sought to
find out how many different ways the system could be used "to promote creative
teaching, to what academic disciplines, and for what educational objectives" (Chu, 1972,
p. 11). Chu's evaluation project documented the use of the audience response system
in a broad range of courses including mathematics, science, government, economics, art,
and psychology. In 2004, Draper and Brown described an overview of their experience
using an audience response system at the University of Glasgow. Similar to Chu, Draper
and Brown sought to "explore both use and adoption across a whole university" (Draper
& Brown, 2004, p. 81). As was done three decades prior, the 2004 examination described
the use of the audience response system in a wide variety of disciplines including
mathematics, science, philosophy, and psychology. A finding common to both investigations was that overall, students and teachers felt the systems were beneficial.
Approval from both staff and students has remained a common result of using audience
response systems for over 40 years (Judson & Sawada, 2002). Less apparent in either case
was strong evidence that the use of the systems led to increased student achievement.
However, Draper and Brown (2004) stressed the importance of being focused on the
pedagogy, not the technology, in order to achieve better learning. They highlighted the

importance and potential of using the systems in tandem with teaching methods that increase student-to-teacher and student-to-student interactivity. Specifically, Draper and Brown recommended contingent teaching (i.e., varying a lecture according to student responses) and peer discussion. Though not as explicit, Chu also outlined benefits of adjusting lectures according to received responses. Chu even mentioned a small-scale study at Skidmore College showing positive student achievement gains when the audience response system was used to collect feedback upon, which individual assignments were based.

Because there seems to be a strong cyclic nature in the way audience response systems are reemerging into today's lecture halls, a closer examination of early, as well as contemporary studies, may assist us in charting new paths with authentic potential to improve student learning, rather than repeating old patterns with new bells and whistles. Reading a historical perspective of these older audience response systems should be more than something akin to thumbing through old sepia photographs. The word *history* itself stems from the Greek word *historia*, which literally means knowing or learning by inquiry (Stein, 1980). The value of exploring the past use of audience response systems comes from our own inquiry. In preparing this chapter, our historical inquiry was guided by three questions:

- Does use of the systems improve student achievement?

- Can using an audience response system yield other types of benefits?

And most importantly:

- What shifts in pedagogy can lead to effective use of audience response systems?

What Research Tells Us

Though the technical differences between older and more modern audience response systems cannot be completely ignored, in reviewing research results, these technical differences will only be highlighted if they affected actual instructional methods. Otherwise, although research on the use of audience response systems has remained a finite field, after four decades, we are able to make some definitive statements and raise far-reaching questions. It is tempting to jump to the question *do they help?* The pragmatists among us would like to immediately know what the benefit-to-cost ratio is. Yet, at the same time, we know this is a ludicrous question. An audience response system by itself can no more improve student learning than any other piece of hardware such as a computer, television or chalk. The question *do they help* needs to be refined. First, we have to ask *has student learning been enhanced or improved with the use of audience response systems.* Then, if we find that indeed there are cases of student improvement, we need to ask *do we know what led to such improvement?*

Motivation and Satisfaction

In general, the research shows that students clearly support the use of audience response systems, finding them motivational, as well as beneficial to learning. Examples of statements reflecting students' reaction to audience response systems are listed in Table 1.

Interestingly, Brown (1972), who also found a more positive attitude toward instruction when an audience response system was in place, additionally discovered there was no significant difference in anxiety levels between control and experimental student groups. This raises the question as to why students who feel no more at ease in class still have a more positive attitude. It is, perhaps, too easy to dismiss this as a halo effect associated with the novelty of the technology. However, the data on positive attitudes should not to be dismissed because, as shown by several researchers (Bennett, 2004; Cue, 1998; Engelder, 2004; Littauer, 1972), positive attitude can manifest in a most desirable outcome — increased student attendance.

Academic Achievement

For many educators, academic achievement is the bottom line litmus test for justifying a purchase. Whether it is spending money on new textbooks or purchasing media equipment, educators and administrators alike often want to know if there is a link between expenditure and student achievement. In the past, this link has been examined for other technologies such as educational radio, classroom television, filmstrips, and laserdiscs. Similarly, the onus today is on manufacturers and other proponents of audience response systems to demonstrate the merits of the systems in terms of genuine academic achievement.

In order to examine academic achievement, it is necessary to distinguish between earlier research and more recent investigations because, among the studies examining academic achievement, the instructional methods documented in the 1960s and 1970s were considerably different from those methods advocated later. In the 1960s and 1970s, audience response systems were seen largely as lecture pacing devices (Bessler, 1969; Brown, 1972; Casanova, 1971; Garg, 1975). Though this often remains the case today, this

Table 1. Statements reflecting students' reaction to audience response systems

Statement	Researcher(s)	Year
The Response-System has been useful to the teaching-learning process	Chu	1972
More like a game than a quiz. I think it is excellent; it tests, but is not as frightening as pop tests.	Garg	1972
Knowing the responses of my classmates raises my interest	Cue	1998
More likely to work out a problem in a lecture if the class was asked to vote using the ARS handsets	Draper & Brown	2004
[ARS] improves my problem solving skills.	Greer	2004

Figure 3. Instructor's panel. Gauges indicate percentage of students responding to each choice (Bessler, 1969).

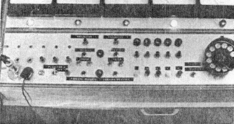

instructional approach is not in accord with current research. Rooted in stimulus-response learning theory, earlier audience response systems were seen as an ideal lecture-pacing tool. In most reported investigations, instructors would pause a lecture, ask students a multiple-choice question, request a response from students, and then look at a panel of gauges to assess the overall "comprehension" of students (i.e., percent recording a correct response) (see Figure 3). If the instructor felt a sufficient proportion of students had correctly responded, then the lecture would continue. If too few students responded correctly, then the instructors interpreted this as a cue to go over information again (i.e., present a brief relecture).

At the time, this seemed a common sense application for audience response systems: By using the systems to monitor and adjust the pace of the lecture, it was believed that students would receive information at a tailored pace. Whether informing the instructor to slow down or to speed up, the lecture's tempo was controlled via the electronic gadgetry. Although there are a few cases reported of the audience response system being used as a means to promote discussion (Chu, 1972; Littauer, 1972), by and large, the lecture hall became a sophisticated stimulus-response Skinner box. However, instead of a pigeon being rewarded for desirable behavior with seed, the instructor was apparently rewarded for an understandable lecture with correct student responses. Yet, this common sense approach of information delivery did not yield the anticipated achievement results. Taken as a whole, students in the 1960s and 1970s who participated in this type of operant conditioning use of audience response systems reaped no academic achievement benefits (Bapst, 1971; Bessler, 1969; Bessler & Nisbet, 1971; Brown, 1972; Casanova, 1971). Consider the achievement results in Table 2.

If the reason for using audience response systems in the 1960s and 1970s was to increase academic achievement, then clearly the devices were not delivering on the intent. Many educational theorists of this time were rooted in this type of stimulus-response or trial and error pedagogy, and it seems that audience response systems were grafted onto what was then seen as a most productive method for teaching students. What the results demonstrate is that if students find information unintelligible the first time, although he or she may learn to peck on a different response when the information is redelivered through more lecture, the student does not gain a better understanding of the content. Maybe this is not unlike a traveler being provided directions repeatedly in a foreign

Table 2. Some representative achievement differences when using ARS and not using ARS

Researcher, year	Description	Results
Bapst, 1971	One control (non-ARS) section and one experimental (ARS) section from the areas of economics, chemistry, physical science, and anthropology were studied. Sections from each discipline were taught by the same instructor. In both the control and experimental sections, students responded to ARS questions, and provided the instructor continual updates on their comprehension level. In the experimental sections, the instructor received feedback of student responses and comprehension level. In the control sections, students inputted responses, but the readout displays were not visible to the instructors. Instructor developed tests were used to measure academic achievement.	No significant difference was found among any of the content areas
Bessler, 1969	Six hundred and sixty four students enrolled in sections of freshman biology were enrolled in control (non-ARS) and treatment (ARS) sections of the course. Ten instructors taught both control and treatment sections. Instruction was based on principles of programmed instruction. SAT scores were used as the covariant. Achievement was measured by four biology exams during the semester.	No significant difference was found
Brown, 1972	General mathematics freshmen students were assigned to the control group (non-ARS) or the experimental group (ARS). In the experimental section, most periods began with a series of questions answered with the ARS. The material was then rediscussed or drilled. Throughout most lectures, further questions would be posed, and responses resulted in the instructor altering the pace of the lecture. A course placement test was administered during the first and last weeks of class.	No significant difference was found
Casanova, 1971	Students enrolled in experimental (ARS) and control (non-ARS) sections of organic chemistry. For the experimental sections, students were asked to respond approximately every 15-20 minutes to a question regarding the preceding lecture material. Questions did not require elaborate deduction. If less than 50% of the students were correct, the same topic was reviewed again. Quizzes and exams were compared.	Control students exhibited a small but consistent superior performance

language by an overly helpful Samaritan: Eventually, the traveler will obligingly smile and be on his or her way without a clue of where to go, but the Samaritan will feel satisfied in having completed a good deed.

Moving forward in time to the 1990s and later, a few more studies examined the effect audience response systems had on academic achievement (Abrahamson, 1998; Cue, 1998; Poulis, Massen, Robens, & Gilbert, 1997; Van Horn, 2004). More precisely, these studies examined the effect on student achievement when the audience response systems were used as a means to allow a public display of responses, facilitate discussion among students, and share thought processes aloud. In short, the type of pedagogy being examined in the past decade is aligned with constructivist tenets.

While achievement results from recent studies are certainly more positive than those from the 1960s and 1970s, it should be cautioned that these studies are few, and are concentrated largely in the science courses (Abrahamson, 1998; Abrahamson, 1999; Cue, 1998; Greer, 2004; Judson & Sawada, 2002; Meltzer & Manivannan, 2002; Poulis et al., 1997). These studies tend to focus on the process of interactive engagement, sometimes facilitated by an audience response system, and do not place the equipment at the focal point of the study. For example, Meltzer and Manivannan (2002) indicated the viable use of a very low-tech audience response system — having students use flash cards to indicate their response. Meltzer and Manivannan found this low-tech approach and the electronic systems equally effective: The key is to emphasize authentic minds-on engagement. They reported extremely impressive achievement results with groups of students attaining normalized gains (g) ranging from 0.46 to 0.69 on tests of conceptual understanding of electricity. Poulis, Massen, Robens and Gilbert (1997) also reported striking student gains when using an electronic response system, with pass rates in physics moving from 57% to 70%. If evidence of future studies can demonstrate similar results in a variety of subjects, then skeptics may have to take a closer look at the applicability of audience response systems within the framework of active engagement.

As mentioned, a purpose of considering the use of audience response systems over a period of 40 years is to learn how the systems can make a difference. Though some recent investigations have shown application of the systems leads to improved academic achievement, many other recent papers do not touch on the topic of academic achievement, and overall, the older studies revealed a null effect. Following an inquiry approach, it is now important to examine the differences among the uses of audience response systems documented in these studies in search of the more promising uses for audience response systems.

Elements of Successful Use

A technical difference between older and more modern audience response systems is that today's systems allow effortless display of student responses as histograms. These graphs can be easily displayed, and under the guidance of a constructivist-minded teacher, can become the focus of intense discussion as students defend their reason for selecting a particular answer. This is particularly true if the questions have been well crafted, and possible responses represent common misconceptions. This one technical difference between older and newer systems exemplifies the underlying pedagogical differences between then and now. This is not to say that today's college lecture halls are not still dominated by straightforward lecturers delivering masses of information to student receptacles, but it can at least be said it is no longer the trend to conduct research on the effectiveness of pacing lectures with electronic feedback. Instead, the field of educational research has moved toward student-centered instruction that highlights the importance of students making connections among ideas, and developing understanding by grappling with ideas which may, at times, seem to be in discord. Learning is not viewed as a private enterprise. Rather, it is now thought that learning can be rooted in the dialogue students have, not only with instructors, but with other students who too are struggling with the same concepts. The field of education does not emphasize a mechanical delivery model of instruction with a series of information satchels to be doled out to students, but instead values learning as a complex process confronting preconceptions, developing mental models, and engaging in meaningful conversation with other learners. So, this seemingly simple, technical difference of student responses displayed as histograms fits ideally with the student-centered classroom. No longer is the audience response system marketed primarily as a diagnostic tool for instructors. It has also become a public broadcast system, permitting students to literally see peer responses.

But the histogram display, as a distinguished technical advance in the past 40 years is, by itself, really not so remarkable. Without the proper pedagogical method in place to take advantage of this technical aspect, the histogram accompanying each question becomes only a mildly interesting report. What really facilitates learning is an adept instructor, and a roomful of students who are comfortable with sharing thoughts.

We've grown accustomed to the cost of new technology dropping dramatically following its introduction, and such has been the case for wireless response systems. Textbook companies can now convince buyers that an audience response system *upgrade* will add minimally to the per student cost. Besides, a textbook hawker might add, the clickers will come shrink-wrapped with the textbook! With images abounding of stimulated participation and increased comprehension, it is tempting to begin writing a check for immediate delivery. However, if improved achievement is the primary goal, then from research studies utilizing audience response systems and reporting positive academic gains, the following elements of successful implementation can be discerned.

- Displayed questions address conceptual understanding of the subject

- Possible responses include commonsense wrong answers

- Students may discuss the question with other students before and/or after submitting a response

- Student responses are publicly displayed

- The instructor facilitates discussion among students

- Students defend responses and voice their reasoning

- Socratic discussion among students and instructor leads to consensus

This list fits well within the principles of constructivism. An effective instructor does not use the audience response system simply as an electronic feedback collector, but uses student data as a means to encourage reflection, explanation, and justification among students. Fostering such student-to-student and student-to-instructor interaction is no simple task, and anyone considering the purchase of an audience response system must understand that the systems do not come with constructivism built in. Instead, developing and/or selecting thought provoking questions, and the skill of promoting discussion and even debate among students requires a high level of expertise and perseverance on the instructor's part. The benefits of a truly interactive classroom and increased comprehension among students will be the rewards.

Recognizing Interactivity

Having outlined the principles of effective use of audience response systems over the years, it would be a mistake to assume all instructors of the past strictly adhered to a stimulus-response model (Chu 1972; Littauer, 1972). Likewise, though current educational theory advocates student-centered classrooms, audience response systems are often still used in the most perfunctory manner. At the same time, it is interesting to realize that audience response systems are often seen by others outside of campus life as devices to facilitate a game show setting. In recent newspaper articles, audience response systems were presented by the press, essentially, as devices to help students with short attention spans, labor through a lecture (Brocklebank, 2000; Fraser, 2000). The notion that audience response systems can be used to promote a deep discussion about concepts is brought to a startling halt when reading the comments of a quoted professor who said, "I support it wholeheartedly for fact-based subjects but its uses are extremely limited. I would be very cautious about extending it to subjects where you have to develop an argument" (Brocklebank, 2000, p. 16).

To be fair, this professor does value the idea of students developing their own arguments, but the newspaper reporter paints a picture of a professor who does not see how audience response systems can help facilitate this goal. Granted, the newspaper article is far from a scholarly essay, and newspapers are notorious for reporting uncomplicated arguments, so it would be interesting to actually discover where this professor's epistemological beliefs lie, whether he adheres more to direct or exploratory learning. However, in the case of James Fitch (2004), his stated beliefs are clear. James Fitch is a professor at Auburn University and in his article "Student feedback in the college classroom: a technology solution," he clearly supports the value of constructivist and interactionist models of teaching. He supports student-centered classrooms, advocating for a learning which "takes place best when constructed within the framework of the learner's own understanding" (Fitch, 2004, p. 72), and calls for a high level of interaction "between the learner and the learner's environment" (Fitch, 2004, p. 72). Fitch strongly emphasizes the importance of classroom interactivity, and fits this well within a constructivist model. However, upon reading about Fitch's classroom experience with an audience response system, scrutiny reveals his actions are far from constructivist. Fitch provides this example audience response question, "How many bones are in the middle ear?" (Fitch, 2004, p.74), with the accompanying information to be displayed being, "The bones of the middle ear are the smallest bones in the body" (Fitch, 2004, p. 74). If Fitch's example problem is representative, then the questions simply require students to recall factual information. Fitch also explains that his audience response system is programmed so that after students are presented with a question and the possible responses, the students have a set amount of time to select a correct answer. Following the viewing time, a counter begins to count down from 1,000 to 0 in nine seconds. As the counter winds down, incorrect possible responses are eliminated from the choices. The quickness of a student's response corresponds directly to the amount of points (1,000 maximum) credited. Finally, the correct answer is displayed, and a summary of student responses is projected so "students can compare their performance with that of the rest of the class" (Fitch, 2004, p.74). While this may, for some students, be an exciting game-like activity, this certainly does not represent constructivism or even interactivity. Nevertheless, the author uses both of these terms to describe the system.

The purpose here is not to single out James Fitch, but to point out a common mistaken belief among many educators: student activity does not equal constructivist learning. This fallacy is perhaps no more evident than in science classes where students are seen busily moving lab equipment about, following directions, and recording data. Upon closer inspection, one often finds little mental engagement on the part of these science students who actually are following a cookbook lab recipe that has no significance to them. This type of activity-mania too easily can occur when using audience response systems. Compared to a traditional lecture, at first glance, using an audience response system to facilitate students repeatedly answering multiple-choice questions seems a great leap in the direction of student engagement. However, the goal of student engagement is to have students actively engaged with ideas, not equipment. So while Fitch's research showed student approval ratings of the audience response system similar to what have been described in other studies, not surprisingly "there was not a significant difference in the grades of the classes using [the audience response system]" (Fitch, 2004, p. 76).

Fitch is right, though, to value interactivity. The few studies that show positive academic achievement when using an audience response system are intimately connected to student interactivity. However, interactivity needs to be better defined. Interactivity means far more than a lecture hall full of students pressing buttons in response to questions. A highly interactive classroom implies students are interacting with several ideas and several individuals all at once. Consider the following example question (Kansas State University, 2003).

A new moon occurs when no lighted portion of the Moon is visible to an observer on Earth. This occurs because:

a.   an object completely blocks the Moon.

b.   the Moon is completely covered by the shadow of the Sun.

c.   the Moon is completely covered by the shadow of the Earth.

d.   the Moon is between the Earth and the Sun.

e.   Both a and d

f.   Both b and d

g.   Both c and d

For a few students, the question would be answered through a simple recall of the definition of "new moon." However, for almost all students, including those who answer through recall, a mental representation of the positions of the Moon, Earth and Sun are imagined. If prompted by the instructor, the student may even quickly sketch a diagram and share his or her thoughts with a fellow student. After all the students have selected a response, the instructor can display the class' answers, and begin to elicit students to elaborate on why they chose a particular response. Even if there is a general consensus about the correct answer, a skillful instructor can deepen the conversation by asking students why the wrong answers might seem plausible. Following up with questions about the causes of various crescent shapes would further enrich the conversation, and promote deeper understanding of lunar cycles. As students listen to other students explain their conception of the Earth-Moon-Sun system, and as they articulate their own thinking, the instructor can ask pointed questions, and lead students to a deeper, more genuine understanding of lunar phases. Thus, the electronic response system is not the star of the lesson: It is a tool, and enriched student thinking is placed center stage. If audience response systems are to make a difference in student learning, then it will be because the instructor has taken the time to plan lessons.

Looking Ahead

Though research has been examined here, the goal of this chapter was not to be an exhaustive review of all conducted research. Rather, the intent here has been to consider lessons learned, consider the relation of technology and pedagogy, and to highlight elements of effective use. This chapter has emphasized the crucial role of pedagogy in determining whether audience response systems can lead to greater student achievement. In particular, it has been noted that a pedagogy that supports minds-on engagement makes a difference. Additionally, the presence of student-student as well as student-teacher discourse as a setting for active engagement is extremely important. In closing, and without further comment, we would like to suggest that the above two pedagogical practices would be even more supportive of student achievement if students were deliberately formed into learning communities.

Acknowledgments

This work is supported by the Center for Research on Education in Science, Mathematics, Engineering, and Technology (CRESMET) at Arizona State University. Any opinions, findings, and conclusions or recommendations expressed in this publication are those of the authors, and do not necessarily reflect the views of CRESMET. The authors would like to express gratitude to Dr. Marilyn Carlson, director of CRESMET, for her support and guidance.

A special thanks is extended to Dr. William Bessler of Minnesota State University, Mankato, who extended permission to reprint photographs from his dissertation. Thank you, Dr. Bessler, for your pioneering work in the investigation of audience response systems for educational purposes.

Chapter III

The Use and Evolution of an Audience Response System

Ray A. Burnstein, Illinois Institute of Technology, USA

Leon M. Lederman, Illinois Institute of Technology and
Illinois Mathematics and Science Academy, USA

Abstract

This chapter reports the authors' use and refinement of a wireless audience response system (ARS) over a 10-year period. The motivation for this effort was to replace the traditional passive lecture with a more interactive classroom. Our classroom procedures and the evolution of these procedures are detailed. The authors also illustrate how ARS systems can be applied in a variety of ways, including the use of modified multiple-choice questions. ARS systems allow for both formative and summative assessment in real time, which is a unique and desirable property. The use of ARS systems similar to the ones described has increased rapidly in the past few years. A brief survey of current and proposed commercial wireless keypad systems is included.

Introduction

The study of audience response systems is closely related to the process of teaching itself, and as such, it has had a long history. In this article, we discuss the subject, starting from the time when electronic teaching tools just became available, about 30-40 years ago. However, most of the activity with these audience response systems has been within the last 10 years. In these recent years, interest has been focused upon keypad systems (Burnstein & Lederman, 1996, 2001, 2003; Dufresne, Gerace, Leonard, Mestre, & Wenk, 1996). Such systems can be used to quiz students in real time during class, thus engaging students more directly in the lecture. Nonetheless, until recently, widespread use of such keypad systems has been limited. The reason for this is that the original keypad systems were relatively expensive, and perhaps additionally, there was reluctance on the part of faculty to change from the existing passive lecture format. For a number of reasons, there has been a significant change in opinion in the last few years, and consequently, there has been a very large increase in the use of wireless keypads. At the same time, there have been rapid changes in the number and type of commercial wireless products available. In this chapter, we discuss a wide range of these related topics.

Background for Change from Passive Learning

The proposals for the revitalization of the physics lecture by involving the students more in the lecture itself started over 10 years ago (Fuller, 1994; Hudson, 1984; Mazur, 1997). It was our belief in the early 1990's that the introductory lectures in physics to engineering, science and nonscience students were ineffective. This was largely due to the size of the lecture, which was rarely less than 40 students, and in some cases, as many as several hundred students. The financial problems in both private and public universities made it safe to predict that the class size problem would only get worse in the future. Further, it was known that large-scale dropouts would usually impact aspiring minority students most seriously. Hewitt and Seymour (1991) had studied the attrition rate among first-year science and engineering students, and they noted that this was about 50%. Blame for this unfortunate loss of students was most often attributed to teaching associated with the large, impersonal lecture format, rather than with the subject being taught.

The reasons for the lack of success of students in a large lecture were understandable, but we felt the problem could be overcome by changing the lecture format. Our approach was later supported by the research articles of Hake (1998) and Poulis, Massen, and Gilbert (1998) that established the value of modifying the passive lecture with "interactive engagement." Although many suggestions and innovations have been proposed and tried, for example, Van Heuvelen (1991), Beichner (2000), and Sokoloff and Thornton (1997), judging by numbers alone, wireless keypad systems are currently the most widely used option, and therefore the main focus of this chapter.

A History of the Development
of ARS Systems

A history of audience response systems (ARS) begins with the early work of Littauer (1972), at Cornell, who produced a simple, homemade, hardwired, push-button keypad system. Horowitz (1998) proposed, and used at IBM, an advanced technology classroom using keypads. A commercial, hardwired keypad system, called ClassTalk[1], was produced and sold by the Better Education Company. The keypads were Texas Instruments calculators that were loaned or bought by the students. Results of their use were reported by Dufresne et al. (1996) and Mazur (1997).

The first, wireless, radio-frequency (RF) keypad system was developed and successfully used in the corporate business world in the late 1980s by Fleetwood Industries.[2] It was purchased and used at the Illinois Institute of Technology (IIT) for engineering classes in about 1991. In 1993, Burnstein and Lederman started to use this wireless, radio-frequency system in physics lectures at IIT after making major software modifications. Later in the same decade, substantially cheaper commercial systems appeared using wireless, infrared (IR) technology.[3,4] The commercialization continues today with further technology improvements and cost reductions. We are now at the point where there are several, low-cost, reliable wireless RF keypads being produced. In a later section, we present a brief, up-to-date comparison of the currently available wireless keypad systems.

While wireless keypads have been the focus of this discussion, it is important to note that other keypad-based interactive systems exist. Wireless communication can be achieved with PDAs, cell phones, and laptop computers (Cox & Junkin, 2002). These devices can also, in principle, be the basis for a wireless response system. Further, the classroom receiver can be replaced by a remote or local wireless Internet host. However, none of these alternative systems has, as yet, gathered widespread adoption, but one can expect continuing development in this area. Our discussions of ARS use are general enough to apply to these systems as well.

The Evolution of Wireless ARS at IIT

The discussion of the IIT effort with wireless ARS is presented as a chronological account that reveals the evolution of our ideas and methods. When we began in 1993, we insisted on a wireless system, in spite of the fact that a wired system, ClassTalk, was the system of choice at that time. We felt it was essential to have an ARS system with mobility, which could be moved from lecture room to lecture room with ease. In addition, we required a system that was two-way; which sent a confirmation signal to the student indicating that his/her response was received. This yielded a system with high reliability, and allowed us to use the data for grading purposes, to use keypad scores as a significant portion of the term grade.

In 1994, an ARS system was used in our elementary physics classes at IIT starting in the spring semester, and in subsequent semesters. In these classes, with 40 to 90 in each class, students were assigned a numbered keypad for the course, which they picked up at the beginning of each class. Loss prevention consisted of requiring the student to exchange his/her ID card for a keypad at the beginning of class, and reverse the exchange at the end of class. In 10 years of operation, only a few keypads were lost either due to theft or failure. Keypads were tested and batteries were changed when necessary, or else about every 4 years.

Questions that could be answered by "yes or no," or multiple choice (1-10), were woven into the lecture, and made relevant to what was just discussed, or what was just about to be discussed. Questions were also asked to test whether students prepared for class. When appropriate, peer instruction (Mazur, 1997) was encouraged by asking students to rework a keypad question through discussion with their teammates (usually two other classmates) and arrive at a consensual response. All questions were displayed on a screen via an LCD projector. Students were given from 30 seconds to a few minutes (depending on the complexity of the problem) to key in responses that were picked up by the RF receiver and input into a PC computer program. The results appeared within seconds as a histogram of class responses that was projected on the screen. A later computer readout or printout was available, which recorded the performance of each student. These results were saved on a spreadsheet, and the scores were available for inspection or grading purposes.

Our first year's experience was positive, in spite of a good number of start-up bugs and inexperience in 'weaving' questions into the lecture. We found that the lecture did cover less material, and the process did, initially, put a burden on the lecturer. Even in the beginning, student acceptance was surprisingly tolerant, and the keypad system always did receive a majority of positive votes. Students had to be alert, with minds on the lecture or demonstration material, but they did not seem to object (in effect, attendance and attention were being monitored). This experience is the usual result: other beginning keypad users, as well as long-term users, have similar positive student responses, for example, Erlich (2005).

In 1995, with a proven system, we made the keypad classroom an important and well-advertised factor in the course grade. In particular, we announced at the beginning of the semester that the keypad questions would count as a substantial part (15-25%) of the final grade. We graded the questions as follows: a correct answer earned the student 10 points, any answer earned 3 points, and no answer received 0 points. The software allows other weighting schemes. With an average of 5-10 questions for each class session, a maximum semester score of over 2,000 points has clear statistical significance. The weighting of homework problem scores in the final grade was reduced somewhat since the keypad questions could test the students on their mastery of homework concepts, as well as test their reading of the text before the lecture. The goal was to motivate students to prepare for the lecture by doing the reading and assigned problems before class. Keypad questions woven into the lecture also reinforced the lecture itself. Teamwork among students (peer instruction) was used by including some team exercises in the mix, and as a procedure for resolving difficult questions.

More Details of ARS Use

A typical class session would begin with an outline of the topics to be covered, and answers to student questions, and then proceed to test the students on their preparation for class with a few keypad questions. These focused on the concepts underlying the homework, and on their familiarity with the reading material. Next, the lecture would begin, and keypad questions would be presented during the lecture, or at the end of a lecture module/topic.

The keypad questions were of a wide variety, and the questions could accommodate a broad range of instructional philosophies and goals. They allow an instructor to determine the following:

a.   Have the students read the text before class?

b.   Are the students paying attention?

c.   Do the students recognize and grasp concepts?

d.   Are the students thinking?

e.   Do the students remember important facts?

f.   Can the students work in a group?

g.   Can the students do numerical exercises?

h.   What do the students say about the pace and the interest of the lecture of lecture?

Instructors can evaluate and get feedback on their performance in real time using questions like "How am I doing?" for example — choose between:

a.   The lecture is very clear so far, no questions.

b.   I have a question or two.

c.   I have a lot of questions.

d.   I am so confused, I don't have any questions.

Using the student responses to the above question enables the lecturer to extend, repeat or modify the discussion of the previous lecture topic.

From experience, we learned that it is not correct to assume that all keypad questions need to be prepared in advance of the lecture. Certainly we feel that it is desirable, and the result improves as questions are more carefully integrated into the lecture. However, the hardware and software allow the creation and insertion of spontaneous questions in a set of prepared questions. For this reason, we expect that a lecturer experienced with the system can, if appropriate, generate questions "on-the-fly." These are, in fact, often stimulated by the class response to some previous question. The ability of the instructor to weave questions into the lecture and generate such questions "on-the-fly" probably takes a semester or so of experience.

Structuring Multiple-Choice Questions in ARS

In more recent lectures, we have experimented with partially correct multiple-choice questions, that is, questions with answers that are only partially correct (Burnstein & Lederman, 2000). These are departures from the traditional multiple-choice question format (Achacoso & Williams, 2003; Burton, Sudweeks, Merill, & Wood, 1991; Frary, 1995). In the next section, we move to a more detailed discussion of multiple-choice questioning, and a more theoretical classification of multiple-choice questions.

The entire universe of assessment techniques is very large, but the tools available to a teacher using an ARS system are more or less restricted to multiple-choice questioning. In the previous section, we presented a list of types of questions that could be presented. This range of questions can be organized in a different way by Bloom's Taxonomy (1956), which is a classification ordered by cognitive levels. There are many representations of these cognitive levels, but a common ordering is: knowledge, comprehension, application, analysis, synthesis, and evaluation, as shown in Table 1.

Structuring multiple-choice questions involves more than selecting the cognitive level of the question: it involves selecting a format for the question. There is a so-called traditional format that is rather rigid. We propose variations in the traditional multiple-choice question format for several reasons: First, the limitation to four or five choices is not necessary, and probably reflects the fact that the original grading devices, typically optical scanners[5], usually handled a maximum of only five answers. Equally relevant is the fact that those scanning machines only allowed credit for one correct answer with no credit or partial credit for any other answer. The situation has now changed: the current wireless keypad systems, and other real-time data entry systems are computer based, and the software for grading allows more flexibility. For example, up to 10 alternatives are possible for each question with most keypad based ARS systems. In addition, each alternative answer can have a different score related to its "correctness." Also, the style of multiple-choice questions can change in order to create new questions

Table 1. The classification of cognitive levels (adapted from Bloom)

Level of Understanding	Nature of Understanding in the Level
Knowledge	Recognizing and recalling information
Comprehension	Restating, interpreting the information
Application	Applying principles to new problem
Analysis	Identifying the underlying organization
Synthesis	Creating new and original connections
Evaluation	Assessment and resolution of issues

that would address a wider range of cognitive skills, and further, new questions of varying format can be created in real time to take advantage of the rapid feedback provided by keypad response systems. All these factors suggest that now a greater variety and more varied format for multiple-choice questions are possible and useful. Some examples are given by Dufresne and Gerace (2004). We name this new type of question an enhanced, or partially correct multiple-choice (PCMC) question. The main advantages of these PCMC questions are:

- PCMC removes the restriction of only five choices per question.
- PCMC removes the limitation of one "correct" answer per question.
- PCMC introduces the possibility of awarding partial credit for answers.
- PCMC, with more choices, allows one to simulate short essay type responses.
- PCMC allows a more refined evaluation of student learning.
- PCMC allows higher-level questions in Bloom's Taxonomy.

Assessing Teaching and Learning Using ARS in Colleges

Traditional multiple-choice questioning is one of the most commonly used assessment formats, and is used in many disciplines. Its use extends to large college classes because of the automated grading features provided by optical scanning devices. Wireless keypad systems and other polling devices can be used in an identical way as assessment tools, since the questions can be multiple-choice or PCMC, and the grading is automated. This type of assessment is referred to as *summative,* and is used when achievement has to be summarized and reported. While summative assessment may measure learning, learning is not improved if performed in a passive learning environment. This conclusion can be inferred from the publication of Hake (1998) that demonstrated that passive learning produces inferior results relative to interactive engagement when student achievement is measured by the Force Concept Inventory test (Hestenes, Wells, & Swackhamer, 1992). While there are various methods to produce interactive engagement, the use of wireless keypads has become the most common method. Interactive engagement, in effect, involves the use of *formative* assessment, which has been recognized as an essential requirement for large learning gains (Black & Wiliam, 1998). Traditional multiple-choice questioning with delayed machine grading was originally designed for summative assessment, and is not a good vehicle for formative assessment. On the other hand, wireless keypads can do both types of assessments, and are particularly well suited for formative assessment in large classes because it makes possible rapid feedback. The exact choice of questions depends on the instructor's teaching style and assessment goals. A wide range of multiple-choice and PCMC questions are available. There could be a variety of questions with different levels of complexity (Bloom Taxonomy levels). For example, one might ask first traditional Bloom level 1 questions (facts) about the reading assignment for the day, to check whether students prepared before class. Other higher-level (Bloom) questions/problems in traditional and PCMC format would normally be given.

There is an additional type of question that is useful, but does not fit into the usual Bloom's classification scheme, and that is the keypad question to elicit student opinion/ evaluation. Since wireless keypads operate in real time, one can ask a question (in an anonymous mode, if desired) and instantly get student feedback (formative assessment information) on the progress of the lecture. A simple question that we have used many times is:

Question: Evaluate the physics topic just presented

a.   Score 7-10   needs no further clarification.

b.   Score 5-7   a few points need clarification.

c.   Score 3-5   many points need clarification.

d.   Score 1-3   can't even ask a question because I understand so little.

How does one grade a keypad session with a mixture of different types of multiple-choice questions? It is the instructor's decision; but some will maintain that all keypad questions should be graded to insure student attention and effort. Others will conclude that the IR hardware and software are not reliable enough for serious grading (this will no longer be the case for the next generation of RF keypads). A different approach, based on classic education research (Angelo & Cross, 1993) would conclude that formative assessment questions should not be graded, to insure the genuineness of the feedback process. A scheme where some questions are graded and some are not graded is not a difficult technical challenge for the instructor and computer, but it is a challenge to make clear to the student beforehand the underlying philosophy — which problems are to be graded and which are not to be graded, and why.

Limitations and Objections to ARS

The basic limitations or disadvantages of ARS are its costs. First, there is the financial cost of providing a classroom with an LCD projector, a computer, and a keypad receiver. This is not an isolated cost, since this is not much more than the equipment required for an up-to-date classroom. The keypads themselves can be purchased by the institution outright or the students can lease/buy/resell them at the bookstore. While an outright keypad purchase is less than the cost of today's textbook and can be used in several classes, nonetheless, some are reluctant to require additional student expenditures. The instructor's software for the keypad system is usually cost-free from the keypad vendor. The other significant cost is the learning overhead of the faculty member using the system. Although this is not a very demanding task, there are still objections.

A Minimal Approach to Using ARS

Many academics find it difficult to abandon the conventional, passive lecture in favor of using an ARS system. Some will never be comfortable with a change, but for others it can be made attractive if made convenient enough. A minimal approach is suggested with this in mind. There are two components involved in the process of using an ARS system. The first component is the actual setup of the system, namely the keypads, LCD projector, computer, RF/IR receiver, and so forth. In many cases, the classroom is equipped with everything except the keypads, and they can either be supplied or rented/purchased from the bookstore. In other cases, it might take some time and effort to set up the ARS system in a barren classroom. That is no more difficult than setting up a for a science demonstration. As such, it is a task that can be performed by an assistant, or if necessary, the lecturer himself, in 5-10 minutes. Operational glitches in the system are frustrating to the beginning user, but are almost always forgiven by the students. The second component in a minimal ARS is the actual lecture plan itself. In the minimal model, it is a conventional lecture plus a small number of keypad questions. The questions can be very simple at first. One might ask keypad questions about the assigned reading at start of lecture. This automatically checks attendance as well as encourages preparation. Then, a few questions could be presented during the lecture to check understanding and alertness. The recording and storing of data is the task of the software, and yields day-to-day scores that could count toward a grade, if desired, but more importantly, yields feedback to the instructor. In this model, prior preparation can be small, and hopefully one will progress to develop more sophisticated questioning in time. A minimal approach might be thought of as a slow (adiabatic) transformation away from the conventional lecture.

An Application of ARS to Grades K-12

While much of the previous sections has discussed undergraduate college education, ARS can play an important role in middle- and high-school education. Under the No Child Left Behind Act (NCLB), enacted in the United States, a test is given, originating from State or Federal sources, at the end of the year in every grade in almost all subjects. The result of this summative assessment test shapes decisions about the future of the school, its teachers, and students. Rather than focusing on testing, it seems much more productive to integrate instruction and assessment, as previously discussed. When testing is an integral part of pedagogue, one is actually not teaching to the test: rather one is teaching **with** the test.

By embedding wireless keypad testing into the teaching process, one can help insure that the student is focusing on the subject. An optimum marriage of questioning and explaining can bring these elements together in the learning process. Here we propose the possibility of using the keypad testing technology to partially satisfy the new accountability requirements imposed on schools by district, State and Federal programs to improve the quality of education. We believe that keypads, plus the use of Internet technology can achieve embedded assessment, day by day, even hour by hour, without imposing the deadly burden of exclusive high-stakes tests. If this interactive student response system does, say, 50% of the job of assessing the progress of the student in the grasp of concepts, understanding and enthusiasms, a summative test (the Federal, NCLB, or State test) can be used to satisfy the accountability authorities with about one-half of the trauma.

Here is how we propose it would work: keypad quizzes throughout the year, at a minute or two per quiz, contribute data so that there would be as many as 300-600 scores for each student during the year. This is enough to give the teacher a very good evaluation of each student's status and progress. The keypad quizzes may, of course, be supplemented by one or two hour-long additional tests from the teacher or external sources. With reasonable coordination between teacher, school, and say, accountability headquarters, the State or Federal education experts can formulate their own multiple-choice tests that can be included via an Internet download at the correct phase of the class. There are numerous ways in which this process can provide accountability, with teacher, principal, and so forth, totally out of the loop. The authorities can leave, unchanged, plans for semester or annual tests, but it will no longer be high-stakes, since the keypad data can be available for a significant portion of the assessment.

This example illustrates how educational technology, in particular ARS, has applications at a different level of education, K-12, and can promise alternative and improved methods of teaching and learning at these grade levels as well.

Survey of Commercial Wireless Keypad Systems

The research and production of one's own wireless keypad system, together with appropriate software, is not impossible, but it is usually far beyond the resources of most noncommercial enterprises. For this reason, we confine the discussion to commercial products. The decision of which system to choose should be made after an analysis using a list of criteria such as the one provided in Table 2. A list of the principal, commercial, keypad[6-8] manufacturers is furnished.

For one-way systems (usually IR), there is a problem with keypad entry confirmation. When the user responds to a question by pushing a button on the keypad in a one-way system, the keypad number can be seen in an array of keypad numbers on a screen. For confirmation, the student has to observe the appearance of his/her number. This does not always occur, due to range limitations, line of sight problems, signal interference, and so forth. The usual two-way RF system has a greater range, and there is a signal sent back to the keypad itself, confirming receipt of the keypad entry. RF systems were more expensive until very recently, but several lower cost systems are about to be marketed and field tested. There are no results available at this time.

In addition to accepting keypad input, some new systems will accept numeric input, and eventually there will be text input. Clearly, the technology is continually improving, but even today's models can already function as sophisticated classroom instructional tools.

Table 2. A listing of important properties of wireless ARS systems

Properties of wireless ARS systems	
Cost of keypad	Range of $25-$100
Type of radiation	Infra-red (IR), radio frequency (RF)
One-way /two-way	IR (usually 1-way), RF 2-way
Range of keypad	IR< 50 ft, RF ~ 200 ft
Software Quality	Ease of use for PC/MAC compatibility
	PowerPoint compatibility
Hardware Quality	Resistance to failure, battery life
Company reputation	Number of keypads sold and support
	Reliablity - testimony of users

Conclusions

Audience response systems are being used by hundreds of thousands of students in large lecture halls at many institutions. This is because the interactive lecture has been shown to produce increased learning gains. The technology is changing very rapidly in this area, and increased reliability, lower-cost, commercial two-way RF keypads are about to appear. Other possible wireless technologies based on PDAs and cell phones are in the development stages.

Keypads can be used for dual purposes in an ARS system. That is, they can be used to perform either formative or summative assessment, or both, in any given class. The learning overhead for the operation of keypad systems is relatively small, and most vendors provide convenient quizzing software.

References

Achacoso, P., & Williams, C. (2003, Spring). *Writing effective multiple choice tests.* University of Texas Learning Center. Retrieved June 2, 2005, from www.utexas.edu/academic/cte/efs2003/achascoso/achacoso.ppt

Angelo, T. A., & Cross, K. P. (1993). *Classroom assessment techniques.* San Francisco: Jossey-Bass.

Beichner, R.(2000) Student-centered activities for large enrollment university physics (SCALE-UP). *Proceedings of the Sigma Xi Forum, Reshaping Undergraduate Science and Engineering Education: Tools for Better Learning*. Minneapolis, MN.

Black, P., & Wiliam, D. (1998). Inside the black box: Raising standards. *Phi Delta Kappan, 80*(2), 139.

Bloom, S. J., (1956) *Taxonomy of educational objectives: The classification of educational goals: Handbook I, Cognitive domain*. New York; Toronto: Longmans, Green.

Burnstein, R. A., & Lederman, L. M. (1996). Report on progress in using a wireless keypad response system: The changing role of physics departments in modern universities. *Proceedings of the ICUPE*. College Park, MD.

Burnstein, R. A., &. Lederman, L. M. (2000). *AAPT Announcer, 30*, 85.

Burnstein, R. A., & Lederman, L. M. (2001). Using wireless keypads in lecture classes. *Phys. Teach., 39*, 8-11.

Burnstein, R. A., & Lederman, L. M. (2003). Comparison of different commercial keypad systems. *Phys. Teach, 41*, 272-275.

Burton, S. J., Sudweeks, R. R., Merill, P. M., & Wood, B. (1991). *How to prepare better multiple-choice test-items: Guidelines for university faculty*. Brigham Young University Testing Services and the Department of Instructional Science.

Cox, A. J., & Junkin, W. F., III. (2002). Enhanced student learning in the introductory physics laboratory. *Physics Education, 37*(1), 37-44.

Dufresne, R. J., & Gerace, W. J. (2004). Assessing to learn: Formative assessment in physics instruction. *Phys. Teach. 42*, 428.

Dufresne, R. J., Gerace, W. J., Leonard, W. J., Mestre, J. P., & Wenk, L. (1996). Classtalk: A classroom communication system for active learning. *Journal of Computing in Higher Education, 7*, 3-47.

Erlich, R. (2005). Classroom response systems, the good, bad and the ugly. *AAPT Announcer, 24*, 84.

Frary, (1995). More multiple-choice item writing do's and don'ts. *Practical Assessment, Research & Evaluation, 4*, 11.

Fuller, R. G., (1994, Spring). Using interactive lecture methods to teach physics. *American Physical Society Form on Education*.

Hake, R. (1998). Interactive-engagement versus traditional methods: A six-thousand student study. *Am. J. Phys., 66*, 64-74.

Hestenes, D., &. Wells, H. (1992). A mechanics baseline test. *Phys. Teach., 30*, 3.

Hestenes, D., Wells, H., & Swackhamer (1992). Force concept inventory. *Phys. Teach., 30*, 141. and ibid 159.

Hewitt, N., & Seymour E. (1991). Factors contributing to high attrition rates among science and engineering undergraduate majors. *Alfred P. Sloan Foundation Report*. University of Colorado.

Horowitz, H. M. (1998). *Student response systems: Interactivity in a classroom environment.* IBM Corporate Education Center.

Hudson, H. T. (1985). Teaching physics to a large lecture section. *Phys. Teach., 23,* 88.

Littauer, R. (1972) Instructional implications of a new low-cost electronic student response system. *Educ. Tech.,* p. 69.

Mazur, E. (1997). *Peer instruction: A user's manual and concept tests.* Englewood Cliffs, NJ: Prentice-Hall.

McDermott, L.C. (1991). What we teach and what is learned-closing the gap. *Am. J. Phys., 59,* 301.

Meltzer, D. E., & Manivannan, K. (1996). Promoting interactivity in physics lecture classes. *Phys. Teach., 34,* 72.

Poulis, J., Massen, C., Robens, E., & Gilbert, M. (1998). Physics lecturing with audience paced feedback. *Am. J. Phys., 66,* 439-442.

Sokoloff, D.R. & Thornton, R.K. (1997). Using interactive lecture demonstrations to create an active learning environment. *Phys. Teach., 35,* 340.

Tobias, S. (1992). *Revitalizing undergraduate science education: Why some things work and most don't.* Research Corporation, Tucson, AZ.

Van Heuvelen, A. (1991). Learning to think like a physicist: A review of research based instructional strategies. *Am. J. Phys., 59,* 10.

Endnotes

[1]   See Better Education, Alexandria, VA Web site: http://www.bedu.com

[2]   See Fleetwood Furniture Company; Holland, MI. Web site: http://www.replysystems.com

[3]   See EduCue (now owned by InterWrite, Columbia, MD) Web site: http://www.gtcocalcomp.com

[4]   See e-instruction, Denton, TX Web site: http://www.einstruction.com

[5]   See, for example, Scantron Web site: http://www.scantron.com

[6]   Manufacturers of IR keypad systems: References 3, 4, and Quizdom, Puyallup, WA, (2-way), http://www.quizdom.com; Turning Technologies LLC, Youngstown, Ohio;www.turningtechnologies.com. H-ITT, Fayetteville, AR, http://www.h-itt.com

[7]   Manufacturers of RF keypad systems: References 2, 4, and Quizdom, Puyallup, WA, http://www.quizdom.com; Turning Technologies LLC, Youngstown, Ohio, www.turningtechnologies.com.

[8]   For a listing with additional keypad system entries see: http://www.techlearning.com/story/showArticle.jhtml?articleID=56900180

Chapter IV

ARS Evolution:
Reflections and Recommendations

Harold M. Horowitz, Socratec, Inc., USA

Abstract

This chapter describes my 25-year journey and experience with audience response systems (ARS), starting with my first realization of the potential of ARS while teaching at a University as an adjunct professor. A synopsis of the initial ARS experiment conducted in the mid-1980s at IBM's Management Development Center serves as a baseline. The conclusions from this study justified the use of keypads in the classroom at IBM, and after publication, set the stage for the growth of the ARS industry. The ARS activities pursued after retiring from IBM in 1988 are described, including the advances that my companies made in software, graphics, and keypad technology, which we incorporated into our products. Finally, the chapter offers 10 recommendations for higher quality questions developed by ARS users. I conclude that these recommendations are critical prerequisites to the continued growth of the ARS industry in academia.

Introduction

A recent Internet search for "Audience Response System" related keypads yielded over 14,000 hits, and displayed over 200 companies that market ARS related products and services. The diverse applications included meetings, strategic planning, corporate training, and education (elementary, secondary and higher). Numerous articles praise the merits of audience response systems, but from my long experience in this field, I sense that many potential users are still on the sidelines.

With the introduction of infrared transmitters, costs of interactive classroom systems have dropped dramatically. Certain publishers even give transmitters free with new textbooks. So why are not clickers, handsets, keypads or transmitters more widely used in classrooms as an intricate part of the learning process? When used, the primary ARS application is to answer test questions one after another to save time in data collection and scoring. For the most part, keypad questions have not been seamlessly integrated into the instructional course design and PowerPoint slide shows. The reason may be that instructors feel that the educational payback is not worth the time required. Another reason may be that high quality questions that stimulate the students' thought processes during lectures are difficult to develop.

My corporate training consulting-support activities to clients over the years have been in course instructional design and development. Their existing courses needed to be redesigned, in order to engage students with creative questions that would stimulate thought and increase participation. Integrating quality questions into a course is referred to as "interactive instructional design," and I am convinced that this represents an important threshold to expanding ARS in academia.

This chapter provides an overview of my reflections and experiences with ARS since the early 1980s. I conclude with 10 recommendations and criteria for producing higher quality questions.

ARS: Where Are You?

My first awareness of the differences among students' participation levels and the possible need for an ARS happened while I was teaching at the University of Maryland. I recall explaining to my class how the Italian economist, Vilfredo Pareto, developed the 80/20 Principle to explain Italy's wealth in the early 1900s. He concluded that 80% of Italy's wealth was controlled by 20% of its population. The business world has since extended Pareto's Principle to assist in addressing its most important issues. I asked for personal examples that could support or dispute this Principle. An excellent discussion followed, but involved about 6 of my 30 students. How ironic to be discussing Pareto's Principle and its applicability to business decision making, and at the same time observing that the phenomenon was happening right in my class! Only about 20% of my students volunteered their experiences. The remaining 80% just listened and took notes.

In subsequent classes, I used simple "ARS-like" experiments to see if I could engage the class into higher levels of participation. I gave my students "Flash Response Cards" at the beginning of class, and they were required to answer a few multiple-choice questions based on homework reading assignments. For example, a case study would have four possible approaches for a manager to consider. Each student would display his or her selected response (1, 2, 3, or 4) and I would tabulate the results with the assistance of a student. An advanced version had each number color-coded to help in tabulation. This question and response did stimulate discussion about the case studies and increase the level of participation. However, the overall process took excessive manual effort to tabulate results, and detracted from the classroom's primary mission. As I look back now, I had no idea that this simple experiment would create an interest that would last the rest of my working life!

IBM Advanced Technology Classroom (ATC)

In the mid-1980s, I lead a research and development effort at the IBM Management Development Center at its Corporate HQ in Armonk, New York. This was an ideal research environment for my interests in classroom learning dynamics. Each week, IBM locations from around the United States send 100 newly appointed managers to this training facility for 5 days of comprehensive training on every aspect of basic management. IBM selected its instructors from various functions throughout the company. They were all outstanding performers with exceptional presentation skills. Most of them were selected for 2-year temporary assignments, and then moved on to continue their careers in their specialty areas.

Each of the five classrooms consisted of 20 students. The same instructor pool presented the same course material in each classroom each week. This was a perfect environment to set up a classic experimental and control group experiment and study. Part of the study was to justify moving from overhead transparencies to computer-based graphics and computer-controlled multimedia. The other part of the study was to justify an audience response system and student activities during the learning process: A summary of the findings follows.

- **Student interaction:** In a typical class, a few students dominated the discussion, that is, these vocal students asked the most questions, offered most of the unsolicited comments, and were more likely to volunteer to answer the questions posed by the instructor. The majority of the students elected to contribute only occasionally to the discussion, unless specifically asked to do so by the instructor.

- **Attentiveness:** Students' interest and observed attentiveness decreased over time, especially if the instructor's style did not encourage participation. Instructors who encouraged more participation did stimulate more interest, and observed attentiveness increased.

- **Pilot interactive classroom system:** This consisted of three subsystems: multimedia presentation, automated control-panel podium, and audience response. This pilot was constructed, modified as necessary, and used as an experimental center. The ARS used in the pilot was a basic, wired ARS system purchased from Reactive Systems. The keypad was custom mounted into each desk, and required special cabling and crimp connections.

The biggest challenge at that time was the effort to create the presentation graphics and the questions to be included for student response. Almost all existing visuals were in the form of overhead transparencies and flip charts. A few instructors were experimenting with computer-based slide shows such as Harvard Graphics, but the quality and resolution of the displayed images were marginal.

This was before the major advances in PC graphics cards and Microsoft's PowerPoint™. In the mid-1980s, General Parameters marketed the best available presentation system with a product called VideoShow™. All overhead transparencies and flipcharts were converted to VideoShow™ graphics. Keypad questions were added to the training material to engage the students during the presentations.

The transition from overhead transparencies and flipcharts to VideoShow™ graphics was difficult and challenging, as was the insertion of properly worded questions. If a keypad response sequence did not achieve the results as planned, it was redesigned or reworded and tried again the next week. The continual flow of students each week was ideal for improving the process.

After its completion, the ATC became a benchmark for IBM. Industry training groups, government agencies, and IBM customers visited the ATC to receive hands-on demonstrations. When asked about their reaction to the concept, visitors were generally positive about the concept, and indicated a desire to implement some form of it in their organizations.

Our conclusions from the ATC experimentation were that students were more positive than the instructors were. The five-point Likert rating questions given students after each class solicited their reactions about the interactive experience. The results were typically between 4.5 and 4.8 (where "5" was Excellent). Student attentiveness improved, as did their test scores, when compared to non-ARS classrooms. The instructors' reactions varied. Some saw great value and others felt threatened. The biggest concern raised at that time by the instructors was the additional course preparation required, and additional class time required.

Interactive Group Presentation Systems

In 1988, I requested early retirement from IBM, and independently began developing and marketing "Interactive Group Presentation Systems" for corporate training applications. I provided consulting services to clients in the application of ARS, and founded three companies that developed complete "turnkey" systems (of which ARS was a major subsystem). These companies (ICN, Inc., HMH Associates, and Socratec, Inc.) developed five different software applications for use with personal computers. The initial software package was a DOS application, and subsequent offerings were PC Windows-based. They were marketed under the trade names of Respondex™, Automated Testing System (ATS™), and RxShow™. Our companies formed alliances with various ARS manufacturers/distributors, and interfaced our software with eight different ARS keypads and transmitters (and worked with numerous private label variations of these units).

From the beginning, our marketing strategies stressed the marriage of presentation graphics and ARS as an integrated solution. Our systems automatically and seamlessly switched from our user's presentation to the question sequence and back to presentation. Our company did not market ARS as a standalone product, but rather as part of a total system.

Evolution of Presentation Graphics

High-resolution images and media were required by our approach, since the interactive results were displayed seamlessly within slide shows. The best quality presentation display products available in the 1988 to 1992 time-frame were an advanced version of VideoShow™ made by General Parametrics. The images, multimedia, and refresh rates were outstanding, but the equipment cost was extremely high. VideoShow™ was a separate graphics processor, and our system still needed a PC for the ARS subsystem.

We evaluated early versions of Microsoft's PowerPoint™, Harvard Graphics™, and Lotus Freelance, and at that time, concluded that these products could not compete with VideoShow™ for our applications. However, we did start development of our next generation product design based on PowerPoint™. We were in no hurry to expedite a product announcement because VideoShow™. was still selling very well. In a few years, the percentage of presenters preferring PowerPoint™ started to grow rapidly, especially after the announcement of PowerPoint 3.0. Shortly after this announcement, General Parametrics went out of business. We converted all of our software products to PowerPoint slide shows, and developed a seamless interface with all of our compatible ARS units.

Our first products used the PowerPoint Viewer to advance the interactive slide show. Next, we incorporated our product into PowerPoint directly as an "Add In." Our presentation software products function quietly in the background during the slide shows. After detecting an interactive visual, the keypad activities are automatically processed for the user. The inputs are processed, results are displayed, and slide show control is returned to the presenter.

Evolution of Keypads and Transmitters

This section summarizes my personal experiences with wired, radio frequency, and infrared technology keypads: While Socratec sold many systems over the years to higher education institutions, corporate training departments were our target customers through 1999. Cost was not a major factor in their buying decisions, and our customers were willing to pay the premium for radio frequency keypads. After Prs was introduced in 2000, we noticed that selected Corporate Training organizations did not see the line-of-sight limitations as a major barrier for their commercial classroom use. Socratec designed an on-screen confirmation scheme for Prs to provide feedback to the student that the input was received, and the "resending" was not required.

In late 2004, Hyper-Interactive Technology Training (H-ITT) announced a two-way infrared transmitter that provided a two-way confirmation signal back to the student after the input was received. This inexpensive infrared keypad was of special interest to our company. We concluded that it filled an important price and function void in the ARS industry.

Socratec integrated a wide range of compatible keypads over the years into its software products. The units and technologies described below are representative of the types that have evolved since we started the business in 1988.

Wired and Cabled Keypads

Q System keypads by Reactive Systems were the first keypads used with our software systems. Each unit was identified with a unique number from 1 to n. The ARS manufacturer assigned these ID numbers. The user could change them by using special codes entered into the keypad's numeric keyboard. Typically, the presenter or instructor organized these keypad numbers sequentially around the room for easy reference. The wired keypads were cabled together in a daisy-chain fashion, and the last cable was plugged into the keypad receiver: that, in turn, was plugged into the PC serial port. The cables consisted of four-wire telephone wires that were a major improvement over the type of cabling and connectors used in the IBM Advanced Technology Classroom. Q System wired keypads allowed for multiple digit inputs, and had a Send key. They also had an LCD display screen, and allowed our software to send individual messages back to each participant at any time during a presentation.

From a functional standpoint, these wired keypads were reliable and provided all the capability that our customers needed. However, from a logistics standpoint, cabling was our "Achilles heel" because our customers were disappointed with the effort required for setting up the systems. Very few of our customers actually had dedicated rooms with permanently wired keypads. They also took the systems off-site to conference centers and remote training centers. The daisy-chaining concept required every wire and connector to be in perfect working order. Customers needed constant assistance in locating bad connections and cables during setup. Our continued business success required wireless keypads and the sooner the better!

Wireless Radio Frequency Keypads

Functionally, the "Cordless Response Systems" CRS Reply™ by Fleetwood Electronics was the next logical step for our business model. This keypad had a 10-digit input and LED display showing the digit input. When the Reply™ Base Station successfully received the Keypad # and input, it immediately returned a confirmation signal to the originating keypad. This signal turned off the keypad's LED. If the LED remained on (or blinked), the signal was not received properly. This rarely happened because the reliability of Fleetwood's Reply wireless keypad was very high and had an excellent range of 75 feet. Dipole antennas were required to extend this range.

The Reply™ keypad required a 9-volt battery, and we had an initial concern that batteries would have to be continually replaced by our customers. Fleetwood incorporated a clever design to conserve battery life. The keypads did not have on/off switches, but only used power during actual transmissions. This allowed the batteries to last for over a year for typical installations. The high reliability and performance of the Reply keypad opened the door for the development of hundreds of applications by many software developers. At last count, Fleetwood has over 400,000 units in service worldwide.

SideKeys by Current Works, Inc., was added to provide our users with a 5-key RF keypad for smaller classroom applications. An entire 30-unit SideKeys system fits into a small attaché type carry case. SideKeys is limited to classrooms sizes of up to 60 students. A USB Plug and Play Receiver sits next to the PC. The system comes with an RF Presenter remote control.

Respondex Wireless Keypad

Our wired keypad applications already had multidigit questions, and our customers were looking to convert to wireless keypads. However, the standard Reply units only allowed single digit responses. Fleetwood marketed a more expensive model, but we elected to modify the standard Reply to accept multidigit inputs. Our company announced a private label version of the standard reply that had new command codes, and called it the Respondex Wired Keypad. This keypad allowed participants to sign on to a session with an ID using any keypad attached to any seat in the room. Our software would look up the ID in a database, and assign the participant to that keypad number for the remainder of the session. Our customers' applications from the wired keypads now worked with the RF technology including prioritizing lists, computing averages, displaying statistics, and so forth. The major limitation of our RF keypad solution was that it was expensive, and mostly being purchased for commercial and industrial training, and meeting applications. In order to pursue academic market opportunities, a less expensive keypad solution was required.

Infrared Prs Transmitters

In 1999, I became aware of infrared transmitter experimentation at the Hong Kong University of Science and Technology. Dr. Nelson Cue had successfully used Prs infrared transmitters in the university's physics lecture halls. Varitonix, and later Aventec, manufactured and distributed these units in China. They granted distribution rights in the U.S. to EduCue, along with several other companies. In 2000, my company, Socratec, Inc. formed an alliance with EduCue to interface Prs with our Interactive PowerPoint Presentation Systems.

Infrared technology has the limitation of needing a line of sight with the receiver. Based on early tests, we found that Prs had an effective range of from 60 to 75 feet, and 30 transmitters seemed to work well with one receiver. Simultaneously arriving IR inputs from different transmitters did cancel each other out. We cautioned our customers that this limitation might require students to resend inputs several times for the same question.

Input Status Matrix and Marquee Displays

Since infrared transmitters provided no indication of whether or not signals were received, Socratec developed an Input Status Matrix to provide feedback to participants. After responding, each participant checked the Input Status Matrix that was displayed on the presentation screen for a visual indication if his or her input was successfully received. For very large rooms, Reference Numbers scroll across the bottom of the screen in a Marquee fashion, and only show the keypad numbers not yet received.

Programmable Infrared Transmitters

Each unit was given a unique Keypad number very similar to the number scheme used for Wired and RF keypads (i.e., from 1 to n). The Keypad # digits were sent for identification along with each input response. Prs programmable units had 10 keys plus High and Low confidence buttons for conditioning these responses. Note: We never used these confidence buttons in our Prs applications. The Programmable Prs units allowed the participant to use an ID Changer device to "burn-in" his or her ID # in addition to the Keypad #. This ID # would then also be sent along with each response. Very few of our customers used this ID # feature, and elected to use only the Keypad number for identification.

Fixed ID Infrared Transmitters

Each Fixed ID Transmitter contains a serial number already permanently "burned-in" during the manufacturing process. Fixed ID Transmitters always send their serial numbers along with the input data. Therefore, the software logic that correlated seat numbers to keypads used for all previous keypad types was no longer valid. End users typically purchased Fixed ID Transmitters for personal use. Participants carried and used the same transmitter in different classrooms. The software was required to recognize the serial number when inputs were received to determine the participant name associated with the input.

The Fixed ID Prs Transmitters were very appealing because they performed well, and were less expensive than the Programmable units. The downside and challenge to customers was the excessive response times when used with large audiences. Receivers accepted inputs at about 10 responses per second. When input signals hit Receivers simultaneously, they would cancel each other out. This required participants to resend their inputs. Typical questions in large classrooms took at least a minute to accept inputs and process.

In 2004, GTCO Calcomp purchased EduCue, and has subsequently repackaged Prs into its InterWrite Prs product line. They have revised the product and announced several new software upgrades since then.

Figure 1. H-ITT transmitter and receiver

H-ITT Fixed ID Transmitters

H-ITT 2-Way Smarte Link Transmitters has 10 operational keys that send an internal serial number to the Receiver along with the response input. The Receiver sends a confirmation signal back to the Transmitter within half a second, which turns its LED green. If no confirmation is received, the LED remains Red, indicating that the input must be resent. RxShow H-ITT accommodates this new keypad, and has a special function to permit multiple-digit entries. The confirmation feature of these H-ITT keypads allows students to "self-manage" the transmission and receipt of inputs. The presenter can display the status of H-ITT keypad inputs during a question sequence, if desired. However, this on-screen feedback to the students is optional, since each student is given an instant confirmation when input is received.

In 2004, Dr. Harold Stokes, Professor of Physics and Astronomy at Brigham Young University, evaluated H-ITT transmitters in a live classroom environment with 214 students. The newly announced H-ITT design, with its 10-millisecond speed, was of interest to our company because of reported infrared technology "Receiver" throughput improvements in large lecture hall applications. (For more information, see Web site link: http://www.h-itt.com/news_hsr.html.)

The H-ITT 2-Way transmitter sells for $25. Our company tailored software to integrate this keypad into our product line, in order to give customers extra value for their investment. This is a prime example of how competition has benefited the ARS consumer, and will continue to do so in the years to come.

Recommendations for
ARS Question Design

As a consultant, I have provided my services to many clients to improve their ARS applications. I offer my thoughts based on my many years of experience in this area on how to improve the quality of questions displayed for keypad response:

1. Simplify sentences, reduce word count, and paraphrase. When a question is displayed, it should be easy to read and easy to understand in no more than 10 to

15 seconds. Questions that have too many unnecessary words only confuse the audience and produce unreliable results. My rule of thumb is that a question setup for keypad response should never display more than 25 to 30 words.

2.   Use setup question visuals — If a question, by nature, must be wordy, is very complex, or requires figures, use a setup visual before the actual question. The next visual should be the actual keypad question that follows the rules stated in Recommendation #1. The second visual should paraphrase the question, since the audience already understands the details from the setup visual.

3.   Reduce multiple-choice options from five to four. For large audiences, five multiple-choice selections slow down the response process. I have found that four choices work better and are more effective. Also, for True or False type questions, adding a "Not Sure" adds an interest dimension to the outcome, and increases the percent who respond.

4.   Add relevant diagrams, clip art, or pictures. Pictures add an important dimension to a question, and give an audience another point of reference in selecting a response. For example, if a textbook contains a diagram that relates to a question, consider including the diagram (or figure) in the question visual.

5.   Survey for opinions and feelings. Not every question should be a test question with a right and wrong answer. Likert-scale questions (on a scale of 1 to n) provide an important outlet for an audience to express opinions about important topics. Participants want to see how their opinions compare to the rest of the audience.

6.   Interweave questions throughout presentations. Audiences enjoy having the opportunity to provide input, and therefore, questions should be strategically placed and interspersed throughout a presentation, rather than batched one after another. A good rule of thumb is to ask a keypad question for audience response at least once every 10 minutes to keep the audience engaged and interested.

7.   Show results as either graphs or values. Most ARS results are displayed in graphical form, but I have found that showing percentages also provides adequate information to an audience. If space on the question slide is limited, consider showing results as percentage values next to each choice.

8.   Compare results from demographic groups. Divide the audience into groups, and then compare graphical results in subsequent questions. This is a great method to stimulate discussions and conduct meetings. In addition, team competitions and entertainment benefit from this feature.

9.   Extract valuable information from the audience. Over the years, many of my commercial clients used our ARS to support their important annual meetings. Their employees traveled from all over the country (and the world) to a centralized meeting location. These meetings recognized achievements, and discussed plans and progress for the upcoming year. Typically, our system supported the client in this "telling" aspect and some team competition exercises. I always encouraged my clients to consider the audience "a valuable information resource." Collecting information from the audience regarding their perceptions of the "state of the business" and their relationships with customers is a great and untapped use of ARS.

10.   ARS question "Learning Object" Web site. I recommend that the ARS industry establish an ARS Web site that becomes a valuable depository and resource for all ARS users. ARS would share their very best questions with their peers and the entire ARS community. Criteria to define quality questions from an instructional viewpoint need to be developed. Questions would be organized with keyword searching to account for the many topics, textbooks, disciplines, and so forth, that users may require. Contributors would be encouraged to submit cleverly designed questions (with some explanations) that worked well in their classrooms, and achieved pedagogical and cognitive objectives. The ARS industry, in cooperation with universities and publishers, should sponsor this Web site. Any registered user should be able to access this Web site and download question ideas in PowerPoint format to use in their slide shows. In my opinion, this database would be enlightening to new users, and would open the door for the future ARS expansion.

Conclusions

The evolution of ARS over the past 25 years has been an amazing and interesting journey, and I am pleased to have had the opportunity to be a part of the process. Competition and creative minds have improved the quality of our products, and reduced the cost of offerings. An infrared transmitter today costs less than 10% of an RF transmitter a decade ago, and the performance of these inexpensive devices is nothing short of amazing.

Now that ARS is so affordable, continued progress and expansion of the concept will be a challenge. My sense is that the barriers to growth will be primarily in the application of the concept. In my opinion, the full potential of ARS will not be achieved if the application continues to be restricted primarily to test taking. Therefore, I wish to conclude by reiterating my point that the key to future success and growth for the ARS industry is to focus our energies into the quality of questions that we ask of our students, and the integration of these questions into instructional material.

Additional Reading

Connor. G. (1996 January/February). Too much training, too little time. *Corporate University Review,* 24-25.

Galagan, P. A. (1989 January) IBM gets its arms around education. *ASTD Training & Development Journal,* 36-37.

Horowitz, H. M. (1993). Jump-starting interactive classrooms for improved effectiveness and productivity. *Journal of Instruction Delivery Systems Spring,* 18-22.

Horowitz, H. M. (1998). Student response systems: Interactivity in a classroom environment. *Proceedings of Sixth Annual Conference on Interactive Instruction Delivery. Society for Applied Learning Technology,* 8-15.

Section II

Chapter V

Practical Lessons from Four Years of Using an ARS in Every Lecture of a Large Class

Quintin Cutts, University of Glasgow, UK

Abstract

This chapter explores pedagogical and logistical issues arising from the extension, using an audience response system (ARS), of an existing module based on traditional 1-hour lectures, over a period of 4 years. The principal issues involve the limited time for equipment setup; the significant time taken to present each ARS question, and hence, the need to maximise the learning gain from each question asked; the importance of considering the pedagogical rationale for using the ARS; the complexity of remediation and the acknowledgement that not all student misunderstandings highlighted by the ARS can be addressed effectively within the lecture. The chapter offers suggestions on the following aspects of ARS use: the setting up in theatres, and distribution to students of ARS equipment; a range of pedagogical rationales underpinning question design; guidelines on session format and question structure; remediation issues both within and outside the lecture context.

Introduction

The adoption of new technology in teaching and learning, as in other settings, often follows a trial-and-error path as the early adopters attempt to discover effective methodologies for use. This often discourages early widespread take-up of new technology. Attempts to rollout audience response systems across the University of Glasgow, while being relatively successful, have highlighted this blockage to take-up. Using an ARS for the first few times is problematic, since the adopters are lecturers who typically (a) have little spare time, (b) do not want to contemplate "failure" in front of their classes, and (c) have no personal experience of this technology from their own education. Successful adoptions at Glasgow have come partially from our being able to pass on the growing personal experience of the brave, early adopters to other interested individuals. Reviewers of our papers on evaluations of the technology's use have commented on a number of occasions that they would like more straightforward logistical and pedagogical information and learning about how the systems were used: information that may not have been relevant to the particular focus of the paper. It appears that the reviewers themselves, not surprisingly, were new to the technology, could see the potential benefits, but then had many questions not answered in the papers.

This chapter, therefore, attempts to answer such questions as they apply to one particular educational setting: that of using the ARS in *every* session of an existing lecture-based module. Many early adopters choose to use the technology in just one or two lectures, or in a large-group tutorial, to try it out, but this chapter describes a 4-year use of the technology where, from the outset, the aim was to use the ARS in as many lectures as possible in an existing lecture-based module. Note the crucial difference here, compared to other reported uses of ARS in a whole course (e.g., Dufresne, Gerace, Leonard, Mestre, & Wenk, 1996; Mazur, 1997; Nicol & Boyle, 2003), where the course and session structure was radically redesigned to incorporate the use of an ARS. For pragmatic reasons, the course under discussion here has largely retained its original structure, a feature that is likely to be valuable to other potential adopters. My aim here is not to presumptuously tell readers how the technology should be used, but rather to highlight issues that have arisen over 4 years of this style of use, issues that I would have found useful to know more about at the start of the process. Addressing these issues has had an effect on the course, and the importance of the ARS, at least as reported in student feedback. The bar chart of Figure 1 shows how students have responded to the question "How useful do you think the handsets are?" over the first 3 years of use, and shows a steady increase in their perceived usefulness over this period.

The chapter presents the context in which the use of the ARS was embedded, and then explores various educational rationales behind the questions that were presented to students. A number of tips on how to format a 50-minute lecture with ARS questions are then presented, along with a range of differing styles of question. Remediation issues are then discussed, (a crucial aspect of any ARS use) followed by the physical requirements for creating ARS-enabled lectures. The chapter concludes with a summary of the major issues and questions that should be answered when considering using an ARS in the style under examination here, and an outline of areas for further work.

Figure 1. Answers from 3 successive years to "How useful do you think the handsets are?"

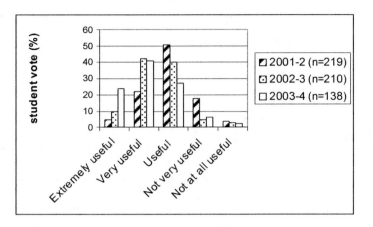

Context

The chapter concerns a 4-year use of an ARS in an introductory, computer-programming module. Enrollment varies between 200 and 450, being taught in a single classroom or in two classrooms consecutively, according to the class size. Ability levels in the cohort have ranged widely from complete beginners, to those who have a high level of computing proficiency from earlier education. The module structure is traditional, with 24 1-hour lectures delivered by a single lecturer, and a range of tutorial and laboratory sessions run by a group of tutors. The course was not radically redesigned to incorporate the use of the ARS.

The subject is partially one of skill development, both the solving of small computing problems and the translation of those solutions into programming code. In addition, the deep concepts underlying the structure of programming languages must be thoroughly understood, since they underpin these skills. There is very little rote learning on offer.

I am the lecturer on this module, but also have been closely involved with a large-scale rollout of ARS technology across the University of Glasgow, reported principally in (Draper & Brown, 2004; Draper, Cargill, & Cutts, 2001). As a computer scientist, a committed teacher, and with an interest in educational technology, I was fascinated to see how an ARS could improve my classes. At the first use, there were very limited reports in the literature of this style of ARS use, and even now, I know of no detailed reports of use in a programming class. Hence, much of what is presented here has inevitably come from personal experience.

Pedagogical Rationales
for ARS Questions

At Glasgow, our experience has shown that when the educational purpose for using the technology is firmly in place, the results in terms of student and lecturer satisfaction are better than when the technology is used for its own sake. I have been using the technology to address the following four education issues.

Engagement in Lectures

An over-arching purpose for using the ARS in this class has been on student engagement. Recognition of student engagement as a fundamental issue came from an earlier study of the same class (Cutts, 2001). Lectures are rarely seen by students as an environment where they work hard to understand the material: instead they are viewed as a collection point for content and materials, to be engaged with later. The ARS breaks up a lecture into manageable chunks, and the students often report that they appreciate the changes in pace, resulting in their being more attentive and awake in classes. A general increase in engagement is the most often cited benefit of using an ARS. Student responses and my experience as the lecturer certainly back this up in this class. We have found in Glasgow that the same is true in many subjects, from statistics to English literature.

Focus on Study Habits

The skills-based nature of this course requires that students are practising their skills all the way through the semester, and regularly reflecting on their progress. Just as a complex piece of music cannot be mugged up at the last minute before a music lesson, so these skills cannot be learned the night before an exam. For many students, this stands in stark contrast to their experience in other academic subjects. Hence, I was keen to use the handsets to get students to reflect on how much time they were putting into their studies outside the lecture, on how hard they were finding the course, on how and when they were going to commit to work on a particular topic, and so on. Hence, I presented many questions on these matters. My intention was that in giving me an answer, the students would be required to reflect on and adjust their own study behaviour. It appears that I did not manage to convey this intention effectively, as many students saw these questions as a means of checking up on them and of my collecting data on student behaviour, data that could be used to adjust delivery in future years. Clearly, they didn't see the personal benefit to themselves in considering and answering the questions, a crucial issue for successful adoption. Although still fascinated by this area, I stopped using the ARS for this purpose after the first year in favour of the other rationales outlined here, principally because only a few questions can be asked in any one lecture, and the students were engaging better with questions rooted in these other rationales. There was simply not time to address this issue as well.

Early Engagement with Course Material

Computer programming is a highly practical subject, and the best way to learn about the concepts involved is to make use of them in some way. A lecturer can introduce concepts and demonstrate how they can be used, but deeper learning happens when students are required to make use of the concepts themselves in order to solve a problem or answer a question. Indeed, before the introduction of an ARS to this course, I had already taken the step of breaking the lecture into sections, and setting short questions for the students to work on for a few minutes, with the aim of reinforcing the topic I had just introduced. However, my observation was that a significant number of students persistently avoided doing the work, staring ahead and waiting for other students to come up with the answer. Additionally, I could only receive responses from a small number of students, most likely only those students who were confident of their answer, and hence, I was largely unable to assist students who were in difficulties.

The anonymity of the responses given with an ARS encouraged me to believe that the students would be more willing to work out an answer and respond, a view borne out in student evaluations, where they indicated that they were twice as likely to construct an answer to a question when asked to respond with the ARS compared to hands-up (Draper & Brown, 2004).

An example of this kind of question is as follows.

Consider the following code:

```
A, B, C : Integer;
...
A : = 2;
B : = A * 2 + 4;
A : = 12;
B : = A * 2 + B;
C : = B – A + 3;
```

What values do A, B, and C have after executing this code?

1.   A=8, B=36, C=31
2.   12, 36, 27
3.   12, 168, 159
4.   12, 32, 23
5.   None of the above
6.   Don't know

Prior to asking this question, I had just covered the rules for executing this kind of code, and worked through an example myself. The principal aim of asking the question is to encourage the students to work with the rules I had just introduced.

The students reported very favourably on this style of use. The questions tend to have a single correct answer, and the students liked the reassurance of an immediate check on their level of understanding.

Testing Fundamental Concepts

Some of the most mature uses of voting technology in lectures (e.g. Dufresne, Gerace, Leonard, Mestre, & Wenk, 1996; Mazur 1997) are based on using seemingly simple questions to get at the fundamental concepts of the subject. The researchers, based in physics education, found that many students could mechanically work their way through the problems to get the right answer, but had little understanding of what the result really meant in terms of fundamental physics. Their seemingly simple questions tend to split the class, and then students argue with each other as to the correctness of their own answer. This articulation of their reasoning process is believed to be highly effective in promoting a deep engagement with the concepts. A second vote determines how the class is progressing and whether the lecturer needs to step in. The initial vote is crucial because it encourages each student to commit to an answer, an essential starting point from which to launch into a serious discussion.

While the students in my class liked the engagement questions presented above, it is relatively easy to learn the rules on how to derive the answers to such questions. They promote a feel-good factor and early practice with the material, but not necessarily deep learning. Just as the physics students needed to appreciate how the concepts underlying the formulae related to the problem, so my students need to appreciate how the computational concepts underlying the programming language relate to a particular problem they are trying to solve.

For computer programming, I was unaware of a record of the areas of the subject typically found to be most challenging by students. However, with a growing range of my own questions covering most of the course, I hit upon a few key issues with which the students were struggling, and each year, increasingly tuned the course to address the fundamental misconceptions underlying their problems.

Because the students could see how important these issues were to me, they tended to become more animated and involved when presented with related questions. Sometimes I used the Mazur (1997) method of getting students to discuss their answers in twos or threes, known as Peer Discussion; at other times, I led a Class-Wide Discussion (a term coined by Dufresne et al., 1996) where typically only the more confident students spoke out, but the whole class appeared to be invested in working their way to the correct answer.

Tips on Session Format and Question Styles

Some generally useful hints for using an ARS in multiple lectures have emerged from the use described here, falling into two categories: how to structure a session making use of an ARS, and issues around question structure and the interpretation of responses.

Session Format

A universally valuable use of the ARS is the insertion of a question at the very start of the lecture. As soon as I can get the equipment set up, usually by about 2 minutes after I walk into the lecture theatre, I get this question up for the students to answer. At this point, some students are still coming into the lecture theatre, and so normally, those already present would be sitting chatting to their neighbours or staring into space. The question projected at the front of the class draws their attention forward and starts to focus their mind on the coming lecture. The topic of the question typically focuses on an aspect of the material covered in the previous lecture that ARS questioning showed to be problematic.

I occasionally use a question right at the end of the session also. This can be a straightforward test of material covered in the session, or else a teaser that encourages them to do further work after the lecture.

One of the most surprising aspects for myself and others when first using the technology is how few questions can be asked in a typical 50-minute lecture. When an ARS is used to augment an existing lecture, as was initially the case for me, it is easy not to realise how much time each question takes. First, the question must be presented to the students. Depending on the question, it may be enough simply to display it and let the students read and answer, or else some explanation may be required. Second, the students need time to formulate an answer to the question and then submit it. For questions of any size or complexity, the students' processing time outweighs the time taken to receive the responses — and so the speed of the ARS is not crucial. This is fortunate for the PRS system, where the collection of 300 votes will inevitably take at least a minute. Processing time may be a few minutes. I believe it is easy for any lecturer to underestimate how long it takes to process a question for a student who may have only first set eyes on the topic a few minutes before. Certainly, some students struggle with the time limit. Finally, once the responses have been collected, the lecturer must interpret the graph in order to decide what feedback to provide. This may be as short as acknowledging the correct answer, or as long as a class-wide discussion around the issues which the question raises. I would say that the shortest time for a question is about 2 minutes, a typical time is 5 minutes, and occasionally they can take a lecture-derailing 10-15 minutes.

Question Format

As outlined earlier, a primary use of ARS questions is for the formative evaluation of student learning. Based on the responses received, the lecturer will provide a level of remediation appropriate to the understanding shown by the class. The decision as to what remediation is required must be made in real time while standing in front of the class, and should attempt to assist as many of the students as possible in the limited time available. The use of multiple-choice questions (MCQ) in an ARS context is therefore in contrast to their use in: exams, for summative assessment, where no remediation is required; and online learning environments, where feedback is only required for one student on the basis of their single response. My experience of asking and responding to questions leads to the following suggestions for question design and analysis.

Simple is best. In line with good MCQ design, keeping the questions as simple as possible, in terms of length and number of response options, limits the time taken to interpret the question and responses by students and lecturer respectively.

Explanations for distractors. Having prepared explanations for why the distractors are wrong, as well as why the right answer is correct, speeds up and sharpens the interpretation of the responses. Picking distractors that result from typical student misconceptions highlighted in earlier runs of the course gives the best chance of catching and correcting them this time around.

Beware on-the-fly questions. An ARS will typically allow a question to be generated on the spot: perhaps spoken out by the lecturer or written on the board, perhaps making use of student suggestions for the answer options. Although the students' suggestions give validity to the question since they are "real" options, I have not found this method to work well in general. It is hard to come up with a good explanation for the wrong answers, because there usually is not time to determine the thought process underlying them.

Take time over analysis of the response graph. I have found it easy to misinterpret the response graph. Say a question has six responses. If half the class opt for the correct answer, with the remaining students spread across the remaining options, the graph will show one significant peak. I have misread a graph of this general structure as showing that a large majority of students got the right answer, when in fact less than half did. This is a consequence of the pressure and limited time available when standing in front of the class with a new set of responses on display.

A style of question I have found particularly hard to interpret includes, say, five numbered statements in the main question text. The student must decide which of the statements are true. The answer options consist of various subsets of the five numbers. A related question style asks more than one question in the main question, and then each answer option contains an answer for each of the subquestions. The benefit of these styles of question is that the students are required to do a lot of mental processing while only a single break in the lecture is made. The drawback for interpreting the answers is that it is hard to see exactly how many students thought each individual statement, using the first example, was correct. To do this, I have to add up the votes for all the answer options containing that statement. Without being able to perform this kind of analysis, it is hard to determine what remediation is really required. Note that some ARS software packages support analysis of the answer data in real time in the middle of the lecture. If such an option is available, then the answers can be analysed to give a count, for each statement, of those students who thought it was true. Such counts permit much more accurate remediation.

Providing a "Don't Know" response option. If a student genuinely does not know the answer to the question, I would rather they could register this, rather than either not voting at all or just guessing an answer. In so doing, I get the most accurate representation of the students' collective understanding, and have the best chance of giving useful feedback. Note, however, that students are conditioned, from endless exam MCQs, never to leave a question blank. In discussion with students, I have discovered that they consider a "Don't Know" response in the same league as not answering at all, and so rarely, by default, use the option.

From the point of view of encouraging cognitive engagement, it may indeed be best for students to attempt to answer something, even if largely a guess, and then additionally provide a method for the students to signal their confidence in their answer. Hunt (1982) showed that the simple addition of stating a confidence level in an answer was significant in improving learning, proposing that those who monitor their learning do better. The PRS equipment allows confidence levels to be submitted at the same time as the response, and displayed on the results graph. Since Hunt's result has only come to my attention recently, I cannot report on personal experience of using confidence levels, but I will experiment in the next run of the module. If Hunt is correct, my feared scenario of increased complexity in interpreting a graph with confidence levels is unfounded, since in my explanations I need not differentiate between responders with different confidence levels. It is the act of choosing a confidence level that is crucial to the increased learning, rather than the presentation of this information to the teacher.

Remediation Issues

As embodied in the educational rationales for using an ARS described earlier, a key use of the technology is to flush out student misunderstandings, and then to offer remediation. Once the question has been presented and the students have processed it and responded with their handsets, the lecturer must decide on the appropriate remediation. Typically, he/she indicates which answer is correct and why, and talks through the incorrect answers, making use of previous insights into why students tend to pick them, in the hope of getting right to the heart of their misunderstanding. In the cyclical learning models of, for example, Laurillard (2002) and Kolb (1984), it makes sense to follow up this remediation with a second question of a similar nature, to determine whether the new understanding is now in place: in fact, to keep going around the cycle until it is.

The choice of how much feedback to offer to the students depends on a trade-off between ensuring that every student has the correct understanding, and that the students, as a body, are moving forward in their learning. This will depend on the context of use of the ARS. In Wit's use (Wit, 2003), in a large group tutorial setting, the aim was principally to deepen and correct students' understanding, and so offering remediation was the main point of the class. In the lectures described here, there is a conflict between offering remediation and presenting new material. Two principal issues have arisen:

- **Limited re-asking.** Because of the time issue in the style of use under discussion here, I have very rarely asked a second, related question immediately after remediating on a question the students found hard. By giving the remediation, I have often tricked myself into thinking that the students now understand the material, but in fact I have not checked this with a second question. The issue has been bourn out on those occasions when I asked a related question at the start of the next lecture: some students still answered incorrectly.

- **Not all misunderstandings addressed.** When half the class choose a single incorrect answer option, it is clearly worth investing time with the class to work out why they chose that option. I often instigate a class-wide discussion, asking students to tell me their thinking process. In so doing, I have uncovered many fundamental misunderstandings common to those students. However, when only a small proportion of the class pick a particular incorrect option, say less than 5%, it is hard to justify the time required to remediate with these students. There is a problem here. I have asked the students to work on a question and answer it, and their motivation is that they will receive feedback on their answer. Although they will get the feedback that it is wrong, if they chose a low-scoring response option, they are unlikely to get any further detailed feedback other than why the correct answer is correct. Their specific misunderstanding hasn't been addressed, and motivation to use the system may therefore be diminished.

Styles of Remediation

I have tackled the issues raised above by providing remediation in a number of different ways, as follows:

- **Immediate feedback.** I will always discuss the responses to a question at least to some extent. This can involve my working through the problem being asked, showing how I derive the correct answer. If I know of typical misconceptions on this topic, and have designed the distractors to incorporate these misconceptions, then I can talk directly to those misconceptions.

- **Class-wide discussion.** As described above, if I see that a large number of students have the wrong answer, but I am unsure why, then I will encourage the students to tell me their thought processes underlying the answer. This works with varying success. Usually only a small proportion of the class are willing to speak out in this way, although this is often enough to ascertain the problem.

- **Restructuring future lectures.** On some occasions, the class-wide discussion raises issues important enough that I am willing to adjust the structure of future lectures in order to fully address the misunderstanding. Hence, while the lecture course has essentially remained the same over the years, the use of the ARS has resulted in my being responsive to the needs of the students in any particular year.

With the response data in hand, I certainly consider each lecture in the sequence more carefully than of old. Whilst I think the results are better, it is an inevitable cost of using an ARS and being responsive to the students' needs, as evidenced by their answers.

- **Provision of assistance outside the lecture.** It is clear from the issues raised above that I cannot address all misunderstandings in the lecture. Additionally, I suspect that both the students and I are misled by my remediation into thinking that they understand the topic correctly now. When I have worked through a problem, it is easy for a student to think "ah, yes, that's clear now, I've got it." For these reasons, I believe that the work completed by students in the lecture should be linked to closely-related work outside the lecture. One attempt at such a system is described in Cutts and Kennedy (2005), where ARS questions and responses from lectures are posted on a Web site, to be used by lecturer, tutors, and students, to direct learning activities outside the lecture. The system has not been in place long enough to make definitive statements about its effects, although initial feedback from students is promising. The key here is that some way of connecting learning activities in the lecture with external learning activities is necessary, and the ARS response data is a rich, and potentially personalised, description of the learner-based activity.

Physical Setup

The physical setup consists of the hardware and software required to operate the system and its configuration. A tenet by which the group promoting ARS in Glasgow operates is that *the lecturer's activities should be minimally disrupted by the introduction of the equipment*, particularly at the start of a lecture. We are keen to avoid the destructive effects often caused to a lecture by, for example, failed attempts to connect a laptop successfully to a data projector. For one-off uses, we are able to give our time to assist the lecturer. However, in a multiple use like the one described here, we don't have the personnel to assist at the start and end of every session, and so have to find another solution.

The hardware used is the Personal Response System marketed by GTCO Calcomp (GTCO, 2005). The PRS consists of an infrared transmitter, or handset, one per student, and a number of infrared receivers connected to the lecturer's laptop. About one receiver is required for every 50-60 students, and these are connected with wires in a chain. The principal issues for deployment are as follows.

Distribution of Handsets

With such a large number of students, and a requirement for the handsets to be available in every lecture, I wanted the students to be allocated a handset at the start of the term, and then personally to bring it to every lecture. The alternative would be to hand them out and collect them in at the start and end of every lecture. Although we have done this for occasional lectures of 300 students, the distribution and collection takes at least 5 minutes in the lecture, and requires a number of helpers. I was keen to avoid both the time disruption and the need for assistants. So, a handset was distributed to each student at the start of the year, on the understanding that if they did not return it in good order at the end of the module, they would be unable to continue to the following academic year until they had paid a replacement fee of £20 sterling. While this setup undoubtedly achieved the requirement of minimum disruption to lectures, there are two ramifications of such a policy: the students can forget to bring their handset, and handsets are lost if students drop out of university completely without returning theirs. From a rough show of hands, it appears that up to 20% of students forget their handset each lecture, and further, there may be as much as a 5% attrition rate for handsets that are not returned and for which we do not get a replacement fee. Alternatives to this policy are to stock handsets in, for example, the university bookshop, and require students to buy a handset, much as they do for required textbooks. This alone will not guarantee that they bring the handset to every lecture, but a further twist is to make one or more of the questions in each lecture contribute to an assessment element — a carrot to encourage students to bring handsets — as adopted by Burnstein and Lederman (2001), for example, but not as yet in this class. Such a scheme carries the overhead of maintaining accurate records of all responses.

Receiver Setup

Initially, four portable receivers, each about the size of a large cigarette packet and mounted on a camera tripod, were connected together for each lecture in the 300-seat lecture theatre. This proved unsatisfactory for a number of reasons: they weren't high enough for students to get their votes accepted since infrared requires line of sight for successful communication; they took too much time to set up; and the resulting wires running up the steps of the lecture theatre were deemed a safety hazard. After the first few lectures, we committed five receivers to this theatre, and had them wired permanently into the ceiling with a convenient connecting jack socket near the lecturer's podium. Setup now was no more than connecting wires between the laptop, a power supply, and this receiver network, and took no longer than a minute to complete. In the second, 150-seat, lecture theatre, I initially engaged a student helper from the class to set up and dismantle two receivers at the start and end of each lecture, but after the first year of use, I was able to do this myself without major disruption.

Laptop and Software

With respect to the software used, the aim has been again to avoid significant pertur-bation to my typical lecture style. I have been a user of Microsoft PowerPoint™ for many years. The ARS group at Glasgow employed a programmer to develop a connection between the PRS software that supports the gathering of responses, and the display of the response graph and PowerPoint™. The aim here was to allow questions to be authored and presented in PowerPoint™, and then for control to be passed seamlessly to the PRS software for response collection and display. We used this system for a year before finding that the level of control over the PRS software was insufficient, at which point we entirely rewrote the software ourselves, resulting in smoother integration with PowerPoint™ and improved flexibility on question styles, response collection, and response analysis and display. Further details of our software system, known as QRS, are available (QRS, 2005). Control over the software allowed for experimentation with the system as a whole, since ideas that came to me during use could quickly be incorporated and tried out in the live system.

The software was installed on my laptop. With handsets held by students, and with the receivers installed in the large lecture theatre, my setup arrangements at the start of a lecture were almost unchanged from how they had been prior to using an ARS.

Conclusions

This chapter has attempted to provide the reader with an insight into some of the complexities of using an ARS with a large class in a traditional, lecture-based course. The ARS provides much needed interaction in the otherwise largely one-way flow of information still required by the existing module structure. The principal issues that have arisen from examination of this use of an ARS, along with questions that should be answered if considering a similar adoption, are as follows:

- The setting up, handing out, and retrieving of equipment takes time. How will it be optimised in the short 1-hour lecture slots?

- Only a small number of questions can be asked in a session, as presentation of the question by the lecturer, processing and response by students, and the final explanation of the responses take a significant time. On what pedagogical basis will questions be developed, in order to maximise the effectiveness of the time used to present them?

- Use of an ARS is unlikely to fix all problems in understanding within the lecture itself. What remediation techniques will be used in lectures? How will the results of the students' initial engagement with the material be transferred into other learning environments, to enable the dialogue initiated in lectures to be continued?

Further Work

As a lecturer using an ARS in most of my lectures, (and as I have heard from other lecturers who do the same) I find I am now frustrated to be in a class without the ARS. I see the benefits to the class of being activated by the ARS, in terms of their heightened attention and willingness to speak out, and I now find traditional monologue delivery increasingly pointless.

This is a pioneering time: the more that ARS-enabled lectures are examined, the more we see there is to examine. Whilst this chapter has reported on basic logistical and educational strategies for use in a single context that have gained favour in student feedback (see Draper & Brown, 2004), further research work is required to understand their effects. Few researchers have made clear links specifically between the use of an ARS and improved learning outcomes. (The impressive 6,000-student study by Hake (1998) covers not only ARS, but a wide range of differing techniques under the umbrella term Interactive Engagement, that all aim to improve interaction, and so, it is impossible to pin the positive effects they report to the ARS alone.) One of the first reported attempts to make such a link appears elsewhere in this publication, and is based on the same use of an ARS as examined in this chapter. Additionally, it is unclear which specific learning strategies are triggered by answering ARS questions. Nor yet is there a corpus of field-tested questions for every discipline. And finally, the precious dialogue on learning initiated in the lecture is rarely carried beyond that environment. There is still much to be done.

Acknowledgments

I acknowledge Chris Mitchell, in particular, for his support of this work over the last 4 years. He is the developer of the QRS software used with the PRS hardware during this period, and has been invaluable before, during, and after lectures, both technically and through his insight into the process. Steve Draper, with whom I have helped roll out ARS technology at the University of Glasgow, has made many excellent suggestions on styles of use over the years, and Margaret Brown's observations have been very helpful. The University of Glasgow has supported this work through awards from both the Learning and Teaching Development Fund and the Chancellor's Fund.

References

Burnstein, R. A., & Lederman, L. M. (2001). Using wireless keypads in lecture classes. *The Physics Teacher, 39*, 8-11.

Cutts, Q. (2001). Engaging a large first year class. In M. Walker (Ed.), *Reconstructing Professionalism in University Teaching* (pp. 105-108). Open University Press.

Cutts, Q. I., & Kennedy, G. E. (2005). Connecting learning environments using electronic voting systems. In A. Young and D. Tolhurst (Eds), *Proceedings of the Seventh Australian Computer Education Conference, Newcastle, Australia. Conferences in Research and Practice in Information Technology, 42*.

Draper, S. W., & Brown, M. I. (2004). Increasing interactivity in lectures using an electronic voting system. *Journal of Computer Assisted Learning, 20*, 81-94.

Draper, S., Cargill, J., & Cutts, Q. (2001). Electronically enhanced classroom interaction. *Australian Journal of Educational Technology, 18*(1), 13-23.

Dufresne, R., Gerace, W., Leonard, W., Mestre, J., & Wenk, L. (1996). Classtalk: A classroom communication system for active learning. *Journal of Computing in Higher Education, 7*, 3-47.

GTCO (2005). GTCO Calcomp, Columbia, Maryland. http://www.gtcocalcomp.com

Hake, R. R. (1998). Interactive-engagement vs. traditional methods: A six-thousand-student survey of mechanics test data for introductory physics courses. *American Journal of Physics, 66*(1), 64-74.

Hunt, D. (1982). Effects of human self-assessment responding on learning. *Journal of Applied Psychology, 67*, 75-82.

Kolb, D. A. (1984) *Experiential Learning: Experience as the source of learning and development*. Englewood Cliffs, NJ: Prentice Hall.

Laurillard, D. (2002) *Rethinking university teaching: A conversational framework for the effective use of learning technology* (2nd ed.). London: RoutledgeFarmer.

Mazur, E. (1997) *Peer instruction: A user's manual*. Upper Saddle River, NJ, Prentice-Hall.

Nicol, D., & Boyle, N. (2003). Peer instruction vs. class-wide discussion in large classes: A comparison of two interaction methods in the wired classroom. *Studies in Higher Education, 28*(4), 458-473.

QRS (2005). http://www.dcs.gla.ac.uk/~quintin/QRS

Wit, E. (2003). Who wants to be... The use of a personal response system in statistics teaching. *MSOR Connections, 3*(2), 5-11.

Chapter VI

Using an Audience Response System to Enhance Student Engagement in Large Group Orientation:
A Law Faculty Case Study

Sally Kift, Queensland University of Tecnology, Australia

Abstract

This chapter discusses an innovative use of an audience response system (ARS) to address the vexed learning and teaching problem of how to manage effective student engagement in large group academic Orientation sessions. Having particular regard to the research that informs transition practice to enhance the first-year experience, the chapter addresses the pedagogical basis for the decision to adopt the ARS technology as integral to the learning design deployed. The Orientation exemplar discussed is drawn from practice in a law faculty; however, the general approach illustrated is capable of replication regardless of discipline or institution. In the hope that this case study might be transferred to other applications, the enactment of the learning design involving the ARS is described, and an analysis of the evaluation conducted is also presented.

Introduction: A Learning and Teaching Problem

Bass (1999) has usefully drawn attention to the difference it makes to have a "problem" in research (a problem in research being the necessary prerequisite to the start of the investigative process), to that of having a "problem" in learning and teaching (which is usually conceptualised as some form of failure that requires immediate remedial action): "[c]hanging the status of the *problem* in teaching from terminal remediation to ongoing investigation is precisely what the movement for a scholarship of teaching is all about" (Bass, Introduction, para. 1).

This chapter will describe a learning and teaching problem that has continually vexed my faculty at the commencement of every new teaching period. How do we engage our large and diverse student cohort in their transition to their first year of tertiary study, at that first point of critical faculty contact — the all-too-brief academic orientation session — when everything can coalesce to militate against students making the requisite cognitive connection with the important, "start-up" messages we seek to convey? As encouraged by Shulman (1998, p. 6), this teaching scholarship publication will present a "public account of ... the full act of teaching [involved] — vision, design, enactment, outcomes, and analysis — in a manner susceptible to critical review by ... professional peers and amendable to productive employment in future work by members of that same community."

This case study will describe the pedagogical approach that has been adopted to harness the technological affordances presented by an audience response system ARS as applied in the context of first year orientation for two distinct groups: internal students (n~350) and external students (n~110). The orientation exemplar discussed is drawn from practice in a law faculty; however, the general approach illustrated can be applied regardless of discipline or institution. This particular ARS application is one aspect of an integrated package of transition strategies, deployed throughout the course of the whole transition year, for the benefit of the first year student in law (that has been more fully described elsewhere (Kift, 2004)). It has been designed specifically to take account of the reality that, as the faculty's Assistant Dean, Teaching & Learning, the author is only one in a progression of "talking heads" attempting to connect with new students in an intense two-hour faculty orientation session. In designing for learning in this unique and quite fraught environment, the necessity to place the learners' needs as central to the learning design is paramount (as should always be the case), while the focus on the technologies and delivery approaches is a secondary consideration. The particular context for the learning — orientation — requires careful thought, including especially "who the learners are" and what prior knowledge, learning styles, expectations/misconceptions, and goals they bring with them to the learning environment. In this latter regard, there is much that we already know about transition complicators and other obstacles faced by at-risk groups and students generally that are likely to impede their retention, progress, or learning success: much research on which we can draw in this regard has been conducted in relation to the "first year experience" (FYE). This chapter will briefly discuss that body of knowledge, as it has influenced the transition pedagogy deployed through the design-in of the ARS. The enactment of an ARS in orientation will then be described; following which an analysis of the evaluation conducted will also be presented.

The First Year Experience and Transition Pedagogy

The problematic nature of transition for students new to a discipline (for example, *from* high school *to* law, or *from* engineering *to* law, etc.) or level of study (latter including transition *from* vocational education or secondary school *to* higher education or *from* undergraduate *to* postgraduate study, etc.) has been the subject of much research and study over recent decades, both nationally and internationally (for example, Krause, Hartley, James, & McInnis, 2005; Kuh & Vesper, 1997; McInnis, 2001; McInnis & Hartley, 2002; McInnis & James, 1995; McInnis, James, & Hartley, 2000; Pargetter, McInnis, James, Evans, Peel, & Dobson, 1998). The massification of the Australian higher education sector, and the consequent diversity of the student cohort (in terms of both background and preparedness for study) have exacerbated transition hot spots in more recent times, though it is also clear that patterns of student engagement have been changing dynamically for some time. For example, research tells us that students today spend less physical time on campus, and more time dealing with a diverse range of priorities (such as paid employment, family, and other extracurricula activities: Krause et al., 2005; McInnis & Hartley, 2002) that compete with their development of a "student identity" (Krause et al., 2005; McInnis et al., 2000). Other factors — environmental, social, and cognitive — also combine in a complex interaction to affect first year students' sense of belonging within their university community, or connectedness to their course of study. It is also clear that various demographic subgroups have further specialised needs requiring discrete support interventions, especially as regards diversity (commonly referring to age, gender, social, and educational background; engagement in work; family status; ethnicity: McInnis 2001; McInnis & James, 1995; McInnis et al., 2000) or equity group membership (James, Baldwin, Coates, Krause, & McInnis, 2004 and Krause et al., 2005, referring to students from low socioeconomic backgrounds; from rural or isolated areas; from a non-English speaking background; with a disability; women in nontraditional areas of study and higher degrees; also Indigenous students).

Relevantly for present purposes, this extensive research has identified that, additional to the external inhibitors and complex commitments mentioned above, students-in-transition often experience extreme difficulty with the initial period of academic and social adjustment, especially regarding the mediation of "orientation issues," examples of which include:

- feeling lonely or isolated, though they are not necessarily interested in participating in community building or extracurricular activities that might lead to greater social or academic engagement, and which have been found to have a positive correlation with retention and success (Krause, McInnis, & Welle, 2002; Krause et al., 2005; Tinto, 1998);

- having little understanding of tertiary expectations as regards academic standards, course objectives, and assessment methods, while also experiencing difficultly negotiating the administrative requirements of the new tertiary environment (James, 2002);

- what it means to assume personal responsibility for managing their own learning as independent learners (especially for school leavers);

- having initially high expectations and levels of enthusiasm that often give way to motivational problems and disillusionment;

- that once they fall behind in their studies they often fail to catch up;

- that they suffer from information overload in orientation;

- that there are some recognisable milestones in the life cycle of a first-year student (for example, "hit-the-wall-week" around about weeks 5-7);

- that first-year students typically have no understanding of the hierarchy of knowledge, generally fail to understand the depth of preparation required for tertiary study, and often lack the necessary study and academic skills required for success. Associated with this also is the tendency of early tertiary learners to assess information as "black" or "white" — Perry's basic duality of "right" or "wrong" — and being confused about making judgements about information from apparently equally convincing sources (Perry, 1970);

- that they are generally unaware of the range of student support services and library resources available, negotiation of which they will usually attempt in times of stress and pressure.

If we know these things about our students at the time they first come to us, then we should use that knowledge to design better orientation and support for them for their period of adjustment to, and integration with, their new academic community. In the United States, for example, the National Resource Center for The First-Year Experience and Students in Transition (2003) reports that, in 2003, 81.6% of the American higher education institutions responding to the sixth, national survey of first-year seminar programming offered a special course for first-year students called a "first-year seminar," "colloquium," or "student success course." The three most frequently reported goals for such seminars were:

1. to develop academic skills (63.5%),
2. to provide an orientation to campus resources and services (59.6%), and
3. self-exploration/personal development (39.8%).

In support of these goals, the most frequently reported seminar topics were: study skills (62.8%), campus resources (61.5%), time management (59.7%), academic planning/

advising (58.1%), and critical thinking (52.3%) (National Resource Center for the First Year Experience and Students in Transition, 2003).

Such approaches provide examples of how teachers might acknowledge the context of the new tertiary learner, and bring their teacher "evidence of experience" to bear in learning design: given what we know about the transition experience of our students, we are able to "recognise and preempt some of the plausible misconceptions, or naïve approaches in [our] students" (Laurillard, 2002, p. 184).

It is not suggested that one person who has one part in a single orientation session will be able to address all of these various issues in an effort to attend to each individual student's social and academic transition needs. But it is not unreasonable to expect that the faculty academic orientation has a pivotal role to play, particularly in welcoming new students into the learning community of their new discipline of study: clearly this learning experience can be better tailored to provide a more effective plank in an overall transition platform of improved just-in-time information delivery, general support, and specific academic skills support, as further mediated over a longer transition period (Kift, 2004).

As Pargetter et al. (1998) remind us in these times of increasingly virtual engagement:

... the consistent [student] stress on 'social transition', on feeling 'welcomed' and on the ability to make friends and feel 'at home' on often dauntingly large and diverse campuses suggests that universities should seek to provide a range of opportunities for social interaction shortly before and shortly after the beginning of each year, that the importance of orientation as a social and *academic transition be highlighted in university information for newly-enrolling students and be recognised through funding and good planning, and that strategies to welcome and value first-year students, as well as promote their interaction with each other (through informal project work, small-group teaching, 'icebreaker' sessions and other more interactive and shared forms of learning) should form an important part of teaching, especially in the first few weeks, and especially in large, general faculties where few students will share the same classes. (chapter XIII, para 10)*

However, it is one thing to identify such features as desirably included in a transition pedagogy; it is another entirely to enact a learning design that will effectively take account of these myriad factors in a manner that will have impact for positive student learning outcomes.

Designing for Orientation Learning

Educational research tells us that teacher-focused, sage-on-the-stage, didactic transmission of large amounts of content, where students are passive in their learning, is largely ineffective. Students will learn best, and have higher quality learning outcomes, when they are actively (individually) engaged or *inter*active and collaborative (with others); for example when they are *doing* something. Discussion methods, for example, "seem more successful when it comes to higher cognitive learning and attitude change" (Cannon, 1992; Dunkin, 1983, p. 75).

In orientation sessions, therefore, where we are looking for an effective and efficient mechanism by which to achieve high levels of cognitive engagement and attitudinal change as regards transition issues, we need to reconsider the efficacy of the traditional expository lecture: it is unlikely to achieve the learning outcomes we would seek (Cannon & Newble, 2000). Biggs and others have also pointed out (sounding the death knell for traditional orientation practice) that the attention span of students in lecture mode can be maintained for approximately 10-15 minutes, after which, at about the 20 minute mark, "learning drops off rapidly" though, encouragingly, a "short rest period, or simply a *change* in activity, after about 15 minutes, leads to a restoration of performance almost to the original level" (Biggs, 2003, p. 102).

What then to do with the large group class of new learners in orientation? Boud, Cohen and Walker (1993, cited in Boud & Prosser, 2002, p. 239) identified five propositions about learning that encapsulate a learning-centred perspective, and which have been very useful in formulating the learning design for orientation that ultimately involved the use of the ARS.

- Experience is the foundation and the stimulus for all learning.

- Learners actively construct their own experience.

- Learning is a holistic process.

- Learning is socially and culturally constructed.

- Learning is influenced by the social and emotional context in which it occurs.

With these indicia in mind, the vision for an orientation learning design, therefore, was to create a learning environment that encouraged students to be involved, and to make sense of their learning (in the constructivist way), relevant to their current context (as new learners in discipline X), and taking advantage of the socioemotional potential for positive peer influence. Duffy and Cunningham (1996, p.171 cited in Laurillard, 2002, p. 67) recently reduced current views of constructivism to two simple but common conceptions that are of use in focusing learning and teaching approaches.

1. Learning is an active process of constructing rather than acquiring knowledge.

2. Instruction is a process of supporting that construction rather than communicating knowledge.

In any learning situation, it is what the student *does* (cf *is* or what the teacher *does* [Biggs, 2003, pp. 22-25]) with the various resources/inputs they are given — how they construct their own understandings and new knowledge — that is critical. The more educationally-aware teachers conceptualise their professional teaching role in this context as that of "designers of learning environments" in a learn*ing*-centred model. They may be the guide-on-the-side or, as my colleague Erica McWilliam (2005) has more provocatively put it, "meddler in the middle":

... the idea of teacher and student as co-creators of value is compelling. Rather than teachers delivering an information product to be consumed by the student, co-creating value would see the teacher and student mutually involved in assembling and dissembling *cultural products. In colloquial terms, this would frame the teacher as neither sage on the stage nor guide on the side but* meddler in the middle. *The teacher is* in there doing and failing *alongside students, rather than moving like Florence Nightingale from desk to desk or chat room to chat room, watching over her flock, encouraging and monitoring. (p. 10)*

It is in this type of carefully designed learning environment, where the learning is central to the student experience and the experience is carefully structured with the technology designed-in *if it adds value*, that students are most likely to have "transformational" learning outcomes, and where their understandings and ways of dealing with and interacting with (transition) knowledge will, most likely, be shifted.

The above outlines the theoretical and pedagogical basis for a learning design that lends itself easily to harnessing the affordances of an ARS (and its intrinsic interactivity) as a device to break up a lengthy, large group session, and to move away from passive exposition. It is also not irrelevant to note that, with some very minor exceptions, traditional face-to-face teaching modes (for example, the large group lecture, small group classes, seminars, *etc.*) have been relatively untouched by technology. Therefore, it was also attractive that the ARS was deployed in our students' first interaction with their new faculty in their university of *technology*. Bringing to bear our teacher "evidence of experience," as informed by research on transition issues, the design vision was for a mix of tailored information, ARS questioning, and (hoped-for) consequential animated discussion. The hypothesis was that the enactment of such a design would lead to a substantially more effectual learning environment with considerably improved learning outcomes for students; the latter in terms of student reflection on, or at least engagement with, the concepts presented as relevant to their individual contexts, with additional gains in increased student interest and satisfaction with this novel form of delivery.

The Enactment of ARS in Orientation

Against this vision, the use of an ARS offered a logical delivery response to the desire to encourage student reflection on their own preconceptions and (mis)understandings about their impending first-year experience. The objective was to utilise an ARS as a mechanism to bring about in students a new metacognitive awareness of, and prepared-ness for, the actuality of their experience in the coming days, weeks and months.

An ARS also goes a long way to addressing the two aspects of "large-class technique" identified by Biggs (2003, p. 106) when he draws attention to the "managerial aspect of dealing with the large cohort including dealing with questions" (or, as is more likely in the Orientation environment, the absence of questioning) (2003, p. 104), and the educational aspect of using the large-class time and space for effective teaching. An ARS is well suited to managing both of these aspects, especially when blended with a tailored PowerPoint™ presentation that has also been designed to grab students' attention visually, and let them know what their *peers* last year (not academics, so as to be more accessible for Generation Y students) said about transition and the FYE. For example, in this way, the "hit-the-wall" week(s) that students generally tend to experience at about weeks 5-7, when the full realisation of what they had undertaken seems to dawn on them, was normalised in advance by anticipating this usual transition reaction, and offering pre-emptive strategies for students to utilise in managing their adjustment period.

When the pedagogy (and not the technology) is central to the learning design, the ARS, by posing questions embedded at various stages of the PowerPoint™ presentation, is able to address the following particular aspects of learner engagement in this context:

- The traditional and absolute absence of interactivity in large group orientation sessions: previously, questions to students routinely elicited no response, while pauses for students to ask questions (with a view to gaining some insight into what they were thinking about the topics presented) similarly had no reaction. In short, prior faculty orientation sessions (n~350) involved no discursive level of engagement, a problem exacerbated each year by the increasing diversity of the cohort.

- To prompt the beginnings of an ethos of a "community of learners," where students collaborate and interact to construct new understandings; this obviously was not going to occur spontaneously, so some form of peer interaction or opportunities for connectedness needed to be designed-in.

- Orientation participants routinely present as (any, or all of) bored, bewildered, or baffled — indeed many students in the large internal session seem to be just plain scared; hardly an environment conducive to positive engagement taking place.

- Similarly, effective learning and teaching practice includes creating friendly or comfortable classroom climates (Hativa, 2000, p. 21): the particular educational setting in which orientation learning is expected to take place — the large impersonal O-week lecture — is not the friendliest of possible learning environments.

- To find a viable, preferably interactive, alternative to the passive, one-way transmission model of exposition of material, which we know from the educational literature is largely ineffective for learning engagement.

- To structure opportunities for students to be actively engaged with the accepted wisdom about the FYE, and to involve them in some cognitive processing (in a constructivist way) about what their likely experience will be in the semester ahead.

- The problematic engagement issue of how to strike the right note in orientation with our external cohort (n~110), most of whom have successfully studied part, if not full, degrees externally, previously, and find it difficult to accept that they may have any transition issues in this new discipline in the external context.

What the ARS allows for is a synchronous communication between teacher and students, no matter what the class size, enabled instantaneously and at a critical time of the semester (orientation). The tabulation of the student responses to the questions posed, and the immediate graphical display of results to the class, is the launchpad for a discussion that has just not occurred previously in this environment. The great beauty of the system is that to participate, students are required to read the question and possible answers, think about a response, and chose an answer to communicate to the receiver by way of (in my institution's case) use of a "keypad" ARS. In the large internal orientaion group, the added bonus of having students pair up and share thoughts to transmit the final response, also added to the sense of belonging and creation of a learning community.

The use to which the ARS was put in this case, though unique in the specific orientation context, is similar to that as has been described elsewhere (for example, Draper & Brown, 2004) and incorporates the following aspects:

- mutual community-awareness building as to the cohort's demographics and/or perceptions/expectations (Draper & Brown, 2004, p. 83);

- teacher evaluation of students' understanding of concepts;

- a basis for obtaining students' views on various topics as discussion-starters;

- to increase discussion, especially in sensitive areas where students may be reluctant to contribute their views on, for example, ethical, moral, or legal issues, where admissions or doubts about ability may be construed as a sign of weakness.

The questions that were asked in both sessions (internal and external) are reproduced in Table 1, together with the percentage of responses for each possible choice. In the larger, internal, full-time group, mainly constituted by Generation Y students, the emphasis was to break up and relax that group, to get them talking to one another (to answer the questions posed), and then, with the teacher, to start the "community of learners" ethos, and to mix in some transition issues that could then be the springboard for further discussion. With the other, usually more mature group (external), fewer questions were posed, and the questions were used almost always as discussion starters after the group had registered their answers, rather than any being an end in themselves. Finally, some of the possible responses were slightly modified for the two different cohorts. This explains why, in Table 1, some questions have no recorded responses internal/external — those questions may have been modified and/or not asked of one group or the other.

The style of questions asked was very focused on using the limited lecture time available to meet the diversity of contextual needs in the orientation setting. Many "question styles" have been identified in the emerging literature (for example, Gunderson & Wilson, 2004; Philipp & Schmidt, n.d), some of which are picked up in this case study, including:

- to help students to reconsider prior views and/or think about their motivations for the first time (for example, questions 7A, 7B);

Table 1. Questions posed using the ARS technology and student responses

Questions and possible responses	Internal group response % (n~350)	External group response % (n~110)
1. *Are you having a good time?*		
A. Yes	56%	67%
B. No	10%	0%
C. Don't know	12%	9%
D. Do I get my degree now?	21%	24%
2. *Which of the following best describes YOU?*		
A. High School OP	63%	8%
B. Alternate Entry/QUT Special Entry	10%	4%
C. International Student	1%	0%
D. Mature Age (no pervious Tertiary)	1%	4%
E. Mature Age (part Tertiary studies)	17%	12%
F. Mature Age (grad Tertiary course)	8%	73%
3. *Your age?*		
A. 18 or younger	68%	6%
B. 19-23	26%	17%
C. 24-30	3%	29%
D. 31-40	2%	40%
E. Over 40	1%	8%
4. *Are you?*		
A. Male		40%
B. Female		60%
5. *Do you intend to practise law when you graduate?*		
A. Duh … Yes	77%	70%
B. Doh … No	23%	30%
6. *The textbook set for CONTRACTS A has more pages than the fifth HARRY POTTER BOOK (which had 766 pages)?*		
A. True	73%	87%
B. False	27%	13%
7A. Why are you studying law?		
A. My parents made me do it	5%	
B. I have to spend my day somehow!	8%	
C. To make buckets of money	49%	
D. To meet other people just like me	2%	
E. To make a difference to society	35%	
7B. Why are you studying law?		
A. Am sick of my day job		9%
B. Intellectual stimulation		51%
C. To make buckets of money		12%
D. To meet new people		0%
E. To make a difference to society		26%
8A. Which factors do YOU think will impinge on your study?		
A. Work, home, family etc	45%	
B. Loneliness	4%	
C. Drinking and partying	24%	
D. Motivation	27%	
8B. Which factors do YOU think will impinge on your study?		
A. Work, home, family etc		80%
B. Loneliness		2%
C. IT skills		0%
D. Motivation		18%

Table 1. Cont.

9. 450 1st year students last year each provided ONE piece of advice for you for 2005. Which was their top advice?		
A. Be organised/keep up to date	39%	64%
B. Make friends/meet ors/enjoy	14%	14%
C. Do all the readings/read more	8%	6%
D. Ask for help/ask questions	23%	2%
E. Party on with good study technique	15%	14%
10. Which of the following is the type of PLAGIARISM (=cheating) that could actually make you fail a unit?		
A. The type where I get caught!	3%	2%
B. Paraphrasing without referencing	4%	4%
C. Cutting and pasting from the WWW	1%	2%
D. 2 of us putting in similar/same work	0%	0%
E. All of the above	92%	90%
11. Which one of the following IS a High Court Judge?		
A. Lawrence Springborg	5%	
B. Quentin Bryce	20%	
C. Daniel Macpherson	3%	
D. Michael Kirby	71%	
12. What's the difference between Uni and High School?		
A. Haven't thought about it	0%	
B. Knowing/understanding is not enough	6%	
C. No difference between them	2%	
D. Expected to take responsibility for my own learning	90%	
13. What are you expecting Uni teaching staff to be like?		
A. Teachers who'll help if I'm proactive	88%	
B. Famous researchers in the field	4%	
C. Friends who worry that I mightn't pass	0%	
D. My mum	5%	
E. My old high school teacher	3%	
14. What's the difference between a Lecture AND a Tutorial ("a tute")?		
A. Between a what & a what?	0%	
B. Lects are big; tutes are little	3%	
C. Lects are boring; tutes are scary	1%	
D. Lects: where all students in a unit come together to learn; Tutes: small groups of students (25ish) & I'm expected to talk (a lot)	96%	
15. What is LOLI?		
A. A sweetie	2%	2%
B. QUT's idea of helping	57%	87%
C. The next govt student loan scheme	18%	7%
D. Something not to be taken from a stranger in a car	22%	4%
16. Which of these Qs did a barrister NOT ask a witness in court?		
A. Were you alone or by yourself?		28%
B. Is that the same nose you broke as a child?		3%
C. Do you have children or anything like that?		28%
D. Q: You are 3 months pregnant & 8 August was the conception date? A: Yes Q: What were you doing at that time?		38%

- to develop insights that link prior and introduced ideas, or restructure ideas to enhance connections (for example, questions 5, 9, 10, all of which topics had previously been mentioned in the session);

- raise awareness of diversity (for example, questions 2-4 especially, but all generally);

- promote some ideas over others (for example, questions 11, 12, 13);

- apply new constructions to personally-relevant issues (for example, questions 8A, 8B, 10, 12, 13);

- clarify and expose misconceptions (for example, questions 6, 12, 13, 14);

- engage and focus students' attention (for example, questions 1, 6, 10, 11, 15, 16);

- enhance the retention of information (all); and

- give immediate feedback to students (all).

Evaluation and Analysis

The ARS technology also permits an immediate evaluation to be carried out regarding students' perceptions of the efficacy of the learning environment they have just experienced. This has been performed for two years now in both groups in the law faculty with the results (as recorded on the KEEpad PowerPoints™) shown in Figures 1 and 2.

Figure 1. For 2004

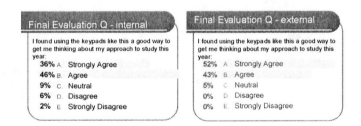

Final Evaluation Q - internal

I found using the keypads like this a good way to get me thinking about my approach to study this year:

- **36%** A. Strongly Agree
- **46%** B. Agree
- **9%** C. Neutral
- **6%** D. Disagree
- **2%** E. Strongly Disagree

Final Evaluation Q - external

I found using the keypads like this a good way to get me thinking about my approach to study this year:

- **52%** A. Strongly Agree
- **43%** B. Agree
- **5%** C. Neutral
- **0%** D. Disagree
- **0%** E. Strongly Disagree

Figure 2. For 2005

Final Evaluation Q – external:
I found using keypads a good interactive activity to start me thinking about my approach to study this year.

- 48% A. Strongly Agree
- 42% B. Agree
- 6% C. Neutral
- 0% D. Disagree
- 4% E. Strongly Disagree

Final Evaluation Q – internal:
I found using the keypads like this a good way to get me thinking about my approach to study this year.

- 31% A. Strongly Agree
- 44% B. Agree
- 20% C. Neutral
- 2% D. Disagree
- 2% E. Strongly Disagree

Remembering that this represents one part only of an overall staged transition, these data are very encouraging. Certainly, the staff perception of the external orientation is that it is much improved, and that students are far more engaged, more willing to be discussants, see greater relevance in the way the material is presented to them, and are receptive to the messages being conveyed, without feeling patronised. As regards the full-time internal orientation, in both years, the blended visual and ARS PowerPoint™ presentation has been made after they had been sitting passively for the first 50 minutes of talking heads. The way in which the students relaxed when we started doing this exercise was palpable: the energy level in the room rose immediately, they were prompted to introduce themselves to a person nearby who had a keypad (with whom they could share), and they were buzzing about the responses to make.

What this case study again evidences is that the ARS technology can be a device for putting learning and teaching theory into practice: students engage more readily and learn more easily when they are active in pursuit of their learning, rather than passive. In short, everything that Biggs exhorts (and the author was hoping for) was reasonably and efficiently achieved: the class moved immediately from stunned silence to (individual) active and (paired) interactive engagement. The relevance of both sessions was established by its being built around a survey that was conducted of first-year students in 2003, where that cohort gave advice on what should be said to their peers in the following years, while the ability to contribute with nonthreatening anonymity at this early transition point, the sense of fun and novelty around the technology, were added bonuses.

Many of these reflections resonant with the positive practices identified by Draper and Brown (2004, p. 86) and with the transition literature.

- As a faculty in a university of technology, it seemed an obvious solution to utilise the technology of the ARS to excite and motivate our students to embrace their chosen course of study.

- The ARS design broke up the traditional, passive, exposition-style orientation lecture, and got students to relax and have some fun, without academic compromise on getting across some serious messages.

- This learning design makes it possible to involve the whole class in interesting interaction, in an environment from which it has proved difficult in the past to elicit this type of involved engagement. In the terms mentioned above, taken from Boud, Cohen, and Walker (1993, cited in Boud & Prosser, 2002, p. 239), the learners are actively constructing their own knowledge and experience.

- This was a structured opportunity for new students to contribute to a large-group session by offering their opinion, the anonymity of which shielded them from any embarrassment. The response mechanism not only provided feedback to the teacher on what students were thinking, but also permitted students to see where their peers were at, in the same process. In terms of the Boud, Cohen, and Walker propositions referred to earlier, the learning is being socially and culturally constructed, and is influenced by the social and emotional context in which it is occurring, as a holistic (whole person) process.

- As Draper and Brown identify (2004, p. 89) — "asking questions via the handsets makes far more students actually think through and decide on an answer than presenting the question in other ways."

- A final, if secondary benefit to this application, in this context, is that it models the potential for this use of technology to the other academic and professional staff present (which, at an orientation session, is quite a number), some of whom are, in turn, inspired to replicate the practice they have seen deployed so successfully.

Conclusions

From the learning-design point of view, the use of an ARS in the orientation context has been a great success, and a highly efficient and effective tailored application of technology for a specific strategic purpose that has substantially improved the student experience of orientation. Rather than the technology being the *mode* of the education, it was rather the *means* by which the education was delivered, albeit a fun and novel means, but delivered in this way because it suited the learning tasks that had been designed. If such considerations remain at the forefront of ARS applications, asking the question not what teaching fits with the technology, but which technology fits with the learning and teaching objectives sought to be achieved, then the interactive future for our students, who are provided with opportunities to engage with these learning tools, is as bright and shiny as the new technology itself.

References

Bass, R. (1999). The scholarship of teaching: What's the problem? *Inventio, 1*(1). Retrieved June 5, 2005, from http://www.doiiit.gmu.edu/Archives/feb98/randybass.htm

Biggs, J. (2003). *Teaching for quality learning at university* (2nd ed.). Berkshire: SRHE and Open University Press.

Boud, D., & Prosser, M. (2002). Appraising new technologies for learning: A framework for development. *Educational Media International, 39*, 3/4, 237-245.

Cannon, R. A. (1992). *Lecturing HERDSA Green Guide No.7* (2nd ed.). HERDSA: Campbelltown.

Cannon, R., & Newble, D. (2000). *A handbook for teachers in universities and colleges: A guide to improving teaching methods* (4th ed.). London: Kogan Page.

Draper, S. W., & Brown, M. I. (2004). Increasing interactivity in lectures using an electronic voting system. *Journal of Computer Assisted Learning, 20*, 81-94.

Dunkin, M. J. (1983). A review of research on lecturing. *Higher Education Research and Development, 2*(1), 63.

Gunderson, M., & Wilson, G. (2004). *Effectively planning and using student response systems in the classroom.* Educational Technologies at Missouri (ET@MO). Retrieved June 3, 2005, from http://etatmo.missouri.edu/toolbox/doconline/SRS.pdf

Havita, N. (2000). *Teaching for effective learning in higher education.* The Netherlands: Kluwer Academic Publishers.

James, R. (2002). Students' changing expectations of higher education and the consequences of mismatches with the reality. In *Responding to student expectations* (pp. 71-83). Paris: OECD.

James, R., Baldwin, G., Coates, H., Krause, K.-L., & McInnis, C. (2004). *Analysis of equity groups in higher education 1991-2002.* Centre for the Study of Higher Education (CSHE): Melbourne.

Kift, S. (2004). Organising first year engagement around learning: Formal and informal curriculum intervention. Keynote address in *8th International First Year in Higher Education Conference*, 14 - 16 July 2004, Melbourne. Retrieved June 6, 2005, from http://www.fyhe.qut.edu.au/program.html

Krause, K-L., Hartley, R., James, R., & McInnis, C. (2005). *The first year experience in Australian universities: Findings from a decade of national studies.* Canberra: DEST Retrieved June 6, 2005, from http://www.dest.gov.au/sectors/higher_education/publications_resources/profiles/first_year_experience.htm

Krause, K-L., McInnis, C., & Welle, C. (2002). Student engagement: The role of peers in undergraduate student experience. In *SRHE Annual Conference.* Retrieved June 6, 2005, from http://www.cshe.unimelb.edu.au/APFYP/pdfs/KrauseSRHE.pdf

Kuh, G. D., & Vesper, N. (1997). A comparison of student experiences with good practices in undergraduate education between 1990 and 1994. *The Review of Higher Education, 21*, 43-61.

Laurillard, D. (2002). *Rethinking university teaching* (2nd ed). London: Routledge.

McInnis, C. (2001). *Signs of disengagement? The changing undergraduate experience in Australian universities.* Melbourne: CSHE. Retrieved June 6, 2005, from http://www.cshe.unimelb.edu.au/APFYP/research_publications3.html

McInnis, C., & Hartley, R. (2002). *Managing study and work: The impact of full-time study and paid work on the undergraduate experience in Australian universities.* Canberra: AGPS.

McInnis, C., & James, R. (1995) *First year on campus: Diversity in the initial experiences of Australian undergraduates.* Canberra: AGPS.

McInnis, C., James, R., & Hartley, R. (2000). *Trends in the first year experience in Australian universities.* Canberra: AGPS.

McWilliam, E. (2005). Unlearning pedagogy. Keynote address in *ICE2: Ideas in Cyberspace Education Symposium* at Higham Hall, Lake District, 23-25 February 2005.

National Resource Center for the first year experience and students in transition, (2003). *Summary of Results from the 2003 National Survey on First-Year Seminars.*

Retrieved June 6, 2005 from http://www.sc.edu/fye/research/surveyfindings/surveys/survey03.html

Pargetter, R., McInnis, C., James, R., Evans, M., Peel, M., & Dobson, I. (1998). *Transition from secondary to tertiary: A performance dtudy*. DEST: EIP 98/20. Retrieved June 3, 2005, from http://www.dest.gov.au/archive/highered/eippubs/eip98-20/contents.htm

Perry, W. G. Jr. (1970). *Forms of intellectual and ethical development in the college years: A scheme*. New York: Holt, Rinehart, and Winston.

Philipp, S., & Schmidt, H. (n.d). Optimizing learning and retention through interactive lecturing: Using the Audience Response System (ARS) at CUMC. Columbia University: Centre for Education Research and Evaluation. Retrieved June 5, 2005, from http://library.cpmc.columbia.edu/cere/web/facultyDev/ARS_handout_2004_overview.pdf

Shulman, L. S. (1998). Course anatomy: The dissection and analysis of knowledge through teaching. In P. Hutchings (Ed.) with L. S. Shulman, *The course portfolio: How faculty can examine their teaching to advance and improve student learning* (pp. 5-12). Washington, DC: American Association for Higher Education.

Tinto, V. (1993). *Leaving college: Rethinking causes and cures of student attrition* (2nd ed.). Chicago: University of Chicago Press.

Chapter VII

Question Driven Instruction:
Teaching Science (Well) with an Audience Response System

Ian D. Beatty, University of Massachusetts, USA

William J. Leonard, University of Massachusetts, USA

William J. Gerace, University of Massachusetts, USA

Robert J. Dufresne, University of Massachusetts, USA

Abstract

Audience response systems (ARS) are a tool, not a magic bullet. How they are used, and how well they are integrated into a coherent pedagogical approach, determines how effective they are. Question Driven Instruction (QDI) is a radical approach in which an ARS-mediated "question cycle" organizes classroom instruction, replacing the "transmit and test" paradigm with an iterative process of question posing, deliberation, commitment to an answer, and discussion. It is an implementation of "real-time formative assessment." In QDI, an ARS is used to facilitate and direct discussion, to engage students in active knowledge-building, and to support "agile teaching" by providing the instructor with constant feedback about students' evolving understanding and difficulties. Class time is used primarily for interactively developing understanding, rather than for presenting content: in QDI, an instructor is more an engineer of learning experiences than a dispenser of knowledge. This requires new teaching skills, such as moderating discussion and managing the classroom dynamic, interpreting students' statements and modeling their learning, making real-time teaching decisions, and designing ARS questions that teach rather than test and that target process as well as content. Above all, it requires understanding and communicating that ARS use is diagnostic and instructional, rather than evaluative.

Introduction

Educational use of audience response systems, also known as "classroom response systems," is exploding in high schools and universities. One vendor claims over a million of their system's keypads have been used, in all 50 U.S. states and 10 countries worldwide, in thousands of K-12 schools, and hundreds of universities (eInstruction, 2005). Several universities are beginning centralized programs to introduce and coordinate response system use across campus. A fringe technology 10 years ago, ARS are entering the mainstream.

ARS have the potential to radically alter the instructional dynamic of our classrooms, and impact student learning. However, for an instructor to realize this potential requires much more than merely learning to operate the technology. Response systems are a tool, not a solution. Their benefits are not conferred automatically: *how* they are used matters tremendously. To be fully effective, their use must be integrated into a larger, coherent pedagogic approach.

As part of the UMass Physics Education Research Group (UMPERG), we have worked with response systems for over a decade. In 1993, we began using Classtalk, a groundbreaking "classroom communication system" by Better Education Inc. In 1994, we received a U.S. National Science Foundation grant (DUE-9453881) to deploy, develop pedagogy for, and study the impact of Classtalk (Dufresne, Gerace, Leonard, Mestre, & Wenk, 1996). In 1998, we began Assessing-to-Learn, an NSF-funded project (ESI-9730438) to seed response systems in secondary school physics classrooms and help teachers develop suitable pedagogic skills and perspectives (Beatty, 2000; Feldman & Capobianco, 2003). In 1999, we brought EduCue *PRS* (since purchased by GTCO CalComp and renamed InterWrite PRS) to UMass, and began its dissemination across campus. As a sequel to Assessing-to-Learn, we are beginning a 5-year NSF-funded project (ESI-0456124) to research secondary school science teachers' learning of response system pedagogy. Based on 12 years of experience with ARS — teaching, researching, and mentoring — we have developed a comprehensive perspective on the effective use of such systems for the teaching of science at both the secondary school and university levels.

In this chapter, we will introduce that perspective. We will not attempt to describe how response systems work, report our personal experiences using them, or discuss detailed logistical issues. Other chapters in this volume address those topics, and we have

A *community-centered* learning environment recognizes that students belong to communities of colearners at the course, program, institution, and society levels, and promotes constructive interaction to further learning between individuals. In particular, it encourages students to view each other as compatriots rather than competitors, and takes advantage of the pedagogic benefits of cooperative activity, disagreement resolution, and articulation of ideas.

As Roschelle and collaborators have noted (Roschelle, 2003; Roschelle, Abrahamson, & Penuel, 2004), ARS use tends to transform the classroom dynamic in a way that makes instruction more student-centered, knowledge-centered, assessment-centered, and community-centered. To put it simply, an ARS can be used for frequent formative assessment (assessment-centered) that lets teaching and learning be tuned to the needs of individual students (student-centered). As students ponder questions and engage in dialogue with each other and the instructor (community-centered), they are building and enriching a network of structured, useful, principle-based knowledge (knowledge-centered). In general, using an ARS in a way that enhances these aspects increases teaching effectiveness, while using one in a way that dilutes them, undermines it.

Question Driven Instruction

Active learning and strengthening of the "four centerednesses" is a possible outcome of ARS use, but it is not automatic. Furthermore, the degree to which these are achieved — impacting the quality of student learning — depends on how an instructor makes use of an ARS.

An ARS is a tool that can be used for many different, sometimes incompatible ends. It can be used as an attendance-taker, coercing students' presence in class. It can be used as a delivery system for quizzes, testing students' comprehension of assigned reading. It can be used to punctuate lecture with opportunities for student thinking, encouraging attention and engagement. It can be used to spur interstudent discussion, promoting sharing of knowledge. It can be used to gauge students' initial understanding of a topic, influencing subsequent coverage.

We see a much more ambitious possibility: that ARS-based questioning can become the very core of classroom instruction, replacing the "transmit and test" paradigm with a cyclic process of question posing, deliberation, commitment to an answer, and discussion. We call this *question driven instruction*.

Our perspective on QDI derives from years of research and development work in multiple contexts (Dufresne & Gerace, 2004; Dufresne, Gerace, Leonard, & Beatty, 2002a; Dufresne et al., 2001a; Dufresne et al., 1996; Dufresne et al., 2000; Dufresne, Gerace, Mestre, & Leonard, 2001b; Dufresne, Leonard, & Gerace, 1992; Dufresne et al., 2002b; Gerace, 1992; Gerace, Leonard, Dufresne, & Mestre, 1997; Gerace et al., 2000; Leonard et al., 2001; Mestre, Dufresne, Gerace, & Leonard, 2001). "Question driven" refers to the fact that we place the posing, answering, and discussing of questions via response system at the center of the instructional dynamic, to act as an engine of engagement and learning. "Active learning" is the student's end of the dynamic, and "agile teaching" is the instructor's (see Figure 1). "Active learning" has been introduced previously.

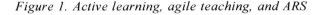

Figure 1. Active learning, agile teaching, and ARS

"Agile teaching" refers to the practice of teaching with a very tight feedback loop, almost continually probing students to ascertain and monitor their learning progress and difficulties. It means modeling them as an array of diverse individuals with diverse needs, and making minute-by-minute decisions about what actions to take to maintain an optimally beneficial learning environment. This contrasts with the common practice of teaching according to a "ballistic" lesson plan: designing a plan for an entire class meeting, "launching" the plan, hoping that it hits reasonably close to its target, and waiting for the next exam to know for certain.

Question driven instruction is a perspective, an instructional style, and a set of pedagogic techniques. It is founded upon the following beliefs:

- The primary goal of instruction is a rich, deep, robust, durable understanding of the subject's essential content from which the student can reason, not "coverage" of a prescribed list of topics.

- Learning is a multipass process, during which ideas must be revisited several times in varying contexts, and with varying degrees of sophistication, to build structured, expert-like knowledge. Students should not be expected to fully grasp any idea or topic on their first exposure.

- The construction of understanding is an effortful process that necessarily involves confusion, frustration, conflict resolution, and unlearning undesirable ideas. Perfect instruction that makes a subject obvious and learning easy is unachievable.

- Instructors must do more than simply present and expound upon knowledge they wish students to master. For efficient learning, they must actively seek out and destroy the impediments to student's understanding: conflicting notions, missing or weak foundational concepts and skills, unhelpful perspectives, and the like.

- Correctly predicting any one student's response to an instructional stimulus is difficult; doing so for an ensemble of students in a class is impossible. An instructor must continually probe, monitor, and model students' knowledge state, progress, and difficulties on a minute-by-minute timescale, and adjust teaching behavior accordingly.

- The very act of articulating an idea or argument, whether correct or incorrect, is of value to both the speaker and to listeners. Analysis of such articulations, and resolution of conflicts between different students' statements, adds significant value, even when an instructor is not participating.

- An instructor cannot provide enough customized interaction with each student in a moderate-sized or large class for efficient learning, and so must foster interaction and cooperative learning among students. Small-group activity and class-wide discussion are both valuable.

- The most potent way to foster learning is to empower students by providing them with the skills and perspective to assess their own knowledge and learning, and to actively seek out beneficial activity and stimulus. In this way, the instructor becomes a learning coach rather than a content provider.

Formative assessment is central to the approach: it provides students with feedback to guide their learning activities and provides instructors with feedback to guide their teaching decisions. In particular, we use an ARS to implement *real-time formative assessment*, in which the instructor and students gain minute-to-minute feedback, enabling productive student engagement and the high level of responsiveness sought by the agile teacher.

What Does *Question Driven Instruction* Look Like?

The Curriculum

From a high-level vantage, the curriculum of a course taught according to QDI principles need not look much different from that of a traditionally taught course. QDI is a perspective on methodology, not on content. However, instructors who adjust topic coverage to students' learning progress often find that, over time, they devote more of a course to building solid understanding of core concepts, and less to peripheral or advanced topics. This does not mean that students learn less about these topics. One of the most powerful effects formative assessment has on instructors is to shatter their illusions that student learning correlates with "coverage" of material. It reveals just how much of what an instructor presents is never really understood or retained by most students.

Additionally, a linear course syllabus only crudely approximates the multipass learning that occurs during effective QDI. Recognizing that students are building and reorganizing a complex and richly cross-linked knowledge structure, an instructor will frequently include forward and backward references, connecting current topics to future and past ones. At times, occurrences in a classroom will cause an instructor to revisit and redevelop prior ideas, not just to "do it again" and hope students "get it this time," but to let students reconsider the ideas from a broader, more sophisticated perspective.

The Classroom

To the uninitiated, a QDI classroom may seem chaotic. QDI treats the instructional process as a collection of dialogues: between the teacher and the class, between the teacher and individual students in the class, and between students. This tends to make the QDI classroom a noisy place. Side chatter among students generally indicates discussion about some point raised by the course — active engagement.

Furthermore, a QDI instructor does not follow a ballistic lesson plan, but continually probes the class for clues about how best to proceed towards a general objective. To an observer accustomed to polished presentations, QDI may appear meandering or even floundering. The QDI instructor is, in fact, following a circuitous and improvised route to shepherd students along, whereas the traditional lecturer is traveling a relatively straight path to a destination whether or not students follow.

A central tenet of QDI is that an instructor must continually probe students for clues; construct, correct, refine, and evolve a model of their changing knowledge states and difficulties; and decide what instructional actions that model indicates. Most teachers unconsciously practice this in one-on-one tutoring or with sufficiently small groups. Some innately adept instructors can also manage this with a dozen or 20 students, but many of us cannot effectively communicate with and model so many individuals. Instead, we fall back on teaching to the mean, and rely on occasional questions, eye contact, and body language for guidance. In large university lectures, most of us give up on even that, and present a truly ballistic lecture. This is the "scaling problem" of QDI: it depends on an instructor's ability to communicate with individual students and model their learning and needs, which an unassisted instructor can only manage for small numbers of students.

Realizing QDI in a full-sized class depends on having and using an audience response system of some kind. Response systems present a partial solution to this scaling problem by providing a supplemental, technology-mediated channel of communication between an instructor and students, helping the instructor assess student understanding, maintain student engagement in the questioning process, and manage the classroom interaction. An ARS can also help with time management in the classroom, and improve the efficiency of interactive, formative assessment-based instruction. More sophisticated response systems called *classroom communication systems*, such as the venerable and now discontinued Classtalk, provide additional helpful capabilities such as self-paced question sets, open-ended question types, and — most importantly — support for collective answers from small collaborative student groups (Roschelle et al., 2004).

A Class Session

A typical QDI class session is organized around a *question cycle*, represented in Figure 2.

The instructor begins by presenting a question or problem to the students, and giving them a few minutes to discuss it among themselves. (Note that we do *not* begin with a lecture.) Students then enter responses into the ARS, and the instructor displays a histogram of class-wide results for all to see. Without revealing the correctness of any answers, the instructor solicits volunteers to argue for the various answers, and moderates a class-wide discussion. The immediate objective is to draw out students' reasoning and vocabulary, expose students to each others' ideas, and make implicit assumptions explicit: *not* to tell students whether their answers and arguments are correct. This may seem inefficient, but allowing students to confront other conceptions and sort out contradictions in their own vocabulary is the fastest, most durable way to build understanding. And helping students develop a general understanding of the subject matter, not just learn the answer to the immediate question, is the instructor's ultimate purpose.

The instructor may then decide to re-pose the same question and see whether and how students' responses have changed. Alternatively, she may present related questions that extend a concept, highlight a distinction, or otherwise build on the prior question. She may explain how the ideas just discussed fit into a high-level picture of the subject. She may summarize key points, helping students to distill what they've learned and take notes. Or, she may deliver a micro-lecture on some point of subject matter or problem-solving practice that seems necessary. She can draw on detailed information about students' thinking to make this decision, and the class is well primed to receive the message, appreciate its relevance, and integrate it with other knowledge.

We find that iterating through this cycle of question, group discussion, answering, moderated class-wide discussion, and wrap-up three or four times in a 50-minute class is optimal. A higher rate leads to rapid-fire quizzing and loses most of the approach's benefits. Our objective is to have students ponder and discuss, not just answer, and sufficient time must be allowed for full engagement to occur.

Instructor flexibility is important. Some questions will prove surprisingly easy to students and merit little discussion or follow-up, while others will raise unanticipated issues that deserve extra time. Such uncertainty is not a drawback of the approach, but

Figure 2. "Question cycle," a design pattern for QDI classes (Dufresne et al., 1996)

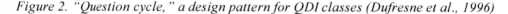

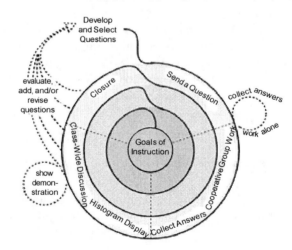

forms the very essence of "agile teaching": genuine discovery of and spontaneous adjustment to students' pedagogic needs.

The question-cycle methodology is focused on helping students explore, sort out, and come to a deep understanding of subject matter, and provides little time for initial presentation of the material to be explored. Instead, students are exposed to and work with material before and after coming to class, via textbook reading, multimedia resources, homework assignments, and other activities. They should appreciate that they are not expected to fully comprehend the material while reading it, but rather to begin the process of making sense that will continue during class and in follow-up homework assignments. This exposure phase is only one loop in the multipass learning spiral.

An Exam

"Assessment drives instruction" is an oft-heard phrase in educational reform circles. A QDI approach targeting deep, conceptual understanding, reasoning skills, and transferable knowledge will fail if undermined by traditional exams that emphasize answers (product) over reasoning and analysis (process) by testing information recall and high-speed performance on recognized problem types.

Superficially, a QDI-compatible exam may resemble a more traditional one. It may even be a machine-graded multiple-choice test. However, many of the questions contained will target conceptual understanding, reasoning, and transfer. For example, a multiple-choice question may direct students to "Select which of the following principles would be most useful in solving the following problem," or to "Indicate which of the following statements about the given situation are true." Most problems to solve are conceptually subtle rather than computationally complex. In addition, QDI-friendly exams are likely to include innovative or unusual aspects, such as a collaborative group component (Cohen & Henle, 1995) or "select all that apply" marking (Leonard, 2005).

How Does One Practice Question Driven Instruction?

QDI requires a very different array of skills than does traditional, ballistic, transmissionist instruction. In addition to the obvious technical skills for operating an ARS, an instructor must set appropriate pedagogic goals; design formative assessment items for in-class use; manage a dynamic and highly interactive classroom environment; probe and model students' learning; make instant decisions based on this evolving model; and guide students as they grow into their roles as active learners.

Strategic Decisions: Setting Instructional Goals

From the QDI perspective, instructional goals are viewed as statements about what we want students to *learn*, rather than about what material we intend to *cover*. The distinction between "this course will cover orbital motion" and "this course will teach students to understand and reason with the principles underlying orbital motion" may be subtle, but it is crucial. At the very least, it highlights the absurdity of marching ahead to cover a prescribed syllabus of topics when formative assessments indicate that students aren't getting it. We want to keep the students, not the curriculum, at the center.

To foster active learning, we must think of ourselves as engineers of learning experiences rather than presenters of knowledge. When setting instructional goals and translating them into learning experiences, we should explicitly target mental behavior and skills as well as subject content. Bloom's "Taxonomy of the Cognitive Domain" (Anderson & Krathwohl, 2001; Bloom, Englehart, Furst, Hill, & Krathwohl, 1956) can be suggestive, but is overly general for this purpose. We find it helpful to itemize 12 *habits of mind* that students should seek to develop and teachers should seek to inculcate (Dufresne et al., 2000). The successful practice of these habits of mind, integrated with content knowledge, is the essence of expert-like behavior in science. The 12 habits of mind are:

- seek alternative representations;
- compare and contrast;
- explain, describe, and depict;
- predict and observe;
- extend the context;
- monitor and refine communication;

- generate multiple solutions;
- categorize and classify;
- discuss, summarize, and model;
- plan, justify, and strategize;
- reflect and evaluate;
- metacommunicate.

These habits of mind can be folded into the curriculum by thinking of them as "what we ask students to do," and the subject matter as "what we ask them to do it with." For example, rather than viewing a question or problem (exam, homework, or in-class formative assessment) merely as a fact for them to recall, or a result for them to calculate, we can ask them to:

- construct a graphical representation of a relationship described algebraically or in words;
- compare and contrast two processes or situations;
- describe the behavior of an evolving system;
- predict the effects of changing one parameter of a system;
- solve a problem twice, with different approaches;
- classify a set of situations according to some criterion;

- describe a strategy for solving a problem without actually solving it; or

- write an essay summarizing the most valuable things they learned during the course, and what they wish they'd known at the outset.

We also can, and should, demonstrate these habits of mind for students as we teach, showing them how an expert in the field thinks.

In accord with the principle of multipass learning, we should resist treating a course's curriculum as a linear syllabus. Rather, we need to think of it as a complex structure of interconnected, organized ideas and skills that we guide students through, visiting and revisiting sections in various ways as they become conversant with both the global organization and the structural details.

Designing Questions

The criteria for an effective QDI question are quite different from those for exam, quiz, and homework questions, and questions for formative assessment use should be engineered with great care. Elsewhere, we detail a theoretical framework for designing questions (Beatty, Gerace, Leonard, & Dufresne, in press). In this section, we present some general principles and suggestions.

Every question should serve an explicit pedagogic purpose: a specific activity to induce in students' minds, not just a piece of topic matter to cover. For example:

- drawing out students' background knowledge and beliefs on a topic;

- making students aware of their own and others' perceptions and interpretations of a situation;

- discovering particular confusions, misconceptions, and knowledge gaps;

- distinguishing similar concepts;

- realizing connections or similarities between different concepts;

- elaborating the understanding of a concept; and

- exploring the implications of an idea in a new or extended context.

Computational or simple factual questions, and those that probe memory rather than understanding and reasoning, are of little value. Questions that have students compare two situations, or make predictions and explore causal relationships, are particularly powerful. Good questions push students to reason qualitatively and draw conclusions from a conceptual model. If an instructor can anticipate likely misunderstandings and points of confusion, he or she should design questions to "catch" students in those, get them articulated, and resolve them through discussion.

Unlike exam questions, ARS questions for QDI benefit from ambiguity. An ambiguous feature sensitizes students to the feature's importance and implications, teaches them to pay attention to subtleties, and motivates discussion of what aspects of a question are important and how they matter. In this way, students can be led to contemplate not just one question, but a family of related questions. Similarly, including irrelevant information or omitting necessary information can be beneficial, helping students learn to evaluate what information an answer requires. Questions need not be "fair" or even well defined, since we seek not to evaluate students, but rather to help them learn to reason, think defensively, and answer future questions — especially the vague, fuzzy kind often encountered outside the classroom. (However, some questions should be straightforward, and provide students with confirmation that they do, in fact, "get" a particular topic: this is useful feedback to them, and also good psychology.)

A question that elicits a spectrum of answers is generally more productive than one all students agree upon: it provides fodder for discussion and disagreement, leading to engagement and learning.

When designing sets of related or sequential questions, instructors should remember that students experience significant "cognitive load" when reading and interpreting a new scenario. Reusing a situation for multiple questions is efficient, allowing students to concentrate on the relevant aspects of the question at hand and realize the implications of features that do change. Conversely, asking questions with the same conceptual content set in completely different circumstances helps students learn to see through a situation's "surface features" to its "deep structure" and to distinguish the core principles from the details.

When and how a question is presented can shape the depth, quality, and character of resulting student thought and interaction. Students tend to assume that the question relates to whatever has recently transpired in the course, and will apply knowledge accordingly. This can lead to "pigeonhole" learning in which concepts are assimilated chronologically and only accessible within a narrow context, rather than being organized into an interlinked, versatile hierarchy. A careful instructor will mix questions of varying types and topics, and include integrative questions that connect recent ideas with earlier ones.

Classroom Management

Perhaps the most initially daunting (and ultimately exhilarating) aspect of QDI is the necessity of giving up control of the classroom. A lecture is predictable and controlled, with attention safely focused on the instructor. QDI, however, necessarily turns the classroom over to students for dialogue and debate. We must learn to manage the apparent chaos rather than attempting to rigidly control it. Furthermore, the principle of "agility" means we must be prepared — even eager — to modify or discard a lesson plan and extemporize.

Some basic attention-management techniques help considerably. For example, one challenge is to recapture students' attention after they have been discussing a formative assessment question among themselves. An ARS helps dramatically here: by collecting answers (with a time limit) and projecting the resulting histogram on a large screen, attention is redirected to the front of the classroom. Students are naturally curious about each other's answers. Another challenge we face is determining how much time to allow students for small-group discussion of a formative assessment question. Noise level is a clue: when a question is shown, the class is initially quiet as students read and digest it; the noise level then rises as they discuss the question, and begins to fall as they reach resolution. This is an appropriate time to collect answers, display the histogram, and begin the whole-class discussion.

Encouraging students to speak up during the whole-class discussion is crucial. When soliciting volunteers to argue for various answers, we should maintain a strict poker face and not divulge which answer (or answers) is (or are) correct (if any). Allow the students to challenge each other's arguments. If nobody will defend a particular position, ask if anyone else will speculate on the reasoning that might lead to such an answer. (Nothing motivates a student to speak up like having someone else misrepresent his position.) Paraphrasing a student's statements can be valuable, perhaps even necessary in an acoustically challenging room, but we must be careful to stay as close as possible to the student's vocabulary and check with the student that the paraphrase is satisfactory.

When we decide to drop our poker face and offer a little illumination of our own, we should downplay notions of "correct" and "incorrect," lest we focus students' attention too much on getting the right answers rather than on reasoning and understanding. Instead of commenting that a particular answer or argument is wrong, we can often say "that would be correct *if...*," indicating some similar situation or question for which it would be valid. This is not only less disconfirming to the student and less deterring to others, it is also more pedagogically productive for all the reasons that "compare and contrast" questions are powerful. We have found that often, students who appear to be offering a wrong answer are actually offering the right answer to the wrong question. Unless they are sensitized to this, telling them they are simply incorrect is confusing rather than enlightening.

Moderating a whole-class discussion presents us with the great danger of making the class instructor-centered rather than student-centered. Working from within students' perceptions and arguments, rather than making assertions from authority, helps to avoid this. Similarly, if a question contains ambiguities or errors, allowing students to discover these or drawing them out during discussion is preferable to announcing corrections as the question is presented. We should strongly resist any temptation to read a presented question out loud or to talk while students are engaged in small-group dialogue and answering. If we seek active learning, we must give them space to do it!

Tactical Decisions: Modeling Students' Needs

Though managing the classroom may be the most daunting aspect of QDI, modeling a classful of students and deciding how best to interact with them is the most enduringly difficult aspect, and it is the very heart of the approach. It requires two distinct skills: modeling and interacting with an individual student, and handling an ensemble of individuals in parallel. Neither comes easily, and both can be truly mastered only by repeatedly trying, occasionally missing the mark, reflecting, and trying again. However, we offer some general advice to help the interested instructor get started.

Interacting "agilely" with a student is a modeling process closely analogous to the scientific method: observe, form a model, make a prediction based on the model, test the prediction, refine the model, and iterate (Gerace, 1992). In this context, we want to model both the student's knowledge (especially the gaps) and his or her thinking processes (especially the weaker skills). In contrast to a traditional lecture, we must practice "active listening": listening carefully and patiently to what is said and how responses, questions, and other behaviors vary from what we expect. Even when we think we know what she is in the process of asking, we should let her finish: both out of respect, and because every nuance of her utterance is valuable data. We will often answer a question with a question, not just rhetorically, but to understand better why the student needs to ask hers. Our goal is not to answer the question, but to understand why she needs to ask it.

Rather than concentrating on the knowledge we wish to communicate, a less direct approach is often more effective: trying to figure out what prevents understanding, and then attacking the obstacles. This sleuthing out of the roots of confusion is an iterative and thoughtful process on our part. Of course, a rich knowledge of pedagogic theory and common points of confusion are useful. If we find ourselves stumped trying to help an individual, other students in the class can assist. They often understand their peers better than we.

Clearly, carrying out such an attention-demanding, thorough process with every student in a full-sized class is impossible. We must try to track an array of typical or likely student mentalities, test the class for the accuracy of this array, and teach to it. For example, if a formative assessment question elicits a range of answers, we can ascribe a putative explanation to each one for why a student might select it, and that becomes our working model. Since we have probably prepared the answer set in advance, we should already have ideas about why each answer might be chosen. The distribution of class answers "fits" the model to the class.

This approach does not attach a model to any specific individual in the class. A complementary approach is to mentally identify certain students as representatives of various subpopulations within the class, and then build and maintain as rich a model as possible of each. This can be very powerful: it is easier for us to think in detail about a real, specific individual than an abstract entity, and yet students generally have enough in common that by addressing one student's needs, we impact many. As a side benefit, the more we treat students as three-dimensional individuals, pay real attention to them, and try to understand their thinking, the more they will believe we care about them personally and are "on their side," and the less adversarial the instructional dynamic will be.

Coaching

QDI requires students to adopt a role they might not be accustomed to from more traditional instruction. Our experience is that the vast majority of students express positive feelings about ARS use and QDI after they have adjusted to it, but this adjustment takes time, and some initially greet it with fear and resentment. Students habituated to success under traditional instruction are most likely to be hostile: they have "mastered the game," and now the rules are being changed. Others object out of simple laziness: they are being asked to engage in thought and activity during class, and that is effortful and at times frustrating. They are also expected to complete assignments beforehand so as to be prepared for class. Many are uncomfortable with the idea that they are accountable for material not directly presented in lecture. Inducing students to become participating, invested learners is vital to the success of QDI, and metacommunication is our most powerful tool for achieving that. We can explain to students why we are doing what we are doing, at both the immediate and strategic levels, and how students will benefit. We can talk frankly about the obstacles students will likely encounter and how they can most effectively surmount them. In other words, we can explicitly address learning and communication as part of the "course material."

Some student perceptions merit particular attention. Initially, students will probably view formative assessment questions as minitests to be passed or failed. If this attitude is allowed to persist, it will sour them on the formative assessment approach and prevent them from fully and constructively engaging in the process. We must explicitly discuss the purpose of formative assessment and stress that the point is not to answer correctly, but to discover previously unnoticed aspects of the subject and of their own understanding. We must consistently reinforce this position by deemphasizing the correctness of answers and emphasizing reasoning and alternative interpretations. Assigning course credit for "correct" answers is massively counterproductive.

Another perception many students have is that problems are solved quickly or not at all: either they "know" how to do the problem, or they do not. The notion that problems may require protracted cogitation and discussion to figure out, and that these efforts are inherently worthwhile, is alien. They must be convinced of this also before they will lose their resistance to active learning. Again, explicit communication helps.

In general, there is nothing about the course or its content, methods, and objectives that is inappropriate to discuss openly with students. Perhaps "Introductory physics" and "Cellular biology" are less accurate titles than "Learning introductory physics" or "Understanding cellular biology."

Conclusions

An audience response system is a powerful tool, but it is only a tool. To make the best use of one, an instructor needs a coherent, comprehensive, pedagogic framework that indicates what ends ARS use should serve and how it can be employed to achieve them. Question driven instruction is such a framework. It is radical, in that it advocates making an ARS-mediated "question cycle" the core of classroom activity rather than augmenting traditional instruction with occasional or periodic ARS use.

We know — from personal experience and from assisting others — that mastering QDI is hard and takes time. In our experience, about three years of sustained effort is required for an instructor to really feel comfortable with the approach. However, we also know that it *can* be mastered, and that the journey and result are transformative for both instructor and students. The change goes deeper than the simple matter of what occupies classroom time: feedback gained about student learning, and the rethinking of pedagogic beliefs this leads to, can impact a teacher's very "way of being a teacher" (Feldman & Capobianco, 2003).

To an instructor beginning to explore ARS-based teaching or looking to get more out of it, the best advice we can offer is to get support. First, try to arrange for mentoring from someone experienced in response system use. Sit in on her classes and ask her to sit in on yours. You may develop your own style and perspective, but the feedback and ideas will be stimulating. Second, if you can find others also interested in developing their response system pedagogy, form a peer support group to help each other learn through practice, experimentation, discussion, and reflection. One of the great benefits of formative assessment is that the data provide a wealth of feedback about student learning and the effectiveness of pedagogic techniques — feedback that can power ongoing professional development. For this reason, we remind ourselves that we enter the classroom as much to learn as to teach.

Teaching the QDI way, with a response system, can be addictive. Every class is different, surprises abound, and genuine interaction is *fun* for the students and for the instructor.

References

Anderson, L. W., & Krathwohl, D. (Eds.). (2001). *A taxonomy for learning, teaching, and assessing: A revision of Bloom's taxonomy of educational objectives*. New York: Longman.

Beatty, I. D. (2000). Assessing-to-Learn Project Website. Retrieved from http://A2L.physics.umass.edu

Beatty, I. D. (2004). *Transforming student learning with classroom communication systems* (Research Bulletin No. ERB0403). Educause Center for Applied Research.

Beatty, I. D., Gerace, W. J., Leonard, W. J., & Dufresne, R. J. (in press). Designing effective questions for classroom response system teaching. *American Journal of Physics*.

Bell, B., & Cowie, B. (2001). The characteristics of formative assessment in science education. *Science Education, 85*(5), 536-553.

Black, P., & Wiliam, D. (1988a). Assessment and classroom learning. *Assessment in Education: Principles, Policy and Practice, 5*(1), 7-71.

Black, P., & Wiliam, D. (1988b). Inside the black box: Raising standards through classroom assessment. *Phi Delta Kappan, 80*(2), 139-148.

Bloom, B., Englehart, M., Furst, E., Hill, W., & Krathwohl, D. (1956). *Taxonomy of educational objectives: The classification of educational goals. Handbook I: Cognitive domain*. New York: Longmans, Green.

Bonwell, C. C., & Eison, J. A. (1991). *Active learning: Creating excitement in the classroom* (ASHE-ERIC Higher Education Report No. 1). Washington, DC: ERIC Clearinghouse on Higher Education, The George Washington University.

Boston, C. (2002). *The concept of formative assessment* (No. ED470206). College Park, MD: ERIC Clearinghouse on Assessment and Evaluation.

Bransford, J. D., Brown, A. L., & Cocking, R. R. (Eds.). (1999). *How people learn: Brain, mind, experience, and school.* Washington, DC: National Academy Press.

Cheek, D. W. (1992). *Thinking constructively about science, technology, and society education.* Albany: State University of New York Press.

Cohen, D., & Henle, J. (1995). The Pyramid Exam. *UME Trends,* (July), 2, 15.

Dufresne, R. J., & Gerace, W. J. (2004). Assessing-to-learn: Formative assessment in physics instruction. *The Physics Teacher, 42*(6), 109-116.

Dufresne, R. J., Gerace, W. J., Leonard, W. J., & Beatty, I. D. (2002a). *Assessing-to-Learn (A2L): Reflective formative assessment using a classroom communication system.* Paper presented at Pathways to Change: An International Conference on Transforming Math and Science Education in the K16 Curriculum, Crystal City, Arlington, VA.

Dufresne, R. J., Gerace, W. J., Leonard, W. J., & Mestre, J. P. (2001a). Creating an item for in-class formative assessment. *The Interactive Classroom, 1.*

Dufresne, R. J., Gerace, W. J., Leonard, W. J., Mestre, J. P., & Wenk, L. (1996). Classtalk: A classroom communication system for active learning. *Journal of Computing in Higher Education, 7,* 3-47.

Dufresne, R. J., Gerace, W. J., Mestre, J. P., & Leonard, W. J. (2000). *ASK-IT/A2L: Assessing student knowledge with instructional technology* (technical report No. UMPERG-2000-09). Amherst: University of Massachusetts Physics Education Research Group.

Dufresne, R. J., Gerace, W. J., Mestre, J. P., & Leonard, W. J. (2001b). *Assessing to learn (A2L): Research on teacher implementation of continuous formative assessment.* Paper presented at the Winter Meeting of the American Association of Physics Teachers, San Diego, CA.

Dufresne, R. J., Leonard, W. J., & Gerace, W. J. (1992). *Research-based materials for developing a conceptual approach to science.* Paper presented at the Workshop on Research in Science and Mathematics Education, Cathedral Peak, South Africa.

Dufresne, R. J., Leonard, W. J., & Gerace, W. J. (2002b). Making sense of students' answers to multiple-choice questions. *The Physics Teacher, 40*(3), 174-180.

eInstruction. (2005). *Who's using CPS?* Retrieved January 24, 2005, from http://www.einstruction.com

Feldman, A., & Capobianco, B. (2003, April). *Real-time formative assessment: A study of teachers' use of an electronic response system to facilitate serious discussion about physics concepts.* Paper presented at the Annual Meeting of the American Educational Research Association, Chicago.

Fosnot, C. (1993). Rethinking science education: A defense of Piagetian constructivism. *Journal of Research in Science Teaching, 30*(9), 1189-1202.

Gerace, W. J. (1992). *Contributions from cognitive research to mathematics and science education.* Paper presented at the Workshop on Research in Science and Mathematics Education, Cathedral Peak, South Africa.

Gerace, W. J., Leonard, W. J., Dufresne, R. J., & Mestre, J. P. (1997). *Concept-based problem solving: Combining educational research results and practical experience to create a framework for learning physics and to derive effective classroom practices* (No. UMPERG-1997-09). Amherst: University of Massachusetts Physics Education Research Group.

Gerace, W. J., Mestre, J. P., Leonard, W. J., & Dufresne, R. J. (2000). *Assessing to Learn (A2L): Formative assessment for high-school physics.* Paper presented at the Winter Meeting of the American Association of Physics Teachers, Kissimmee, FL.

Hake, R. (1998). Interactive-engagement vs. traditional methods: A six-thousand-student survey of mechanics test data for introductory physics courses. *American Journal of Physics, 66*(1), 64-74.

Hestenes, D., Wells, M., & Swackhamer, G. (1992). Force concept inventory. *The Physics Teacher, 30*(March), 159-166.

Hobson, E. H. (1997). Formative assessment: An annotated bibliography. *Clearing House, 71*(2), 123-125.

Laws, P. W. (1997). Millikan Lecture 1996: Promoting active learning based on physics education research in introductory physics courses. *American Journal of Physics, 65*(1), 14-21.

Leonard, W. J. (2005). *Every decision counts for better assessment.* Retrieved May 26, 2005, from http://kb.physics.umass.edu/edc

Leonard, W. J., Gerace, W. J., & Dufresne, R. J. (2001). Questions First (Q1st): The challenges, benefits, drawbacks, and results of asking students questions prior to formal instruction. In S. Franklin, J. Marx, & K. Cummings (Eds.), *Proceedings of the 2001 Physics Education Research Conference* (pp. 41-44). Rochester, NY: Rochester Institute of Technology.

Leonard, W. J., Gerace, W. J., Dufresne, R. J., & Mestre, J. P. (1999). Concept-based problem solving. In W. J. Leonard, R. J. Dufresne, W. J. Gerace, & J. P. Mestre (Eds.), *Teacher's guide to accompany "Minds•On Physics: Motion".* Dubuque, IO: Kendall/Hunt.

Mazur, E. (1997). *Peer instruction: A user's manual.* Upper Saddle River, NJ: Prentice Hall.

McDermott, L. (1991). Millikan Lecture 1990: What we teach and what is learned — Closing the gap. *American Journal of Physics, 59,* 301-315.

McDermott, L. (1993). Guest comment: How we teach and how students learn — A mismatch? *American Journal of Physics, 61*(4), 295-298.

Mestre, J. P. (1991). Learning and instruction in pre-college physical science. *Physics Today, 44*(9), 56-62.

Mestre, J. P. (1994). Cognitive aspects of learning and teaching science. In S. J. Fitzsimmons & L. C. Kerpelman (Eds.), *Teacher enhancement for elementary and secondary science and mathematics: Status, issues and problems* (NSF 94-80) (pp. 3.1-3.53). Washington, DC: National Science Foundation.

Mestre, J. P., Dufresne, R. J., Gerace, W. J., & Leonard, W. J. (2001). *The multidimensionality of assessing for understanding.* Paper presented at the Winter Meeting of the American Association of Physics Teachers, San Diego, CA.

Milner-Bolotin, M. (2004). Tips for using a peer response system in a large introductory physics class. *The Physics Teacher, 42*(4), 253-254.

O'Loughlin, M. (1993). Some further questions for Piagetian constructivists: A reply to Fosnot. *Journal of Research in Science Teaching, 30*(9), 1203-1207.

Penuel, W. R., Roschelle, J., Crawford, V., Shechtman, N., & Abrahamson, L. A. (2004). *Workshop report: Advancing research on the transformative potential of interactive pedagogies and classroom networks.* Menlo Park, CA: SRI International.

Redish, E. F., & Steinberg, R. (1999). Teaching physics: Figuring out what works. *Physics Today, 52,* 24-30.

Roschelle, J. (2003). Keynote paper: Unlocking the learning value of wireless mobile devices. *Journal of Computer Assisted Learning, 19,* 260-272.

Roschelle, J., Abrahamson, L. A., & Penuel, W. R. (2004, April 16). *Integrating classroom network technology and learning theory to improve classroom science learning: A literature synthesis.* Paper presented at the Annual Meeting of the American Educational Research Association, San Diego, CA.

von Glasersfeld, E. (1991). A constructivist's view of learning and teaching. In R. Duit, F. Goldberg, & H. Niedderer (Eds.), *Research in physics learning: Theoretical issues and empirical studies: Proceedings of an International Workshop.* Kiel, Germany: Institute for Science Education at the University of Kiel.

von Glasersfeld, E. (1992). Questions and answers about radical constructivism. In M. Pearsall (Ed.), *Scope, sequence, and coordination of secondary school science, Volume II: Relevant research* (pp. 169-182). Washington, DC: National Science Teachers Association.

von Glasersfeld, E. (1998). Cognition, construction of knowledge, and teaching. In M. R. Matthews (Ed.), *Constructivism in science education.* Dordrecht, Germany: Kluwer.

Chapter VIII

Anonymous Polling in an Engineering Tutorial Environment:
A Case Study

Steven M. Durbin, University of Canterbury, New Zealand

Kristi A. Durbin, University of Canterbury, New Zealand

Abstract

As a means of improving student participation, an infrared remote based audience response system was trialled in a second-year introductory level engineering tutorial. This chapter presents a case study of the initial implementation that directly followed a semester that employed a traditional tutorial format. Student response was consistent and generally positive at both the beginning and end of the semester, and the opportunity for live (anonymous) assessment proved useful from an instructional perspective, despite some limitations of the system. Interestingly, the new tutorial format appeared to encourage discussion after *each question was concluded, driven in part by the fact that a histogram of responses to the multiple-choice questions was displayed.*

Introduction

Introductory-level engineering courses continually struggle to balance the need for delivering theoretical content against developing problem-solving skills, both of which compete intensely for classroom time. A common approach taken at the University of Canterbury is to meet twice weekly for formal lectures largely focused on theory (attended by approximately 100 students), with a third meeting time set aside for less formal tutorials that focus specifically on working problems. This tutorial slot is particularly important in the theory-oriented electric circuit analysis course (ENEL 202), which is not accompanied by a set of laboratory experiments. In previous years, students were separated into four or five classrooms to reduce the student-instructor ratio at the tutorial. Homework-type problems were distributed in advance, and a member of academic staff, along with a postgraduate teaching assistant, were available at the tutorial to answer questions as students worked individually.

Ostensibly, this approach was adequate for many years, but newer generations of students, many with poor time management skills, less traditional backgrounds, and varying degrees of preparation, quickly opt to not attend tutorials in lieu of procuring the solutions from other students. Several attempts to revise the basic format, including a single instructor in each room directing problem sessions and answering questions on a whiteboard, did nothing to improve attendance, and participation was often limited to the same small group of students unafraid to ask questions in front of their peers. As a rule, students are reluctant to appear unprepared or to be having difficulty with the material, so that the primary feedback mechanism to the instructor is a series of tests and the final examination. Although homework assignments are collected and marked throughout the year, plagiarism and overly enthusiastic collaboration tends to blur any distinctions that might otherwise be drawn between student abilities.

In an attempt to improve student participation, as well as the effectiveness of the tutorials for ENEL 202, an infrared-based audience response system (ARS) was implemented during the second semester of this two-semester paper. Although electronic student response systems are by no means new (see, for example, Bessler & Nisbet, 1971, and references therein), the current technologies remove restrictions on lecture theatres being prewired, offer more variety in terms of displaying results, and have the potential to be more easily used in conjunction with other presentation software packages.

As put forward by Mayer (2002), if our goal is meaningful learning in the classroom, then the emphasis must be on more than just remembering the facts. Teaching strategies should also promote *retention* (remembering material at a later time) and *transfer* (using what was learned to solve new problems). Learning is a demonstrably meaningful process when students can construct knowledge by making sense of their classroom experiences, leading to the development of cognitive processes to be used in successive problem solving activities. In this fashion, tutorials having a different classroom format than the corresponding lectures can, if properly devised, assist the student in both knowledge retention and transfer, the latter being particularly critical in an engineering curriculum. Clearly, students must attend and participate in the tutorials, however, for this to occur. Although checking rosters is one method of encouraging attendance, it consumes valuable classroom time, is imperfect, and does nothing to encourage participation.

Several institutions (Shapiro, 1997) have reported implementing an ARS in order to attempt to do both: if each student's handset is given an electronic serial number, and the ARS software can track student performance, a nonparticipating student can be identified and penalised (assuming one student does not bring 10 handsets to class). A much better alternative, however, is to design and adopt a strategy to which students positively respond as a result of enjoyment or finding it useful. For this reason, we chose to implement the ARS in an anonymous fashion — the instructor had no means to identify which student was using which (serial number encoded) handset.

Research on multimedia delivery techniques (Mayer, 2003) has shown that traditional, "verbal only" instructional methods are not as effective as those that combine both words and pictures (or graphics, in the case of audience response technology that provides histograms or related summaries after polling). This is because humans process information through both auditory and visual channels: alone, each has capacity limitations, but effectively utilised together, they can promote and enhance active learning. Therefore, an ARS-based approach to engineering tutorials has the potential to help students achieve "deep learning," as it consistently and predictably exploits both visual and verbal media. Significantly, the student is transformed from passive observer to active participant, because the anonymity of audience response should encourage participation without fear of exposure (e.g., giving the "wrong" answer). There are positive aspects from the instructor's perspective, as well: audience response can provide the means for focusing on conceptual questions and concepts that may sometimes be overlooked on numerical, problem-driven homework and exams (Shapiro, 1997), and extends the opportunity to respond to the entire class as opposed to a few selected at random.

Another key issue is the significant variation that can occur between multiple, parallel, tutorial sessions (typically three to five for a class of one hundred) run by different instructors, some of whom are not involved directly in the lecturing. While it is generally a positive experience for students to be exposed to alternative problem solving strategies, it can be confusing when too early in the learning process. Attempts to align the sometimes disparate approaches of multiple instructors often lead to resentment, as it engenders the feeling that academic freedom is being infringed upon. Ideally, the lecturer should run the tutorials; equally ideally, each student should be motivated to actively participate (as opposed to passively copying solutions). An additional benefit from an administrative perspective is a reduction in staff full-time equivalents (FTEs) that must be assigned to the course. The results of the initial trial indicate that such goals are within reach of the technology, if properly implemented.

Methodology

For this study, an infrared remote based ARS from eInstruction Corporation (Denton, TX, USA) was trialled during the second semester of 2004 (Figure 1). The basic framework of the system employs handsets with individual serial numbers that can be linked to a student database for performance tracking and/or examination purposes, if desired. To

Figure 1. Top: Example histogram displayed after question end. A running tally of the number of students responding is displayed during the question. Middle: Initial reaction was clearly positive. Bottom: Example infrared handset, approximately the same size as a typical television remote control. Each unit has a unique serial number for student tracking.

provide full student anonymity in our implementation, each student picks up a randomly selected handset on the way into the lecture theatre, with two wide-angle infrared receiver units at the front of the room; the handsets are returned at the end of each tutorial session. All students are therefore combined into a single tutorial session that meets together, led by one instructor.

Questions can only be in a multiple-choice, true/false, or yes/no format, which places some significant restrictions on the complexity of questions, as well as the question format. One very interesting aspect of implementing this technology was that at the end of each question, a histogram was immediately displayed showing the percentage of students who chose each possible answer, with the correct answer highlighted in green. Both students and instructor, therefore, were provided with information regarding which problems the majority of the class was struggling with, and which topics seemed well in hand. This precluded too much time being wasted working problems in detail with which the majority were already comfortable. It also allowed students an indication of where they were in the class, performance-wise.

A typical 50-minute tutorial consisted of approximately 10 technical questions run through sequentially, each with a preset maximum time limit (nominally 8 minutes) and usually terminated manually by the instructor when either the full set of handsets had responded, or the frequency of responses decreased to one or two per minute (the experience is surprisingly similar to choosing the stopping time for cooking microwave popcorn). Underneath the question window, an array of boxes, each with a number corresponding to a handset number (printed on the underside of the unit), flashed when the software registered a response from a specific handset. This allowed students to see if they needed to rekey their response. The software recorded only the most recent student response, so that answers could be changed while a particular question was active.

With two receiver units and students generally nonuniformly dispersed throughout a lecture theatre having capacity for twice the enrollment, each tutorial began with several "throw away" warm-up questions not pertinent to the course material. These questions allowed the instructor to align the infrared receiver units, if necessary, for a particular day's student seating pattern, and, early on, for students to become familiar with the operation of the ARS. Topics queried included sports figures in the news, identification of characters in a popular cartoon televised during prime time, geography, and current events purposely nontechnical, to set the mood more to that of a game show. On one occasion, the lead-in question asked students which area of specialisation offered by the department was most attractive to them: communications/information processing (17%); computer engineering (11%); electronics (23%); power systems (14%); and undecided (18%). This anonymous survey capability was later exploited to sample student attitudes towards the implementation of the ARS, but the specific question also showed that even early in their academic career, four out of five students were intent on a rather narrow field of study. This directly impacts how a student will respond to a specific course, as less attention will be devoted to a subject whose links to the student's objective are unclear. Standard end-of-term course surveys typically do not poll on such issues, and doing so using the ARS can provide the means to test attitudes throughout a term, tracking changing responses or simply avoiding "survey fatigue."

Design of questions was impacted to some extent by the need to adhere to a multiple-choice format, and also by the desire to retain student attention (so that initially, at least, simple questions were asked which required minimal or no calculation). An example question is shown in Figure 2. More difficult questions would provide the basis for analysing a particular circuit in response to a given excitation function, or similar information requiring calculation. However, as a rule, the targeted "time to solve" was kept to a minimum, so that the majority of students finished at approximately the same time, or the noise level in the room could become too distracting to students still working.

Figure 2. An example question

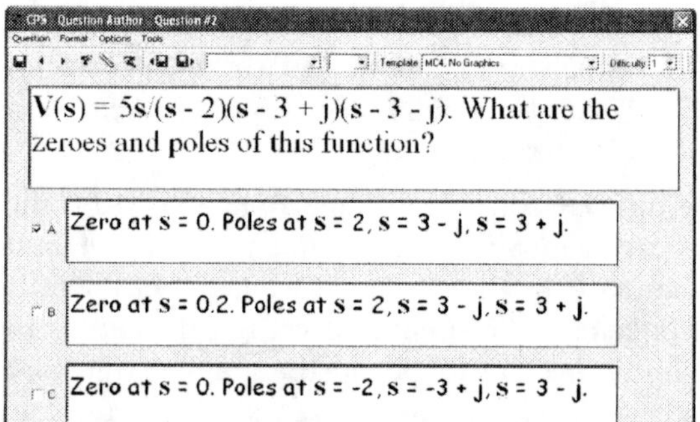

The general emphasis was on practical problem solution, given the purpose of the tutorial, and not theoretical questions, which would be appropriate in a lecture environment. Beyond straightforward questions, with perhaps one answer clearly impossible and others closely related — giving the instructor an opportunity after the question to briefly touch upon theory by discussing the impractical choice — other options exist. For example, one answer can be included which results from making a common error. In this fashion, a brief discussion can naturally follow even questions where many answered correctly, without the danger of losing momentum.

Discussion

Every tutorial, typically one or two students would arbitrarily choose a response key that did not correspond to an allowed answer (e.g., choosing "F" for a four-answer multiple choice question). This was borne out in the post-tutorial summaries, where several students each time responded to less than four questions. Attendance varied, but was usually between 75% and 90% of the official enrollment number. For the first tutorial, 67% of the respondents answered all 15 questions, 15% answered 14 questions, and 13% answered between 9 and 13 questions. Including warm-up questions, and not adjusting for tardy students, 12% of the final number of students at the tutorial answered less than 9 of the 15 questions, comparable to the number who ultimately did not pass. Interestingly, the same percentages were also essentially reflected in the distribution of responses. The average score for the first tutorial was 72%; later tutorials had somewhat lower averages, as more challenging problems comprised the bulk of the questions. For each tutorial, the most challenging questions were placed at the very end, in order to build student confidence, and to not prematurely reduce their attention span.

As should be expected whenever working with new technology, especially in an educational setting, several problems were encountered. The most notable was that the particular version of the Classroom Performance System (CPS) software from eInstruction Corporation did not import image files into the question database partitioned by tutorial date; rather, a pointer to a specific location on the laptop hard drive was used to build image-based questions. This reduced ease of portability, but more importantly image quality was relatively poor, due to the way the software imported the image at the time the corresponding question was activated, making line drawings and equations generated using other software virtually impossible to include. As a result, use of images was minimised in later tutorials, and the instructor was forced to verbally point out key features of images that were used. It was suggested that perhaps the questions (along with any images) could be run in another software package, such as PowerPoint™, in parallel with the eInstruction software handling response logging and display of the histogram after each question. This was attempted during one tutorial, but since questions had to be programmed into two separate software packages, and the computer system crashed during the tutorial, all subsequent tutorials were confined to the single software package.

Many institutions are able to install the hardware components of their ARS permanently into the classroom or lecture theatre, but in our case, the receiver units and associated hardware were on loan as part of the software licensing agreement, and the lecture theatre used by many departments throughout the week. As such, it was necessary to bring the two receivers, mounting poles, associated cables, power supply, and laptop each week. With only approximately 10 minutes between classes, it proved somewhat of a challenge to assemble and disassemble the system for each tutorial. Also, unlike PowerPoint™ and similar software in which double-clicking a file icon launches the software, with only one further mouse click required to launch the presentation, a sequence of windows was required to launch each tutorial. The combination of set up time and presentation launch time has implications for capturing and retaining student attention.

The same ARS can be used in conjunction with lectures as well, although time constraints and logistical issues mean that efficient implementation would have to coexist with lectures developed in PowerPoint™, or other computer-based presentation software. However, with lecture content heavily weighted towards diagrams and equations, students often respond more positively to whiteboard-written lecture delivery rather than projected slide shows. Also, there was a clear "novelty factor" associated with introducing the new technology, and there was some concern that the clear benefits of this would be diminished from overuse. For this reason, initial testing of the ARS was confined to the tutorial setting.

As a standard practice in the department, this course was scheduled for an end-of-year survey designed to assess student opinions of workload, difficulty, organisation and interest generation issues. Three supplementary questions specifically targeting the tutorials were added, the results of which are shown in Figure 3. Students were asked to evaluate whether they felt the tutorials, in general, were a valuable aid to their learning, whether they were helpful in clarifying lecture material, and whether the new ARS-based format represented an improvement. Also provided for comparison is the result from one of the standard questions: "Overall, this was a good quality course." Using a weighting algorithm of 1 = strongly disagree, 2 = disagree, 3 = neutral, 4 = agree and 5 = strongly agree, the standard question result — an overall opinion on the quality of the course —

Figure 3. Results of end-of-year course survey conducted on October 4, 2004

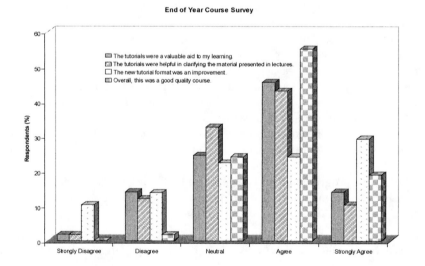

corresponds to a weighted response of 3.9, with the average over all engineering faculty being 3.8. Generally speaking, the tutorial-specific questions track the response of the course quality question, but with a noteworthy fraction (in excess of 10%) indicating rather strong negative opinions of the new technology replacing the more traditional tutorial format. It is interesting that this is essentially the same percentage of students who did not actively participate in the tutorials, although several factors prevent a direct correlation from being drawn as a result of both tutorials and the paper-based survey being completed anonymously. Overall, students appear to assign value to the tutorials, with a slightly higher fraction strongly agreeing specifically that the new format is an improvement.

Of course, one benefit of using an audience response system in anonymous polling mode is that such surveys should, in theory, be administrable without paper, providing nearly instant feedback if desired. At the end of one of the initial tutorials, 2 months prior to the course survey summarised in Figure 3, a single such survey-type question was added at the end of the circuits tutorial: "This new tutorial format is: (A) An improvement over last semester; (B) About the same; (C) Less helpful than last semester's format; (D) I'm not sure yet." The polling results are plotted in Figure 4, which show over 50% of the students felt the change was an improvement over the previous semester's traditional multiple room format. The same number of students (10%) responded that they were either ambivalent or as yet undecided, with about 10% of the students indicating that they found the new format less helpful.

Interestingly enough, the same percentage agreed that the tutorial was an improvement during the anonymous polling survey and the course survey administered 2 months later. This suggests that if a student responded positively to the introduction of the ARS system early on, this did not change significantly as some of the novelty factor began to diminish. At least one student indicated on the written survey that despite perfect anonymity, he/she felt compelled to ask a peer for the correct answer. Not surprisingly, the students experience some degree of frustration when they do not know how to work a problem, and the ARS does not directly address this. Generally, however, during the

Figure 4. Results of survey conducted using eInstruction system on August 2, 2004

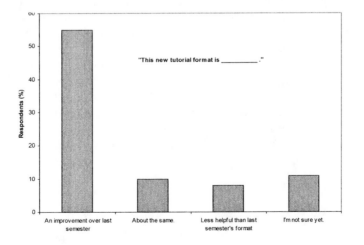

tutorial, the students appeared in a good mood — several commented to an outside interviewer that they enjoyed the opportunity to talk among themselves, as the ARS tutorials were more casual. The noise level was typically higher than the previous tutorial format, growing as more and more responses were logged. This particular outcome was unanticipated: that students would discuss their answer with their peers most commonly after responding, preferring to log a response (participate in the game) first.

What do students think about high-tech approaches in the classroom, generally? A recent survey conducted by the Educause Center for Applied Research (2004), a consortium of 300 colleges and corporate sponsors interested in academic technology, found that 72% of student respondents preferred classes with moderate to significant use of information technology. Interestingly, a breakdown of responses, by major, showed that engineering students had the highest preference for technology use (67.8%). In terms of the perceived impacts of educational technology, student respondents endorsed "communication with the instructor" and "prompt feedback from the instructor" most frequently. This is consistent with the course survey results from ENEL 202: more than half of those responding indicated that they were comfortable with, and generally positive about, the changeover to an ARS-based tutorial format, although some students did perceive that it had the negative consequence of further separation from the instructor.

That said, students are sometimes critical of the lack of skill shown by their professors in utilising technology, lamenting that class time can be wasted in getting it to actually work. As a case in point, this was the experience when the ARS software was combined for one tutorial with PowerPoint in an attempt to provide higher resolution images. However, a paradox ensues, as the same students often complain when professors make no attempt to use academic technology at all. This creates pressure on the faculty to "deliver the goods," so to speak, even though they may feel uncomfortable and underprepared to use the latest technological innovations (Young, 2004).

What makes professors unwilling to utilise the latest technology in their teaching? In the words of Prensky (Educause Center for Applied Research, 2004) faculty are "digital immigrants" when it comes to technology, not having grown up with it. Although many colleges have spent millions of dollars upgrading facilities and creating "smart" classrooms, they have failed to invest the necessary time and money in faculty skill development. Warren Arbogast, an academic technology consultant, notes that "most faculty learned in an environment much like Charlie Brown's teacher — I talk, you listen. Now we roll in an electronic gadget and say 'Use this.'" Additionally, when tenure and promotion committees place so little emphasis on teaching, an untenured or junior professor would be hard pressed to invest time and effort in new approaches that may not contribute to career advancement (Young, 2004). Interestingly, however, it is, the junior faculty in the department who expressed the most interest in trying the ARS in their classes. Feeling more comfortable with similar technology, it may, in fact, seem more natural to them, and not something completely new that must be learned.

Conclusions

The student response and instructor experience at the conclusion of this initial trial of an ARS in an engineering tutorial environment was sufficiently positive to encourage the continued use for the 2005 academic year. Direct measurement of the overall success will require more consistent use over a longer time period, where comparisons to similar courses not using the ARS can be made in terms of student performance on final examinations. Interestingly enough, however, it did not take long for the university administration to pick up on the potential marketing aspects of the trial. Several other departments have already begun exploring the feasibility of implementing a similar system for their introductory-level courses, although the start-up and licensing costs are nontrivial and may significantly impact how soon this can transpire, regardless of instructor enthusiasm.

Still, at the October 2004 meeting of Educause, James J. Duderstadt, President Emeritus of the University of Michigan at Ann Arbor, likened universities in the digital age to "dinosaurs looking up at the incoming comet," and commented that extinction threatens, should they fail to understand and respond to technological advance. Like it or not, technology has already drastically transformed the classroom of the 21st century. Duderstadt described the professor in the current technological climate as "becoming more of a guide or coach, while students have gone from being passive learners to active learners" and "synthesizers of knowledge" (Carlson & Carnevale, 2004). Whether instructors or department budget managers are ready, and independent of the impact of ARS technology on learning, it is more probable than not that some type of ARS installation in campus lecture theatres will be common in the near future. A passing fad? The answer to this question will depend on whether instructors actually use the systems, which depends at least in part on whether the students want them.

References

Bessler, W., & Nisbet, J. (1971). The use of an electronic response system in teaching biology. *Science Education, 55*(3), 275-284.

Carlson, S., & Carnevale, D. (2004, October 29). Technology threatens colleges with extinction, ex-president warns. *The Chronicle of Higher Education.*

Educause Center for Applied Research (2004, September). *ECAR study of students and information technology, 2004: Convenience, connection, and control.* Retrieved June 17, 2004, from, http://www.educause.edu/ecar

Mayer, R. (2002). Rote versus meaningful learning. *Theory into Practice, 41*(4), 226-232.

Mayer, R. (2003). The promise of multimedia learning: Using the same instructional design methods across different media. *Learning and Instruction, 13*, 123-139.

Shapiro, J. (1997). Electronic student response found feasible in large science lecture hall. *Journal of College Science Teaching, 26*(6), 408-412.

Young, J. (2004, November 12). When good technology meets bad teaching. *The Chronicle of Higher Education.*

Chapter IX

Using Audience Response Systems to Develop Critical Thinking Skills

Robert Webking, University of Texas at El Paso, USA

Felix Valenzuela, Yale Law School, USA

Abstract

This chapter describes an approach that integrates audience response systems into the social science classroom. The pedagogy uses the technology to produce active and engaged participation, encouraging the development of students' critical analysis skills, and facilitating high-level discussion within the classroom setting. The authors present their use of multiple audience response systems, along with the results they have observed, with a view to showcasing a variety of ways in which instructors at institutions of higher education might utilize these systems in their classes.

Introduction

Previously, in university classroom settings, student participation tended to diminish as class size grew. Class size also tended to change the way instructors could approach the material they taught. In larger settings, there was less give and take between professor and students: the instructor was likely to present the material in lecture style, and students were more likely to become passive observers. Incorporating new technologies, including audience response systems, into the classroom helps to shrink the gap between professor and student. Working with that technology in humanities and social science classes enables and leads to new pedagogies that can help to guide students, in classes of any size, to develop more sophisticated understandings of difficult material, by helping to make the reasoning process explicit to them.

This chapter will discuss the use of these systems in classes that fall partially in humanities and partially in social sciences, focusing in particular on three benefits of the systems: encouraging active participation, developing critical analysis skills, and stimulating high level classroom discussion.

The development and use of an audience response system in college classrooms, and particularly in larger lecture sections, has accelerated beginning in the 1990s, and especially with the invention of the Classtalk system by Better Education, Inc., which encouraged, and continues to encourage, reflection and research about effective ways to use these systems (Abrahamson 1998). Initially, this increasing use of interactive response systems occurred in science (especially physics) classes, and the research on their use and effect reflects that fact. This is confirmed by the material presented in Judson and Sawanda's 2002 study of the literature, which notes at the outset that these systems have been "primarily used in science courses" (2002). Several papers are available to detail such uses.[1] In recent years, the literature also reflects significant and growing use of the systems in medical education.[2]

The pedagogical uses of the audience response systems in these science classes are well established. Burnstein and Lederman (2001) provide a list of the things the keypads allow the instructor to determine:

a.   Have the students read the text before class?

b.   Are the students paying attention?

c.   Do the students remember important facts?

d.   Are the students thinking?

e.   Can the students recognize concepts?

f.   Can the students work in a group?

g.   Can the students do numerical exercises?

h.   What do the students say about the pace and interest of the lecture?

To these points, physicist Eric Mazur has added that the electronic response systems can facilitate peer instruction, though he rightly emphasizes that the pedagogical technique can be used without the technology. We believe that using interactive response systems in the humanities and social sciences can certainly take good advantage of these techniques to improve the lecture hall experience, but also can go further, in some cases with methods that would not be available without the technology, to help students develop a sophisticated understanding of conceptually difficult and complex issues about human beings, the universe in which they live, and the relationships between the two.

We began using audience response systems in political science classes at the University of Texas at El Paso in 1998. We have used these systems both in very large sections of required introductory classes, as well as in smaller, upper-division sections that focus on understanding of political philosophy and development of analytical skills. We have made extensive use of three different systems: we began with Classtalk, a hardwired system that uses graphing calculators as response pads for students,[3] and have also used the wireless Classroom Performance System.[4] In addition, we have created our own system, "Cephalus," which uses wireless networks, and computers or pocket PCs as input devices for students.

Simple Things

Audience response systems are especially helpful in large lecture classes in a couple of ways that become immediately apparent upon recognizing what the technology allows. Since the systems simplify record keeping for large numbers of students, they make it easy to check on attendance and participation. The ability to ask the students questions frequently, and to have them respond, helps to address the problems of anonymity and passivity in large lecture settings, involving each student more actively in each day's class. Moreover, frequently asking questions can help the lecturer to understand whether explanations have been grasped with clarity, or whether, on the contrary, it is advisable to explain the course's problems or issues more thoroughly, or from a different perspective.

Active Participation

A great advantage to using an audience response system, especially in larger lecture classes, but also in smaller classes, is that it makes each student continually active in working with the material and the lecturer. With each question, each student in the class is "on the spot" and required to make an assessment in order to answer. The temptation to sit back and listen — or not listen and do one's calculus homework or surf the Internet — that is so easily given in to in the large impersonal lecture hall, must be resisted in order to fulfill the requirements for the course. As in many cases, the short-term motive of grades can provide the initial reason for attention and participation, perhaps culturing a genuine interest in the material that might offer a more sophisticated and mature motive.

It is sometimes suggested that an advantage of these systems is that they encourage participation by students who would not ordinarily participate readily, because they are more retiring or unsure of themselves, or perhaps because there are other students in the class who tend to dominate, making participation too difficult for the others. The response system makes it possible, indeed necessary, for all students to participate actively in the work of the class session. It is also suggested that one of the keys to this benefit is the anonymity that can come with the systems: each student responds, but it is not known who submitted which particular response. Indeed, there are times when the response system can be used to ask questions of a personal or embarrassing nature, at which times it is essential that those answering the questions have the confidence that their particular responses will not be divulged. In fact, some of the systems do not allow the instructor to identify the particular answers of particular students during a class session (though the particular answers of particular students can be seen after the class session has ended). But there are some systems that permit the instructor to identify students by name, or seat, or both during the session, and to see what they answer as they answer it. The instructor can use this information judiciously to call upon particular students and ask them to explain the answer and the reasoning behind choosing it or writing it (in the case of an open-ended question for systems that allow that sort of input). The prospect of knowing that he or she might be called upon can make an individual student seek to participate even more actively, so as to be able to explain or defend a position.

Analysis

The use of audience response systems in large lecture classes can also help students to engage in the process of analysis, and to understand what they are doing as they do so. The analysis of texts involves reading critically to understand and embrace the statements and arguments that are there, considering those statements and arguments together to discover apparent contradictions or things that do not seem to be clear when put together, and then learning from those apparent contradictions or difficulties to develop a conceptual understanding that will help to account for the data of the text more completely. Using the audience response system, an instructor can help students through this reasoning process, and also lead them to appreciate what they have just done, and help them to be conscious of how the reasoning process works.

As an example from an introductory class, consider a problem from the play *Antigone*. When charged by the king to explain her choice to disobey his prohibition against burying her brother's body, Antigone offers two arguments: first, she explains that the only authority that she is required to obey comes from the gods and not human rulers; second, she claims that in this case she must disobey the king, since divine law requires her to bury a dead relative's body. Antigone is often seen as a noble figure to be praised for her devotion to do what the gods tell her is right, and from her statement, her actions do seem to be driven by her piety. Indeed, in the context of the play, she seems to be nearly the only character who is driven by anything other than the narrowest of self interests. But a problem arises in the text as Antigone is being led off to her punishment, when she bemoans her fate and explains that the only reason she challenged the king was due to her brother's body lying unburied. In fact, she makes the audacious statement that had it been merely her husband's body or her child's body lying unburied, she would not have "withstood the city to its face" and attempted to bury it, since she could get another husband or produce another child. The meaning of this statement and its implications for Antigone's motivations are things that readers tend to overlook because of their convictions about who she is and why she does what she does. But using an audience response system to pose a series of questions can help students see the difficulty, and then come up with an explanation that helps to resolve it.

We start with a question that asks the students to clarify what Antigone actually says:

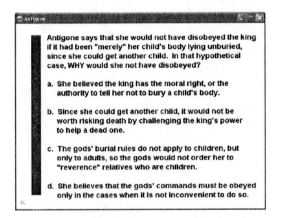

When the students have answered with choice "b" and have made what she says clear to themselves, a next question applies that understanding and draws out a concept:

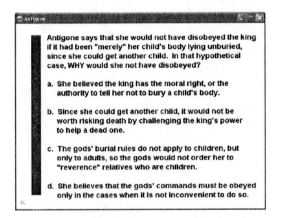

Again the answer is "b," and the students tend to see that readily at this point. Now they combine this deduction with the information that at the beginning of the play, when Antigone resolves to disobey the king yet does not even mention divine law, and must account for her claim that a reason for her disobedience is a resolve to obey the gods. They are asked this question:

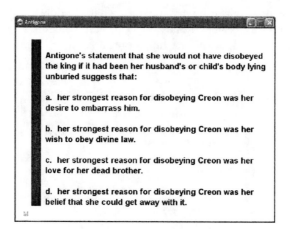

Now they realize that a care for divine law is not sufficient to make Antigone risk self preservation, as she has said, and so not a sufficient cause to make her disobey. Thus, one must look for some other difference between the two cases of her brother and her hypothetical child (and for the problem to exist, it is enough that the child be hypothetical — it could be the case, as students will occasionally object, that a real child would make her feel differently) and answer "c" makes the two choices consistent whereas answer "b" does not. And that is the key point: that complete devotion to divine law is not consistent with Antigone's statements and actions. Students at this juncture can see the point about Sophocles' play, and, with some explanation, can see the reasoning process that led them to that realization about the play and, thus, can begin to be conscious of that reasoning process.

Perhaps by now the reader of this piece is more engaged in questions or disputes about the interpretation of the play *Antigone* than thinking about physical technologies. That, in fact, is a critical point. Very quickly, the technology becomes transparent to the individual student and to the group as a whole. What it enables is a direct engagement that involves the student's active participation in interpreting and understanding the issues in the text.

Another example leads students to use the system to see an apparent contradiction, and then come to a more sophisticated understanding in order to resolve it. In the *Apology of Socrates*, Plato's account of the philosopher Socrates' defense of himself at his trial in ancient Athens, Socrates begins a central speech by claiming that one should not think of life and death when deciding how to act, but only about whether one is acting rightly or wrongly. Later in the same speech, Socrates asserts that he has avoided getting involved in politics because had he become so involved, he would have insisted on justice and, for that reason, would have been killed by the people. He asserts, in fact, that no one, in Athens or elsewhere, can survive if he opposes much injustice in the community. Individual questions can be used to be certain that the students are clear on each of these points. Then, once those questions are asked and answered, students tend to be fairly clear on the data in the speech that appeared to be contradictory. Then, in thinking about those data, they can move to a higher level of understanding by attempting to account for them as not being contradictory through a question like this:

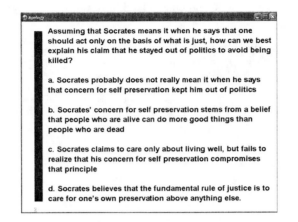

Because it enables a clear understanding of the problem, the technology enables the movement to a more conceptual level in understanding the point that, perhaps, Plato is trying to make.

Sometimes the data that need to be explained to encourage understanding are beliefs that are held on the part of some or all of the students. The audience response system is useful in helping the students to be aware of, and to think about those beliefs, to see the difficulties that they might present, and to work to resolve those difficulties. A question polling students on the meaning of happiness, for example, can lead to a discussion about the different definitions that students choose, and about the possibility that any individual student is incorrect in his or her feelings on the point, leading to the recognition of the need for a more careful analysis.

A similar poll is useful in discussing *Federalist* 10 and its efforts to explain the Constitution's efforts to shape beliefs to be compatible with the commercial republic. Students are asked a question such as this:

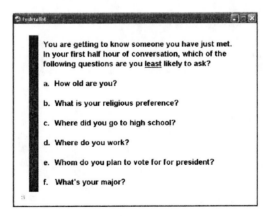

Invariably the graph of the answers comes back looking like this graph generated by Classtalk:

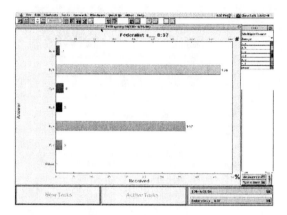

It is striking to the students not only that, with few exceptions, each has said himself or herself that either politics or religion is the least important thing to know about in getting to know someone, but also that in looking at the graph, it is apparent that this is the case with nearly everyone. It does not take much reflection to realize what a curious opinion this is, and it disposes students to want to seek possible explanations for this phenomenon.

A question with similar impact is asked at an earlier point during the semester. Students are asked to consider their actions in a hypothetical situation:

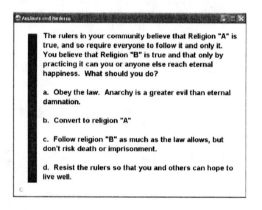

Again, invariably, the distribution of the answers comes back looking like this graph generated by Classroom Performance System:

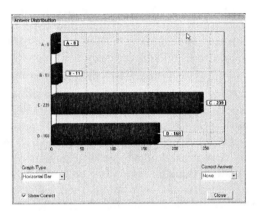

It does not take extensive discussion for the students to appreciate that in this case, answer "c" is simply insane since it says that one would rather choose the certainty of damnation over the possibility of spending some time during life on earth in prison (assuming something that it is very difficult for many to assume: that one would genuinely and sincerely believe what the question asks them to assume they believe). Later, in the course of a discussion of *Federalist* 10, it is possible to bring this answer up again to help students appreciate what it is in the regime that tends to make them and their colleagues answer as they do. Again, here, the reader of this piece is probably not thinking about technology, but in the classroom setting, it is especially these systems' ability to project a graph showing the whole class's distribution that enables students to appreciate the problem, and to begin to try to grapple with it conceptually.

Stimulating Discussion

In a large, introductory level class, the audience response system can stimulate discussion among students, particularly if the students are arranged in groups and answer, either as a group or as individuals, using the same device. In this circumstance, students will try to convince one another of the right answer, and the instructor can encourage such behavior, especially in an instance where there is a great diversity of answers among the students in the room, or in the circumstance where a majority, perhaps even a large majority, has initially answered a question incorrectly. The instructor can point that out, and then ask the students to work together to determine what was wrong about the incorrect answer and, perhaps from that, what a correct answer would have to involve. In cases in which the instructor induces the students to choose a particular answer, discussion and analysis can point to the opinions and dispositions in the students that the instructor seeks to make the students aware of in so doing.

But it is in a smaller class that the system is at its best in encouraging discussion and precise argument. Students can be asked to consider a difficult passage in a text, and then they can be presented with a very difficult multiple-choice question, or even an open-ended question that requires them to consider the text with great care as they answer. Working either alone or in groups, students will then choose an answer, and, if the system allows, the instructor can see which student has chosen which answer, which students have changed their answers, and, if the students are working in groups, which students have gone along with the other members of their groups and which have not.

Once the answers are in, the instructor can either choose to show the distribution to the whole class or not, and then call on individual students, asking them to explain their answers and the thought process which took them there, focusing on any number of things: groups which had difficulties in reaching consensus, students or groups which answered particularly quickly or particularly slowly, students who disagreed with their groups, students who changed their answers, and so on. Each student feels like he or she may be called upon to present an argument on each question. Students are encouraged to change their minds in the course of the argument, and often that is exactly what happens. A student will begin to analyze the text and the position taken, and realize during the course of the argument that in fact that position is weak. In time, and actually not very much time, students learn to care more about the strength of the argument than about having their initial position defended as right. They would prefer to appreciate the superiority of a better argument than simply to be told that they are right. Students learn to see the text for what it says, rather than for what they feel it ought to say, and to identify the difficulties that they have in coming to an answer from a question about it.

In this kind of setting, questions can be made more difficult and challenging than, perhaps, might be fair on an actual multiple-choice exam. But in working with those questions, students learn the analytical difficulties they face and, thereby, improve their critical thinking skills. Consider, for example, this passage from Plato's *Euthyphro*:

SOCRATES. Now this is the sort of thing I was asking when I was speaking before: is it "where 'just' is, there too is 'pious'"? Or "where 'pious' is, there too is 'just,'" but "where 'just' is, everywhere is not 'pious'"? Is the pious part of the just? Shall we say so, or does it seem otherwise to you?

EUTHYPHRO. No, but this is so. You appear to me to speak correctly.

SOCRATES. Then see what comes after this. If the pious is part of the just, then we need to discover, as is likely, what part of the just the pious would be. Now if you were asking me about one of the things mentioned just now, such as what part of number is the even and what this number happens to be, I would say "whatever is not scalene but rather isosceles." Doesn't it seem so to you?

EUTHYPHRO. It does to me.

SOCRATES. You too, then, try to teach me what part of the just is pious, so that we may also tell Meletus not to do us injustice any longer and not to indict us for impiety, on the ground that we have already learned sufficiently from you the things both reverent and pious and the things not. (West & West, 1998)

Having been assigned to read this passage as part of a slightly larger selection, students are then asked this question:

According to the agreement of Socrates and Euthyphro

a. piety is a more comprehensive standard for human action than justice.

b. a just person is necessarily pious.

c. a pious person is necessarily just.

d. piety and justice are unrelated standards for human action.

e. there is sometimes conflict between what justice requires and what piety requires.

The correct answer here is answer "b" since, according to the passage, one can be pious without being wholly just, but one cannot be wholly just without being pious. Thus, a just person must be pious, but a pious person might be simultaneously unjust, according to the passage, regarding things not having to do with the gods. But because of the difficulty of the interpretation, and to a lesser degree because the question is stated in language that makes the question itself challenging to interpret, students have difficulty with the question. This graph indicates the distribution of their answers:

Students who select answer choice "e" tend to do so because they believe, from their experience or perhaps from other texts, that there is some conflict between justice and piety. But when challenged to show the textual support for Socrates and Euthyphro's belief in that, they fairly quickly realize that their own opinion is not supported by this text. Indeed, after a few days of exercises like this, students take satisfaction in recognizing their own errors in reading things into the texts and are happier to seek a better argument, when that is appropriate, than to try to defend one that they have come to see is not supported. So at that point, about a third of the class is ready to listen and analyze to find the better argument.

Now it is possible to have students, who chose answers "b" and "c," explain the reasoning behind their choices, and argue with one another. It is useful to identify individual students who chose one of the answers first and then changed to the other, just as it is useful to identify and call on students who answered particularly quickly or particularly slowly. During the discussion, which on this question is often quite spirited, it is possible to refer to the students who had initially chosen answer "e" and ask whether they are being convinced of anything and if so why. Students quickly make the case that the issue is the relationship between piety and justice, and that the problem is to be clear on that relationship. In the course of attempting to reach and express that clarity, students will actually "invent" categorical logic and use something approaching Venn diagrams to explain their positions. Of course this discussion has absolutely nothing to do with the technology of the audience response system, but that technology enables us to encourage the classroom discussion by calling students to account for their answer choices, and by enabling them to change their answers during the course of the discussion as they think appropriate, and then to call on them to make arguments justifying such changes. This particular question has been used effectively to lead into a theoretical discussion of categorical logic to help students acquire the tools that they need to be more precise in their analytical thinking and in their expression of it.

Here the differences in the audience response systems become important. It is crucial to be able to know who answers what as the answers come in, and to allow additional time for changing answers, and also to see those changes, to be able to spot the active changes in reasoning, and to ask that they be explained. It makes every student an active participant, and helps everyone to develop the reasoning skills needed to appreciate and express the categorical relationship.

Conclusions

Audience response systems provide tools to improve the level and quality of the students' engagement in different sized classes. They permit instructors to actively encourage participation in a way that is comfortable for the students. Because each student must participate, and because, at least in some settings, each student's rational odyssey with each question can itself be analyzed as part of the effort to understand an issue or argument, the technology allows the use of innovative pedagogical techniques. This encouragement has contributed remarkably toward developing the critical analysis skills students' need. Finally, students actively participate in the classroom discussion because of the ability to address individual or groups of students during the presentation of the material.

Viewed in this light, the technology is merely the means for leading more students to engage in careful analysis of problems. The capability for seamlessly integrating the systems with class and lecture discussion enables the students to become actively engaged in the texts and argument. While the students' use of any of these systems takes merely moments to master, they benefit in the long term by becoming accustomed to rigorous analysis as they interpret texts and posit, defend, and adjust arguments about them.

References

Abrahamson, A. L. (1998, June 3-6). *An overview of teaching and learning research with classroom communication systems*. Paper presented at the International Conference of the Teaching of Mathematics, Village of Pythagorion, Samos, Greece, Conference Proceedings. John Wiley & Sons.

Burnstein, R. A., & Lederman, L. M. (2001). Using wireless keypads in lecture classes. *The Physics Teacher, 39*(1), 8-11.

Burnstein, R. A., & Lederman, L. M. (2003). Comparison of different commercial wireless keypad systems. *The Physics Teacher, 41*(5), 272-275.

Judson, E., & Sawada, D. (2002). Learning from past and present: Electronics response systems in college lecture halls. *Journal of Computers in Mathematics and Science Teaching, 21*(2), 167-181.

Latessa, R., & Mouw, D. (2003). Use of an audience response system to augment interactive learning. *Innovations in Family Medicine Education, 37*(1), 12-14.

Mazur, E (1997). *Peer Instruction*. NJ: Prentice Hall.

Meltzer, D. E., & Manivannan, K. (2002). Transforming the lecture-hall environment: The fully interactive physics lecture. *American Journal of Physics, 70*(6), 639-654.

Uhari, M. Renko, M., & Soini, H. (2003). Experiences of using an interactive audience response system in lectures. *BMC Medical Education, 3*(12).

West, T. G., & West G. S. (1998). *Four texts on Socrates*. Ithaca: Cornell University Press.

Wit, E. (2003). Who wants to be … The use of a personal response system in statistics teaching. *MSOR Connections, 3*(2), 14-20.

Endnotes

[1]   See, for example, Burnstein and Lederman, 2003; Meltzer and Manivannan, 2002; and Wit, 2003.

[2]   See, for example, Latessa and Mouw, 2004; Uhari, Renko, & Soini, 2003.

[3]   http://www.bedu.com

[4]   http://www.einstruction.com

Chapter X

Using the Personal Response System to Enhance Student Learning:
Some Evidence from Teaching Economics

Kevin Hinde, University of Durham, UK

Andrew Hunt, University of Durham, UK

Abstract

Recent increases in class size in higher education have focused more attention on the nature of the face-to-face learning experience. This chapter examines how a keypad technology facilitates active learning in the lecture hall using a number of pedagogically proven approaches. We survey 219 first-year business studies students tackling introductory economics, and find that the technology enhances learning in lectures because, among other things, it improves concentration, provides instantaneous and more effective student feedback, and allows students to make comparisons on how well they fare relative to their peers. Interestingly, we find less statistical support for the benefits of using the technology to allow students to respond anonymously, and explore some reasons for this result. Finally, we demonstrate our use of the tool to engage in teaching the Prisoner's Dilemma game. This forms part of the emerging knowledge on how to teach classroom experiments using keypad technology.

Introduction

This chapter will show how the personal response system (PRS), one form of audience response system, has been used to enhance student learning by improving interactivity and participation in the classroom, particularly the large lecture hall. The tool works in a familiar way: each student is given a small handset, similar to a television remote control. The tutor poses questions and activities and students respond by pressing the appropriate numbered button on their keypad. The responses are received by infrared receivers, and then automatically graphed and displayed on the projection screen for all to see.

We have found the PRS useful in developing and embedding learning, particularly in large group teaching situations, and report on a survey of 219 first-year business studies students who used the technology in economics lectures. Our use of the PRS with this group was fairly extensive. It was used as an icebreaker; as a way to build classroom communities; to engage in formative and diagnostic assessment; to facilitate interactive engagement between peers through deeper questioning; and to direct teaching based on student voting. We have also begun to use this technology to make the student actively and successfully participate in the famous Prisoner's Dilemma game, and report on this later in the chapter.

Our chapter develops as follows. The following section provides a brief environmental context and pedagogical rationale for using the PRS. The third section outlines how we used the PRS with our survey group. The fourth section summarises our survey data, and this is followed by a discussion of the results. The penultimate section shows how we have extended the use of the PRS to teach elementary game theory to economics and business students. We conclude by briefly reflecting on our findings.

The Rationale for Using the PRS

A number of factors have contributed to our increased use of the PRS. Over the past 25 years, the UK has experienced a dramatic growth in the numbers and diversity of the student body in higher education (Dearing, 1997). However, this has taken on a new meaning in recent times as the Government has increased the target participation rate of home based 18 to 30 year olds in higher education to 50% by 2010, and continues to encourage universities to increase their numbers of overseas students (DFES, 2003, 2003a). Students have also become more consumer oriented. This is partly due to increased indebtedness. Postgraduate fees have been raised, whilst home undergraduate students now pay a fee, and have had grants abolished in favour of government-subsidised loans. However, this is also part of the wider societal movement associated with greater consumer rights awareness, and an enhanced desire for value for money, as perhaps best illustrated in higher education by the display of teaching and research league tables in the media.

Though universities' revenues have increased, the cost base has risen more than proportionately with the growth in student numbers. Universities have responded to this by increasing class sizes, and it is a moot point whether UK universities are adopting the American approach of reducing "seat time," that is, class contact time, through large investments in virtual learning environments (VLEs), such as Blackboard, WebCt, and so on (Voos, 2003). VLEs have helped to coin the term "blended learning," the mix of electronic and face-to-face teaching evident in most universities nowadays, and afforded new possibilities in enhancing the learning experience. However, the growth in numbers has placed additional emphasis on face-to-face learning in the classroom which, modern thinking suggests, must be based around a meaningful interactive experience, perhaps even a conversation (Brown & Race, 2002; Laurillard, 2002; Steinert & Snell, 1999).

It is possible to facilitate interactivity in large lecture theatres by a "show of hands" or the use of coloured flash cards, in which each student registers a colour to demonstrate their individual preference. However, the principal problem with these methods is they do not readily demonstrate the numbers who have responded and, in the case of the show of hands, there is always the problem of knowing whether an individual's response is based upon their own or their neighbours understanding (Draper & Brown, 2004). The PRS overcomes these difficulties. The reticent student can register their choice of answer via the handset anonymously and, once all preferences are received by the transmitter, the software displays the aggregated choices on the projection screen. Students and tutor get immediate feedback. Students can see how they fared relative to their peers. The tutor gets accurate information on the numbers who understood the topic being considered. The PRS, like all keypad response systems, allows the tutor to control the pace and direction of the learning, but it also adds to the learning experience for both student and teacher (Leidner & Jarvenpaa, 1995).

A number of studies have shown that the PRS has value for teaching and learning. Elliot (2003) showed that using it to deliver multiple-choice questions in intermediate microeconomics led to improved concentration during lectures and greater enjoyment. Similar findings are reported in mathematics (d'Inverno, Davis, & White, 2003). A study of statistics classes reported some improvements in attendance at tutorials (Wit, 2005). There are also some tentative claims for improved test scores following use of the PRS (Strathclyde Biosciences Department, undated; Stuart, Brown, & Draper, 2004), suggesting confirmation of an earlier study of physics students using a simpler technology (Poulis, Massen, Robens, & Gilbert, 1998). Others have reported how the PRS can be used for engaging students in experiments, as well as to take student feedback from the PRS, and change the shape of the lecture based on the nature of the response (Draper & Brown, 2004). Nicol and Boyle (2003) demonstrate that keypad technology can be used to engage students in deep discussion with their peers, if the questions are thoughtfully posed. Thus, the technology impacts on student cognition, and so facilitates deeper learning. Further, it can create active socialisation among students and staff. In summary, it encourages participation in learning in large group teaching environments in a meaningful and enjoyable way.

How We Used the PRS

We began to use the PRS in 2001 at Northumbria University, and recently at Durham University, after becoming aware of the use of audience response technologies elsewhere. We noted immediately the pedagogic potential of this technology and embarked on using techniques deployed in other universities but tweaking them to our own subject specialism, economics. Similarly, we wanted to see if we could extend the technologies' use in classroom situations, something we are still working on. So far, we have employed the technology to gain feedback about students' prior knowledge and progression; to allow students to express preferences about particular topics, or the direction of lectures; and to engage in deeper learning through meaningful questioning, peer discussion, and games (we report on the use of the PRS in teaching rudimentary game theory later in the chapter).

The following techniques were all captured in the statistical analysis reported in the next two sections.

Opinion polls: By allowing students to express opinions about open-ended and often emotive questions, for example, 'Should the UK adopt the Euro as it's currency?', the lecturer gets a sense of the classroom community and the values it espouses. This allows the lecturer to shape the lecture, stressing the advantages and disadvantages accordingly.

Diagnostic assessment: Prior knowledge and understanding can be tested at the beginning of the class using questions based on previous lectures or past learning from elsewhere. Such tests direct how we proceed with new material.

Formative assessment: By testing knowledge of what is learned in a lecture we can get a sense of our own performance, provide guidance for seminar tutors, and rethink our strategies for directed learning outside of the class — for example, by providing further reading, or a Web resource. It is also possible to use the PRS for summative assessment, though to do so requires using the equipment in named mode. We have used it to prepare students for a multiple-choice exam using questions from previous years, but in anonymous mode, so they do not feel too intimidated in responding. This gives students a chance to reflect on their own performance relative to the group, and consider how they might proceed for the final summative assessment.

Interactive engagement: One variant of the technique involves the lecturer setting complex questions (Mazur, 1997; Nicol & Boyle, 2003). Students make an initial response to a number of possible answers using the PRS. The distribution of answers is seen, but the tutor makes no response other than to ask the students to discuss the question with their peers so that a solution is reached. These complex questions can be set to allow a correct or an open-ended answer. Both of these are ideal for a subject such as economics, and can be used to encourage deep learning through meaningful interactions between peers.

Contingent teaching: Draper and Brown (2004, p. 91) state the defining attribute of contingent teaching as "making teaching (the course of a lecture session) depend upon actions of the students, rather then being a fixed sequence predetermined by the teacher." One way of doing this is to gain feedback from multiple-choice questions, and then to redirect the lecture on the basis of serious misunderstandings. Alternatively, it is possible to allow students to follow a particular direction, given their preference in relation to the story they want to be told. For example, at some point within most economics modules, time is spent covering possible government policy options. It is impossible to cover them all in one lecture. However, if we provide students with a particular scenario, say high unemployment or inflation, we can then ask them to discuss the possible consequences of this problem, and allow them to vote on the one of numerous policy options they wish to adopt. Figure 1 shows the process. Having made a collective decision, we can test their knowledge of the transmission mechanism associated with their policy choice, the likely impact on the policy problem, and the likely consequences of their policy choice on other issues. The downside of this approach is that tutors have to provide numerous routes through the policy maze. This means creating quite complex slideshows. However, this is compensated for by the enjoyment of collective decision-taking in the classroom using interactive engagement techniques, and the opportunity to examine, through independent learning, the consequences of other policy decisions as students analyse the complete slideshow and further reading on the VLE.

Survey Data

We have used the technology with first- and second-year economics and business studies undergraduate students studying mainstream micro- and macro-economics modules, where class sizes can range from 20 to 250. The evaluation we report on in this section relates to a first-year cohort of over 400 business studies students at Northumbria University tackling economics as a part of a module titled "Business organisations and the environment". The system was used over five 1-hour lectures, and 219 students responded to our questionnaire, which was handed out in the fifth session.

The questionnaire was constructed based upon issues previously highlighted within the literature (Cue, 1998; Stuart & Brown, 2004). To help elicit students' actual views on the

Figure 1. Combining "contingent teaching" with "interactive engagement" in economics: A schematic diagram

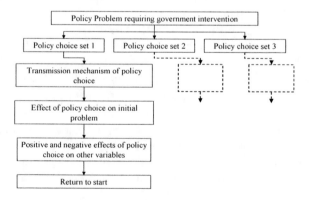

technology, at no point were students provided with a discussion of the lecturer's views on its advantages and disadvantages.

The questions asked were:

- I think more lecturers should use this technology;
- Overall, I have enjoyed using the personal response system;
- I like the way that the personal response system gives instant feedback;
- Discussion of the answers helps to clarify my knowledge about the subject;
- Specific multiple-choice questions are a good way of checking knowledge;
- I like to see how I fared in my response relative to the rest of the group;
- Being able to answer anonymously is important to me;
- The personal response system is a good way of helping me maintain concentration in lectures;
- The time involved in using the personal response system detracts from valuable lecturing time;
- Overall, the personal response system has helped me to learn;
- I found the personal response system easy to use.

Students responded by selecting one option from, "strongly agree", "slightly agree", "neither agree nor disagree", "slightly disagree", and "strongly disagree". Two questions were asked for written answers. These were:

1. Please add a few comments on what you think are the strengths of the system.
2. Please add a few comments on what you think are the weaknesses of the system.

Data Analysis

Table 1 shows the distribution of returns by question. The first column indicates that the vast majority of the student group, 82%, think that more lecturers should use the PRS technology, 7% of the group did not wish to see others using the system, and 11% did not have a firm opinion. The remaining ten columns illuminate student responses to the other questions.

Almost all students (90%) found the system enjoyable; this could be for a wide variety of reasons. Some typical comments suggesting reasons for enjoyment, or lack of enjoyment, included:

- "It's easy to use and remains interesting — being interactive during lectures passes the time in a better way than being talked at."

- Learn about macroeconomics in a fun way. Levels of concentration are much better. Encourages me to listen and pay more attention.

- It's really good, I have enjoyed being able to discuss answers with other people. It's like 'Who Wants to be a Millionaire!' Where are the prizes?

- Doing it every week gets a bit tedious.

- Unfortunately there is always going to be a minority who seek excitement within lectures and found it enjoyable to press their handheld console first regardless of questions. This was a pain and completely unproductive, but hey life's like that.

The fact that the PRS gives instant feedback was liked by 92% of the respondents, while only 4% took the contrary view. That the feedback allows the student to see how they have fared relative to the rest of the lecture group was liked by 84% of students, and it seems reasonable to assert that such a comparison would not be possible without the PRS (or similar system), partly due to 58% of students indicating that being able to answer anonymously was important to them. Typical comments in these areas included:

- Testing knowledge and if you get the question wrong you find out instantly why.

- You can see what other students are thinking and don't feel as stupid if your answer is wrong.

- It shows us where we are going wrong and helps establish areas that need revision.

Eighty-eight percent of respondents felt that specific multiple-choice questions were a good way of checking knowledge. A similar percentage of respondents found discussion of the answers helpful in clarifying their knowledge. This is clearly one of the key areas where the PRS can be of benefit, especially within a lecture session. It allows the material delivered to focus upon areas of misunderstandings or difficulties, rather than upon tutor perceptions. Student comments in this area were:

- Going through why the answer is correct/incorrect helps me to remember and clarify information.

- It allows you to examine your knowledge during a lecture.

- It makes you think about what the lectures are about.

- This helps to highlight important points on a subject and I subconsciously took more in than [during] a normal lecture.

A large proportion, 80%, of respondents found that the PRS helped maintain their concentration. This presumably means that they gain more from the material covered within the session due to a higher level of engagement than would otherwise be the case. Comments in this area included:

- Sometimes it was time consuming but it did keep people interested in wanting to participate in study.
- Interactive learning helps keep concentration up.

A possible disadvantage of the system, which needs to be balanced against the advantages discussed so far, is that the time involved in setting up, using, and removing the system will detract from the total time for "other" activities within the 1-hour lecture slot. Only 23% of students felt that time involved in using the system detracted from valuable lecturing time, and a further 19% provided a neutral response to this question. This may reflect one of two views. First, it may reflect different learning preferences. Some students may be more able to engage with a didactic lecture approach and prefer "a good set of notes", though most appear to favour the active learning style promoted by using the PRS. Second, it may be that students felt that the time involved in setting up and using the system displaced other valuable activities. This said, students are unlikely to be able to fully engage with this question. They did not know what changes had been made to accommodate the PRS. One of the consequences of the PRS within our sessions was that students were given other directed learning. Some student comments in this area include:

Table 1. Distribution of returns by question

	I think more lecturers should use this technology	Overall, I have enjoyed using the Personal Response System	I like the way that the Personal Response System gives instant feedback	Discussion of the answers helps to clarify my knowledge about the subject	Specific multiple-choice questions are a good way of checking knowledge	I like to see how I fared in my response relative to the rest of the group	Being able to answer anonymously is important to me	The Personal Response System is a good way of helping me maintain concentration in lectures	The time involved in using the Personal Response System detracts from valuable lecturing time	Overall, the Personal Response System has helped me to learn	I found the Personal Response System easy to use
Strongly Disagree	2%	1%	1%	1%	1%	0%	5%	4%	16%	1%	1%
Slightly Disagree	5%	3%	3%	3%	3%	2%	9%	7%	42%	8%	3%
Neither Agree or Disagree	11%	6%	4%	8%	9%	14%	28%	8%	19%	15%	4%
Slightly Agree	40%	40%	51%	51%	61%	60%	41%	39%	19%	52%	51%
Strongly Agree	42%	50%	41%	37%	27%	24%	17%	41%	4%	24%	41%

Table 2. Correlations between responses by question

Kendall's tau
Correlation is significant at
*** 0.01 level
** 0.05 level
*0.1 level
All 1 tailed tests

	I think more lecturers should use this technology	Overall, I have enjoyed using the Personal Response System	I like the way that the Personal Response System gives instant feedback	Discussion of the answers helps to clarify my knowledge about the subject	Specific multiple-choice questions are a good way of checking knowledge	I like to see how I fared in my response relative to the rest of the group	Being able to answer anonymously is important to me	The Personal Response System is a good way of helping me maintain concentration in lectures	The time involved in using the Personal Response System detracts from valuable lecturing time	Overall, the Personal Response System has helped me to learn	I found the Personal Response System easy to use
I think more lecturers should use this technology	1.00	***0.60	***0.56	***0.43	***0.48	***0.36	0.02	***0.61	***-0.35	***0.61	***0.39
Overall, I have enjoyed using the Personal Response System		1.00	***0.72	***0.47	***0.42	***0.42	0.01	***0.53	***-0.26	***0.50	***0.34
I like the way that the Personal Response System gives instant feedback			1.00	***0.48	***0.46	***0.48	**0.11	***0.53	***-0.27	***0.52	***0.34
Discussion of the answers helps to clarify my knowledge about the subject				1.00	***0.40	***0.36	**0.12	***0.42	***-0.28	***0.53	***0.42
Specific multiple-choice questions are a good way of checking knowledge					1.00	***0.28	**0.14	***0.38	***-0.27	***0.56	***0.42
I like to see how I fared in my response relative to the rest of the group						1.00	***0.18	***0.38	-0.03	***0.37	***0.29
Being able to answer anonymously is important to me							1.00	*0.09	0.00	**0.11	0.04
The Personal Response System is a good way of helping me maintain concentration in lectures								1.00	***-0.32	***0.64	***0.34
The time involved in using the Personal Response System detracts from valuable lecturing time									1.00	***-0.33	*-0.09
Overall, the Personal Response System has helped me to learn										1.00	***0.38
I found the Personal Response System easy to use											1.00

Note: Correlations greater than 0.5 are highlighted in bold typeface for ease of reading

- I would prefer a normal lecture as I feel I learn more i.e. more is taught as more is covered.

- Not very good for getting notes from.

- People take a long time to stop talking after you've submitted your answers so it takes time away from discussing answers with the lecturer.

- Can cause a lot of distraction and conversation when the handsets are shared.

The final column of Table 1 shows that almost all students found the system easy to use: usage problems seemed to relate to flat batteries and students being unsure if the receivers had registered their response.

Table 2 shows pairwise correlations between the responses to the various questions. Correlations were calculated using Kendall's tau-b, which measures associations between ranked orders. The coefficients can range between -1 and 1, with 1 indicating a perfect positive correlation, 0 the absence of a correlation, and -1 a perfect negative/inverse correlation.

Table 2 can be read across a row (as in the first question, "I think more Lecturers should use this technology"), down a column (as in the last column, "I found the personal response system easy to use"), and a mixture of row and column (as in all other cases). The strongest correlations are related to thinking that more lecturers should use the technology, personal enjoyment, liking instant feedback, maintaining concentration, and helping individuals to learn. There is some additional evidence from Table 2 to show interdependencies between the associations. For example, maintaining concentration is associated with instant feedback, which itself is associated (albeit less strongly) with clarifying and checking knowledge (0.48 and 0.46, respectively) as well as seeing how individuals fared with their group peers (0.48).

Almost all of the distributions of responses for each question are significantly correlated with other questions (81% of the correlations are statistically significant when testing at the 5% level). One of the exceptions relates to the question, "Being able to answer anonymously is important to me". This is not significantly correlated with four questions, and those correlations that are significant are relatively low in size. As there are a relatively large number of neutral responses to this question (28% neither agreeing nor disagreeing) this result is not surprising. If this question is reanalysed, including only the students who are concerned with this issue, that is, removing the neutral responses, the correlations become higher, but they all remain below 0.4, suggesting that using the PRS to remain anonymous may not be one of the most important factors in helping students learn and enjoy sessions. Of course, this does not deny that remaining anonymous may be extremely important for a subgroup of students. Additionally, it seems likely that even though many students claim to not be concerned with being able to answer anonymously, the fact that they have a handset in front of them makes them more likely to participate within the session than would otherwise be the case.

As expected *a priori*, the correlations between all but one of the questions show positive relationships, the exception being, "the time involved in using the personal response system detracts from valuable lecturing time," which has a significant and negative correlation with students wanting more lecturers to use the technology and student enjoyment. However, these correlations were significantly lower in magnitude than the positive correlations relating to most of the positive aspects of the technology.

Further Development in Using the PRS: Teaching the Prisoner's Dilemma Game

Our survey thus reveals that students perceive that the benefits of using this technology outweigh the costs. The results relate to using the technology for sampling classroom opinions, formative and diagnostic assessment, interactive engagement, and contingent teaching. However, we are also finding it useful to explain economic rationality and behaviour in game theory. This forms part of the emerging knowledge of how we can employ the tool to engage in deep learning through experiments (Draper & Brown, 2004). Our best example so far, as indicated by qualitative feedback from first- and second-year students of economics, business, and business finance, is in explaining the long-run outcome in the Prisoner's Dilemma game. The original game showed two (naïve) prisoners brought in for questioning by the police on suspicion of some criminal acts. The police have some information, but not enough for the conviction they believe is deserved. Thus, the police put the prisoners in separate cells, and so the game begins. The two players are the prisoners, and they have two choices, to confess or not confess to the crimes. Confessing to the police is tantamount to one player defecting (or competing) against the other, whilst staying silent is a cooperative signal by a player. The problem for the two criminals is that they do not know what the other is going to do, although they know the payoffs from confessing and not confessing in terms of jail sentences. The Nash Equilibrium in the game (a situation in which one player maximises their payoff, given what they anticipate the other is going to do) is suboptimal. Both players would be better off not confessing, but they rationalise that the other is likely to confess, and so they both confess to the crimes. Of course, we know that the prisoners have learnt to play the game and stay silent, provoking the authorities to consider alternative criminal justice strategies.

The game is fairly ubiquitous across a number of economic and social arenas, for example, in explaining competition and collusion (i.e., the formation of cartels) as well as teamwork and free riding among team members. It is a key concept in economics, and can be taught

Figure 2. The Prisoner's Dilemma game

Column Player			
Row Player		*C*	*D*
	C	(3,3)	(0,5)
	D	(5,0)	(1,1)

using traditional "talk and chalk" techniques. However, we have found that the best way to embed learning in large group situations is to employ an interactive approach in which all students are involved. Further, as we argue below, this is best revealed using the PRS because scores are instantly recorded.

In the lecture, a general form of the game, such as that in Figure 2, is presented on the projector screen. Students are told that they are the Row Player and have two choices, C and D and that the payoff they will get is on the left hand side of the bracket. It is only after the game is finished that students are told that 'C' stands for cooperation and 'D' for defection, or competition, between players. Students are told that the payoffs represent monetary payments, or units of satisfaction for a player. The lecturer declares that they are the column player, and that the class will be playing against the lecturer. The students are then asked to make their choices using the PRS handsets (the lecturer has already written their choice — C — on a piece of card hidden from view). The students' choices are declared on the projector screen for all to see, and the lecturer reveals their choice. Students are then asked to make a note of their payoff and that of the lecturer, who they are playing against. Those who chose D clearly have a payoff of 5 whilst the lecturer has a payoff of 0. On the other hand, those who chose C have achieved an identical payoff to that of the lecturer, 3. The lecturer says nothing, but asks the students to play another round of the game against the lecturer, as depicted in Figure 2. This time, the lecturer has a sheet that declares "If you [the student] chose C in the first round, then I have chosen C in this round, but if you chose D in the first round, then I have chosen D in this round." Here the aim is to play a "Tit for Tat" strategy, so identified as being the optimal strategy to adopt in infinitely played games because it punishes defection quickly, but allows reconciliation in the event that another player switches back to acting cooperatively (Axelrod, 1984). Again the student is asked to record their score and that of the lecturer. The lecturer announces that another round — Round 3 — is to be played. This time the lecturer declares that "If you [the student] chose C in the previous (i.e., second) round, then I have chosen C in this round, but if you chose D in the previous (i.e., second) round, then I have chosen D in this round." The game is played for 20 minutes (students do not know when it will end), and this usually allows for 5 rounds to be played. The scores are totalled, and we discuss the experiment. Those students who had chosen to play C are met with a similar cooperative response and both students and learners get a payoff of 15 after 5 rounds. If a student had played D in all rounds, then they would achieve a payoff of 9 whilst the lecturer would have a payoff of 4. Note, though, that such a competitive approach by the student offers a poorer outcome than acting cooperatively. There are some interesting additional points too. Although it is fairly clear from the changing results on the projection screen, the students are usually asked to respond to a multiple-choice question asking whether they switched their choice as the rounds progressed, to which they usually say they have switched from D to C. However, it is also noticeable that a small number of students realise that the game must finish at some point, and so switch from C to D after round 3 or 4. Both of these outcomes are rational within the context of the experiment.

It is possible to play the game in a lecture theatre by using a show of hands, or asking a few students to play the game against each other and then record these results on an overhead projector transparency before entering into discussion. However, neither of these methods captures the dynamic of the long-run game in a coherent way. A particular objective of the game is to show that the behaviour of individuals may change towards cooperation based partly on the punishment strategy of "Tit-for-Tat," and on the observations of how other individuals are behaving, as represented by scores rapidly displayed on the projector screen. Such instantaneous availability of accurate information is not possible with other techniques. It facilitates intense classroom debate among students as the game unfolds, and allows discussion of social conditioning and rationality in economics. Having played this game a number of times in large seminar and lecture groups, the reaction of students is always very positive, with few concerned about whether it takes up "valuable lecture time."

Conclusions

This chapter has examined our experiences of using the PRS to teach economics in the UK university sector. Much of the rationale for using the PRS relates to the changing context of higher eduction, notably the increased numbers and diversity of students and the development of learning technologies such as VLEs, as well as the pedagogical benefits we perceived. Having used this technology for a number of years we have been able to adapt it in a variety of ways for lecture and seminar sessions, and we are particularly pleased with its use in lectures where interaction can be more difficult to achieve. We have used it to: poll opinions; assess and attain feedback for tutor and student; redirect lessons based on student preferences and the further development of knowledge; facilitate "Interactive Engagement"; and embrace the teaching of elementary game theory. Our survery shows that PRS fosters enjoyment, improves concentration, provides timely feedback and clarifies subject knowledge. An ability to respond anonymously using the PRS was not as important overall though it may be important to a substantial sub-group of individuals.

By creating interactive lectures using the PRS, students are getting more control over the pace and content of the learning process. It takes time to set and answer questions and activities in a live lecture, and there needs to be some flexibility within the lecture to adapt to the changing needs of the audience. However, such an active teaching approach has several positive outcomes. First, involving students more directly has benefits for classroom behaviour, including increased concentration and attention. Where students are asked to interact in the lecture, their responses are more focused on the task. Second, with careful design and thought, students can be more engaged with questions and activities that involve conceptual problem solving and higher-order thinking. Third, there are important impacts on classroom performance, and this should result in an improvement in summative assessments. We noted how students like to check their knowledge of what is taught, know how they fared relative to other group members, and how discussion of the questions posed clarifies individual knowledge. Although we have no direct evidence, we might also surmise that students feel more motivated to learn using the PRS and have a longer-term commitment to the learning process when they are engaged more actively in the classroom.

References

Axelrod, R. (1984). *The evolution of cooperation.* New York: Basic Books.

Boyle, J. T., & Nichol, D. J. (2003). Using classroom communication systems to support interaction and discussion in large class settings. *Association for Learning Technology Journal (Alt-J), 11*(3), 43-57.

Brown, S., & Race, P. (2002). *Lecturing: A practical guide.* London: Kogan Page.

Cue, N. (1998, December 10-12). *A universal tool for classrooms?* Paper at the First Quality in Teaching and Learning Conference, Hong Kong.

d'Inverno, R., Davis, H., & White, S. (2003). Using a personal response system for promoting student interaction, *Teaching Mathematics and its Applications, 22*(4), 163-169.

Dearing, R. (1997). *Higher education in the learning society.* National Committee of Inquiry into Higher Education. Retrieved March 6, 2005, from http://www.leeds.ac.uk/educol/ncihe

DFES (2003). *The future of higher education.* White Paper, presented to Parliament by the Secretary of State for Education and Skills by Command of Her Majesty, January, Cm 5735.

DFES (2003a). *Widening participation in higher education.* London: HMSO. Retrieved from http://www.dfes.gov.uk

Draper, S. W., & Brown, M. I. (2004). Increasing interactivity in lectures using an electronic voting system. *Journal of Computer Assisted Learning, 20*, 81-94.

Draper, S. W., Cargill, J., & Cutts, Q. (2002). *Electronically enhanced classroom interaction.* Retrieved June 11, 2005, from http://www.psy.gla.ac.uk/~steve/ilig/handsets.html

Elliot, C. (2003). Using a personal response system in economics teaching. *International Review of Economics Education, 1.1*, 80-86. Retrieved June 11, 2005, from http://www.economicsnetwork.ac.uk/iree/i1/elliott.htm

Laurillard, D. (2002). *Rethinking university teaching: A conversational framework for the effective use of learning technologies* (2nd ed.). London: Routledge.

Leidner, D. E., & Jarvenpaa, S. L. (1995). The use of information technology to enhance management school education. *MIS Quarterly*, September, 266-291.

Mazur, E. (1997). *Peer instruction: A user's manual.* NJ: Prentice Hall.

Nicol, D. J., & Boyle, J. T. (2003). Peer instruction versus class-wide discussion in large classes: A comparison of two interaction methods in the wired classroom. *Studies in Higher Education, 28*(4), 458-473.

Poulis, J., Massen, C, Robens, E., & Gilbert, M. (1998). Physics lecturing with audience paced feedback. *American Journal of Physics, 66*, 439-441. Retrieved June 11, 2005, from http://www.bedu.com/Publications/PhysLectAPF.html

Steinert, Y., & Snell, S. (1999). Interactive lecturing: Strategies for increasing participation in large group presentations. *Medical Teacher, 21*(1), 37-42.

Strathclyde Biosciences Department (undated). *Report on the evaluation of interactive learning in Bioscience degree courses. The personal response system (PRS) as an aid to student learning.* Strathclyde University. Retrieved June 11, 2005, from http://www.strath.ac.uk/Departments/BioSci/prs.htm

Stuart, S. A. J., & Brown, M. I. (2004). An evaluation of learning resources in the teaching of formal philosophical methods. *Association of Learning Technology Journal - Alt-J., 11*(3), 58-68.

Stuart, S. A. J., Brown, M. I., & Draper, S. (2004). Using an electronic voting system in logic lectures: One practioner's application. *Journal of Computer Assisted Learning, 20,* 81-94.

Voos, R. (2003). Blended learning: What is it and where might it take us? *Sloan-C View, 2*(1), 3-5. Retrieved March 4, 2005, from http://www.aln.org/publications/view/v2n1/blended1

Wit, E. (2005). Further reflections on the personal response system in statistics teaching. *The Higher Education Academy, Maths, Stats and OR Network.* Retrieved June 11, 2005, from http://mathstore.ac.uk/articles/maths-caa-series/june2005

Chapter XI

Evaluating Electronic Voting Systems in Lectures:
Two Innovative Methods

Gregor E. Kennedy, University of Melbourne, Australia

Quintin Cutts, University of Glasgow, UK

Stephen W. Draper, University of Glasgow, UK

Abstract

This chapter provides practical advice on the evaluation of electronic voting systems (EVSs), particularly in relation to two evaluation methods. It begins by considering two potential educational advantages of using EVSs in large-group lectures in higher education. Four evaluation questions that are commonly asked by lecturers who use EVSs are linked to these two pedagogical advantages. The main body of the chapter focuses on two methods, observation and audit trails, and shows how these can be used to innovatively evaluate the use of EVSs. The development of an observational coding schema is described, and a case study of its use in two learning contexts is presented. Practical and technical issues associated with the use of audit trails are then discussed before a second case study is presented. The two case studies presented in this chapter draw extensively on data collected in evaluations of EVS implementations at the University of Glasgow.

Introduction

The use of electronic voting systems (EVSs) in higher education has become more widespread, evidenced by this volume dedicated to the issue. Educators are taking advantage of EVS technology in order to make their lectures more interactive, to promote peer-based and class-wide discussion, to help students prepare for exam questions, and to offer lectures that are contingent on students' learning needs. While there is no *one* way to use an EVS, when an EVS has been implemented, every student in a class can use a handset to respond to questions posed by the lecturer. The lecturer can then collate all the students' responses and present them back to the group.

The increased use of EVSs in higher education has raised the question of how to evaluate their use and impact. We start our discussion in this chapter by considering two potential educational advantages of using an EVS in large-group lectures, and pose four evaluation questions that are frequently asked after an EVS has been implemented. The main body of this chapter discusses two innovative methods of evaluating EVSs. The purpose of the chapter is not to provide an exhaustive discussion of evaluation techniques and methods. Rather, we attempt to give EVS users background information and practical advice on how to employ two evaluation methods that should be readily accessible to them. Our discussion draws on data we have collected in evaluations of EVS implementations at the University of Glasgow.

Authors have suggested a number of benefits to adopting EVS technology (Cue, 1998; Draper & Brown, 2004; Draper, Cargill, & Cutts, 2001; Dufresne, Gerace, Leonard, Mestre, & Wenk, 1996; Elliott, 2003; Mazur, 1997; Nicol & Boyle, 2003). For example, Draper, Cargill, and Cutts (2001) suggest seven "pedagogic categories of use" for EVS equipment, outlining how it could be educationally useful. These categories include facilitating assessment, providing feedback to the teacher and the learner, facilitating real-time experiments, and initiating discussion. However, when the rationales for using EVSs in large-group lectures are distilled, two predominant, direct benefits on teaching and learning processes seem to emerge.

The first of these is the *provision of feedback*. When an EVS is used, students can be given formative feedback, both through lecture-based questioning, and practice summative, assessment sessions. Feedback can be provided by the system, the teacher, or the students themselves. Lecturers receive feedback from students, either explicitly or implicitly, through their EVS responses. This "dialogue" between students and their lecturer makes contingent teaching possible, where the lecturer's presentation is largely driven by the responses of students. The second benefit of EVSs is the *promotion of active learning*. Traditionally, large-group lectures are didactic learning experiences where students are relatively passive bystanders. By asking students to respond to questions, students become active participants in the lecture. Active learning can be promoted through peer-based discussion, or simply through the act of responding to a lecturer's question (Draper et al., 2001; Kennedy & Cutts, 2005).

General and Specific
Evaluation Questions

The introduction of an EVS into a large-group lecture, regardless of the specific implementation or pedagogic rationale, represents the introduction of a new educational technology. The way in which this technology is evaluated is, to a great extent, no different from the way in which we evaluate any educational technology. As such, the first place to start is with a clear evaluation question, as the nature of the evaluation question will fundamentally affect the way in which the evaluation is carried out.

Typically, lecturers who have incorporated new technology within their learning environments are interested in how "successful" their innovation has been. The criteria that evaluators use to gauge "success" can obviously vary. The deployment of an EVS could be judged in terms of its cost effectiveness, the degree to which the EVS integrates with an existing course structure, the efficiency with which the technology is deployed, a cost-benefit analysis for staff and students, the impact of the EVS on students' learning processes and outcomes, or on their attitudes and perceptions. An individual evaluator's background will affect the types of evaluation questions and the criteria of success he or she is interested in. For example, decision-makers and course convenors may be more interested in macro questions of implementation and cost-effectiveness, while educators and developers may be more interested in student learning, and the integration of the EVS with existing instruction methods.

In our experience, the most common questions practitioners ask after they have implemented an EVS in their lectures are "How well is it working?" and "Is it helping my students learn?" Table 1 lists these two general questions, and articulates them at a more specific level in the second column. Considering the second general question, in an educational setting, student learning could be regarded as a valuable marker of whether or not an innovation is "working." Thus, the two questions in Table 1 are not mutually exclusive. Both questions would need to be specified in even further detail before they could be used to guide investigations of an EVS. Further explanation of each question, and the details evaluators may consider investigating is provided below.

Table 1. General and specific evaluation questions commonly asked after EVS implementations

General Evaluation Questions	Specific Evaluation Questions	
1. Now that I have introduced an EVS, how well is it working?	1a.	How are students using the EVS in my lectures?
	1b.	How can my use of the EVS be improved?
2. Now that I have introduced an EVS, is it helping students learn?	2a.	What are students learning from my EVS-enabled lectures?
	2b.	How are students learning from my EVS-enabled lectures?

How students are using an EVS system (Question 1a) is heavily reliant on the way that it is implemented by an individual lecturer. Thus, this question implies the need for lecturers to firstly reflect on how they are asking students to use EVSs in their classes, and what learning opportunities this affords. Regardless, a number of criteria and issues could be investigated as part of this question. As the focus of this question is fundamentally concerned with *use*, a simple audit of how many handsets were dispensed, how many students used the system, the frequency of use, when students used it, and for what period of time, could all be an initial evaluation focus. Once degree of use is established, evaluators may be interested in the barriers (and promoters) to EVS usage. These may include technical issues (e.g., difficulties with reception and displays), teacher-centred issues (providing too little time to vote, gratuitous use of the technology, lack of clarity in questions) or student-centred issues (forgotten handset, attendance, confidence, motivation).

Formative evaluation seeks to refine and improve a programme, intervention, or innovation, and therefore, this is the primary focus of Question 1b. In educational contexts, a formative evaluation will often focus on the programme or innovation itself, investigating how it has been developed, or how successfully it has been integrated into a specific teaching and learning environment (Draper, Brown, Henderson, & McAteer, 1996; Kennedy, 2004). An evaluation that aims to improve the use of an EVS could easily draw on data gathered from responses to Question 1a. By considering how an EVS has been implemented and used — where it succeeded and failed — evaluators can often see where the programme's implementation could be improved. Another critical component of formative evaluation is assessing what people's perceptions of the programme are. Indicators of where the implementation of an EVS can be improved ideally come from the teachers and students who have used the system. Asking students explicitly about both the benefits of using an EVS and, more importantly, any problems they had with using the system, is bound to identify any difficulties, and thus areas that could be improved (Draper & Brown, 2004).

Student learning can refer both to what is ultimately produced in terms of students' achievement (learning outcomes), and also to the processes involved with the learning experience. The question, "What are students learning from my EVS-enabled lectures?" (Question 2a), is predominantly concerned with learning outcomes. Educational researchers often investigate whether or not students have learned what is expected or desired of them. Lectures, including EVS-enabled ones, will typically have clear learning objectives associated with them (students should come to understand specific concepts, principles, or procedures): objectives that should, on the whole, be realised in the assessment of students' learning outcomes.

What is of primary interest with the question, "How are students learning from my EVS-enabled lectures?" (Question 2b), is not so much the achievement of learning outcomes, but rather, an understanding of the educational *processes* underlying the achievement of these outcomes (or lack thereof). Learning processes include cognitive processes associated with learning (e.g., reflection, critical thinking, problem solving, etc.) and contextual processes in the learning environment (e.g., peer-based discussion, degree of feedback, etc.). While learning processes are typically regarded as antecedents or concomitants to students' learning outcomes, researchers often investigate them without assessing learning outcomes at all, content to focus their attention on the patterns of relationships between variables within the learning environment. Learning process variables may be drawn from a number of domains such as the characteristics of the learner, the characteristics of a technological innovation, pedagogical focus, or other contextual variables.

These four commonly asked evaluation questions can be aligned with the proposed learning benefits of EVSs outlined above. Students' activity and interactivity, peer-based discussion, and formative feedback can all become the primary focus of evaluations of how students are using an EVS, and whether or not an EVS implementation can be improved. Similarly, these issues can become the variables of focus in an evaluation of how students are learning from EVS-enabled lectures. While not directly related to the evaluation question "What are students learning from EVS-enabled lectures?", these variables can be seen as antecedents or concomitants to students' learning outcomes.

Evaluating any new technology that is used for teaching and learning is a complex process. While the first step is to carefully consider the evaluation question that is being asked, a number of other decisions need to be made before starting an evaluation investigation. In carrying out an evaluation, Shulman (1988) suggests that "We must first understand our problem, and decide what questions we are asking, then select the mode of *disciplined inquiry* most appropriate to those questions" (p. 15) [italics in original]. In order to carry out an "appropriate" and "disciplined" inquiry, evaluators need to consider both the paradigm of inquiry and the general methodology they are adopting. A discussion of these elements is beyond the scope of this chapter, and we refer the interested reader to Reeves and Hedberg (2003; Chapter 2), Guba and Lincoln (1988), and Patton (1988). The final ingredient in a rigorous evaluation is using appropriate methods to gather information or evidence about the evaluation questions. The remainder of this chapter focuses on two evaluation methods.

Two Innovative Methods for Evaluating EVSs

The most commonly used evaluation methods are questionnaires, focus groups, and interviews. As mentioned above, gathering students' and teachers' perceptions of an EVS is extremely beneficial in understanding its value and impact. Questionnaires are a particularly popular method of doing this, as it costs relatively little to gather a large volume of data. Issues that need to be considered when employing these more traditional evaluation methods have been covered extensively elsewhere and, as a result, our discussion will focus on two more innovative methods that we have used in our own EVS evaluations: observation and audit trails.

Case 1: Observations of EVS Usage

Observation is a method that is useful in the evaluation of educational technology, and can be carried out in a number of ways. When observation is used in educational settings, it is often completed with a single individual, and allows evaluators to determine precisely what he or she does when faced with an educational task. Extensions of this method include techniques such as "think-aloud protocols" and "video-stimulated recall." The former involves observer intervention: participants are asked to explain their actions and thinking while they are completing a learning activity. The latter involves participants viewing a video recording of their learning session, and retrospectively explaining their actions and thinking. In this section, we review our development of an observational coding schema, and show how it has been used to evaluate the use of EVSs in large-group lectures. We present data generated using the schema to show how it enables evaluators to document the time allocated to different teacher and learner activities in EVS-enabled lectures.

It is often assumed that traditional lectures are not very engaging for students. However, many of us would have found some lectures very engaging: while sitting in a lecture hall listening to the presenter, we were "thinking hard" and were actively "trying to take in" the material being covered. This notwithstanding, it has been suggested that this is not the case for many students, and that between 20 and 30 minutes is the time it takes for their attention to wane (Bligh, 2000). One of the primary reasons for introducing EVSs in large-group lectures is that it makes this form of teaching and learning more "active" or "interactive." An anticipated learning benefit of this interactivity is that it will encourage students to cognitively engage with the material presented. We were interested in investigating this further, and in order to do so, we needed to think about what exactly we meant by "cognitive engagement."

Intuitively, we considered cognitive engagement to mean that students were actively thinking about or processing the material presented to them in EVS-enabled lectures. On one level, processing could mean simply attending to the lecturer and the lecture material (rather than dozing off or attending to something else). At a deeper level, processing would involve employing what educational researchers have termed "cognitive" or "learning" strategies (c.f. Weinstein & Mayer, 1986). These strategies reflect greater cognitive engagement, deeper processing, and include strategies such as elaboration, organisation, self-regulation, critical thinking, and problem solving.

Tapping directly into students' thought processes (their use of cognitive strategies) is clearly impossible, given they are covert, hidden from an observer's gaze. Traditionally, the cognitive processes of learners have been assessed either retrospectively through questionnaires (e.g., Heppener, 1988; Pintrich, Smith, Garcia, & McKeachie, 1991) or through the observation and analysis of students' behaviour, responses, or conversations. We were more interested in a method that was immediate, not highly abstracted, and did not rely on the retrospective reports of students. However, using an observational method with a large group of students posed a number of challenges. For example, it is difficult to observe and analyse the conversations of many students at once. Moreover, our previous observations of EVS-enabled lectures taught us that observing students from a distance does not allow us to hear their conversations and, as a result, the kinds of topics they were talking (and thinking) about. We also found that even when evaluators sit in the audience, alongside the students, it is difficult to record conversations. Additionally, in this scenario, there is the danger that students' conversations could be affected by the presence of the observer.

Given the difficulties associated with observing students' discussions directly, we decided to attempt to assess the extent to which EVS-enabled lectures provided students with an opportunity to actively process lecture material. We recognise that these more general observations of lecture-based activities are a weak proxy of students' cognitive activity. They are not particularly sensitive to what individual students actually think and do when asked to participate in the activities of the lecture. However, we saw this type of observation as beneficial because it could show what kinds of learning opportunities the implementation of an EVS affords. It should also reveal how implementing an EVS alters the traditional structure of a lecture.

Thus, we developed an observational coding schema for the activities typically manifest in EVS-enabled lectures. At the outset, we recognised that there was a tension between focussing on either the lecturer's or the students' activities in a class. While clearly related, and often interdependent, what students and lecturers do in class are usually different. For example, when the lecturer speaks, the students often listen. After posing a question in an EVS-enabled lecture, the lecturer often wanders about, while the students discuss the question before voting. In developing a coding schema, we needed to be clear about whether our focus was on the lecturer, the students, or both, as this had implications for how the schema was organised.

To develop the coding schema, the first step was to describe the types of activities lecturers and students engage in during EVS-enabled lectures. Table 2 presents this, and attempts to align lecturers' and students' activities with each other, where possible. Once these activities were established, the taxonomy was simplified into an initial version of the coding schema that contained five categories:

1. Lecturer speaking
2. Lecturer presenting a question
3. Discussion and voting
4. Lecturer presenting an answer
5. Lecturer explaining an answer

This coding schema was pilot-tested with a statistics class at the University of Glasgow (Wit, 2003). The first author attended a lecture, armed with the coding schema and a stopwatch, and placed himself at the front of the class. When the lecture began, the stopwatch was started, and the lecture activities were recorded. When the activity changed, the time was noted, and the new activity was marked on the coding schema. Through this structured observation, the pattern of activities in the EVS-enabled lecture, and the time spent on these activities, were documented. An example of what the completed coding schema looked like for the first 15 minutes of this lecture is presented in Table 3.

It became clear while using the coding schema that the third category of observation, "Discussion and voting," required greater detail in its specification. This became apparent during the observation itself, with the category being refined in situ to incorporate three subcategories: Vote only (v), Discussion only (d), and Question and answer with the group (qa). A summary of the activities of this pilot lecture is presented in Table 4.

Table 2. Potential activities of lecturers and students in EVS-enabled lectures

Lecturer Activity	Student Activity
General presentation (admin/organisational)	Attending to a lecturer presenting something general
Lecture presentation (content)	Attending to presentation
Presenting a question/problem	Attending to a lecturer presenting a question/problem
	Discussing a question/problem with partner
	Discussing something else with partner
	Using the handset to vote
Presenting a distribution of answers	Attending to a presentation of a distribution of answers
Explaining the answer	Attending to an explanation of a correct answer
Explaining something else	Attending to an explanation of something else
	Reading handouts or class notes
	Taking notes
Reflecting/wandering around/time out	Doing something else (e.g. reading diary, texting friend)
Leading a group question and answer	Participating in a group question and answer
	Listening to a group question and answer
Assisting individuals in the class	Receiving assistance from the lecturer

This test of the coding schema established it as a feasible mechanism of structuring observations of EVS-enabled lectures. The schema was modified on the basis of the pilot test, as the three categories of "Vote only," "Discussion only," and "Group question and answer (plenary)" were added as individual categories, resulting in an eight-fold classification:

1. Lecturer speaking (general administration or content)
2. Lecturer presenting the question
3. Students told to discuss (only)
4. Students told to vote (only)
5. Students told to discuss and then vote
6. Group question and answer (plenary)
7. Lecturer presenting the answer
8. Lecturer explaining the answer

Table 3. The coding schema template, and activities documented in the first 15 minutes of a lecture

Time (m.s)	Category					Notes	ΔTime (Secs)
	1	2	3	4	5		
0	x					Intro Handsets	162
2.42	x					Outline lecture	23
3.05		x					32
3.37			x			v	65
4.42				x			31
5.13			x			d	69
6.22					x		145
8.47		x					43
9.30			x			v	69
10.39				x			21
11.00					x		80
12.20		x					33
12.53			x			v	61
13.54				x			30
14.24					x		35
14.59		x					48
15.47			x			v	60
continued...							

This coding schema was then used with a number of other EVS-enabled lectures. The remainder of this section presents the results of using this schema in two different learning contexts.

Contexts of Use

The first context in which the observational coding schema was used was in a subject (Introductory Programming — CS-1P) in a first year computer science course at the University of Glasgow in 2002. The EVS was used to provide students with the opportunity to engage with the new content material of a lecture, to allow them to practically apply the content of lectures to programming problems, and to provide an alternative feedback mechanism to students on their understanding of the course content. The format of lectures was not altered markedly to accommodate the introduction of the EVS, with the lecturer stopping his presentation at preordained points to pose a question to students. Students were given time to respond and while sometimes they

Table 4. A summary of the activities documented in the pilot test of the observational coding schema

Category	Code	Segments of Time (secs)	Total Time (secs)	% of Total Lecture Time
Lecturer Speaking (general)	1	162, 23,27,23	235	8.7%
Lecturer Presenting the Question	2	32,43,33,48,64,17, 81,68	386	14.3%
Voting Only	3 (v)	65,69,61,60,107	362	13.4%
Discussion Only	3 (d)	69,153,135	357	13.3%
Group Question and Answer	3 (qa)	130,205,28,93,117	573	21.3%
Lecturer Presenting the Answer	4	31,21,30,47,22	151	5.6%
Lecturer Explaining the Answer	5	145,80,35,118,54, 84,33,79	628	23.3%
Total			2692	100%

were encouraged to discuss their potential responses "with their neighbour," peer-based discussion was not a major component of the EVS implementation. The second context in which the observational coding schema was used was in a statistics course at the University of Glasgow in 2002. These large-group tutorial sessions (up to 200 students) were designed as revision classes in which students were asked questions about the material covered in earlier, traditional teaching sessions. During these tutorials, the lecturers adapted their presentations in situ, so that the topics covered reflected the needs of students. Students were given options of areas to be covered, and then were presented with a series of questions in these areas. Lecturers would select each question based on students' responses to earlier ones. In this way, these EVS sessions were directed by students' responses (Wit, 2003).

Table 5 presents the observational data from these two contexts (three computer science lectures and one statistics session), and it reveals a number of interesting trends. A comparison of the three computer science lectures in the categories of "Lecturers speaking" shows how the amount of "Lecturing" can vary quite substantially with the same lecturer, and the way the EVS is used in specific classes. The variation across the "Students told to vote" category generally reflects the number of times students were asked questions (e.g., one question in CS-3 compared to seven questions in Stats). The "Group question and answer" category was an activity often employed by the computer science lecturer, and is akin to class-wide discussion. The coding schema is sensitive to variations across lectures, as evidenced by the percentage of time devoted to this activity being as low as 10%, and as high as a third of the lecture. The data show that in computer science classes, the lecturer chose either to explicitly explain an answer (CS-

Table 5. Results from the use of the observational coding schema in four example lectures

Category	Percentage of Lecture			
	CS-1	CS-2	CS-3	Stats
Lecturer Speaking	41.5	24.2	58.5	6.0
Lecturer Presenting the Question	1.3	12.3	3.8	7.8
Students told to Discuss (Only)	0.0	0.0	0.0	4.7
Students told to Vote (Only)	20.6	15.3	6.4	23.6
Students told to Discuss and then Vote	0.0	0.0	0.0	3.1
Group Question and Answer (Plenary)	9.7	33.0	21.5	0.7
Lecturer Presenting the Answer	5.5	10.1	1.2	12.4
Lecturer Explaining the Answer	21.3	5.1	5.7	33.3
Other (e.g. dead time, technical problems)	0.1	0.0	2.9	8.4
Total	100.0	100.0	100.0	100.0

1), as opposed to leading a plenary discussion in which the explanation of answers was inherent (CS-2; CS-3). Finally, the high percentage of time devoted to "Lecturer explaining the answer" in the statistics session indicates that this class was very much driven by the question being posed. The lecturer practiced "contingent teaching," where the responses of students determined what content material was presented. Thus, while there was not much "Lecturer speaking" time, there was a high percentage of presenting and explaining the answer (a combined total of 45.7%).

The original intention of the coding schema was to develop a means of assessing the extent to which EVS-enabled lectures provided students with an opportunity to actively process lecture material. In order to more directly address this aim, we further collapsed the categories in Table 6 so that they represented lecturer-based activities (lecturer speaking, presenting the question, answering the question, explaining the answer), student-based activities (discussing and voting) or both teacher- and student-based activities (group question and answer). The results for the four example lectures are interesting when recast in this way.

While similar in terms of percentages, the lecturer-based category in statistics is dominated by contingent teaching, and the lecturer-based category in the computer science lectures is dominated by more traditional "lecturing." The difference between statistics sessions and computer science lectures, and also the variation within the three computer science lectures, shows that the way in which an EVS is implemented will

Table 6. Results from the use of the observational coding schema in four example lectures using collapsed categories

Activities	Percentage of Lecture			
	CS-1	CS-2	CS-3	Stats
Lecturer-based	69.6	51.7	69.2	59.5
Student-based	20.6	15.3	6.4	31.4
Lecturer and student-based	9.7	33.0	21.5	0.7
Other	0.1	0.0	2.9	8.4
Total	100.0	100.0	100.0	100.0

fundamentally affect the degree to which students are given a dedicated opportunity to process lecture material. While some computer science lectures gave students an explicit opportunity to reflect on the content of the lecture (e.g., CS-1: 20.6%), for others, this time was a small percentage of the entire class time (e.g., CS-3; 6.4%). The data from these four sessions show that the observational schema is sensitive to the different educational structures in large-group teaching sessions and, despite the use of EVSs, some formats require students to be more passive than others.

A number of interesting issues emerge from our development of this coding schema, and the analysis presented. First, it was clear that there could be overlap in the categories of the coding schema. For example, a lecturer may spend a considerable amount of time explaining an answer to a particular question, but included in this time, he or she may spend 5 or 10 seconds asking one or two students for comments about the concepts being addressed in the question. Strictly, this activity should be coded as "Group question and answer." This notwithstanding, in most cases, it was clear what the dominant activity in the lecture was at any point in time.

Second, we indicated that the coding schema was not particularly sensitive to what individual students were actually thinking and doing in lectures. This became particularly apparent for two coding schema categories in computer science lectures. While peer-based discussion was not a major component of the EVS implementation in computer science, when students were asked to vote, the lecturer occasionally suggested students discuss material with their neighbour. Regardless, there was nothing to prevent students from engaging in this activity anyway. This indicates that the "Vote only" category may involve some student discussion. Similarly, while plenary sessions were defined as activities involving "group question and answer," our informal observation showed that the majority of students listen to the plenary discussion, and only a handful of students actually participate in it.

Finally, an interesting question is whether we can assume that classes are generally less didactic because they employ contingent teaching using EVSs. Draper and Brown (2004) suggest that contingent teaching has a motivational effect as it "cheers learners up enormously" (p. 92). An assumption underlying contingent teaching is that if students direct the lecturer to present material they want, or are interested in, then there is a greater chance of them engaging with it. While this may be the case, the degree to which students truly engage with the lecture content may be limited if the lecturer simply lectures at them. That is, if there is no change towards more student-centred learning strategies within the lecture — strategies such as peer-based discussion — students' engagement may be limited, despite them choosing the topic of the presentation. For this reason, the question of whether contingent teaching leads to more active student engagement is worthy of further investigation.

Case 2: Audit Trails of Usage

In educational settings, the term "audit trail" describes an electronic record of users' activities within a digital environment. Audit trails have also been referred to as "log files," and the process of using them has been called "event tracking," "electronic monitoring," and "electronic logging." When used in Web-based or interactive, multi-media environments, an audit trail typically documents the sequence of users' activities (or their "history") within the environment, as well as the discrete user inputs which make up this history (free text input, responses to fixed questions, behavioural responses to activities and tasks). The use of audit trails is becoming commonplace in educational technology research and evaluation studies, and their utility has been shown in a number papers (Evans, Dodds, Weaver, & Kemm, 1999; Guzdial, 1993; Hilbert & Redmiles, 2000, Judd & Kennedy, 2001a, 2001b; Kay & Thomas, 1995; Logan & Thomas, 2001; Misanchuk & Schwier, 1992; Pearce, 2005; Phillips, Baudains, & van Keulen, 2002; Salter, 1995; Weaver, Kemm, Petrovic, Harris, & Delbridge, 1999).

Most commercially available EVSs have a built-in audit trail system. Typically, the minimum audit trail capabilities of a system include the start and stop times of vote collection for each question and all individual student votes on that question, the time taken to vote, and the chosen response. This automatically-generated audit trail of students' EVS usage — the frequency and nature of their responses and the pattern of these responses — is another valuable method of evaluation available to educators.

There are, however, a number of practical and conceptual difficulties associated with using data automatically generated by EVSs. Data generated from any audit trail typically present challenges to evaluators in two areas: data management, and data interpretation (Misanchuk & Schwier, 1992; Reeves & Hedberg, 2003). Often, when data collection is automated, as is the case with EVSs, information will be gathered on every user action. As the number of recorded activities quickly increases, the size of the data-set becomes unwieldy, to the point where it becomes unmanageable. A number of strategies are available to evaluators to avoid this problem. They can be more specific about the exact nature of the data required by designing their evaluation studies and questions more carefully. This, depending on the capabilities of the EVS, will allow them to adopt a more targeted approach to data collection. In the absence of targeted data collection, evaluators can develop parsing routines to extract only a subset of the data originally recorded.

A second difficulty associated with using audit trails as an evaluation tool is data interpretation. At their most basic level, the audit trail data from EVSs measure students' behavioural responses. They capture if and when students responded, how long they took to respond, and what their responses were. While students' answers to multiple-choice questions may be indicative of how students are thinking (their cognitive processes), this cognitive component is typically absent from other data generated by EVSs. For example, data from an EVS audit trail may show that in a large class of students, a subset were consistently taking more time to respond to questions posed by the lecturer. An evaluator may conclude that these students were taking more time to consider their responses. While this may be the case, alternative explanations clearly exist. It may be that this subset of students comprised "strategic voters," who waited until the initial traffic jam of responses had subsided before choosing to have their response more easily registered by the system. The point here is that often a single action represented in an EVS audit trail may be indicative of a variety of student motivations, intentions, and ultimately, learning processes.

Thus, EVS evaluators need to be mindful of the vagaries implicit in audit trail data and, importantly, any assumptions being made when interpreting them. A strategy to facilitate more reliable interpretation of audit trial data is to gather additional information about the learner. Reeves and Hedberg (2003) argue that the interpretation of audit trail data in multimedia environments almost invariably requires the "input of learners" (p. 182), and certainly, the reliability of audit trail data interpretation will be increased by triangulating methods of data collection (Patton, 1990).

Despite these difficulties, evaluators can employ EVS audit trail data to generate useful descriptive statistics of usage, and to establish more complex patterns of EVS usage. The remainder of this section presents a case study from a computer science course at the University of Glasgow (the same as reported in Case 1). The case study provides details of how the audit trail data were gathered, cleaned, analysed, and interpreted, thereby showing how data generated by an EVS itself can be used to support evaluations of EVSs in higher education.

Each student was assigned an EVS handset with a unique identification number at the beginning of the semester, and response data were automatically recorded during the first semester of CS-1P. After each session, the following data were stored in a database: the date and time of the lecture, the text of the EVS questions used in each lecture, individual handset responses to each question, and the time each response took to make. At the end of the semester, these data were extracted from the database and placed in sequential order in an Excel™ spreadsheet to facilitate manipulation. Students' matriculation numbers were then matched with their handset identification numbers, thereby linking EVS responses with individual students in the spreadsheet.

At this stage, the data were cleaned. Three hundred and eighty four handsets, each with a unique identification number, were allocated over the semester. A number of these were one-off allocations for the last lecture that was predominantly an EVS-based evaluation of the course. When responses from these handsets, and those that were not used at all over the semester, were removed from the sample, 318 handset response sets remained. Sixteen cases were removed because the handset identification number could not be matched to a matriculation number. A small number of variables included out of range

Table 7. Descriptive statistics of EVS usage

	Mean	SD	Max	Min	Mode
Number of questions responded to (n = 33)	17.98	8.52	33	1	28
Number of questions answered correctly (n = 16)	2.72	2.19	10	0	1
Proportion of questions answered correctly	.28	.19	1	0	0

values. These were scrutinized on a case-by-case basis, and were recoded where it was clear why the discrepancy occurred (typically a system error). Where it was not clear, the individual data point was removed. Finally, given there were repeat lectures in this subject (i.e. a 12.00 pm lecture was followed by a 1.00 pm lecture to a smaller group of students) students' responses were aggregated across these two sessions. There were only five instances where students responded with the EVS in both lectures. In these instances, the first response was recorded in the data set, and the second response was discarded.

A total of 33 questions were asked using the EVS in lectures, and for each student, preliminary descriptive statistics were computed for (i) the number of questions responded to (ii) the number of questions answered correctly[1] (iii) the proportion of questions answered correctly. A summary of the data for these preliminary statistics is presented in Table 7. Even these simple descriptive statistics provide useful information about how the EVS was used by students. There was a great deal of variation in the number of questions that students answered (as evidenced by the high standard deviation). It is clear that a number of students were not answering many questions, with some students answering as few as 1 of the 33 questions. Note that the data presented in Table 7 does not allow us to tell why students did not respond to questions: whether it was because they did not attend lectures, because they forgot their handset, or simply

Table 8. Proportion of correct responses for each question

Question	Proportion Correct	Question	Proportion Correct
Question 3	.08	Question 15	.19
Question 13	.12	Question 7	.36
Question 16	.13	Question 6	.38
Question 1	.15	Question 2	.39
Question 8	.15	Question 11	.48
Question 9	.15	Question 10	.53
Question 14	.17	Question 5	.55
Question 12	.19	Question 4	.70

*Table 9. Four clusters showing distinct groups of EVS users, * n = 24*

	N	Questions Answered* (M,SD) x 2	Proportion Correct (M,SD) x 2	Description
Cluster 1	62	19.31 (2.66)	.46 (.09)	High Responders Moderate Success
Cluster 2	111	17.87 (2.70)	.21 (.09)	High Responders Low Success
Cluster 3	101	9.03 (2.76)	.36 (.19)	Low Responders Moderate Success
Cluster 4	41	5.34 (2.60)	.00 (.00)	Low Responders No success

because they often did not respond to particular questions within lectures. The success rate of students on the 16 questions with definitive answers was very low (the mean number correct was only 2.72), and the most any student answered correctly was 10 of 16. While students may not have responded to some of these questions, the proportion of questions answered correctly by students was also relatively low.

We also focussed on the questions, rather than students, and calculated the proportion of correct responses for each question. As mentioned previously, 33 questions were asked in lectures across the semester. While all questions employed a multiple-choice format, two different types of questions were used. Nine questions asked students about their general study attitudes and behaviour (e.g., "When will you start preparing for the Practical Class?"). The second type of question (n=24) asked students specifically about the course content. There were two types of "Content" questions: those with definitive answers (n=16) and those without (n=8). An example of the former is "Is this activity sequential, repetitive, or conditional?" and the latter is "Which of the following solutions is best?" (where there are sound arguments for the correctness of more than one response).

The range of error rates for questions with a definitive answer is presented in Table 8. The data clearly indicate that students were finding some questions more difficult than others. Almost no students arrived at the correct answer for some questions, while for others, almost three-quarters of the class got the question right. By using this type of data and carefully scrutinising the questions that are asked, lecturers may decide that some questions need to be revised because they are ambiguous, too difficult, or too easy. Alternatively, they may revise their lecture content in order to more explicitly address the content associated with "difficult" questions.

Another way to analyse EVS-generated data is to see if distinct patterns of responses are manifest in the student cohort. By using exploratory ordination techniques such as cluster analysis or multidimensional scaling, students can be classified into groups on the basis of the natural variation in their responses and use of the EVS. For example, we created two variables for each student: "Questions answered" (the number of content questions responded to) and "Proportion correct" (the proportion of correct responses).

We then used these variables in a cluster analysis (using Ward's clustering method and the squared Euclidean distance as the proximity measure). Four clusters emerged from this analysis that represented distinct groups of users of the EVS. Table 9 shows how these groups are defined statistically, and how we have chosen to describe them. These four groups of users could be used in subsequent analyses to see whether differences existed between groups on other variables such as motivation, amount of lecture-based discussion, or learning outcomes. For example, Kennedy and Cutts (2005) found a positive association between EVS usage and learning outcomes for students who, relative to their class, were more correct in their EVS responses.

Conclusions

In a discussion of evaluation methodology, Patton (1978) says that "The real point is not that one approach is intrinsically better or more scientific than the other, but that evaluation methods ought to be selected to suit the type of program being evaluated and the nature of decision-makers' questions" (pp. 210-211). The two evaluation methods we have discussed can, on the whole, be used to investigate the four commonly asked questions posed at the start of this chapter. The observational schema can be used to effectively document how lecturers and students are using an EVS, and the outcomes of these observations may indicate where the use of the system could be improved. While structured observation cannot shed light directly on students' learning outcomes, it is a method that may be particularly useful in evaluating how EVS usage is associated with students' learning outcomes.

Similarly, audit trail analysis can be a very useful tool in responding to all four evaluation questions. The case study presented previously showed how audit trails were used to establish how an EVS was being used. An analysis of question error rates suggested areas where the EVS implementation could be improved, and also directly assessed students' understanding of lecture material. Finally, by applying ordination techniques to audit trail data, we showed how different groups of EVS users could be established. These groups could then be used in an analysis of differences in both students' learning processes and outcomes.

A final caveat to our discussion of evaluation methods, and implied in Patton's (1978) words above, is that rarely is one method sufficient in carrying out a robust and systematic evaluation. We have aimed in this chapter to provide some practical advice on how to employ two evaluation methods. Educators interested in establishing a clear understanding of how their use of an EVS is working would be well advised to consider triangulating the methods discussed here with others such as questionnaires, focus groups, and interviews.

Acknowledgments

We would like to thank Chris Mitchell for assisting with the extraction of the audit trail data, and Margaret Brown for her insight into the evaluation of EVSs.

References

Bligh, D. A. (2000). *What's the use of lectures?* San Francisco: Jossey-Bass.

Cue, N. (1998, December 10-12). A universal tool for classrooms? In *Proceedings of the First Quality in Teaching and Learning Conference,* Hong Kong International Trade and Exhibition Centre, Hong Kong, SAR, China.

Draper, S., & Brown, M. (2004). Increasing interactivity in lectures using an electronic voting system. *Journal of Computer Assisted Learning, 20*(2), 81-94.

Draper, S., Cargill, J., & Cutts, Q. (2001). Electronically enhanced classroom interaction. *Australian Journal of Educational Technology, 18*(1), 13-23.

Draper, S. W., Brown, M. I., Henderson, F. P., & McAteer, E. (1996). Integrative evaluation: An emerging role for classroom studies of CAL. *Computers in Education, 26*(1-3), 17-32.

Dufresne, R., Gerace, W., Leonard, W., Mestre, J., & Wenk, L. (1996). Classtalk: A classroom communication system for active learning. *Journal of Computing in Higher Education, 7,* 3-47.

Elliott, C. (2003). Using a personal response system in economics teaching. *International Review of Economics Education.* Retrieved from http://www.economics.ltsn.ac.uk/iree/i1/elliott.htm

Evans, G., Dodds, A., Weaver, D., & Kemm, R. (1999). Individual differences in strategies, activities and outcomes in computer-aided learning: A case study. Global Issues and Local Effects: The challenge for educational research. In R. Jeffery & S. Rich (Eds.), *Proceedings of the Joint Conference of AARE (Australian Association for Research in Education) and NZARE (New Zealand Association for Research in Education) 1999.* Melbourne: Australian Association for Research in Education Inc.

Guba, E. G., & Lincoln, Y. S. (1988). Do inquiry paradigms imply inquiry methodologies? In D. M. Fetterman (Ed.), *Qualitative approaches to evaluation in education* (pp. 89-115). New York: Praeger.

Guzdial, M. (1993). *Deriving software usage patterns from log files.* (Tech Report GIT-GVU-93-41).

Heppener, P. (1988). *The problem solving inventory: Manual.* Palo Alto, CA: Consulting Psychologists Press.

Hilbert, D. M., & Redmiles, D. F. (2000). Extracting usability information from user interface events. *ACM Computing Surveys, 32*(4), 384-421.

Judd, T., & Kennedy, G. (2001a). Extending the role of audit trails: A modular approach. *Journal of Educational Multimedia and Hypermedia, 10*(4), 377-395.

Judd, T., & Kennedy, G. (2001b). Flexible audit trailing in interactive courseware. In C. Montgomerie & J. Viteli (Eds.), *Proceedings of ED-MEDIA 2001, World Conference on Educational Multimedia, Hypermedia & Telecommunications* (pp. 943-948). Charlottesville, VA: AACE.

Kay, J., & Thomas, R. C. (1995). Studying long-term system use. *Communications of the ACM, 38*(7), 61-9.

Kennedy, G. E. (2004). Promoting cognition in multimedia interactivity research. *Journal of Interactive Learning Research, 15*(1), 43-61.

Kennedy, G. E., & Cutts, Q. I. (2005). The association between students' use of an electronic voting system and their learning outcomes. *Journal of Computer Assisted Learning, 21,* 260-268.

Logan, K., & Thomas, P. (2001). Observations of students working practices in an online distance educational learning environment in relation to time. In G. Kadoda (Ed.), *Workshop of the Psychology of Programming Interest Group* (pp. 29-38).

Mazur, E. (1997). *Peer instruction: A user's manual.* Upper Saddle River, NJ: Prentice-Hall.

Misanchuk, E. R., & Schwier, R. (1992). Representing interactive multimedia and hypermedia audit trails. *Journal of Educational Multimedia and Hypermedia, 1*(3), 355-372.

Nicol, D., & Boyle, N. (2003). Peer instruction vs. class-wide discussion in large classes: A comparison of two interaction methods in the wired classroom. *Studies in Higher Education, 28*(4), 458-473.

Patton, M. Q. (1978). *Utilization-focused evaluation.* Beverly Hills, CA: Sage Publications.

Patton, M. Q. (1988). Paradigms and pragmatism. In D. M. Fetterman (Ed), *Qualitative approaches to evaluation in education* (pp. 116-137). New York: Praeger.

Patton, M. Q. (1990). *Qualitative evaluation research methods.* Newbury Park, CA: Sage.

Pearce, J., Ainley, M., & Howard, S. (2005). The ebb and flow of online learning. *Computers in Human Behavior, 21*(5), 745-771.

Phillips, R., Baudains, C., & van Keulen, M. (2002). *An evaluation of users' learning in a web-supported unit of plant diversity.* Paper presented at the Nineteenth Annual Conference of the Australasian Society for Computers in Learning in Tertiary Education (ASCILITE), Auckland, New Zealand.

Pintrich, P. R., Smith, D., Garcia T., & McKeachie, W. (1991). *The motivated strategies for learning questionnaires (MSLQ).* Ann Arbor: The University of Michigan.

Reeves, T. C., & Hedberg, J. G. (2003). *Interactive learning systems evaluation.* Englewood Cliffs, NJ: Educational Technology Publications.

Salter, G. (1995). Quantitative analysis of multimedia audit trails. In, J. M. Pearce, A. Ellis, G. Hart & C. McNaught (Eds.), Learning with technology. *Proceedings of the*

Twelfth Annual Conference of Australasian Society for Computers in Tertiary Education (ASCILITE) (pp. 456-461). Melbourne: Science Multimedia Teaching Unit, The University of Melbourne.

Shulman, L. S. (1988). Disciplines of inquiry in education: An overview. In R. M. Jaeger (Ed.), *Complementary methods for research in education* (pp. 3-17). Washington DC: American Educational Research Association.

Weaver, D., Kemm, R., Petrovic, T., Harris, P., & Delbridge, L. (1999). Learning about control systems by model building: A biological case study. In J. Winn (Ed.), *Responding to diversity. Proceedings of the 16th Annual Conference of Australasian Society for Computers in Learning in Tertiary Education (ASCILITE)* (pp. 381-390). Brisbane, Australia: Queensland University of Technology.

Weinstein, C., & Mayer, R. (1986). The teaching of learning strategies. In M. Wittrock (Ed.), *Handbook of research on teaching* (pp. 315-327). New York: Macmillan.

Wit, E. (2003). Who wants to be... The use of a personal response system in statistics teaching. *MSOR Connections, 3*(2), 5-11.

Endnote

[1]   Sixteen questions had a definitive correct answer.

Chapter XII

Selected and Constructed Response Systems in Mathematics Classrooms

Leslee Francis Pelton, University of Victoria, Canada

Tim Pelton, University of Victoria, Canada

Abstract

This chapter examines two types of response technologies (selected and constructed) available to support discussion and participation in the classroom, and describes our experiences using and observing them in a variety of mathematics, science, and computer science classes at various educational levels. Selected response systems (a.k.a., clickers) display multiple-choice questions, and then collect and analyze student responses, and present distribution summaries to the class. Constructed response systems allow students to use handheld computers to generate free-form graphical responses to teacher prompts using various software applications. Once completed, students submit their responses to the instructor's computer wirelessly. The instructor may then select and anonymously project these authentic student work samples or representations to promote classroom discussion. We review the purpose, design, and features of these two types of response systems, highlight some of the issues underlying their application, discuss our experiences using them in the classroom, and make recommendations.

Introduction

In *Principles and Standards for School Mathematics* (NCTM, 2000), the National Council of Teachers of Mathematics identified communication as one of the fundamental processes for learning mathematics. They state that effective communication enables students to organize and consolidate their thinking; practice presenting their mathematical thinking in a clear, coherent fashion; analyze and evaluate the mathematical thinking and strategies of others; and learn to use the language of mathematics precisely. Although these goals clearly indicate that active participation of the students within the classroom promotes efficient learning, communication in the mathematics classroom is frequently a one-way process.

Some teachers still instruct their classes using the "chalk and talk" method, lecturing and working examples on the board, with students taking notes and responding to questions involving a calculation step or fact, or asking for clarification when a concept or process is unclear. Classroom communication and interaction tends to be between the teacher and one or two students, and the questions and responses generally fail to promote real discussion in the class. While students may passively take notes and mechanically follow prescribed procedures, they are often not actively engaged in thinking about the content of the lesson, or its connection to other curricular content, or indeed the world around them. Little or no opportunity exists to discuss the lesson material, students work in isolation to learn it, and exams simply require regurgitation and rote application of procedures with little understanding or experience (MacIsaac, 2000).

Often when teachers make an effort to promote, direct, and mediate discussions, the process is dominated by a few outgoing, or confident students. Those students who remain silent for lack of opportunity, or avoid participation because of fear or other social constraints (Dickman, 1993; Reynolds & Nunn, 1997) are likely to have misunderstandings that are not addressed in a timely fashion, and may not be learning efficiently.

Classroom teachers who seek to engage all students in meaningful and challenging discussions promote greater conceptual understanding than teachers that make little or no use of such techniques (Crouch & Mazur, 2001; Hake, 1998; MacIsaac, 2000; Nichol & Boyle, 2003). Techniques that promote and support student participation yield students who pay more attention in class, use in-depth thinking and reflection, learn from one another's reasoning and mistakes, evaluate their own misconceptions, perform better on tests, have greater retention, and have improved attitudes toward learning (Crouch & Mazur, 2001; Guzdial, Hmelo, Hubscher, Nagel, Newstetter, Puntambekar, Shabo, Turns, & Kolodner, 1997; Hake, 1998; MacIsaac, 2000; Menon, Moffett, Enriquez, Martinez, Dev, & Grappone, 2004).

This chapter describes two types of audience response systems (selected and constructed) that are used to support discussion and participation in the classroom, and then shares observations made by the authors as these emerging technologies were used in a variety of mathematics, science, and computer science classes at various educational levels. In the following sections, we review the purpose, design, and features of these two types of response systems, highlight some of the issues underlying their application, discuss our experiences with these response systems, and make recommendations for increasing their use.

Two Types of Audience Response Systems

Audience response systems introduce both a compelling reason to participate in classroom discussions, and a level of anonymity that makes such participation comfortable for most students. Response systems can be used to support student learning in the classroom by:

- encouraging student centered dialog and questioning which, in turn, encourages critical thinking and active participation;

- providing timely feedback to the students with respect to their own understandings and misunderstandings; and

- supplying teachers with better information on the level of student mastery of curricular content to support lesson adaptation and planning.

Although both selected and constructed response systems have the potential to provide these benefits in the classroom, each tool has unique advantages.

Selected Response Systems

Selected response systems evolved out of a desire to poll audience members (or students) about their opinion on a given topic. Teachers have long used a show of hands to obtain feedback on student understanding or agreement on a subject. Unfortunately, this polling method only provides input for one option at a time, responses are not anonymous, and it is difficult to accurately judge proportions of responses, particularly in large classes (Draper & Brown, 2004). Using flash cards (Meltzer & Manivannan, 1996) or other devices with different colors can allow students to select from a larger number of options, and can support polling for responses to multiple-choice questions, but such an approach only provides limited improvement with respect to privacy and observing. Counting and sharing student responses remains a struggle. Also, as with hands, the data set is gone once cards are lowered.

Electronic selected response systems effectively address most of these issues. They allow the teacher to present prepared or ad hoc questions and response options to the students through a data projector, and then permit students to select and anonymously submit their responses through either an infrared or radio frequency remote control "clicker." Student responses are analyzed, and the compiled results are presented through the data projector as well as stored in a database.

These systems promote distress-free, concurrent participation by all students without substantially increasing the administrative or attentive load on the teacher. Students benefit by evaluating their own understanding in the light of the displayed numerical summary or bar chart illustrating the distribution of responses made by their classmates.

Depending upon the question and the teacher's pedagogical intentions, a correct response may or may not be identified. Because each student has made a choice, they are all interested in the outcome, and the ensuing discussion supports all students by providing an opportunity to either confidently share their understanding, or immediately address and discuss concepts that are unclear to them, and by having many more well focused questions asked and answered (Crouch & Mazur, 2001; Draper & Brown, 2004; Menon et al., 2004).

Students identify increased privacy and anonymity as one of the things they like most about the selected response systems (Draper & Brown, 2004; Menon et al., 2004). Increased anonymity has been found to promote greater academic risk taking by students (Williams, 2003), leading to greater engagement. In addition, because students are less likely to observe others' responses, they are less likely to be swayed in their own responses, providing increased validity over traditional hand-raising.

Other research, and our own experience, suggests that selected response systems are extremely useful in building a cooperative atmosphere in the classroom. When a challenging question is followed by the results from an initial poll, more meaningful discussion ensues, and students have a greater desire to share their understanding so that the overall results on the next poll will improve (Roschelle, Abrahamson, & Penuel, 2004). Finally, the database of student responses can be used by the teacher to support follow-up evaluation of individual participation and progress.

Of course, to maximize these benefits, well-crafted questions and response choices must be prepared in advance. Questions seen as trivial, irrelevant, or unrepresentative of what will be tested, cause student interest to plummet. Similarly, negative reactions result if students perceive that the teacher is more motivated by the technology than the pedagogy (Draper & Brown, 2004). Success does not depend on the system, but on how well it is used to promote thought, reflection, and understanding in the learners.

Constructed Response Systems

One limitation of selected response systems (or even the newer, hybrid response systems that allow students to submit simple numeric or text responses) is that any concepts or questions requiring graphical representations rely heavily on representations provided in the question stem or response choices. These are necessarily generated by the teacher or a curriculum content designer, rather than by students. Often, these representations are difficult for students to understand and apply (Hübscher-Young & Narayanan, 2001), and inauthentic with respect to their experience or the classroom context. Because multiple representations are more effective for promoting problem solving and under-standing than a single representation (Cox & Brna, 1995), it seems reasonable that requesting, selecting, and sharing student representations would also be helpful in the classroom.

Using handheld whiteboards is one popular, simple means of sharing authentic student constructed responses in the classroom. Providing whiteboards to students can promote collaboration, and help students practice problem solving, display their reasoning, and visualize multiple representations. This approach is particularly useful in problem-based learning classes. Unfortunately, handheld whiteboards share two of the drawbacks of hand-raising, and so forth. First, there is the ephemeral nature of the responses: unless work is captured (e.g., digitally), there is no enduring record of the student work. Second, the sharing of work samples on whiteboards is not anonymous, and this again may be stressful to some students.

The authors of this chapter have created a constructed response system for Palm OS 5 based handheld computers (the older term, personal digital assistant, or PDA, is no longer appropriate in light of the flexibility now offered) that builds upon the strengths of whiteboards, while addressing the drawbacks. We call this system the Classroom Interaction System (CIS). With the CIS, students use any application available on their handheld computers to construct responses to the instructor's open-ended questions. These responses are then captured (as a screen image) and submitted to the instructor's computer wirelessly using Bluetooth (2005). The instructor may then select and anonymously project authentic student representations to promote classroom discussion. The handheld computers can be used both as part of the CIS and independently, and instructors can introduce new applications, or even create them, according to the particular needs of their content area.

The CIS overcomes the two main weaknesses of whiteboards (transience, and anonymity) and expands the potential breadth of responses by allowing students to use any one of a multitude of computer applications to support the construction of their responses (Pelton & Francis Pelton, 1996a, 1996b, 2003, 2005). It is important to note that constructed response systems such as CIS have substantially higher thresholds (i.e., the time and effort required to learn new computer applications to support the creation of the responses) and friction (i.e., time and effort on the part of students to create responses) when compared to selected response systems. Thus, the decision to introduce and use a constructed response system requires the teacher to carefully weigh the implementation costs relative to the pedagogical benefits in their particular classroom before selecting the most appropriate tool.

Earlier research with asynchronous (out of class time) graphical response systems suggests that even when a supplied tool provides many features and options for graphical representations, the students tend to converge on a simple style, primarily using simple graphics and text (Hübscher-Young & Narayanan, 2001). Students do not want to use "five different tools for ten different tasks" (Guzdial et al., 1997, p. 92) if one or two tools can adequately accomplish it. We anticipate teachers and students using this type of system will select two or three straightforward applications as the primary response tools for a class, and provide a short introduction to these during the first class.

Observations and Impressions
from the Classroom

In the following sections, we describe our observations and general impressions gleaned from the use of a selected response system in several different settings: a grade-five mathematics class, a grade-five science class, three grade-eleven mathematics classes, four senior-level mathematics education classes, and a large, first-year computer science course. We also describe the use of the CIS, a constructed response system, in a year five mathematical problem-solving course.

Observations on Selected Response Systems in Multiple Settings

The Classroom Performance System (CPS) (eInstruction, 2004) is a selected response system that we found very easy to introduce into the classroom. At all four levels (grade five, grade eleven, first-year university, and fourth/fifth-year university), the students were able to quickly learn how to use the remote controls, submit their responses, and check or change their responses. Although the technology was very easy for students to use, the impact on learning was dependent upon the type of questions asked, and how the teacher used the information received.

One teacher used the tool to mechanically assess student understanding of concepts and procedures. This teacher displayed a question to students, and then used the automatic timer feature to limit the time students were allowed to answer the question. After the time had elapsed, the distribution of responses was displayed, with the correct answer highlighted. The instructor and the students were able to quickly see what proportion of students had selected the correct response. When a large number of students chose an incorrect answer, the teacher explained why that response was incorrect, and how to determine the correct answer. Very little discussion occurred, as the teacher seldom invited the students to explain their thinking, or discuss why a response was incorrect. Although the students likely received some benefit from the visual feedback on the screen and the subsequent explanations, the full potential of the system was not realized.

Teachers in the other settings all used the student responses to promote classroom discussion. The instructors generally did not use the automatic timer or display the correct response. Instead, after seeing the distribution of responses, students were invited to suggest what students who chose a particular response might have thought, as well as how to figure out the answer. Questions with greater variation in the responses generally lead to more discussion to identify the correct response. Students provided many good explanations, and participated readily in the discussions.

Additional ad hoc questions asked verbally (either in a hand-poll or with the CPS) helped to clarify the preset multiple-choice questions. These allowed teachers to identify misunderstandings related to a question, or to response options that were unclear. For instance, one teacher asked students to show, by raising their hands, whether they knew the meaning of one of the terms used within a response option, and when the majority of the students indicated that they were unfamiliar with the particular term, the teacher was able to use the moment to clarify the term. It also identified a question that may need to be modified before it is reused.

Another technique used successfully was to have students discuss the problem and the distribution of responses with a partner, or in a small group, to see how they arrived at their answer and to agree upon a solution. This approach works particularly well when a question has two or three response options selected fairly evenly by students. It is also effective in large classes where it is not possible to hear from all students in a group discussion. Students still get the chance to explain their own thinking, and analyze the thinking and strategies of their peers. After a discussion period, the teacher polls the students again to see how the response distribution changed, and to see if students were coming to a consensus on the answer. Whole class discussion can then be used to confirm or further clarify the question and answer.

Student reaction to the CPS was positive in all four settings, including the one lacking discussion. Participation and engagement was high, and students reported they enjoyed working with the units. All students were encouraged, and even subtly pressed to participate, since both the teacher and students could see how many had submitted responses. Many students responded as soon as the "Start" button was activated. Those less sure of an answer often checked with a neighbor before submitting their response. Students often freely shared their answers with those around them. For older students, it was primarily to confirm answers, but with the grade-five students, one student would determine an answer, and others in his "group" would then select the same response.

Students were more interested, and willing to work more problems using the system. We visited one grade-eleven class using the system in an inner city school during the last block one day in June. With 5 minutes class time remaining, the teacher said to put away the clickers. The students' response was "Oh no, can't we do some more problems?" We were impressed with how motivating the system was. This class had many students who did not participate frequently with traditional instruction, but happily participated with the cooperative way the system was applied in this class.

The system encouraged cooperation, and students were motivated to help everyone succeed. They viewed the questions as a competition between them and the system, rather than them and their classmates. When everyone got the right answer, there was a collective cheer, and when consensus was not found, a buzz of explanation and discussion ensued.

Some issues were identified that may require teachers to make classroom specific adjustments to their use of the system. One issue was that the liberal sharing of answers permitted some students to respond without actually considering the question. A second issue was that the younger students tended to avoid using paper and pencil to work out an answer, even when such was appropriate. For some classes, a rule that each student must be prepared to explain the thinking leading to a particular answer might discourage reliance on others' answers without understanding, and might encourage students to make a record of their thinking. For other classes, an early discussion on the potential learning benefits associated with considering the options, removing the least likely and then selecting the most likely, may be sufficient.

Students did not seem to like the pressure of the clock counting down the time they had left. Image size was also a consideration. The question templates of the software restricted the image size for a question or response option. Images were not always easy to see. Some instructors chose to show images on an overhead, or a linked PowerPoint™ presentation to overcome this problem.

Solutions and Recommendations for Using Selected Response Systems

Based on our observations, we offer the following recommendations for using selected response systems:

- Be clear on objectives and the instructions given to students. If the goal is to assess whether individual students have mastered particular concepts or procedures, or if it is to collect distributions of individual ratings, preferences, or experiences, then the students may be asked not to share answers. If, on the other hand, the goal is to promote class discussion, and help students to build understanding, then instructions should explicitly encourage collaboration.

- Pilot questions before using them. A second set of eyes (e.g., a class teaching assistant) reviewing the questions can help identify questions that are poorly worded, or response options that are not well defined.

- Make liberal use of ad hoc questions in addition to the preset questions. Meaningful discussion requires enough flexibility to allow for tangents to be explored, and teachable moments to be seized.

- Try to encourage thoughtful assumptions. Some questions may be purposely ambiguous. Leave room for students to make some decisions.

- Avoid jumping to show the correct answer. Show the response distribution, and then ask questions that lead students to assert their choice for the correct answer.

- Have students explain why a particular response might be selected (this may or may not have been the response they chose).

- When a question yields varied responses, talk about it. "Convince your neighbor" works well in large classes. Then rerun the question to see if consensus has been reached.

- Not all questions need to have a preset correct answer. Let the students know that more than one answer may be correct. A debate over the "best" answer is often illuminating for both the students and the teacher.

- When a question has been discussed and revisited, have students reflect on the process as well as the answer. Ask: "What was said that caused you to change your answer?"

- Avoid using the timer with questions. Students seem to find it stressful. You can choose to end the question in the same amount of time, but without the pressure of the clock counting down the time. If a nudge is needed, a simple comment a few seconds before examining the results is usually sufficient.

Observations on Constructed Response Systems in a Problem-Solving Course

The prototype CIS was piloted in fall 2004 with a year-five, mathematics, problem-solving class for elementary preservice teachers. This class was a natural fit with the CIS because the content would be better supported by constructed responses than selected responses. A large part of the course focused on strategy selection, and implementation and communication of the problem solving processes used, all of which benefit from a constructed response format.

None of the students in the class had previously used a handheld computer, although all were familiar with other forms of computer technology. The particular handhelds used were Bluetooth (2005) enabled Sony Clies, with 3" diagonal color screens, 320 x 320 pixel resolution, and keyboard, as well as pen input. Activities on the first day focused on tasks requiring students to use a graphics program and a word processing program. This enabled students to become familiar with applications for the handhelds, and to practice using the Neoslate utility to submit a response to the teacher station. Students were able to effectively explore the features of the programs, and become comfortable with the technology in a relatively short timeframe. They enjoyed seeing each other's drawings and writings, and were impressed with the ease of sharing the information.

Discussion and sharing of solutions was a major component of the classes throughout the term. Students enjoyed using the CIS, and frequently expressed disappointment on days the CIS was not used.

Many benefits of using the CIS were identified. One major benefit was that students were able to see a greater selection of strategies and approaches. Traditional instruction only allowed time to share one or two student solutions to a problem at the chalkboard or overhead projector. With the CIS, the instructor could see solutions from all students as they were submitted, and select samples to display that showed common approaches or innovative solutions. Even when similar approaches were used, students benefited from seeing how others organized and communicated their solutions.

Another benefit of the CIS was the anonymous display of work. Incorrect solutions could be displayed, and the ensuing discussion was able to focus on where the errors occurred and possible reasons for those, without embarrassing the student who had made the error. In contrast, on days when the CIS was not in use, solutions presented on the board were not anonymous, so students could suffer the anxiety of the public presentation of their work. Because the instructor tried not to choose students who felt uncomfortable sharing their solutions, students rarely saw erroneous work. This eliminated one rich catalyst for classroom discussion.

The database of solutions collected by the teacher provided a record of class participation, and a source for formative assessment of student progress, growth, and understanding.

As students became more familiar with an application, they used a greater variety of tools, colors, and detail in their solutions, rather than just drawing a freehand image, using pen input. Greater experience in problem-solving, as well as exposure to other students' strategies and presentations, were contributing factors in this change. However, students tended to use the familiar applications when creating their responses, rather than accessing other available applications, suggesting that Hübscher-Young and Narayanan's (2001) findings may apply to synchronous as well as asynchronous communication of representations.

Although the response to the system was overwhelmingly positive, some limitations were noted. Because the current Neoslate application sends only a screenshot of the student's handheld, students had to limit their solutions to one screen of information, or send additional screenshots to complete their solution. Since screenshots appear on the teacher station in the order that they are submitted, a complete solution may require the instructor to scroll up or down the list of responses to search for linked submissions from the same student. Most often, students chose to limit their solution to one screen, requiring students to be selective about the detail they included, or zoom in while creating their response, to allow a finer level of detail and sizing for their work.

Since a response could not be recalled once submitted, students sometimes submitted several responses to a question because they realized they had omitted something or worked something incorrectly. Fortunately, a time stamp on solutions meant the instructor was always able to determine the latest submission for any student. An option to allow multiple responses, or filter the results so that only the last response from each student is visible, may be added to the CIS in a future revision.

Because the problem-solving class was relatively small, there were no transmission issues with the CIS. However, the Bluetooth technology in our equipment only effectively transmits data within 10 meters, and the bandwidth degrades significantly as a function of distance (e.g., at 2 m from the laptop, a 13 KB screen image could be transmitted in <1 second, but at 10 m, the same image might require 5-10 seconds). Thus, the current CIS would work best in classes of no more than 50 students, with the teacher's laptop positioned within 7-8 m of all students. A new Bluetooth protocol has been announced that will greatly alleviate these limitations (Bluetooth SIG, 2005).

Finally, using the CIS changed the nature of the class in subtle ways. Limiting their responses to a single screen required students to make critical decisions about what to include, and how to best present their solutions or understandings. Only then could students begin to compose their response on the handhelds. The instructor then had to efficiently review the submitted images, and quickly make critical decisions about which solutions to display, and how many of them to discuss. All of these decisions have time and content coverage implications. The benefits of the critical, in-depth analysis, decision-making, and discussion have to be balanced against the need (or desire) to cover a broad curriculum.

Looking Forward

Selected response systems are low-threshold, low-friction, mature technologies that effectively support and encourage classroom discussion. Small improvements in the management software and the presentation of questions will further enhance their usability. These systems work well, and will likely see increased usage in the classroom over time.

We have developed the CIS to demonstrate that constructed response systems might also be helpful. Although using the CIS requires more time and effort, we are already seeing benefits when it is applied appropriately. Over time, the feature set will expand, and the efficiency with which students will be able to create and share representations of their understandings will improve. It is anticipated that constructed response systems will also become common in the classroom.

Both selected and constructed response systems have been observed to increase engagement, support discussion, and enhance student learning. While the comments and references included in this chapter provide an informal examination of the pedagogical value of these devices, research is now needed to formally assess their impact on student learning. The "Are they effective?" and "Should we be using one?" questions are changing to "How effective are they?", "When would such tools be most useful?" and "What type of response system would be most effective for supporting learning in my classroom today?"

References

Bluetooth SIG, (2005). *Bluetooth: The official Bluetooth website.* Bluetooth SIG, Inc. Retrieved February 25, 2005, from http://www.bluetooth.com

Cox, R., & Brna, P. (1995). Supporting the use of external representations in problem solving: The need for flexible learning environments. *International Journal of Artificial Intelligence in Education, 6,* 239-302.

Crouch, C. H., & Mazur, E. (2001). Peer instruction: ten years of experience and results. *American Journal of Physics, 69*(9), 970-977.

Dickman, C. B. (1993). Gender differences and instructional discrimination in the classroom. *Journal of Invitational Theory and Practice, 2*(1).

Draper, S. W., & Brown, M .I. (2004). Increasing interactivity in lectures using an electronic voting system. *Journal of Computer Assisted Learning, 20,* 81-94.

eInstruction's Classroom Performance System (2004). Retrieved February 25, 2005, from http://www.einstruction.com

Guzdial, M., Hmelo, C. E., Hubscher, R., Nagel, K., Newstetter, W., Puntambekar, S., et al. (1997). Integrating and guiding collaboration: Lessons learned in computer-supported collaborative learning research at Georgia Tech. *Proceedings Computer Support for Collaborative Learning '97* (pp. 91-99).

Hake, R. R. (1998). Interactive-engagement versus traditional methods: A six-thousand-student survey of mechanics test data for introductory physics courses. *American Journal of Physics, 66,* 64-74.

Hübscher-Younger, T., & Narayanan, N. H. (2001). *Features of shared student-created representations.* Paper presented at AI-ED 2001 Workshop: External Representations in AIED: Multiple Forms and Multiple Roles, San Antonio, TX.

MacIsaac, D. (2000). Active engagement, cooperative learning in large enrollment introductory college physics lectures for preservice teachers. Paper presented at the *NSF Collaboratives for Excellence in Teacher Preparation CETP Conference Past, present, future: Recognizing and Evaluating Best Practices (Sixth Annual Meeting)*, Washington, DC (Vol. 23, pp. 31-33).

Meltzer D. E., & Manivannan K. (1996). Promoting interactivity in physics lecture classes. *The Physics Teacher, 34*, 72-76.

Menon, A. S., Moffett, S., Enriquez, M., Martinez, M. M., Dev, P., & Grappone, T. (2004). Audience response made easy: Using personal digital assistants as a classroom polling tool. *Journal of the American Medical Informatics Association, 11*(3), 217-220.

National Council of Teachers of Mathematics (2000). *Principles and standards for school mathematics*. Reston, VA: National Council of Teachers of Mathematics.

Nicol, D . J., & Boyle, J. T. (2003) Peer instruction versus class-wide discussion in large classes: A comparison of two interaction methods in the wired classroom. *Studies in Higher Education, 28*, 458-473.

Pelton, T. W., & Francis Pelton, L. (1996a). The electronic slate: Including pre-service teachers in research and development. In B. Robin, J. Price, & D. Willis (Eds.), *Technology and teacher education annual* (pp. 519-523). Charlottesville, VA. Association for the Advancement of Computing in Education.

Pelton, T. W., & Francis Pelton, L. (1996b). *The classroom interaction system: Using electronic slates to enhance communication during the lesson process*. Paper presented at the Thirteenth International Conference on Technology and Education. New Orleans, LA: ICTE.

Pelton, T., & Francis Pelton, L. (2003, May). *The classroom interaction system (CIS): Neo-slates for the classroom*. Connections '03. Victoria BC.

Pelton, T. W., & Francis Pelton, L. (2005, March). *Transforming handheld computers into electronic slates to support learning*. Paper presented at the Sixteenth International Conference of the Society for Information Technology and Teacher Education. Phoenix, AZ.

Reynolds, K. C., & Nunn, C. E. (1997). *Engaging classrooms: Student participation and the instructional factors that shape it*. Paper presented at the annual meeting of the Association for the Study of Higher Education, Albuquerque, NM.

Roschelle, J., Abrahamson, L. A., & Penuel, W. R. (2004, April 16) *Integrating classroom network technology and learning theory to improve classroom science learning: A literature synthesis*. Paper presented at the Annual Meeting of the American Educational Research Association, San Diego, CA.

Williams, J. B. (2003). 'Learning by remote control': Exploring the use of an audience response system as a vehicle for content delivery. In G. Crisp, D. Thiele, I. Scholen, S. Barker, & J. Baron (Eds.), *Interact integrate impact. Proceedings of the 20th Annual Conference of the Australasian Society for Computers in Learning in Tertiary Education (ASCILITE)*, Adelaide, Australia.

Chapter XIII

Theorizing the Transformed Classroom:
Sociocultural Interpretation of the Effects of Audience Response Systems in Higher Education

William R. Penuel, SRI International, USA

Louis Abrahamson, Better Education Foundation, USA

Jeremy Roschelle, SRI International, USA

Abstract

This paper explores the theoretical framework needed to explain observed effects of classrooms in which instructors use audience response systems. We consider how current theories of audience response systems cannot adequately explain students' initial resistance to the introduction of response systems, or the emergence of a sense of classroom community. We propose a sociocultural reinterpretation of the networked classroom in which learning is described as a process of transforming participation in classroom activities. We use sociocultural theory to help explain students' changing motivations for participation in class, and the development of scientific concepts through discussion. Finally, we propose some initial hypotheses and approaches to studying audience response systems in higher education within a sociocultural framework.

Introduction

Audience response systems have been in use for several years in higher education, and have shown promise for transforming classroom participation and learning, especially in the sciences. These systems enable students to respond to instructor questions using small handheld devices that employ infrared technology to communicate data to a central computer. Instructors can then display a histogram of student responses, and use this display to discuss students' answers, or to adjust their instruction on the basis of students' level of understanding.

Because they are mature technologies, there has been a considerable amount of research on their effects. In a review of research conducted in 2003 by a team of researchers here at SRI, we identified 25 studies that examined effects of audience response systems (Roschelle, Abrahamson, & Penuel, 2003; Roschelle, Penuel, & Abrahamson, 2004). Of these studies, 15 reported positive effects of using the systems on student engagement. Ten studies reported positive effects on students' understanding of complex subject matter in subjects ranging from physics to elementary level reading. For example, analysis of results from multiple, large, lecture classes conducted at different universities using peer instruction, a teaching method often used in conjunction with audience response systems, indicated that gains of students in peer instruction classrooms on the force concept inventory, a widely used test of students' understanding of the most basic concepts of Newtonian mechanics, were much higher than for students in regular lecture classes (Crouch & Mazur, 2001; Hake, 1998).

There are gaps, however, in systematically measuring and understanding how teaching and learning unfolds in these kinds of networked classrooms, (Roschelle et al., 2004). For example, none of the studies that have examined the effects of systems have also sought to measure, systematically, the contribution of specific pedagogical elements to the effects. Also, some of the more dominant theories and ideas about how instruction in higher education with audience response systems unfolds do not adequately capture the range of experiences reported by practitioners. These are major gaps in the knowledge base guiding research and development in the area of audience response systems, since systematic data on instruction, and its effects, are both necessary to guide improvements in the classroom, and to test prevailing explanations of the effects.

A central explanation for the effectiveness of teaching with audience response systems focuses on the role that systems use plays in facilitating conceptual change. We describe that account, before considering some of the common experiences of instructors and students in classrooms where audience response systems are used, that the account fails to consider in theorizing the effects that have been reported in the literature. We then turn to an examination of how sociocultural theory, which has been used to describe learning processes within networked classrooms at the elementary and secondary level, might be used productively to theorize teaching and learning in higher education settings with audience response systems.

The Conceptual Change Account of Audience Response Systems

More commonly, the research on audience response systems focuses on explaining how teaching with the systems helps bring about conceptual change in students. Conceptual change has been of central interest to researchers in cognitive science, because it is an enduring challenge for educators (National Research Council, 1999). Students tend to bring many conceptions of scientific domains to class from their lived experience that do not match scientists' understanding of those concepts; those conceptions have proven quite difficult to change, especially without involving students in collaboratively constructing their understandings of concepts in such a way that reveals the underpinnings of concepts and shortcomings in their own thinking (Roschelle, 1996). The promise of audience response systems in facilitating conceptual change is, therefore, of central importance to the science education community, because any instructional approach that might improve the odds students will give up their own misconceptions and develop more scientific understandings of concepts, is of great value to the field.

A recent paper by Judson and Sawada (2002) provides a synthesis of arguments that focus on theorizing how conceptual change comes about. These authors, in reviewing research conducted since the 1960s on different generations of audience response systems, argue that in the past 20 years, much more attention has been paid to how systems foster student-to-student interaction. But they argue that the significance of the interaction derives from constructivist learning theory, which in their words has "highlighted the importance of collaborative discourse that allows students to negotiate meaning in science and mathematics classes" (Judson & Sawada, 2002, p. 173).

The Role of Discussion in Facilitating Conceptual Change

Discussion, the authors note, does not inhere in the technology, but must be orchestrated by the instructor in conjunction with use of the audience response system. Discussion can take place after students have seen a question posed by the instructor but before answering, or, as in peer instruction, it can take place once students have answered and seen a display of their answers that indicates wide divergence in responses (see Mazur, 1997). As part of the discussion, students are often encouraged to explain their answers to peers, or to the whole class, and listen to counterarguments to their own position (Abrahamson, 1999; Dufresne, Gerace, Leonard, Mestre, & Wenk, 1996).

As we have noted elsewhere (Roschelle et al., 2003), there are close parallels between the emphasis placed on class discussion and debate, and ideas from cognitive science, about how best to promote conceptual change. In particular, research on self-explanation (Chi, 1996) suggests that in formulating arguments and presenting them to others, students come to a deeper understanding of concepts. Working together with a peer, moreover, can help students to converge on meanings of concepts that more closely resemble those of target understandings in a domain, even if students' discourse does not closely resemble the way scientists might talk about concepts (Roschelle, 1992).

The Role of Questioning in Facilitating Conceptual Change

The conceptual change account also emphasizes that the nature of questioning is particularly important to effective uses of audience response systems (Dufresne et al., 1996; Poulis, Massen, Robens, & Gilbert, 1998; Shapiro, 1997). Questions that target the core concepts of a discipline are believed to be most effective in promoting conceptual change, especially when answer choices reflect common student conceptions that may diverge from target understandings. Eliciting those misconceptions is believed to be particularly important, even necessary, step in the development of scientific concepts, especially because the meanings of words and concepts in everyday settings is often quite different from meanings in the specialized languages of science (Gee, 1999; Lemke, 1990; Vygotsky, 1987).

Judson and Sawada (2002) suggest that these pedagogical elements are what make the use of audience response systems effective. They note that earlier research from the 1960s on such systems — in which instructors used systems to achieve behavioral objectives — found few positive effects on achievement. By contrast, more contemporary uses have shown much more promise with respect to improving achievement, leading them to conclude:

It is more beneficial for the student, who has just arrived at a new conceptual understanding, to explain to peers how he/she struggled and arrived at his/her new rationale than it is for an instructor to simply explain the abstraction. (Judson & Sawada, 2002. p. 178)

Missing Experiences from the Conceptual Change Account

The conceptual change account provides several important insights into what works about teaching with audience response systems. In fact, evidence from studies of peer instruction suggests conceptual change does happen in classrooms where audience response systems support its use (Crouch & Mazur, 2001). Moreover, the kinds of questioning, discussion, and other interactive pedagogies cited in the conceptual change account, have been reported by practitioners in the field, and as we have argued elsewhere, they are consistent with a number of findings from the learning sciences about how people learn (Roschelle et al., 2003). However, there are several aspects of instructors' and students' reported experiences of being in classrooms where audience response systems are used that are not captured fully by the conceptual change account. These experiences are reported primarily in research conducted by scholar-practitioners familiar with the use of the system, and more recently, large-scale survey results have replicated some of their findings. These findings are consistent enough to warrant a careful consideration and reinterpretation of the theories that are necessary to explaining the effects of teaching with audience response systems.

Explaining Early Resistance To Audience Response Systems

One such experience is that early in students' encounters in classrooms where audience response systems are used, students adjust their participation in class to the changed classroom environment, often with mixed feelings. Research by Jackson and Trees (2003), which examined the perception of some 1,500 students enrolled in University of Colorado classes that used response system technology, indicated that many students were anxious about the heightened accountability for learning in networked classrooms. They also found that students who had taken many lecture classes in the past were less positive about the technology, perhaps because they had already developed some strategies for participating in large, lecture classes.

Jackson and Trees' study also revealed that although the use of audience response systems increased class attendance, many students felt ambivalent about this effect. Students who were coming to class for the first time tended to be disruptive: many resented that participation in class could be more accurately measured by the response systems. Students that already attended lecture classes willingly resented the disruption caused by the students who came to class less often.

Experts in teaching with the systems acknowledge these challenges in outlining a set of recommendations for how instructors should address them. In his seminal book on teaching with audience response systems, *Peer instruction,* Mazur writes that it is particularly important for instructors to be prepared for student resistance when audience response systems and interactive pedagogies are introduced into the large lecture:

Students are not likely to accept a change in lecture format with open arms. They are used to traditional lectures and will doubt the new format will help them achieve more (i.e., obtain a higher grade in the course). Since full student collaboration is essential to the success of the Peer Instruction *method, it is important to motivate students early on.* (Mazur, 1997, p. 19)

Mazur's warning is similar to that of Duncan, another higher education user of audience response systems:

Especially in a large university class, students have certain expectations: They will be relatively anonymous; they should sit up front and sometimes raise their hands if they want to be noticed; they should sit in the back of the lecture hall if they want to catch up on homework or read a newspaper; if a lecture doesn't seem it will be worthwhile, they should just stay home — no one will notice, and they aren't graded just for showing up in class. The use of a clicker system shatters these student expectations. (Duncan, 2005, p. 21)

Emergence of Trust and Community In Classrooms with Audience Response Systems

An additional shortcoming of the conceptual change account is that it has not sought to explain the emergence of strong feelings among students that the classroom environment, as a whole, has become one in which it is safe to pose questions and admit difficulties of understanding. Abrahamson and colleagues (Abrahamson, Owens, Demana, Meagher, & Herman, 2003), for example, reported that before the introduction of Texas Instruments' Navigator system into their classrooms (a specific kind of audience response system with advanced affordances for interaction), students reported that they would rarely admit in class, or even to the teacher, when they were having problems understanding the subject matter. They feared that others would think that they were stupid, or that they were the only students having problems. After Navigator became part of the classroom, however, the environment transformed for students, and they began to feel much safer taking risks of admitting that they did not understand something. The public, anonymous display gave them and their teacher immediate knowledge of different class positions. Students came to see that others had the same difficulties that they did, opening the way for class discussion where reasons for actions taken become more important than who took them. The following exchange among students in a focus group, reported in Owens, Demana, Abrahamson, Meagher, and Herman (2002), illustrates how many students experienced the class:

S1: ... whereas in just a regular classroom setting, when the teacher asks, "Does everyone get this material?" And then you look around and everyone is nodding their head, "Yes!" You don't want to be the one that said, "Well no, actually. I don't get it at all! So can you explain to me?" And waste everybody else's time.

S2: That is right! That is so true!

S1: ... without the system you'd feel more I guess ... alone -

S2: Unsure!

S1: Yeah! You're not ... as with the Navigator you're more of a group and you know what everybody else is thinking ... what their answer is.

No new class starts off with such feelings present, and many probably never develop them, but classrooms with audience response systems seem naturally to evolve in this direction. Whether it happens more or less in networked classrooms than in regular lectures has not yet been proven at the level of a randomized study, but there is strong circumstantial evidence that it is so. We take up one possible set of hypotheses as to why this is so in the next section.

Toward a Sociocultural Theory of Audience Response Systems

A more complete theory is needed to explain the diverse experiences of students and instructors in classrooms with audience response systems, which accomplishes three things:

- accounts for how changes in interactions cause students and instructors to adjust their own participation in class;

- accounts for the emergence of new classroom-level dynamics from changed interactions and individual orientation; and

- maintains a focus on communication and individual learning, as evident from changes to intent of participation in class.

In this section, we consider how three different sets of ideas from sociocultural theory can help account for the phenomena reported in research on audience response systems: (1) the idea that learning is a process of transformation of participation in cultural activities that are themselves changing; (2) the idea that learning science involves developing fluency with the forms of talk associated with doing science; and (3) the idea that motivation and interest emerge from particular patterns of social interaction, and from engagement with tasks that have particular kinds of features. Sociocultural theories give prominence to both the *social* dynamics of classrooms in fostering individual learning, and to the role that the classroom and wider *cultures* play in shaping the ways people talk and participate in activities (Wertsch, 1991).

We are drawn to sociocultural theory for an account of audience response systems, because research on classroom network technologies with a different set of affordances — for classroom simulations, for example — has turned to sociocultural ideas about learning and development. For example, Stroup and colleagues (Stroup, 2002; Stroup, Kaput, Ares, Wilensky, Hegedus, Roschelle, et al., 2002) have drawn on Vygotsky's ideas (Vygotsky, 1987; Wertsch, 1979) about *dynamic structuring* of activities to describe how mathematical ideas structure the social space of network-supported learning activities aimed at teaching students about parametric space. Similarly, Kaput and Hegedus (2002) have sought to explain dynamics in such classrooms with reference to students' identification with mathematical projections. Their notion of identification bears a close kinship with sociocultural accounts of identity, as formed in the context of activity and mediated by culturally-situated tools (Penuel & Wertsch, 1995b).

In the next section, we review in greater detail some of the potentially relevant aspects of sociocultural theory to informing a theoretical perspective on the use of audience response systems to support science learning in higher education settings. We discuss how the concept of learning as transforming participation can provide a broad framework for studying learning in classrooms where students and teachers use audience response systems. We also explore how the idea that learning to "talk science" can help explain why classroom discussion is so critical to conceptual change. Finally, we explore how sociocultural accounts of motivation help explain students' varied responses to the introduction of audience response systems.

In this section of the chapter, to illustrate these points, we draw on some examples from elementary- and secondary-education settings. These settings are different in important ways from higher education settings because of their smaller size, however, lecture and teacher-led instruction tend to dominate in both kinds of settings. In addition, some of the technologies that have been developed specifically to support elementary- and secondary-education settings provide new insight on how classrooms transform when audience response systems are introduced.

Learning as a Process of Transformation of Participation

Contemporary sociocultural theories define learning and development as a process of *transforming participation in valued sociocultural activities* (Rogoff, 1995, 2003; Rogoff, Baker-Sennett, Lacasa, & Goldsmith, 1995). Rather than viewing knowledge as a fixed entity that must be transmitted from instructor to students, sociocultural theorists emphasize that people learn when given opportunities to practice using the tools of a discipline — including its discourse, methods, and technological instruments that aid discovery — under conditions in which they can be guided by experts who are either more capable peers or adults (Rogoff, 1990; Vygotsky, 1978; Wertsch, 1979, 1991). Over time, as learners gain experience with particular tools, and become familiar with participation in particular cultural activities, such as those of an academic discipline, their participation transforms from one in which they play primarily peripheral roles with limited responsibility to fuller roles with more responsibility for the activity (Lave & Wenger, 1991). Of particular significance, too, in sociocultural theory, is a distinction made between *intent* and *passive* participation that captures two different ways in which learners listen in and pay attention to cultural activities (Rogoff, Paradise, Arauz, Correa-Chavez, & Angelillo, 2003). Learners tend to participate and observe activities more intently when they are preparing to participate in them: more passive participation is more common, however, in instructional settings in which learners are not expected to take on more responsibility for full participation in the activity. Despite the fact that many instructional settings offer few such opportunities for students, sociocultural researchers have shown that those settings that do allow learners' participation to transform are quite effective with a wide range of students (Doherty, Hilberg, Pinal, & Tharp, 2003; Tharp & Gallimore, 1988).

At the same time that individuals' participation changes over time, their own contributions, and the kinds of interactions that take place within activities, transform those activities themselves (Rogoff, 1995; Rogoff et al., 1995). Individual, interpersonal, and community development are intertwined, and become the focus of sociocultural accounts of development:

... [H]uman development is a process of people's changing participation in sociocultural activities of their communities.... Rather than individual development being influenced by (and influencing) culture, from my perspective, people develop as they participate in and contribute to cultural activities that themselves develop with the involvement of people in successive generations. (Rogoff, 2003, p. 52)

Rogoff's perspective is that the account makes room for examining these activities from what she calls community, interpersonal, and personal (individual) "planes." Her perspective is that these planes are mutually constitutive (Rogoff, et al., 1995b); they do not exist apart from one another, but are separable in principle for the purpose of developmental analysis, like lenses that can have a different focus, depending on the analyst's purpose.

When attention is directed to a particular plane, Rogoff emphasizes that different kinds of learning processes come into focus (Rogoff, 1995a, 1995b). At the personal plane, analysts focus on how it is that individuals change and transform as they participate in activity, and how they orient themselves — as active, passive, or even avoidant — to participation. At the interpersonal plane, analysts examine what people are doing together, and examine how people come to understand each other, and structure participation for each other. And at the community plane, analysts examine the way that people apprentice to larger cultural practices, like becoming an instructor, or learning to use scientific discourse.

By itself, Rogoff's theory provides just a broad outline of what is needed to understand in order to develop a more coherent theory of what is happening in classrooms with audience response systems to produce the kinds of transformations that are claimed for them. We need to take into account the research on the personal, psychological processes typically activated in classrooms with audience response systems — engagement, motivation, and shyness for example — in considering how these systems might change individuals' participation in classroom activities. And we need to take into account what is known about the role of feedback and group participation, processes highlighted in the cognitive account, in considering how participation is guided differently in classrooms with audience response systems. With this new set of lenses, however, we can also develop hypotheses about the "missing experiences" in the conceptual change account, such as the emergence of classroom community, and the experience of disruption often felt by instructors and students when audience response systems are first introduced.

Mediated Action in Sociocultural Theory: Learning to "Talk Science"

Sociocultural theory that draws on Vygotsky's theory emphasizes the special role of language and other symbol systems in mediating cultural activities. Wertsch (1991, 1998), in particular, has argued that the proper unit of analysis for sociocultural research is *mediated action:* by making this claim, he is suggesting that sociocultural research should describe human mental functioning and development in the context of action that is mediated by, or performed by cultural tools that are available within particular historical, cultural, and institutional contexts. The cultural tools that are typically analyzed in sociocultural research include language, signs, and other symbol systems, which were given special attention within Vygotsky's account of human development (Wertsch, 1991). In Vygotsky's view, language was an important advance in human evolution in that it enabled us to create "tools" for manipulating not just objects in the world, but for creating and adapting ideas and systems of ideas (Vygotsky, 1987).

Sociocultural theorists have paid particularly close attention to the role of symbolic representation and discourse in science. For example, Martin (1989) has analyzed the grammars of scientific texts, drawing attention to the way that factual writing in science makes heavy use of nominalizations in describing complex and often abstract processes that are often subjects of sentences, instead of the human agents who performed the scientific work (Hanania & Akhtar, 1985; Rodman, 1994). These grammars, argue sociocultural theorists of science, have the effect of placing distance between the activity of doing science and the scientific communities that conduct it (Gee, 1999; Latour & Woolgar, 1986). In fact, engaging in science and writing scientific texts are fundamentally social activities, and doing them successfully depends on access to, and fluency with, the instruments, methodologies, and languages of science (Bazerman, 1983; Dunbar, 1995; Latour & Woolgar, 1986; Lynch, 1985).

Sociocultural theorists in education have sought to explore the implications of how scientific activity is mediated by language for the study and design of classroom learning environments. Several Australian researchers, for example, have developed and studied strategies for teaching students how to write in the genres of science, and have encouraged teachers to help students recognize when different genres for writing are appropriate, and more or less powerful for purposes of persuading others (Cope & Kalantzis, 1993; Halliday & Martin, 1993). Lemke (1990) has noted that in classrooms where students successfully learn to "talk science," teachers model scientific forms of oral and written language by tending to avoid colloquial, emotive, and figurative language. At the same time, Lemke notes that typical question-posing patterns of teachers in science classrooms, in which the teacher asks students to respond to a question in which the answer is known already, provides students with limited opportunity to develop and elaborate on their understanding of concepts. More extended turns at discourse at generating answers to more open-ended inquiry and practice with inquiry methods may be necessary to promote deeper learning of science concepts (Gee, 2004; Wells, 1993). In addition, students' everyday understanding and language for describing particular constructs is often at odds with scientific ways of speaking, so expanding participation of students in science is likely to require providing students with opportunities to connect everyday concepts to scientific concepts (Gee, 1994; Rosebery, Warren, & Conant, 1992).

Research on students' practice with the academic languages of science by sociocultural theorists provides a bridge to the conceptual change account, which emphasizes strongly the role of discussion in promoting student learning and engagement. Its attention to communicative processes in the classroom, and their role in conceptual development, highlight the important ways to foster participation in classrooms. In emphasizing the forms of science talk that students need to learn, the sociocultural approach shows how conceptual learning, and representing what one knows in speech and in print, are inextricably linked.

Sociocultural Accounts of Interest and Motivation

From a sociocultural perspective, interest and motivation are not simply mental states or orientation of individuals, but rather, are orientations to action that arise from interactions in particular contexts (Hickey & McCaslin, 2001; Hidi, Renninger, & Krapp, 2004; Jarvella & Volet, 2001; Pressick-Kilborn & Walker, 2002). Just as Vygotsky argues that mental functioning, in general, is a transformation of social activity (Wertsch, 1979), sociocultural theorists argue that motivation, in particular, involves a kind of "transformative internalization" of activity and subsequent "externalization" of mental functioning in activity (Walker, Pressick-Kilborn, Arnold, & Sainsbury, 2004). To analyze motivation, then, researchers need to examine more than individuals' mental states and goals: they need to conduct such an analysis in the context of how states and goals emerge from classroom interactions, features of particular tasks, and other features of the sociocultural context (Rueda & Moll, 1994).

Like motivational theorists who have focused on the goal orientation of individuals for academic tasks (e.g., Ames & Archer, 1988), sociocultural theorists are interested in aspects of motivation that persist beyond individual situations for learning. But rather than focus on motivational goals, sociocultural theorists are more likely to study how individuals enact and display particular identities in the classroom through their participation in learning activities (Gee, 2000-2001; McCaslin & Hickey, 2001; Penuel & Wertsch, 1995b). The identities that are enacted draw upon available and typical forms of self-representation and participation in learning associated with being a member of particular kinds of communities. Some of these communities are related to ethnicity and gender, but other categories (e.g., one's status as a "jock" or "burnout") are often relevant to explaining how and why people participate in some learning activities, but not others (Eckert, 1989; Heath & McLaughlin, 1993; Penuel & Wertsch, 1995a). Identities tend to have several "externalizing" markers associated with them — forms of speech, dress, even body position in class — that enable one to infer when they are being enacted as part of a particular activity (Gee, 2000-2001; Shaw, 1994). Analyzing the development of identity in classrooms is an important focus of sociocultural research, because its development, and disciplinary learning, often go hand-in-hand (Wortham, 2004).

Of particular interest to both sociocultural researchers and other motivation researchers are ways in which specific task features contribute to the development of interest and development of motivational orientations (Butler, 1987; Butler & Neuman, 1995; Hackman & Oldham, 1980; McCaslin & Hickey, 2001). Characteristics of tasks that are particularly important for shaping interest and motivation include the kinds of opportunities they afford for student collaboration, the incentives for participation, processes for teacher-student feedback, and rewards and punishments for performance that are associated with particular academic tasks. Learners' perceptions of task features have been shown in motivation research to influence students' motivational goals (Butler, 1987), and also to influence their willingness to participate actively in classroom discussions (Wortham, 2004).

A sociocultural perspective on interest, motivation, and identity can help explain why research studies often report on such dramatic shifts toward increased class participation in classrooms in which audience response systems are used. Just as important, its focus on identity as a lens for examining classroom participation enables us to make hypotheses about how different kinds of students might respond to the introduction of audience response systems. Its attention to the way particular task features contribute to the development of interests and goals among students can help identify what kinds of pedagogical uses of systems are likely to produce the positive effects in the literature, and which uses might yield less positive results. In the next part of this section, we consider in greater detail how sociocultural accounts of motivation, mediated action, and participation can contribute to a more complete model of teaching with audience response system technology.

Initial Hypothesis for Sociocultural Account of Teaching with Audience Response Systems

We can summarize how sociocultural theory can help us by generating some new hypotheses about when, how, and why audience response systems are effective, which can then be tested in future research. We can use Rogoff's theory of learning as transformation of participation can help to *when* systems are effective to generate hypotheses about how changes in the personal, interpersonal, and community planes interact to produce a typical classroom trajectory of use and development. We can use sociocultural theories about the importance of learning to "talk science" to help explain *how* audience response systems might produce gains through peer discussion. Finally, we can use a sociocultural theory of motivation to help explain *why* students' engagement is often so strong, and also why not all students might respond in the same way to the introduction of audience response systems.

Explaining Instructors' and Students' Initial Responses

When response systems are first introduced into a classroom, the most apparent change is at the interpersonal plane of development. These systems introduce a new system of feedback between instructors and students that makes it possible for instructors to pose questions of all students (not just a select few), and to get information on how all students are learning. The interaction is mediated by technology, and not performed simply by oral turn-taking. On the personal or psychological plane, this change leads to a set of initial responses on the part of instructors and students. Students form differing reactions to the change — excitement, anxiety, even resistance — to the extent that they recognize, and are comfortable with their new roles in the classroom. Instructors, for their part, may realize that the questions they pose, and their strategies for addressing student misconceptions, must change.

The introduction of the technological display into the classroom has the possibility for creating a range of effects. If instructors display a histogram of results to students, for example, instructors may feel a new kind of pressure to reteach a concept that few students understand, rather than just the pressure to "move on" to be able to cover more material. At the community plane, we hypothesize that instructors' and students' personal responses lead to what is often experienced as a kind of initial sense that something is awry in how the classroom is flowing. If instructors and students were surveyed about how they think the class is going in the first few weeks after audience response systems are introduced, we would predict that they would, in fact, say things are not going too well. The majority might even say that things are not going so well, and the instructor would report feeling thrown off-balance by the introduction of the system.

The Emergence of Conceptually-Driven Discussion

Some instructors and students may be especially challenged by the requirement to discuss their ideas with peers, if this pedagogical strategy is used in conjunction with audience response systems. Sociocultural theory, however, would hypothesize that peer discussion is a critical component of audience response systems, because it gives students an extended turn at talk with another student that allows them to elaborate on their understanding of a construct. We would also hypothesize, however, that instructors will have limited access to all the peer-to-peer conversations that take place, especially in a large classroom, because they cannot listen in simultaneously to multiple conversations. Audience response systems do facilitate students' developing scientific ways of talking about concepts, but whole-class interaction and discussion of selected student explanations may still be very important to advancing conceptual change, because in such a setting, instructors can provide students with guidance about terminology, forms of speech, and ways of thinking that the particular scientific discipline expects its experts to adopt.

At this point, two kinds of interpersonal interactions in the classroom are required for the kinds of participation patterns reported in the literature to emerge. For their part, instructors must demonstrate by their actions that in fact they *do* adjust their teaching strategies or extend their coverage of particular content when students do not understand the material. The instructors' different response changes the typical sequence of tasks students encounter in the classroom—from responding to instructors' questions, having their individual answer evaluated publicly, and then observing as the class moves on — to enable all students to respond to instructor questions, having aggregate answers answered publicly, and pausing for discussion or reteaching. In this new task structure, students do not have to "perform" their intelligence for others. Rather, they are able to take risks to indicate what they think, knowing that others will not see their answer, and appreciating that the instructor will take the situation seriously if too few students understand the concept to move on. Students, for their part, must take some risks publicly, specifically by sharing their own thinking in peer and whole-class discussion. In such a context, there is no doubt that students are still performing their classroom identities, but the emerging atmosphere of instructor responsiveness is likely to make such risk-taking more palatable, and also to change students' perceptions about the kinds of "performances" that are desired in the classroom. Ideally, at this point, students are expected to "show their thinking" in whatever state of formation it is in, rather than "show their smarts" by providing the correct answer.

As both students and instructors become more familiar with their new expected roles and responsibilities for participation within these task structures, new forms of motivation and interest are likely to emerge. Many students become excited about the new approach, and develop a strong interest in participating in class and in using the audience response systems. Instructors, in turn, develop more comfort with using the system, and become more confident in its benefits because they see that many students are interested. It is likely, at this point, however, that students whose classroom identities do not mesh well with the new roles and responsibilities will not perceive audience response systems or the classroom in such a positive light. At this point, for example, students who are motivated by the idea of demonstrating their knowledge to the instructor by raising their hands early may feel thwarted in their efforts to project an identity as the "smart student." Similarly, students of all ability levels who prefer to "lay low" in the classroom may find the requirement to provide an answer to all instructor questions, and discuss those answers with a peer, may feel quite threatened by the use of student response systems. Students whose family and cultural backgrounds have communication styles and attitudes toward school participation that differ from the new requirements may also find the new forms of classroom interaction problematic. There is, at present, too little research on students' interest and motivation conducted in the middle of a semester or school year to make specific predictions about how particular classroom and cultural identities are likely to influence students' motivation, engagement, and participation, but we would hypothesize that divergence of viewpoints about the benefits of audience response systems is likely to be greatest midterm or midyear.

Community Effects of Audience Response Systems

Toward the end of the school year, repeated instances of interaction with the system, as well as the emerging positive affect toward system use by the majority of students and instructors, leads to the emergence of a new kind of classroom, when viewed from the community plane. Students' increased interest in and motivation for classroom learning helps explain why researchers report increased cognitive engagement and classroom participation by the end of a semester or year. Instructors' own experiences of success with the system and with fostering student engagement lead them to evaluate the experience positively, as well as conferring benefits to them as instructors (improved feedback on learning) and to students (improved conceptual understanding). To the extent that instructors and students have been able to establish a common language for coordinating their efforts (Rogoff, 2003) at producing classroom-wide learning, a positive, new, classroom culture focused on learning tends to emerge of the kind reported so widely in the research on audience response systems.

There emerges in such classrooms, by the end of class, a sense of learning as a shared endeavor among students and the instructor. As one student described it, "We're all kind of in the same boat!" (Owens et al., 2002). It is easy to underestimate the significance of such a remark and dismiss it as a cliché, because of the way it is expressed. But it masks a sentiment rare in education because it refers to a transformed classroom environment including all the students and the instructor as well. One instructor expressed a sentiment similar to the student's above, in noting that the shared display of student responses enabled by the audience response system yields a situation in which students and teachers are *looking together* at the problem of learning, often for the first time:

[I]t's in the sense that we're all looking at it together for the first time so it's not that, 'I've graded them,' and, 'I know what they've done,' and, 'I'm giving it back,' and, 'I'm going over it.' With Navigator, we're basically all seeing the information together for the first time, and that ... it does ... it's hard to explain how it does it, but it's like, 'Oh well, look at that, this is something!!!...' and um, so we're kind of exploring concepts and ideas together.

Testing the Sociocultural Account: Implications for Practice and Further Research

This sociocultural account of audience response systems is an important complement to the conceptual change account that may be of particular use to instructors. A benefit of the conceptual change account is that it is closely aligned with the goals and practices of instructors in higher education. At the same time, instructors may be disappointed in the results if they come to expect that the introduction of systems will lead, in a linear fashion, toward increased achievement, and if they do not understand the complex reactions students are likely to have to the introduction of audience response systems. The benefit of a sociocultural account is that it brings student and teacher participation into focus, and it helps draw attention to the ways that transformed participation is a critical component of conceptual change. Further, the sociocultural account can help instructors understand the likely developmental pathway to a transformed classroom.

A sociocultural reinterpretation of the phenomenon of audience response systems in higher education also has several important implications for how research should be conducted in these settings to examine both implementation and effects. To test the hypotheses identified above, it is necessary to use the theory to specify the kinds of variables that are important to measure, and to identify critical points in the developmental trajectory to observe transformations in participation. In this last section of this chapter, we argue that future research on audience response systems should consider collecting data at multiple points in time on student-instructor interaction, instructor and student perceptions of the classroom environment, and teaching and learning outcomes, to advance knowledge of how, when, and why audience response systems can improve teaching and learning outcomes.

The Need for Measurements of Process and Outcomes

Most studies of audience response systems, to date, have measured two kinds of variables: perceptions of the classroom (from instructors and students) and student learning outcomes. Both perceptions of the environment and measures of learning are still important in a sociocultural account, but they are not adequate to a full account of teaching within the networked classroom. A few studies have sought to *describe* and *interpret* the typical implementation trajectory in classrooms when response systems are introduced, but we are not aware of any that have sought systematically to *measure* aspects of implementation, especially student-teacher interactions. We do believe it is important to measure teacher and student perceptions, but it is just as important to produce systematic analyses of classroom interactions, whether through an analysis of discourse, systematic observation, or review of instructional logs provided by teachers. Such analyses, which could include both quantitative and qualitative measures of classroom practice, are necessary to account for changes in perception of the classroom environment by students and teachers. In addition, it is necessary to measure student motivation and interest more systematically, using measures from psychology (Midgley, Maehr, Hruda, Anderman, Anderman, Freeman, et al., 2000), and in conjunction with analyses of classroom interaction. A sociocultural account would specifically seek to use these kinds of measures of individual functioning and social interaction together to develop an understanding of how particular patterns of interaction lead to changes in student interest and motivation, and how they activate and potentially transform students' classroom identities.

Measurements at Different Time Points are Necessary

Testing the adequacy of the sociocultural account for explaining the pattern of results often reported in classrooms that use audience response systems requires some adjustments be made to the typical course of evaluation research. A common evaluation research design measures key variables of interest only at the beginning and end of a study. Our theory, however, specifies at least four different points in time when it would be important to analyze interactions, and measure individual mental functioning. Baseline data on student understanding of key concepts, motivational goals, and expectations for the course are important to collect before the class actually begins. When systems are first introduced, it is important to measure initial changes to students' motivation and interest, and students' and instructors' perceptions of the classroom environment. After an initial period of novelty has passed, it is particularly critical to examine student-instructor interaction, to see if in fact instructors are adjusting instruction on the basis of what they learn from querying students more often about their knowledge, and if students are taking more risks by discussing their thinking and ideas, however tentative, in class with peers, and in whole-group interactions. Toward the end of class, it is important to measure what students have learned, to gather data again on their interest and motivation, and to survey them again on their overall perceptions of the classroom environment.

Rigorous Research Designs

Theory-testing research also requires rigorous research designs. Ideally, studies that would gather data from such a wide range of data, and at multiple time points, would also employ research designs that employ either random assignment, or use matched control groups. We recognize that budgets for research and evaluation studies rarely afford opportunities to measure both implementation and outcomes, or to employ random assignment. However, future investment in audience response systems, and the advancement of knowledge of effective teaching in the networked classroom, is likely to depend on the field generating a few rigorous studies that can demonstrate impact and account for the impact through documented changes to teaching with audience response systems.

References

Abrahamson, A. L. (1999). *Teaching with classroom communication systems: What it involves and why it works*. Paper presented at the International Workshop on New Trends in Physics Teaching, Puebla, Mexico.

Abrahamson, A. L., Owens, D. T., Demana, F., Meagher, M., & Herman, M. (2003, March). *Developing pedagogy for wireless handheld computer networks*. Paper presented at the Society for Information Technology and Teacher Education International Conference, Albuquerque, NM.

Ames, C., & Archer, J. (1988). Achievement goals in the classroom: Students' learning strategies and motivation processes. *Journal of Educational Psychology, 80*(3), 260-267.

Bazerman, C. (1983). Scientific writing as a social act: A review of the literature of the sociology of science. In P. V. Anderson, R. J. Brockman, & C. Miller (Eds.), *New essays in technical and scientific communication: Research, theory and practice* (pp. 156-184). Farmingdale, NY: Baywood.

Butler, R. (1987). Task-involving and ego-involving properties of evaluation: Effects of different feedback conditions on motivational perceptions, interest, and performance. *Journal of Educational Psychology, 79*(4), 474-482.

Butler, R., & Neuman, O. (1995). Effects of task and ego-achievement goals on help-seeking behaviours and attitudes. *Journal of Educational Psychology, 87*(2), 261-271.

Chi, M. T. H. (1996). Constructing self-explanations and scaffolded explanations in tutoring. *Applied Cognitive Psychology Special Issue: Reasoning Processes, 10*(Spec Issue), S33-S49. Additional info UK, John Wiley & Sons, http //www interscience wiley com/jpages/0888-4080

Cope, B., & Kalantzis, M. (Eds.). (1993). *The powers of literacy: A genre approach to teaching writing*. London: Falmer Press.

Crouch, C. H., & Mazur, E. (2001). Peer instruction: Ten years of experience and results. *The Physics Teacher, 69*(9), 970-977.

Doherty, R. W., Hilberg, R. S., Pinal, A., & Tharp, R. (2003). Five standards and student achievement. *NABE Journal of Research and Practice, 1*(1), 1-24.

Dufresne, B., Gerace, B., Leonard, B., Mestre, J., & Wenk, L. (1996). Using the Classtalk classroom communication system for promoting active learning in large lectures. *Journal of Computing in Higher Education, 7*(2), 3-47.

Dunbar, K. N. (1995). How scientists really reason: Scientific reasoning in real-world laboratories. In R. J. Sternberg & J. Davidson (Eds.), *Mechanisms of insight* (pp. 365-395). Cambridge, MA: MIT Press.

Duncan, D. (2005). *Clickers in the classroom: How to enhance science teaching using classroom response systems*. San Francisco: Pearson.

Eckert, P. (1989). *Jocks and burnouts: Social categories and identity in the high school*. New York: Teachers College Press.

Gee, J. P. (1994, April). *"Science Talk": How do you start to do what you don't know how to do?* Paper presented at the Annual Meeting of the American Educational Research Association, New Orleans, LA.

Gee, J. P. (1999). *Social lingustics and literacies: Ideology in discourse* (2nd ed.). New York: Taylor and Francis.

Gee, J. P. (2000-2001). Identity as an analytic lens for research in education. *Review of Research in Education, 25*, 99-125.

Gee, J. P. (2004). Language in the science classroom: Academic social languages as the heart of school-based literacy. In E. W. Saul (Ed.), *Crossing borders in literacy and science instruction: Perspectives on theory and practice* (pp. 10-32). Newark, DE: International Reading Association.

Hackman, J. R., & Oldham, G. R. (1980). *Work redesign*. Reading, MA: Addison-Wesley.

Hake, R. R. (1998). Interactive-engagement versus traditional methods. *American Journal of Physics, 66*, 64-74.

Halliday, M. A. K., & Martin, J. (1993). *Writing science: Literacy and discursive power*. London: Falmer.

Hanania, E., & Akhtar, K. (1985). Verb form and rhetorical function in science writing: A study of MS theses in biology, chemistry, and physics. *English for Specific Purposes, 4*(1), 49-58.

Heath, S. B., & McLaughlin, M. W. (Eds.). (1993). *Identity and inner-city youth: Beyond ethnicity and gender.* New York: Teachers College Press.

Hickey, D. T., & McCaslin, M. (2001). A comparative, sociocultural analysis of context and motivation. In S. Jarvella & S. Volet (Eds.), *Motivation in learning contexts: Theoretical advances and methodological implecations* (pp. 33-55). Oxford: Pergamon.

Hidi, S., Renninger, K. A., & Krapp, A. (2004). Interst, a motivational variable that combines affective and cognitive functioning. In D. Y. Dai, & R. J. Sternberg (Eds.), *Motivation, emotion, and cognition: Integrative perspectives on intellectual functioning and development* (pp. 89-115). Mahwah, NJ: Erlbaum.

Jackson, M., & Trees, A. (2003). *Clicker implementation and assessment.* Boulder: Information and Technology Services and Faculty Teaching Excellence Program, University of Colorado.

Jarvella, S., & Volet, S. (Eds.). (2001). *Motivation in learning contexts: Theoretical advances and methodological implemcations.* Oxford: Pergamon.

Judson, E., & Sawada, D. (2002). Learning from past and present: Electronic response systems in college lecture halls. *Journal of Computers in Mathematics and Science Teaching, 21*(2), 167-181.

Kaput, J., & Hegedus, S. (2002). *Exploiting classroom connectivity by aggregating student constructions to create new learning opportunities.* Paper presented at the 26th Conference of the International Group for the Psychology of Mathematics Education, Norwich, UK.

Latour, B., & Woolgar, S. (1986). *Laboratory life: The construction of scientific facts.* Princeton, NJ: Princeton University Press.

Lave, J., & Wenger, E. (1991). *Situated learning: Legitimate peripheral participation.* Cambridge, MA: Harvard University Press.

Lemke, J. L. (1990). *Talking science: Language, learning, and values.* Norwood, NJ: Ablex.

Lynch, M. (1985). *Art and artifact in laboratory science: A study of shop work and shop talk in a research laboratory.* London: Routledge & Kegan Paul.

Martin, J. R. (1989). *Factual writing. Exploring and challenging social reality.* London: Oxford University Press.

Mazur, E. (1997). *Peer instruction: A user's manual.* Upper Saddle River, NJ: Prentice Hall.

McCaslin, M., & Hickey, D. T. (2001). Self-regulated learning and academic achievement: A Vygotskian view. In B. J. Zimmerman, & D. Schunk (Eds.), *Self-regulated learning and academic achievement: Theoretical perspectives.* Mahwah, NJ: Erlbaum.

Midgley, C., Maehr, M. L., Hruda, L. Z., Anderman, E. M., Anderman, L. H., Freeman, K. E., et al. (2000). *Manual for the Patterns of Adaptive Learning Scales (PALS)*. Ann Arbor: University of Michigan.

National Research Council. (1999). *How people learn: Brain, mind, experience*. Washington, DC: National Academy Press.

Owens, D. T., Demana, F., Abrahamson, L. A., Meagher, M., & Herman, M. (2002). *Developing pedagogy for wireless calculator networks and researching teacher professional development*. Columbus: Ohio State University and Better Education.

Penuel, W. R., & Wertsch, J. V. (1995a). Dynamics of negation in the identity politics of cultural other and cultural self. *Culture and Psychology, 1*(3), 343-359.

Penuel, W. R., & Wertsch, J. V. (1995b). Vygotsky and identity formation: A sociocultural approach. *Educational Psychologist, 30*(2), 83-92.

Poulis, C., Massen, C., Robens, E., & Gilbert, M. (1998). Physics learning with audience paced feedback. *American Journal of Physics, 66*, 439-441.

Pressick-Kilborn, K., & Walker, R. (2002). The social construction of interest in a learning community. In D. M. McInerney & S. Van Etten (Eds.), *Research on sociocultural infuences on motivation and learning* (pp. 153-182). Greenwich, CT: Information Age Publishing.

Rodman, L. (1994). The active voice in scientific articles: Frequency and discourse functions. *Journal of Technical Writing and Communication, 24*(3), 309-331.

Rogoff, B. (1990). *Apprenticeship in thinking: Cognitive development in social context*. Oxford: Oxford University Press.

Rogoff, B. (1995). Observing sociocultural activity on three planes: Participatory appropriation, guided participation, and apprenticeship. In J. V. Wertsch, P. del Rio, & A. Alvarez (Eds.), *Sociocultural studies of mind* (pp. 139-164). Cambridge: Cambridge University Press.

Rogoff, B. (2003). *The cultural nature of human development*. New York: Oxford University Press.

Rogoff, B., Baker-Sennett, J., Lacasa, P., & Goldsmith, D. (1995). Development through participation in sociocultural activity. In J. Goodnow, P. Miller, & F. Kessel (Eds.), *Cultural practices as contexts for development*. San Francisco: Jossey-Bass.

Rogoff, B., Paradise, R., Arauz, R. M., Correa-Chavez, M., & Angelillo, C. (2003). Firsthand learning through intent participation. *Annual Review of Psychology, 54*, 175-203.

Roschelle, J. (1992). Learning by collaborating: Convergent conceptual change. *The Journal of the Learning Sciences, 2*(3), 235-276.

Roschelle, J. (1996). Convergent conceptual change. In T. Koschmann (Ed.), *CSCL: Theory and practice of an emerging paradigm* (pp. 209-248). Mahwah, NK: Lawrence Erlbaum Associates Publishers.

Roschelle, J., Abrahamson, A. L., & Penuel, W. R. (2003). *CATAALYST: Towards scientific studies of the strategic integration of learning theory and classroom network technology to improve teaching and learning*. Menlo Park, CA: SRI International.

Roschelle, J., Penuel, W. R., & Abrahamson, A. L. (2004). The networked classroom. *Educational Leadership, 61*(5), 50-54.

Rosebery, A. S., Warren, B., & Conant, F. R. (1992). Appropriating scientific discourse: Findings from language minority classrooms. *The Journal of the Learning Sciences, 2*(1), 61-94.

Rueda, R., & Moll, L. C. (1994). A sociocultural perspective on motivation. In H. F. O'Neil & M. Drillings (Eds.), *Motivation: Theory and research* (pp. 117-137). Hillsdale, NJ: Erlbaum.

Shapiro, J. A. (1997). Student response found feasible in large science lecture hall. *Journal of College Science Teaching, 26*(6), 408-412.

Shaw, T. S. (1994). The semiotic mediation of identity. *Ethos, 22*(1), 83-119.

Stroup, W. M. (2002, September). *Instantiating Seeing Mathematics Structuring the Social Sphere (MS3): Updating generative teaching and learning for networked mathematics and science classrooms.* Paper presented at the First International Conference on Wireless and Mobile Technologies in Education, Vaxjo, Sweden.

Stroup, W. M., Kaput, J., Ares, N., Wilensky, U., Hegedus, S., Roschelle, J., et al. (2002, October). *The nature and future of classroom connectivity: The dialectics of mathematics in the social space.* Paper presented at the Annual Conference of Psychology of Mathematics Education in North America, Athens, GA.

Tharp, R., & Gallimore, R. (1988). *Rousing minds to life: Teaching, learning, and schooling in social context.* New York: Cambridge University Press.

Vygotsky, L. S. (1978). *Mind in society: The development of higher psychological processes.* Cambridge, MA: Harvard University Press.

Vygotsky, L. S. (1987). *Thought and language* (A. Kozulin, Trans.). Cambridge: Cambridge University Press.

Walker, R., Pressick-Kilborn, K., Arnold, L. S., & Sainsbury, E. J. (2004). Investigating motivation in context: Developing sociocultural perspectives. *European Psychologist, 9*(4), 245-256.

Wells, G. (1993). Reevaluating the IRF sequence: A proposal for the articulation of theories of activity and discourse for the analysis of teaching and learning in the classroom. *Linguistics and Education, 5*, 1-37.

Wertsch, J. V. (1979). From social interaction to higher psychological process: A clarification and application of Vygotsky's theory. *Human Development, 22*, 1-22.

Wertsch, J. V. (1991). *Voices of the mind: A sociocultural approach to mediated action.* Cambridge, MA: Harvard University Press.

Wertsch, J. V. (1998). *Mind as action.* New York: Oxford University Press.

Wortham, S. (2004). The interdependence of social identification and learning. *American Educational Research Journal, 41*(3), 715-749.

Endnote

- This material is based, in part, on work supported by the National Science Foundation under Grant Number REC-0337793. Any opinions, findings, conclusions, or recommendations expressed in this material are those of the authors, and do not necessarily reflect the views of the National Science Foundation.

Chapter XIV

Wireless Interactive Teaching by Using Keypad-Based ARS

Jiankun Hu, RMIT University, Australia

Peter Bertok, RMIT University, Australia

Margaret Hamilton, RMIT University, Australia

Graeme White, RMIT University, Australia

Anita Duff, RMIT University, Australia

Quintin Cutts, University of Glasgow, UK

Abstract

Lecturing large classes in tertiary education is always a challenge; one of the most difficult tasks being how to gauge students' understanding. Introducing interactivity can alleviate this problem by providing instant feedback that enables the lecturer to clarify problematical points. This is even more crucial and challenging when lecturing to large classes with students from many different cultural backgrounds. This chapter reports the authors' experience with a wireless keypad-based system in different classrooms. New deployment strategies used in this project, and educational foundations on which they were based, are explained. The environment and the experience of using the technology from the educator's viewpoint are also described. Student feedback is also discussed, and improvements for future use are also proposed.

Introduction

It is well known that an interactive approach is the most effective way to achieve a high quality of teaching and learning in the classroom (Happern & Hakel, 2003; McConnell, Steer, & Owens, 2003; Rust & Gibbs, 1996). However, the difficulty of organizing interactive teaching and learning activities with a large, lecturing class size is also well recognised (Mazur, 1997; Panitz, 1998). An increasing number of tertiary students are coming from other countries, especially from Southeast Asia, where the teaching and learning cultural styles are markedly different from the Australian open interactive classroom teaching style. This adds another difficulty to interactive teaching and learning activities in the classroom.

Like Australian universities in general, RMIT University of Australia is a student-centred institution. The School of Computer Science and Information Technology (CS&IT) at RMIT has a typically high percentage, as high as 50%, of international students in many classrooms. The School conducted a reflective research project to explore an effective way of organizing interactive teaching and learning activities in an environment that includes a large number of students from diverse backgrounds. The aims were to engage students in a lecture environment that was traditionally regarded as requiring passive student participation (Neild, 2004; Rodrigues, Bu, & Min, 2000), and to introduce overseas students to a more interactive learning approach. The project team was headed by Dr. Jiankun Hu, and comprised four lecturers, one teaching and learning adviser, one teaching and learning specialist, and one research assistant. The project deployed wireless technology, a keypad-based audience response system (ARS) for the classroom teaching and learning, in the field of computer science and information technology. With the support from KEEpad Australia, this project leased 150 KEEpad wireless voting devices at a heavily discounted price. In the remainder of this paper, we use KEEpad to represent the company KEEpad Australia, and the keypad-based ARS system supplied by KEEpad Australia, interchangeably. The KEEpad wireless voting device has buttons labelled with numbers 1 to 10, and letters A to I. This allows the user to choose an answer to a multiple-choice question. The KEEpad company has also provided TurningPoint software for class and statistical analysis. The TurningPoint application was embedded in the PowerPoint™ software. It can record and display the device ID, and voter selection from this device on the slide. A statistical summary showing the percentage of voting on each possible answer is displayed that can help the lecturer identify the level of students' understanding. TurningPoint operates on Windows 98, 2000, or XP. More details can be found at the KEEpad company Web site (KEEpad).

The objective of this chapter is to report some of the experiences, case studies, issues, controversies, and critical problems encountered in using this wireless interactive technology. In this chapter, we cover background, case studies, implementation issues, lessons learnt, and future thoughts.

Background

Lecture classes at many universities worldwide have very large numbers, and the situation is worsening due to shrinking funding. Having 300 to 600 students in lectures is common, which makes it very difficult for lecturers to actively engage with students. The need for more staff/student interaction was identified as the top student concern at RMIT in 2001, and remained an important issue in 2002 and 2003 (RMIT Report, 2003). Additionally, Australian universities face a cultural hurdle to achieving quality interactive teaching in the classroom. Australian universities have attracted large numbers of students from the Asia-Pacific region. The School of CS&IT at RMIT has more than 850 international students from the Asian region, who have different cultural learning backgrounds. Typically, these students do not like to be placed in front of the class, which makes it more difficult to apply conventional interactive teaching techniques such as requesting students to answer a question.

There is much literature on the different styles of eastern and western learning, and how this can impede the international students' learning (Ballard & Clanchy, 1997). Much discussion has taken place on the apparent differences in approaches between eastern and western ways of accumulating knowledge. In this discussion, there has been an emphasis placed on rote and memory learning vs. critical thinking and independent research learning (Ballard & Clanchy, 1997; Pearson & Beasley, 1996). The features of the learning environment prior to tertiary education vary in different cultures, and this strongly influences how students approach their tertiary education in Australia (Chan, 1999; Nield, 2004; Rodrigues et al., 2000). In the field of computer science and IT, teaching and learning needs to cover both highly abstract theory-based courses and highly hands-on experimental courses, which requires different teaching and learning styles. It is unclear from the literature how to enhance effective interactive teaching and learning in the classroom when all of these complicating factors are present. More literature is being presented addressing the problem of large lecture classes, and how to develop strategies to make these lectures more interactive and increase student participation (Bruno, 2002).

Wireless, interactive teaching promises an innovative solution to these learning problems. When the lecturer asks a question, students can use this technology to answer such questions anonymously. From the percentage of correct answers, the lecturer can identify any learning problems immediately, and so, take remedial actions. The peer instruction teaching technique can also be used to allow students to discuss ideas with their neighbours, and to challenge one another on the veracity of their answers. This new teaching and learning scheme is based on Mazur's ConcepTest (Panitz, 1998). Dr. Eric Mazur developed the 15-minute lecture, and ConcepTest, for the teaching of physics to large classes (Mazur, 1997). These ideas have been further developed, and are used in other science subjects (Apple, Nygren, Williams, & Litynski, 2002; McConnell, Steer, & Owens, 2003). Although it has been successfully used at a number of universities in the US and Europe, no systematic method of deployment appears to have been followed.

The School of Accounting and Information Systems at the University of South Australia has used this technology for peer review of collaborative group-work (Banks, 2003).

Banks reported that such an application caused uncomfortable feelings for students, and received negative feedback. Such applications can cause even more problems for Asian students, indicating the need for further research before implementation. RMIT University, through its teaching and learning portfolio, encourages the development of strategies that improve learning outcomes for all students. It supports best teaching practices, which include interaction between students and facilitators; quality, appropriate feedback to all students; meeting the different needs of different students; appropriate pacing of the delivery of materials; encouraging the development of lifelong learning skills; higher student participation, which helps to motivate and engage students in their own learning. Within its charter, RMIT provides grants and seed funding to encourage and support learning strategies such as active learning. In 2004, the Academic Development Group in the RMIT Science and Technology (SET) Portfolio provided funding for several action research projects in teaching and learning during the second semester. This ARS application is one of these research projects.

Case Studies

The wireless, interactive teaching technology has been deployed in five different courses conducted by four different lecturers. In this chapter, we select two courses to report as case studies. The first course is programming oriented, and the other one is concept oriented, which is representative of the discipline of computer science and information technology.

Case Study I: Programming Oriented Course

The course is Web Page Construction, taught by the third author. For many students, this is their first course at our University. It was designed as a postgraduate course, and the lecture is given from 9 am till 12 noon on Saturday morning. However, there are many undergraduate students, as well as the postgraduate students, in the course. For many students, this is an elective, so not all are students of computer science or information technology degrees. There is no prerequisite for this course, so students may have no knowledge of programming. The lecture for which the students used the KEEpads was entitled "Introduction to JavaScript."

During the previous lecture, the students had completed the ethics form, and all the data from the class had been collected onto a spreadsheet. There were 51 students altogether, and they appeared interested to join in the KEEpads trial. From this data:

- 11 were from China, 8 from Australia, 8 from Indonesia, 4 from Malaysia, 2 from Sweden, 11 other, and 3 were left blank.

- 14 spoke English as their first language, 3 spoke English plus another language, 31 had other first languages, and 4 left this section blank.

Thus, the class was predominantly of Asian origin, and mostly spoke languages other than English. The staff designed questions for the end of each major concept to see if the students had understood that concept.

At the beginning of every lecture, using this technology, the lecturer displayed the registration slides to determine the cultural mix at the beginning of that lecture. This was not the first lecture to trial the KEEpads, and the previous lecturer had suggested that the students liked to experiment with the KEEpads at the beginning, so perhaps we should ask some "fun" questions. The initial data collection appeared not to work, as the registration boxes on the bottom of the screen were not going red. However, the graph did appear. The lecturer changed the background, reset the slide, and asked the question again, and a similar graph appeared. Therefore, the lecturer believed that at least the students were answering truthfully, as the same response was provided the second time. Unfortunately, the polling bar at the bottom of the screen did not work for the registration slides.

After covering the material for the first concept, the lecturer displayed two summary questions:

- Which of the following is NOT true? (followed by several options from A to F)
- Which is not a typical use of JavaScript?

For the first question, 65% got the answer right, and for the next one 94 % got the correct answer, so it appeared that students had understood that section well.

During the next section on JavaScript language control structures and operators, when the review question slide was displayed, it was not announced, but the students answered immediately with 77% correct. As 14% had given an incorrect answer, the lecturer provided further explanation of the misunderstood concepts. Students were confused by the next summary slide, where they selected alternatives A, B, C, D with the following percentage distribution: 16%, 13%, 39%, and 32%. This slide had one alternative answer split over two choices, and so the 39% and 32% options were really the same option, which was the correct answer. Those who selected the 16% and 13% options had not understood that particular language concept. Therefore, the lecturer reviewed this section.

During the break, two students approached the lecturer and asked about that question, explaining their incorrect selections. This was a useful outcome, as the explanation had enabled these students to gain a better understanding of these concepts. It also indicated that these students were shy about asking their question in front of the whole class.

The final section went reasonably quickly, but the students were now more talkative. They asked if these types of things were to be in the exam, and they voluntarily replied to some rhetorical questions. Ninety-four percent of the students got the second to last summary slide correct, and 100% the last.

The final evaluation slide gave the following results:

- 14%   Shorter lectures with discussion time enabled me to learn more.
- 45%   The use of technology during lectures helps me to learn.
- 7%   I thought that student participation in peer discussion was of value to me.
- 17%   I prefer the whole of the session to be lecture time.
- 14%   So long as there are detailed notes, the lecture/discussion time is not important to me.
- 0%   I found the session disruptive to my learning.
- 3%   I found the lecture difficult to follow using this technology

These statistics indicate that the majority of the students liked the technology.

The lecturer believed more discussion could be generated in the lecture, and so plans to organise more thought provoking, difficult, and tricky questions, requiring students to make more effort, and think to find a solution. However, on the whole, the lecturer is happy with the results of this lecture. Beforehand, the lecturer had been very unsure whether or not the technology would work. But despite a few difficulties with the registration slides, the technology appeared to work well. It did involve extra time setting up before the lecture on the day, and also handing out the KEEpads. Retrieving them was also time-consuming, as all the students 'piled down the front' together at the end. A lot of time was involved beforehand for those involved in learning the software and installing it. The lecturer needed to borrow a laptop with the software working, and organise suitable questions. However, the time and effort was worthwhile to find out that the students had followed and participated much more than the lecturer had realised, rather than simply looking out on what often seems to be "a sea of faces."

Case Study II: Concept Oriented Course

This course is Broadcast Network Engineering, taught by the first author, and has 108 enrolled students. It covers intermediate-level material in the fields of data communication and networking. Most of the concepts, such as TCP/IP protocols, digital encoding, and so forth, are rather abstract. Such features make it very hard to obtain timely feedback regarding how well the students have understood these concepts. Therefore, introduction of wireless, interactive teaching technology to identify the problems, on the spot, is valuable. This is a second semester course with 12 2-hour lectures.

The lecturer started to use the wireless, interactive technology from lecture five onwards. In the prior lecture, ethics forms had been distributed and collected. In the 58 completed forms, nearly 90% of the students were shown to have a non-English speaking background. No literature has been found showing how to prepare experimental slides. We decided to display five registration slides to collect information about the participants' learning background, such as nationality, country of origin, language used in primary education, and so forth. At the end of the lecture, we placed evaluation slides to collect students' feedback regarding this technology. Feedback questions included "By using the KEEpad, I was able to answer questions without embarrassment." The evaluation feedback from the first lecture was excellent. However, several problems have been observed in the subsequent lectures.

1.   **Registration problem:** It was found that a significant number of students came to the class a little bit late, and hence, missed the registration phase, which could cause problems in collecting accurate voting data. It was also found that students may get bored with the registration phase, which has up to five slides that are irrelevant to the course.

2.   **Evaluation problem:** The evaluation slide was placed at the end of the lecture. However, it is very difficult to control lecture timing, so there may be no time left at the end of the lecture to arrange this part. This might occur if the lecturer allocates extra time to cope with unexpected problems found in the question answering process.

3.   **Timing problem of the lecture:** The deployment of the wireless, interactive teaching and learning has introduced enormous uncertainty into the lecturing. As the voting process takes a significant fraction of time, the lecture notes had to be redesigned. Sometimes the voting clearly indicated that students' understanding was well below the lecturer's expectation, in which case, the lecturer has to take extra time to make remedies. Although this interactive response phenomenon is exactly one of the advantages of deploying the wireless, interactive teaching and learning technology, it renders the task of controlling the flow of the lecture nearly impossible.

Interestingly enough, such problems and solutions have not been reported in any published literature. Although Mazur's ConcepTest has been used in a scheduled timely manner, based on a "15 minute learning fatigue period," it has not involved the time uncertainty for making unexpected remedies. The lecturer has also found it infeasible to adopt such a prescheduled, timely, Mazur ConcepTest, as it is extremely difficult and costly to arrange the flow of the lecture material in such a way. Even if the lecture material can be arranged in such a way, the timing uncertainty problem mentioned above can easily destroy the lecture schedule. Upon reflection, the lecturer took several actions for the last three lectures. The first action was to reduce the number of registration slides from five to two. Other actions included redesign of all lecture notes to better accommodate the voting process, and the redesign of the voting questions based on controlling the flow of concepts in the lecture, instead of Mazur's conventional fatigue timing. To accommodate the timing uncertainty, the lecturer has also limited the number of voting questions to four in each 2-hour lecture, and has designed an optional question to adjust the lecturing timing dynamically. A snapshot of the evaluation obtained is given below:

The final evaluation slide gave the following results:

- 25%   By using the KEEpad I was able to answer questions without embarrassment
- 16.67%   Shorter lectures with discussion time enabled me to learn more.
- 41%   The use of technology during lectures helps me to learn.
- 8%   I thought that student participation in peer discussion was of value to me.
- 0%   I prefer the whole of the session to be lecture time.
- 0%   So long as there are detailed notes, the lecture/discussion time is not important to me.
- 0%   I found the session disruptive to my learning.
- 8.3%   I found the lecture difficult to follow using this technology

These statistics also indicate a very positive result from our deployment strategy for this technology.

Implementation Issues: A Practical Approach

Hardware Issues

One set of equipment was leased from the KEEpad Company for the duration of this project, and used by all faculty members participating in the project. The hardware comprised

- three, wireless receivers with attached networking device and stands,
- one, wireless network hub,
- USB port connector and USB security key,
- 160 student transmitter devices (for student responses).

Also, the School provided a staff notebook computer with PowerPoint™ installed. KEEpad software was installed on this computer by the research team. The four lecturers involved in the project used the KEEpad devices for a different course. Three of these courses involved lectures at RMIT City Campus, with one course involving lectures across two campuses.

KEEpad student response transmitters were usually placed on a table at the front of the lecture theatre, in the plastic storage pockets provided by KEEpad. Students were instructed to collect one of these devices, depositing either their student card or a driving licence in the location from where they collected the transmitter. In most cases, the process of installing, distributing, collecting, and dismantling hardware requirements for this teaching approach decreased the amount of time available for lecture delivery by approximately 10 minutes. The same hardware configuration was appropriate for all four courses in which the KEEpad equipment was used, therefore, the one set of equipment was shared by all faculty members involved in the project. This required cooperation amongst the staff to ensure that the equipment was available when required for all lecture groups involved, and this generally worked quite well.

Faculty and staff participating in this research project were already well versed in the use of PC computers, and also connecting and configuring peripheral devices. After a demonstration of the components comprising the KEEpad system, and the overall configuration of the system, staff were encouraged to experiment with setting up and dismantling this equipment so that this could be done in a timely manner during the lectures.

Staff Issues

The KEEpad Company provided staff training in the use of the hardware and software components of the wireless, interactive system for all lecturers involved in this research project. This training covered installation of the software, development of multichoice questions, and their inclusion into lecture presentations. Lecturers were provided with access to the equipment and software during the preparation stage. Staff were encouraged to undertake practice "setups" of the gear, even if just in their office, and to conduct trial runs of their lecture presentations, with the student feedback or voting questions incorporated.

In almost all cases, the "voting" questions incorporated in the lecture presentations were multichoice questions. Typically, a "question slide" was incorporated into the lecture presentation following the coverage of a key or important concept. This required review of lecture material to identify clearly when key concepts were covered during lectures.

Incorporation of feedback questions into the lecture sequence changes the nature of lecture delivery, decreasing the time that lecturers spend on decreeing. An important consideration for the development of questions for lecture delivery, and modification of lecture materials to include these, is determining the number of key concepts to be covered, the distribution of these within the lecture sequence, and the number of feedback questions which can practically be incorporated in relation to these concepts.

Use of technology that encourages or requires students to interact on a regular basis throughout the lecture time, in effect, forces a change in the lecturing strategy. The change in focus is away from a purely decreeing model to a lecturing mode that requires students to engage more actively with the lecture material, and to decide answers to feedback questions either as an individual, or from discussion with neighbouring students. By allowing more student interaction, lecturers might also be concerned that they will lose a degree of control of the lecture, and possibly that the "voice" of the lecturer will be lost in the interactive nature of the lecture. Faculty and staff involved with this project all expressed concerns of this nature during the preparation stages of this project. However, with appropriate sequencing of content, and the inclusion of appropriate voting questions to promote student feedback, faculty and staff were provided with information to gauge the level of students' understanding, allowing them to modify the emphasis and time spent covering concepts in their lectures. Rather than causing the lecturer's voice to be lost, this can allow some gain in efficiency, as lecturers can modify their lecture sequence in response to feedback, placing emphasis, or spending more lecture time, on concepts that students have shown that they do not understand.

Student Issues

Students were required to complete "ethics documents," confirming that they wished to participate in this trial. As part of this process, all students were provided with an introductory document explaining the rationale for educational research projects, for this project in particular, and the strategy that would be used for delivering lectures.

Lecturers showed the KEEpad interactive devices to their lecture groups, and explained the process that would take place during lectures. Students were assured that any information that they might provide relating to their personal background and educational history would remain confidential.

Students in each of the lecture groups were introduced to this lecturing strategy that required student input and feedback to a greater degree. The students showed interest in the equipment, and the level of interaction that it allowed with only minimal direction.

Students provided the feedback requested of them, and participated in discussions with their peers. For the duration of this trial, students generally demonstrated that they were enjoying participating in lectures in this manner. Results from focus groups conducted at the end of this trial showed that students valued increased interaction during lectures, and indicated that their level of understanding had been greatly improved.

Lessons Learned

- Student participation enhances lecture delivery, and provides improved learning outcomes. From student interaction enabled by KEEpad interactive devices, lecturers are able to gain a much better insight into the students' level of understanding of lecture material. This enables lecturers to modify the sequence of lecture content to address student-learning needs.

- At the same time, students are engaged more fully with the lecture material, solving problems and answering questions either individually, or on the basis of discussion with peers. Student feedback from this project has shown that students believe they have a greater level of understanding of the lecture material from lectures where this strategy of increased interactivity is employed.

- Students are more comfortable answering questions anonymously with KEEpad wireless interactivity devices, and are more likely to respond to lecturers' questions than if required to answer orally.

- International students from a wide range of cultural backgrounds are more likely to interact within a large lecture class when using interactivity devices that allow them to answer anonymously.

- This type of educational technology can be a useful teaching and learning tool, both in undergraduate and postgraduate education, as shown by the above benefits both to lecturers and students.

- To further implement what we have started will need planning, professional development, and financial support. All change takes time, effort, and commitment.

- This trial indicated that the complexity involved in deployment of this lecturing strategy is much greater than our initial expectation. There is much room for further improvement.

Future Thoughts

This project demonstrated that KEEpad interactive wireless devices can be introduced into lectures with a successful result. Several of the issues that arose during this project are a result of the experimental conditions of this trial. Only one set of equipment was available, to be shared between a number of staff, delivering lectures within a busy teaching schedule.

A number of possible improvements have been identified, including the following:

- **Buying or renting hardware.** One possible approach is to install the wireless receivers and networking equipment required for the KEEpad system into a number of lecture theatres. This would substantially decrease the amount of work required to use this technology. At the same time, a major source of unreliability, equipment being set up hurriedly, with the possibility of incorrect connections and damage due to movement and constant handling, would be eliminated. Establishing specialist lecture theatres introduces timetable constraints, so one or more sets of equipment could also be made available for use in other lecture theatres.

- **Encouraging students to rent/buy/hire/borrow hardware.** A number of strategies could be used to ensure that students each have a KEEpad interactive wireless device. Strategies could be developed to allow students to rent, buy, or borrow a KEEpad interactive wireless device at the commencement of their study. Alternatively, such devices could be "bundled" with textbooks. Assistance programs could also be made available for students unable to afford one of these devices.

- **Develop a bank of concept questions for the School:** To encourage faculty and staff to adopt a teaching strategy incorporating increased interactivity, banks of concept questions appropriate for courses offered within the School could be developed.

- **Joint development projects between faculties:** Linking strategies might also be developed between faculties to develop software.

Acknowledgments

We would like to thank Robyn Lines and Cecily Walker for their involvement in this project, Ewan Wilson for his effort as our project mentor, and also Sally Bateman, and the technical support staff from her company, KEEpad. Finally we would like to thank Rosemary Chang for her support as the program leader. We are grateful for the funding support from our SET portfolio, and the support from our School.

References

Apple, D., Nygren, K., Williams, M., & Litynski, D. (2002). Distinguishing and evaluating levels of learning in engineering and technology instruction. *Proceedings of the 2002 Frontiers in Education Conference*, Boston.

Ballard, B., & Clanchy, J. (1997). *Teaching international students: A brief guide for lecturers and supervisors*. Deakin, Australia: ACT IDP Education.

Banks, D. (2003). Using keypad-based group process support systems to facilitate student reflection. In G. Crisp, D. Thiele, I. Scholten, S. Barker & J. Baron (Eds.), *Proceedings of the 20th Annual Conference of the Australasian Society for Computers in Learning in Tertiary Education (ASCILITE): Interact Integrate Impact,* Adelaide, SA (pp.37-46).

Bruno, M. (2002). *Student active learning in a large class setting.* Project Kaleidoscope, 2000 Summer Institute. Retrieved June 1, 2005, from http://www.pkal.org

Chan, S. (1999). The Chinese learner: A question of style. *Education and Training, 41*(6/7), 294-304.

Halpern, D., Hakel, & Milton (2003). Applying the science of learning in your teaching. *Change, 35*(4), 36-40.

KEEpad Australia. (n.d.). Retrieved June 1, 2005, from http://www.keepad.com

Mazur, E. (1997). *Peer instruction: A user's manual.* Englewood Cliffs, NJ: Prentice Hall.

McConnell, D., Steer, D., & Owens, K. (2003). Assessment and active learning strategies for introducing geology courses. *Journal of Geoscience Education, 51*(2), 205-216.

Nield, K. (2004). Questioning the myth of the Chinese learner. *International Journal of Contemporary Hospitality Management, 16*(3), 189-196.

Panitz, B. (1998). The 15-minute lecturer. *American Society for Engineering Education, 7*(6), 17.

Pearson, C., & Beasley, C. (1996, July 8-12). Facilitating the learning of international students: A collaborative approach. *Proceedings of the HERDSA Conference,* Perth, Western Australia.

RMIT (2003). Student feedback, top ten report. *RMIT Report.*

Rodrigues, C., Bu, N., & Min, B. (2000). Learners' training approach preference: National culture as a determinant. *Cross Cultural Management - An International Journal, 7*(1), 23-32.

Chapter XV

The Audience Response System:
A New Resource in Medical Education

Vivienne O'Connor, University of Queensland, Australia

Michele Groves, University of Queensland, Australia

Sandy Minck, University of Queensland, Australia

Abstract

There are general, educational benefits of audience response systems (ARS), although relatively little application (or evaluation) in medical education. We briefly review changes in medical education worldwide over the last two decades, highlighting areas in which new tools, such as ARS, are valuable. We evaluated an ARS for more than 300 first-year, graduate-entry medical students, used in four 2-hour educational sessions, summarising the benefits and limitations of the system.

Introduction

The recent, radical changes in medical education were stimulated by the demand for more doctors, increased community demands for accountability, the increasingly diverse demands of modern medical practice, and the exponential expansion of scientific and medical knowledge. For example, in the UK and Australia, there has been a significant expansion in both the number of medical schools and the number of medical students in existing schools.

In 1997, the University of Queensland introduced an integrated, 4-year, graduate-entry medical degree, "the MBBS Program," to overcome the limitations of its 6-year under-graduate-entry, traditional predecessor, which included:

- perceived deficiencies in preventive medicine and population health,

- didactic teaching discouraging active learning,

- basic sciences teaching (preclinical) disconnected from its application (clinical),

- limited encouragement to integrate and apply learning clinically,

- poor lifelong learning skills, and

- inadequate teaching of communication skills.

The new curriculum emphasises the parallel acquisition and integration of biomedical knowledge and clinical skills through problem-based learning (PBL) (The University of Queensland, 1995).

Now, teaching staff may be involved with teaching in all or any years of the course, instead of confined to a specific one. The lack of any increase in academic staff (indeed sometimes a decrease), together with increased small-group teaching, the integration of the curriculum, and the increase in student numbers, drove a search for innovative teaching and assessment. We also responded to student suggestions, one of which was for more formative assessment. The ARS was an efficient solution, once a question bank was developed.

Audience Response Systems
and Learning

Medical education at all levels (undergraduate, graduate and postgraduate) is shifting from the traditional model where the expert/teacher determines what is learned, and delivers it didactically, to a learner-focused interactive model (teaching adapted to the learner's needs). Questioning is an important mode of such learning (Thalheimer, 2003), especially if the learner processes the question, and participates in the learning activity. Those motivated to answer questions are more likely to learn than those not (Frase, 1971; Frase, Patrick, & Schumer, 1970). This ability to transform a lecture to interactive learning makes ARS effective (Copeland, Longworth, Hewson, & Stoller, 2000; Homme, Asay, & Morgenstern, 2004; Miller, Ashar, & Getz, 2003; Nasmith & Steinert, 2001; Turpin 2003), increasing attendance by 50% (Homme et al., 2004) and enhancing participant's attention and enjoyment (Homme et al., 2004; Latessa & Mouw, 2005; Miller et al., 2003; Uhari, Renko, & Soini, 2003). Nearly all participants formally commit an answer to the keypad: probably more than paper-based or hand-raising polling methods (Homme et al., 2004). However, it is less clear that this results in better knowledge retention in medical education, the evidence being limited and conflicting: a prospective crossover study of postgraduate medical trainees (between ARS interactive and traditional lecture) found an improvement in learning (postlecture quiz) for ARS (Schackow, Chavez, Loya, & Friedman, 2004). The effect was durable at 1 month, with factual retention in those attending the ARS lecture still surpassing those at the basic lecture. Conversely, a randomised, controlled trial (RCT) of participants in clinical round tables showed no increase in knowledge between the ARS intervention and control groups (Miller et al., 2003), although the process measures (quality of the presentation and speaker, and the level of attention) rated more highly for the ARS participants. An evaluation of 15 clinical meetings in which 40-50 postgraduate, internal, medicine trainees found ARS improved their convergence in answering evidence-based medicine questions, and significantly changed their proposed management of a patient after presentation of the evidence. They allow instant assessment of the quality of the clinical question, and the degree of uncertainty among the audience (Eggert, West, & Thomas, 2004). Asking multiple rather than single questions on a single learning point improved learning results by 29% (Boyd 1973). The importance of feedback in producing learning benefits has been shown several times (Bangert-Drowns, Kulik, Kulik, & Morgan, 1991), and these are sometimes huge, especially when corrective feedback is provided for incorrect answers (Guthrie, 1971).

The anonymity and confidentiality of the ARS encourages participation and honest answers, especially important in sensitive or controversial areas such as reproductive health to teenagers (Winsor, Case, Kwon, & Reid, 1999).

Medical Education Today

Medical Knowledge

Medical information has expanded exponentially. It is no longer possible for a medical student to graduate with a "total knowledge" of medicine. For decades, medical programs have produced undifferentiated graduates with broad medical knowledge who then specialise with additional training in their chosen field. But more than that, today's medical graduate needs a knowledge of the principles of health and disease, clinical skills, and especially, the ability to look for, evaluate, and utilise new information, and a lifelong commitment to continuing education.

Access To Patients

Student access to patients for clinical learning is reduced by much shorter hospital stays, and early discharge from the hospital. A greater use of alternatives includes patients in the community, and the presentation to students of visual patient experiences.

Changing Community Attitudes and Expectations

The most important change in community is that of improved communication. In addition, patients themselves are better informed, and demanding a greater role in decisions affecting them, (Muir Gray, 2002). Recent qualitative research has classified "professionalism" into three themes: interpersonal, public, and intrapersonal (Van de Camp, Vernooij-Dassen, Grol, & Bottema, 2004). Each requires rising standards of professionalism, emphasising accountability and cost-effectiveness (in diagnosis as well as treatment) in both medical practice and education (Murray, Gruppen, Catton, Hays, & Woolliscroft, 2000; Winkens & Dinant, 2002).

Clinical Reasoning

The major objectives in the majority of medical consultations are to determine the nature of the patient's complaint (diagnosis) and to formulate a plan (treatment). Diagnosis requires two interrelated masteries: clinical knowledge and clinical reasoning. Clinical reasoning is the cognitive process that analyses and interprets data to enable a diagnosis and treatment decision (Barrows & Tamblyn, 1980). It involves the synthesis and integration of information about the patient, with the doctor's knowledge and experience (Newble, Norman, & van der Vleuten, 2000). A major innovation of modern medical curricula is the nurturing of clinical reasoning skills through formal tuition, role-modelling on experienced clinicians, and formative and summative assessment.

Medical Error

Safety in clinical practice is emerging as a very serious public and professional concern (Wilson & Sheikh, 2002). The main areas are diagnosis, prescribing, communication, and organisational change. Diagnostic errors can be improved by an understanding of the uncertainty inherent in medical practice, and better clinical reasoning. Improved training and assessment in the area of drug interaction and prescribing can minimise error, and the ARS could be utilised for this.

Pedagogy of PBL

PBL was first introduced at McMaster University's medical school 40 years ago in response to concerns about the level of applied knowledge displayed by students graduating from the existing didactic, discipline-based course, and differs fundamentally from conventional forms of teaching (see Table 1).

PBL is grounded in adult-learning theory, and conforms to the constructivist model of education. It is based on six principles important for effective learning (Schmidt, 1993):

Table 1. Comparison of conventional teaching and PBL

Conventional teaching	Problem-based learning
1. Content is identified and structured explicitly by a teacher as a series of topics	1. Content is identified implicitly and communicated as learning objectives and by problems
2. Content boundaries are set explicitly by the teacher	2. Students set boundaries by identifying their own learning objectives although overall objectives are set for them
3. Teaching learning progresses from transfer of information +/or knowledge to application	3. Identifying information, knowledge, understanding is more closely connected with using it
4. Problems, scenarios, case studies are mostly used to illustrate theories, methods, techniques	4. Problems are at the heart of learning and knowledge is identified and used to provide solutions
5. Problems are often 'closed', routine and limited to a particular theory, method or technique	5. Problems are open-ended, fuzzy, not clearly defined and simulate real-life situations

1. Prior knowledge is the most important determinant both of the amount of new information that can be processed, and the quality of the processing (i.e., the depth of understanding).

2. For processing to begin, this prior knowledge must be activated by cues in the context of which the information is being studied.

3. Activation is dependent on the way knowledge is structured in memory, and this determines its accessibility and availability for use. Knowledge is organised as conceptual networks connected by links which specify the relationship between concepts (causal, temporal, conditional, etc.) (Patel & Groen, 1986). It is the size and complexity of a network that determines the depth and accuracy of understanding.

4. Knowledge networks develop through an elaborative process that is part of active learning. Elaboration is the construction of new associations or links between concepts where none previously existed. The creation of these new links increases the number of ways knowledge can be activated, and therefore, enhances understanding (Anderson & Reder, 1979)

5. Activating knowledge stored in long-term memory, and its retrieval, depends on contextual cues. Incidental information about the context in which knowledge is learnt is stored in long-term memory at the same time as intentionally-learned information (Godden & Baddeley, 1975). Learning, then, is most effective if it takes place in the context in which it will be applied.

6. Motivation to learn increases study time, and therefore, achievement. Two types of motivation have been described, extrinsic (such as fear of failure), and intrinsic (natural or epistemic curiosity). Epistemic curiosity is more likely to produce deep learning, and moreover, is stimulated by group discussion, where existing ideas are challenged and clarified (Johnson & Johnson, 1979; Lowry & Johnson, 1981).

PBL in medical education aims to achieve several important cognitive effects: enhanced problem-solving skills, increased acquisition, retention and use of knowledge, integration of basic science and clinical knowledge, the development of self-directed learning skills, and enhancement of any intrinsic interest in the subject matter (Barrows & Tamblyn, 1980; Norman & Schmidt, 1992; Dolmans & Schmidt, 1996).

The PBL cases in the MBBS program mirror, as closely as possible, typical medical consultations whose broad objectives are to reach a diagnosis, and make associated treatment decisions. The have two components: the acquisition of knowledge that can be applied appropriately; and the development of clinical reasoning skills sufficient to integrate this knowledge, apply it to the case, and solve the patient's problem.

PBL cases are presented sequentially, revealing a series of triggers corresponding to the patient's presentation, history, physical examination, and investigations (laboratory tests, x-rays, and so on). Tutors facilitate the small, group discussion and independent learning. Resources such as lectures, tutorials, practical laboratory sessions, and an extensive clinical skills program support the specific clinical area of the case.

The Audience Response System Pilot Studies

We tested the use of the 'KEEpad©' ARS in the first year of the medical course in large-group clinical symposia. These were introduced to illustrate the importance of basic science to clinical practice, and of modelling expert clinical reasoning, and held at the end of each "block" of learning (for example, the respiratory system). They extend and develop topics of interest from the preceding PBL cases, and are conducted (in similar fashion to a hypothetical) over 2 hours with a chairperson and a panel of four or five academic staff, experts in a relevant discipline, to provide immediate feedback, explanation, and expert opinion about the clinical issues emerging (Table 2). These symposia are highly interactive, and therefore popular, both students and panel encouraged to question, and discuss issues.

We undertook an evaluation of this application of ARS with about 300 students in three case-based sessions. A final session was held, covering learning areas throughout the year, *without an expert panel present*, with its answers and specific feedback provided given on the Web.

Constructing the ARS Questions

An important requirement for successful and enjoyable application of ARS is the construction of high quality questions that address the learning objectives. Companies supplying the ARS often provide excellent, common-sense resources on the theory of designing effective questions, and information on their use with the ARS, and there are other independent resources (University of Columbia, 2004; Robertson, 2000). However,

Table 2. Audience response system evaluation

Symposium	PBL Case	Panel Members
1	Chest pain	Cardiologist, general practitioner, emergency medicine physician, anatomist, pharmacologist
2	Asthma	Respiratory physician, general practitioner, pharmacologist, adolescent psychologist
3	Domestic violence/teenage suicide	Psychiatrist, pharmacologist, emergency medicine physician, general practitioner
4	none (whole year)	none (feedback available on the EWeb)

a great deal of preparation is required before a session, which should be planned, and with the chair and panel, well before (see Appendix) to allow agreement on the main learning outcomes, and minor problems, such as question ambiguity, to be eliminated. This does not mean that a rigid session structure is required: changes on the day are welcome and easily accommodated, provided both chairman and panel are confident and familiar with their material.

The ARS Session Format

Individual keypads were distributed to the students as they entered the lecture theatre. The name of each student was recorded against the number on each keypad to reduce loss, as well as track individual responses. A few introductory slides were shown to explain how the system worked, check that it was performing correctly, trial some basic questions, and gather demographic data from the group (Figures 1 and 2).

The chairperson then introduced the PBL case and the first "trigger," and asked the panel to comment on the presenting patient symptoms (Figures 3 and 4).

As new information is introduced, questions are given to the students, along with a number of possible responses. The students are given 30 seconds to answer on the keypad, and a graph of all the responses to each answer is displayed on a screen. Different types of questions were used to evaluate a range of learning activities.

Assessment of Knowledge

Simple, factual knowledge is the easiest type of question to produce (Figures 5 and 6). The immediate display of results allows students to see whether or not their response is in line with that of their peers. The expert panel commented on each of the possible answers, with an explanation of facts that contributed to a correct or incorrect response, giving the students the scientific information behind the answers.

Figure 1. Example of the demographics of the group using a bar graph to display the results

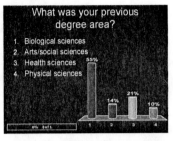

Figure 2. General question using a pie chart to display the results

Figure 3. Case presentation — video demonstrating laboured breathing

Figure 4. First 'trigger' of information

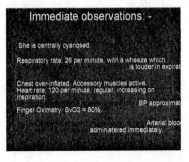

Further information can then be given about the case, the scenario progressed, and further questions asked (Figures 7 and 8).

Alternatively, the students can be asked a question first, and then tested. For example, the students were asked if they all understood the procedure of spirometry (used to test respiratory function), and whether they had any questions they would like answered. After a few simple questions, the students were then given an ARS question to answer. This demonstrated that, even though the students thought that they understood the procedure, there was some confusion (Figures 9 and 10).

Misinformation

The unique combination of the ARS and an expert panel to provide feedback and answer queries meant that not only were students who did not know the answer able to learn,

Figure 5. Example of a simple question

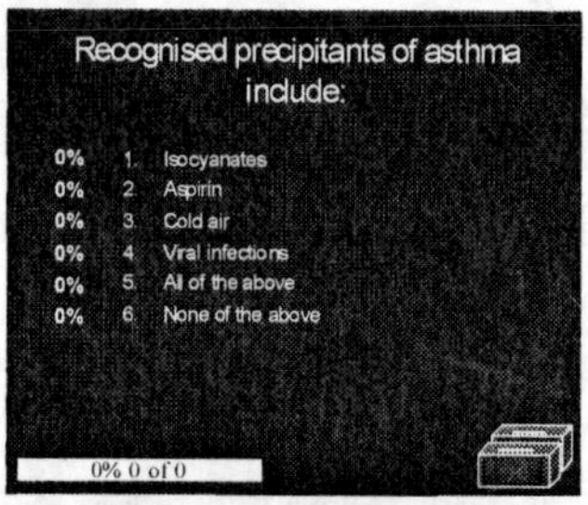

Figure 6. Response to question

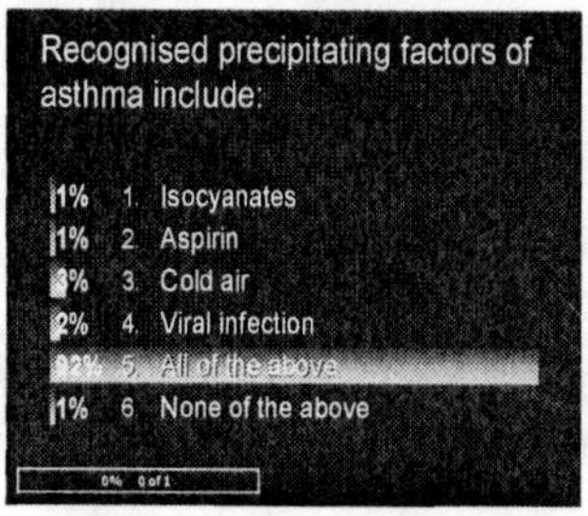

Figure 7. Immediate management

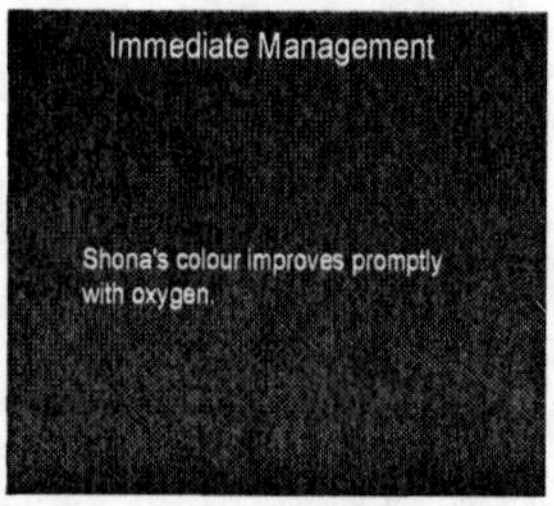

Figure 8. Which of the following is false?

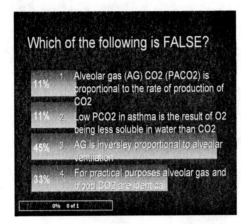

Figure 9. Students were asked if they had any questions on spirometry

Figure 10. The response indicated that there were indeed some misunderstandings

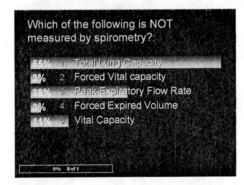

but students who had misinformation were able to correct themselves. This was demonstrated by asking the same question before and after discussion (Figures 11, 12).

Clinical Reasoning

Clinical reasoning could be assessed by giving students clinical scenarios (Appendix 1), and asking for the most likely diagnosis from a list. Responses were discussed with the panel (Box 9). The presence of both general practitioners and specialists on the panel highlighted the fact that the most likely diagnosis would vary according to the context. If the scenario was set in general practice, the diagnosis of a given presentation may be different to that in the accident and emergency unit, due to differences in the range and nature of problems encountered in these different settings (Figures 13 and 14). Discussion followed that illustrated how clinical reasoning was changed by the context and acuteness of the presentation.

Medical Errors

Prescription errors include use of inappropriate drugs or dosage, inadequate consideration of common side effects, and ignorance of essential information about the action of drugs. The ARS provides a system whereby students' knowledge about drugs, their dosage, and side effects, can be improved by questions with a series of options to answer (Figure 15).

Figure 11. Responses before discussion

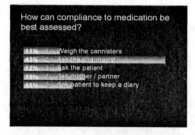

Figure 12. Responses after discussion

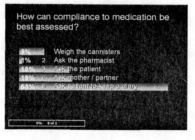

Figure 13. Clinical reasoning

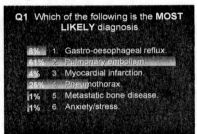

Figure 14. Clinical reasoning

> **Q2** Which of the following is the **MOST LIKELY** diagnosis
>
> 41% 1. Gastro-oesophageal reflux.
> 1%   2. Pulmonary embolism.
> 4%   3. Myocardial infarction.
> 0%   4. Pneumothorax.
> 54% 5. Metastatic bone disease.
> 1%   6. Anxiety/stress.

Figure 15. Which of the following statements are true re bronchodilators?

> **Which of the following statements regarding bronchodilator drugs is FALSE?**
>
> 10% 1. Salbutamol decreases c-AMP levels to relax bronchial smooth muscle
> 23% 2. Nebulised ipratropium causes marked systemic antimuscarinic side effects such as a dry mouth
> 35% 3. Ipratropium is a selective antagonist of the M3 muscarinic receptors in the airways
> 7%   4. The delay in the bronchodilator effect of salbutamol can be avoided by giving it with ipratropium
> 25% 5. Montelukast is a competitive antagonist at the receptor for cycsteinyl leukotrienes

Ethical Issues

Questions of an ethical nature — where no one right answer is evident — are common in clinical practice. These often both produced a range of responses, and stimulated the greatest debate. We found that an open question about the clinician's role, where domestic violence was disclosed, stimulated little response. However, when this was followed by an ARS question that required students to decide on a specific course of

Figure 16. ARS on domestic violence

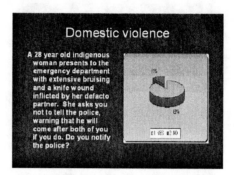

action, there was enormous discussion stimulated, with a variety of opinions voiced (Figure 16).

This allowed all students — including those with an extreme view at either end of the spectrum — to hear all the arguments and evidence. Adequate time is important, not only for the audience to formulate their response, but to allow the ensuing discussion to cover key points learning objectives.

Use of Supporting Materials, For Example, Pathology or Results of Investigations

Clinical photos, pathology slides, or video-clips of patients (for example, an unusual gait), or procedure (Figures 17 and 18) can be interspersed within the session to maintain interest, add new information, or reinforce existing knowledge. They can also be used to demonstrate a particular disease or test that would otherwise not be seen, and this can then be followed by questions related to the condition or procedure.

Figure 17. Pathology of a myocardial video clip

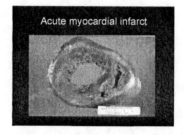

Figure 18. Illustration of a procedure with an infarction

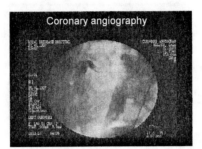

Figure 19. Question on asthma

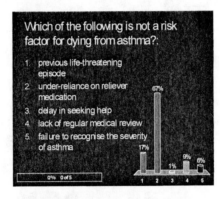

Figure 20. Example of information from research

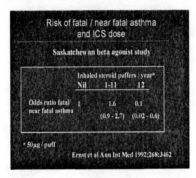

Evidence Based Practice

The ability to search, evaluate, and utilise information from the research literature can be shown to influence clinical practice. For example, after posing a question about asthma and the students have responded, information from the research literature can be used to indicate the value of applying research to clinical practice (Figures 19 and 20).

Retention of Knowledge

Symposia were held about monthly for 3 months. The final revision session (with answers placed on a Web site) included some questions already used previously. Corrected information was retained by the students over the period of 1-3 months. A largely incorrect answer at the first session, corrected by the expert panel, remained correct 6 weeks later when re-tested, Figures 21 and 22.

Discussion

The Benefits of the ARS

Benefits for both staff and students can be broadly categorised as follows (Table 3):

1.   **Immediate feedback**

The provision of an immediate answer to a question, with expert feedback, clearly improves student knowledge, corrects misinformation, and enables students to

Figure 21. Responses at initial session

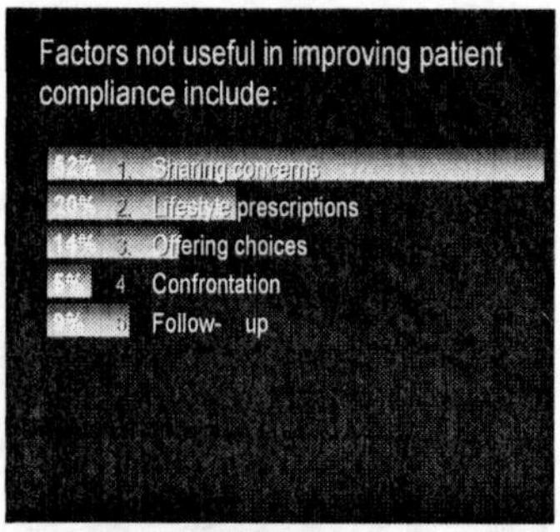

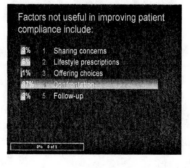

Figure 22. Responses to same question 6 weeks later

Table 3. Benefits of the ARS

1. Immediate feedback	
To students on	
	o Their knowledge
	o Peer comparison
	o Clarification of misconceptions / incorrect information
To staff on:	
	o The effectiveness of the learning resources
	o The quality of the assessment
	o Identification of areas requiring more teaching effort
2. Interactivity	
	o Highlights clinical relevance of the material
	o Focuses on essential points
3. Cost-effectiveness	
	o Managing/assessment a large group
	o Cost saving with marking
	o Time saving for student feedback
	o Cover knowledge of multiple disciplines over a short time period

compare their responses with their peers. Staff benefit: they get direct feedback of the effectiveness of their teaching; identify areas that require additional resources; and receive evaluation about assessment questions. The presence of staff from both basic sciences and clinical areas encourages interaction.

2. **Interactivity**

Areas where students miss issues (such as investigating and prescribing) are immediately identified, redressed, and rechecked. These are also areas of error and overuse (overtreatment and overinvestigation). Again, ARSs can identify them.

Clinical reasoning can be stimulated by presenting different, clinical scenarios for the same, differential diagnoses. Asking the students for the most likely diagnosis, followed by panel discussion of the options, illustrates different approaches of clinicians in different clinical settings. For example, a general practitioner (GP) faced with a patient with chest pain has a different differential diagnosis list to the cardiologist, who sees a range of patients already triaged by a GP.

3. **Cost-effectiveness and efficiency**

The ARS is cost-effective: it covers a wide range of subject matter to many students relatively quickly; time is saved from marking, and utilised in the construction of the "perfect" question bank because the results of the session are automatically generated (and can even be related to individual students).

Limitations of the ARS

The Format

PowerPoint™ presentation limits the amount of information that can be given in both questions and answers. The first of Robertson's 12 tips (keep questions short to optimise legibility) (Robertson, 2000) can be difficult to achieve with complex, case-based scenarios. Yet it is these that challenge the students the most, not only by highlighting deficiencies or misinformation in knowledge, but in demonstrating the difference between theory and practice (i.e., what the textbooks say you should do, vs. what is actually done in practice), and the often "grey" nature of medicine, where there is not always one correct answer. The "not enough room on the slide" problem can be overcome by using two screens (two data projectors or acetate film), one providing case information, and the other the questions (and answers).

Anonymity

Some students were concerned about anonymity. Perhaps improving their understanding of adult learning and formative assessment might allay these fears. Alternatively, results could be given individually for the students to monitor their own progress.

Writing a Good Question

To formulate appropriate, unambiguous questions takes time with ARSs, like any other form of assessment. A poorly constructed question that may have slipped through the presession meeting will be immediately exposed, and allow immediate redress. Over time, a bank of high-quality questions can be developed, as tutors become more adept.

Logistics

Setting-up time may be too long to fit in between lecture slots. The ideal arrangement is a permanently installed ARS, with students responsible for their own keypads.

Time

The establishment of an ARS in a course requires investment of time and effort by an enthusiastic core group in learning the necessary skills. For most of our sessions, it was difficult to get feedback from busy clinicians on the questions that the core group had developed earlier. Consequently, questions emerged as incorrect or confusing during the sessions. Nevertheless, this in itself stimulated useful discussion!

It is easy to overestimate the amount of information that can be covered in the allotted time, (Winsor et al., 1999), which itself can hardly go beyond 2 hours (for both the students' and staffs' attention span). Increased experience of the tutors, refinement of the format, and collection, over time, of an extensive bank of questions should mitigate this.

Evaluation

Students provided evaluation surveys after the sessions. Most reported that it enhanced interaction, they liked it, and would like to use it again (Table 4). At the end of the year, a brief survey was sent by e-mail evaluation to students and panel members. Sixty-eight answered every question, with two students answering no questions, but providing comments that are included with the others.

Positive Comments from Students

- The ARS provides some novelty which makes learning just a little more exciting. Having your knowledge assessed immediately is very helpful. Lots of fun!

- I have no problem with the system, it is good and does give us some questions from the school. However my only issue is when the clinicians are disagreeing with the school on those answers and therefore the dilemma of us being given wrong information.

Table 4. Evaluation of the ARS at the end of the first session (300 students) (1) and end of year responses (70 students) (2)

evaluation after first session = 1 after end of year = 2		Responses (%) 1 n = 300 2 n = 68				
Evaluation question		SA	A	N	D	SD
Enabled me to compare my	1	32	45	11	10	4
knowledge with that of my peers	2	39	54	6	1	0
Highlighted areas of	1	21	46	20	8	5
misinformation	2	20	54	14	7	1
(where I had unknowingly						
misunderstood)						
Brought to my attention my	1	18	56	12	9	5
knowledge deficits	2	13	69	13	4	1
The keypad and subsequent	1	51	30	11	3	5
discussion highlighted that there	2	44	37	14	1	3
is not always a single answer to						
a clinical problem						
The keypad enhanced	1	37	33	10	9	11
interaction	2	42	33	16	9	0
I would like to use the keypad	1	Yes 67			No 33	
system again	2	Yes 94			No 6	
Key: SA Strongly Agree, A Agree, N Neutral, D Disagree, SD Strongly Disagree						

- The AR system has a lot of potential, it is good for estimating the immediate effects of lecture content, with appropriate timed and worded questions concerning topics covered in the lecture.

- I thought it was an excellent system to keep you focused on the types of things we are meant to know. It is easy to get off track on a learning objective, or not to know the types of clinical applications we are meant to know. I felt that the keypad system and the associated quizzes were very beneficial in this way.

- There are a lot of misconceptions that are never addressed in medicine. It would be extremely useful to have such questions every week.

- It should be used as much as possible. It livens up the lecture, and is a great way to test students after the lecture. A quick 10 min ARS session in the middle or at the end of each lecture would definitely increase student interest and attendance at the lectures. It would also increase the "interactive learning," and I think many more students will be more interested in learning with the ARS.

- It's the best thing since PBL.

Negative Comments from Students

- Sometimes more time needs to be allowed for question reading and answering.

- I liked the idea behind ARS but if you're going to use it, we must have the time to discuss answers, and more importantly those questions that arouse debate.

- I found it very frustrating in the last revision session we had using ARS in that there was no one who could tell us the answer, and discuss why (which is what I have found is the biggest benefit in using ARS).

Overall, the students thought that the ARS had a place in medical education (Table 5). In general, the students favoured the use as a revision session. Students showed a preference for the sessions involving immediate feedback and discussion, compared to the final session, where they had to look at the answers on a Web site at a later time.

Table 5. Uses of the ARS in medical education — student responses

I think the ARS could be used for the following	Student responses, n (%)				
	Panel symposia	Lectures	Small groups	Revision sessions	Other practice exams
	59 (84)	21 (30)	11 (16)	63 (90)	1 (1) –

Table 6. Evaluation by the tutors

	Tutors responses, n (%)				
	Strongly agree	**Agree**	**Neutral**	**Disagree**	**Strongly Disagree**
1. Using the ARS brought attention to the students' knowledge deficits	3 (43)	4 (57)	0	0	0
2. The ARS enabled the students to compare their knowledge with that of their peers	6 (86)	1 (14)	0	0	0
3. The ARS highlighted areas of misinformation (where the students had unknowingly misunderstood)	2 (29)	5 (71)	0	0	0
4. The ARS and subsequent discussion highlighted that there is not always a single correct answer to a clinical problem	4 (57)	1 (14)	1 (14)	1 (14)	0
5. The ARS enhanced interaction	2 (29)	4 (57)	1 (14)	0	0
6. I enjoyed utilising the ARS	0	6 (86)	1 (14)	0	0
7. I would like to utilise the ARS again	Yes			No	
	7 (100)			0	
8. I think the ARS could be used for the following	Panel symposia	Lectures	Small Groups	Revision sessions	Other
	7 (100)	7 (100)	0	5 (71)	1 – Clinical reasoning

The tutors felt that the ARS was a valuable tool in medical education (Table 6). A few tutors commented that more time needed to be spent preparing good questions and checking that the wording was correct and not ambiguous.

The ARS in Medical Education

The ARS can enhance the students' learning experience in the following ways:

- expose and clarify students' misconceptions;
- differentiate between easier and more difficult concepts;
- promote interactivity and discussion in large group, case-based learning;

Table 7. Question: Have you used a key pad response system before today?

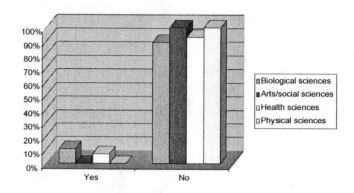

- elicit and discuss diverse points of view when there is no correct answer (e.g., ethical issues);

- administer an effective review session/mock exam (formative assessment);

- assess mastery of content;

- longitudinal monitoring of students, and the quality of teaching and resources;

- provide expert opinion — immediate or later;

- use for summative assessment;

- identification of individual students requiring additional assistance with their learning.

In the medical context, the ARS promotes discussion of contentious issues, and highlights the diversity of opinion and management in clinical practice. The immediate feedback provides an opportunity for deeper discussion of the evidence, and follow-up questions to clarify difficult concepts (Eggert et al., 2004). The value of instant feedback to both students and teachers is clear.

Although the anonymity is attractive, there are a number of advantages in being able to match the responses with individual students. We were able to cross-reference the answers with the demographic responses (Table 8). This is useful in looking at the impact of specific features (age, gender, previous training, or academic level) on the learning outcomes. In addition, by recording the same keypad number for an individual student with every session, it would be possible to track a student's progress. This would contribute to early identification of a student with a problem, and enable timely remediation to assist that student. By providing the cohort responses to all students, individuals would be encouraged to take control of their own learning, and monitor their own progress with that of their peers.

Table 8.

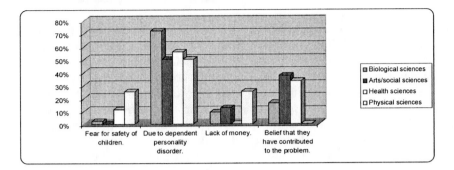

Future Use in a Medical Course

Future Educational Directions

Possible future educational directions include using the ARS to confidentially record responses to assessment. Focus could be on core topics (as indicators of the quality of learning), areas of expertise, and gaps in knowledge. Individual students could be monitored for early remediation. It could be used to vote on issues after brainstorming, or where there is controversy. The ARS also allows for "on the spot" questions to be asked that require a simple "yes/no" response to clarify points. It could be a useful tool not just for formative assessment, but also summative assessment, provided a method can be devised to prevent students looking at their colleagues' answers in the session!

Future Technical Directions

Future technical directions include the use of personal digital assistants (PDAs, also called hand-held computers) with "wireless Bluetooth cards" to allow access to a central server (Menon, Moffett, Enriquez, Martinez, Dev, & Grappone, 2004). Increasingly, medical students and physicians are using PDAs in their daily lives as reference tools, drug databases, and learning supplements (Moffett et al., 2003), as well as personal organisers. Use of wireless-enabled PDAs would enable the use of the techniques of the ARS system, that is, interaction, instant feedback and so forth, without the need for touch-pads, which are usable only for this single purpose.

Conclusions

Medical courses today need to maximise the use of new technology to enhance the teaching and learning of the increasing numbers of students, and to best utilise staff expertise. We found that the ARS may be a key component, important for adult learning, active participation (interactivity and commitment to an answer), timely feedback, correction of misconceptions, and highlighting key concepts by the "expert". This is accomplished in a nonthreatening, anonymous environment. In addition to knowledge, the ARS is useful for development of clinical reasoning, avoiding medical error, and exploring ethical issues. Further longitudinal studies are required, and these may highlight even more uses for this valuable resource, particularly in the area of clinical reasoning and prevention of medical error.

References

Anderson, J., & Reder, L. (1979). An elaborative processing explanation of depth of processing. In L. Cermak & F. Craik (Eds.), *Levels of processing in human memory* (pp. 524-586). Hillsdale, NJ: Lawrence Erlbaum.

Bangert-Downs, R. L., Kulik, C-L. C., Kulik, J. A., & Morgan, M. (1991). The instructional effect of feedback in test-like events. *Review of Educational Research, 61*(2), 213-238.

Barrows, H. S., & Tamblyn, R. M. (1980). *Problem-based learning: An approach to medical education.* New York: Springer Publishing.

Blandford, L. & Lockyer, J. (1995). Audience response systems and touch pad technology: their role in CME. *Journal of Continuing Education in the Health Professions, 15*(1), 52-57.

Borduas, F., Gagnon, R., Lacoursiere, Y., & Laprise, R. (2001). The longitudinal case study: From Schon's model to self-directed learning. *Journal of Continuing Education in the Health Professions, 21*(2), 103-109.

Boyd, W. M. (1973). Repeating questions in prose learning. *Journal of Educational Psychology, 64,* 31-38.

Copeland, H. L., Longworth, D .L., Hewson, M. G., & Stoller, J. K. (2000). Successful lecturing: A prospective study to validate attributes of the effective medical lecture. *Journal of General Internal Medicine, 15,* 366-371.

Copeland, H. L., Stoller, J. K., Hewson, A. G., & Longworth, D. L. (1998). Making the continuing medical education lecture effective. *Journal of Continuing Education in the Health Professions, 18,* 227-234.

Dolmans, D., & Schmidt, H. (1996). The advantages of problem-based curricula. *Postgraduate Medical Journal, 72*(851), 535-538.

Eggert, C. H., West, C. P., & Thomas, K.G. (2004). Impact of an audience response system. *Medical Education, 38*(5), 576.

Frase, L. T. (1971). Effect of incentive variables and type of adjunct question upon text learning. *Journal of Educational Psychology, 65,* 371-375.

Frase, L. T., Patrick, E., and Schumer, H. (1970). Effect of question position and frequency upon learning from text under different levels of incentive. *Journal of Educational Psychology, 61,* 52-56.

Gagnon, R. J., & Thivierge, R. (1997). Evaluating touch pad technology. *Journal of Continuing Education in the Health Professions, 17,* 20-26.

Godden, D., & Baddeley, A. (1975). Contextual dependent memory in two natural environments. *British Journal of Psychology, 66,* 325-331.

Guthrie, J. T. (1971). Feedback and sentence learning. *Journal of Verbal Learning and Verbal Behavior, 10,* 23-28.

Homme, J., Asay, G., & Morgenstern, B. (2004). Utilisation of an audience response system. *Medical Education, 38*(5), 575.

Johnson, D., & Johnson, R. (1979). Conflict in the classroom: Controversy and learning. *Review of Educational Research, 49,* 51-69.

Latessa, R., & Mouw, D. (2005). Use of an audience response system to augment interactive learning. *Family Medicine, 37*(1), 12-14.

Lowry, N., & Johnson, D. (1981). Effects of controversy on epistemic curiosity, achievement and attitudes. *Journal of Social Psychology, 115,* 31-43.

Massen, C., Poulis, J., Robens, E., Gilbert, M. (1998). Physics lecturing with audience paced feedback. *American Journal of Physics, 66,* 436-441.

Mazur, E. (1996). *Peer instruction: A users manual.* Upper Saddle River, NJ: Prentice Hall

Mennin, S. P., Kalishman, S., Friedman, M., Pathak, D., & Snyder, J. (1996). A survey of graduates in practice from the University of New Mexico's conventional and community-oriented, problem-based tracks. *Academic Medicine, 71*(10), 1079-1089.

Menon, A. S., Moffett, S., Enriquez, M., Martinez, M. M., Dev, P., & Grappone, T. (2004). Audience response made easy: Using personal digital assistants as a classroom polling tool. *Journal of the American Medical Informatics Association, 11*(3), 217-20.

Miller, R. G., Ashar, B. H., & Getz, K. J. (2003). Evaluation of an audience response system for the continuing education of health professionals. *Journal of Continuing Education in the Health Professions, 23*(2), 109-115.

Moffett, S. E., Menon, A. S., Meites, E. M., Kush, S., Lin, E. Y., Grappone, T., et al. (2003). Preparing doctors for bedside computing. *The Lancet, 362*(9377), 86.

Muir Gray, J. A. (2002). *The resourceful patient.* Oxford: eRosetta Press Ltd.

Murray, E., Gruppen, L., Catton, P., Hays, R., & Woolliscroft, J. O. (2000). The accountability of clinical education: Its definition and assessment. *Medical Education, 34*(10), 871-879.

Nasmith, L., & Steinert, Y. (2001). The evaluation of a workshop to promote interactive learning. *Teaching and Learning in Medicine, 13*(1), 43-48.

Norman, G. R., & Schmidt, N. (1992). The psychological basis of problem-based learning: A review of the evidence. *Academic Medicine, 67,* 557-565.

Patel, V. L., & Groen, G. J. (1986). Knowledge-based solution strategies in medical reasoning. *Cognitive Science, 10,* 91-116.

Robertson, L. J. (2000). Twelve tips for using a computerised interactive audience response system. *Medical Teacher, 22*(3), 237-239.

Samuelowicz, K. (2004). PBL versus conventional teaching. (personal communication)

Schackow, T. E., Chavez, M., Loya, L., & Friedman, M. (2004). Audience response system: Effect on learning in family medicine residents. *Family Medicine, 36*(7), 496-504.

Schmidt, H. G. (1993). Foundations of problem-based learning: Some explanatory notes. *Medical Education, 27*(5), 422-432.

Thalheimer, W. (2003). *The learning benefits of questions. A work learning research publication.* Retrieved from http://www.work-learning.com

Turpin, D. L. (2003). Enhance learning with an audience response system. *American Journal Of Orthodontics And Dentofacial Orthopedics, 124*(6), 607.

Uhari, M., Renko, M., & Soini, H. (2003). Experiences of using an interactive audience response system in lectures. *BMC Medical Education, 3*(12). Retrieved from http://www.biomedcentral.com/1472-6920/3/12

University of Columbia, Center for Education Research and Evaluation (n.d.). *Effective use of the audience response system: A primer.* Retrieved from http://library.cpmc.columbia.edu/cere/web/facultyDev/ARS_handout_2004_tipsheet.pdf

The University of Queensland, Faculty of Medicine. (1995). *The Graduate Medical Course Curriculum.*

Van de Camp, K., Vernooij-Dassen, M. J. F. J., Grol, R. P. T. M., & Bottema, B. J. A. M. (2004). How to conceptualize professionalism: A qualitative study. *Medical Teacher, 26*(8), 696-702.

Wilson, T., & Sheikh, A. (2002). Enhancing public safety in primary care. *British Medical Journal, 324,* 584-587.

Winkens, R., & Dinant, G. J. (2002). Rational, cost effective use of investigations in clinical practice. *British Medical Journal, 324,* 783-785.

Winsor, S. H., Case, A. M., Kwon, J. S., & Reid, R. L. (1999). Touch-pad technology: Immediate feedback for resident educators in teenage reproductive health. *Obstetrics and Gynecology, 93*(5, Part 1), 790-794.

Appendix

"Choreography" of a Symposium Session

Tutorial 1 Chest Pain: Trigger 1
PRESENTING COMPLAINT   Ralph M., age 53, awakes at 5.40 a.m. with chest pain.
PANEL DISCUSSION   **STUDENT QUESTIONS**

For the Panel   *Discussion points:*
- Structures in chest that can cause pain
- Pain pathways
- Age and chest pain
- Characteristic features of pain
- Length of history of pain

Tutorial 1 : Trigger 2
HISTORY OF PRESENTING COMPLAINT (on overhead)
Ralph was driven by his wife to Accident and Emergency half an hour later. At first he insists that his pain is just bad indigestion.
The pain is a dull, crushing ache in the centre of his chest, extending up into his neck. It awoke him 30 minutes ago, and has been constant. He is sweaty and short of breath, but is not coughing or wheezing. He denies any palpitations. He is becoming increasingly anxious, and is soon telling the A&E staff that he feels like he is going to die.
Ralph says that he had similar pain the previous evening after dinner, but it was not as bad, and had passed with rest and antacids. When he woke with it this morning, he took some antacid and a glass of milk, but the pain was not relieved.

DIFFERENTIAL DIAGNOSIS OF CHEST PAIN
Aim: Students should be familiar with structures in the chest that can cause pain. This series of Qs aims to determine if they are able to identify common causes of chest pain based on history.
Please note that with these cases, we are aiming for one diagnosis that is significantly more likely than others, although some ambiguity can be used as discussion points:

For the students   *Clinical reasoning: Consider the following diagnoses*
1   Gastro-oesophageal reflux
2   Pulmonary embolism
3   Pneumothorax
4   Metastatic bone disease
5   Anxiety/stress
For each of the following case scenarios, indicate what you believe would be the **MOST LIKELY** diagnosis

---

Q 1   Ann is a 35-year old international travel consultant returning from a "bonus" trip to the USA following her recent promotion. She is fit, and takes the oral contraceptive pill to control her periods. Ann smokes 15 cigarettes a day. She presents to the Accident and Emergency unit of the local hospital, and complains that since walking back from lunch with her boss, she has a sharp pain in the left side of the chest, worse on breathing in, and a productive, irritating cough of recent onset

---

Q 2   Michael, aged 63 years, is a labourer on a property at St George. Michael had recently visited Brisbane for an endoscopy to investigate a one-year history of weight loss and anorexia. He had just been into town, and had a curry and a few beers with the "boys". He visits the general practitioner, and complains of a sudden onset of severe pain in the left side of the chest and into the thoracic spine. On questioning, he has had a nagging pain on and off in the same area for the last 6 months.

Panel discussion on clinical reasoning leading to each diagnosis

---

Chapter XVI

Learning and Anxiety:
Exploring Individual Judgement Processes in a Learning Environment with a Group Support System

Sam Groves, University of Glamorgan, UK

Tony Gear, University of Glamorgan, UK

Cath Jones, University of Glamorgan, UK

Michael Connolly, University of Glamorgan, UK

Martin Read, University of Portsmouth, UK

Abstract

This chapter explores the process of making individual judgements within a group meeting environment that employs a "low-impact" form of group support, based on handset technology. A series of field-based case studies are reported in summary, and one in postgraduate education in more detail. These serve to demonstrate the potential for suitably designed group support systems (GSSs) to aid groups to overcome certain fundamental difficulties with which they have to contend. The protocol used is described, and a conceptual framework is proposed with which to explain practice. The framework centres on the encouragement of conversation that is focussed on the reasons for differences, coupled with the reduction of personal anxiety, achieved with flexibility offered through the GSS meeting environment.

Introduction

A broad spectrum of group-decision (or process) support technologies (or systems) has been developed since the early 1980s, which is referred to using the generic term, group support system.Most of these GSSs utilise some form of network of room-based computers, wherein each member of the group uses an individual workstation. Research has shown that these systems may be extremely useful to brainstorm ideas and help support the group process (Nunamaker, 1997; Nunamaker, Dennis, Valacich, Vogel, & George, 1991).

We have developed a more portable GSS that makes use of a wireless handset approach in order to maintain face-to-face interactions, augmented by the additional channel of communication provided by the technology, known as Teamworker (Gear & Read, 1993). Each member of a group is provided with a wireless handset. This comprises a 0-9 numeric keypad, styled to mimic a telephone layout. We term this type of system as a "low-impact" GSS, because the technology has a lower profile within the group when compared to networked systems, and focus is maintained on a single, group screen. The difference in technology between networked systems and "low-impact" type systems, and the resulting differences in the group process, means that results of studies with the former, cannot, necessarily, be transferred to the latter.

At appropriate points of a meeting, a group member can enter their judgement, vote, or opinion on an issue, by pressing a key on their handset. The messages are all received at a single, personal computer running selected software for the meeting type. The computer is linked to a large screen in order to display the set of judgements that have been entered back to the group, in various graphical formats. Typically, this feedback might be a histogram showing the range and distribution of inputs, while maintaining personal anonymity. The handsets can be used to enter a range of judgement types, including scoring, voting, or comparing options; assessing parameters such as risk; and assessing feelings or emotions.

This "low-impact" GSS is designed to overcome emotional barriers to the use of technology, whilst maintaining face-to-face communication, aided by a single, group screen. The chapter is aimed at extending existing theory, stemming from observations of a series of field applications using this GSS design. One educational application, the use of business cases with postgraduate business students, is developed briefly. We introduce a conceptual framework that builds on ideas that seek to explain how a "low-impact" GSS environment can enhance individual and group learning in face-to-face group sessions.

The perspective adopted proposes that a group of individuals working on a task can learn (develop or change their beliefs, ideas, etc.) by exploring the reasons for differences of opinion in conversation, provided each member is able to express their feelings without inhibition from the social pressures that such a process may produce. In other words, the anonymity provided by the GSS environment enables participants to express their view without the risk of being publicly undermined. When making personal judgements in a less "risky" environment, learning, or taking on new ideas and changing opinions, may be more likely to occur without jeopardising one's standing within the group.

GSS Group Processes

In an influential review of GSS group processes by Nunamaker (1997), it was noted that the last two decades of research had established the improved productivity of GSS groups compared to those without technological support. In a comparison of a number of field studies from around the world, it was found that a significant saving could be made in both labour costs, and time spent through the use of this intervention. The reasons for this saving were explained through the effect that GSS had on both reducing "process losses" and augmenting "process gains" (Nunamaker et al., 1991). *Process losses* describe the problems experienced by groups that produce a negative effect on the interaction and, consequently, the group outcome (e.g., free-riding, production blocking, evaluation apprehension, domination, etc.). *Process gains* refer to the qualities of group interaction that can enhance the process, and contribute positively to the group outcome (e.g., synergy, stimulation, learning, democratic involvement, etc.)

These issues have been addressed through the introduction of managed process techniques, such as Delphi Technique (Dalkey, 1969); and Nominal Group Technique (NGT) (Van de Ven & Delbecq, 1971). Nunamaker et al. (1991) and others since have also found that a GSS process employing forms of NGT effectively enhances the group process beyond manual process techniques, by reducing some process losses, and improving the potential for process gains, for example, Reagan-Cirincione, 1994. The group meeting scenario is often fundamentally described as comprising main *input* (resource) categories, including the participants, the place, the time, the task, and any technological process aids used by the group. These components operate together toward the group *outcome* by means of a central *process*. As previous research advises, it is within the process that we can find a description of the relationship between these inputs and outcomes. (See Figure 1- Gear, Read, & Minkes, 1996.)

However, Weingart (1997) commented that related management research rarely focuses on the intricacies of participant communication processes, but tends to reduce the procedure to input-output relationships, or more static measures of validity. Rohrbaugh (1989) agrees, stating that "Any assessment of the effectiveness of a group decision process … requires directing primary attention to the process itself, not to subsequent outcomes." Finlay (1998) makes the point that validation of a GSS has to involve the development and testing of a theory of process.

We contend that validation of GSS involves the development of explanatory theory, emerging from research of three aspects: the details of process, the perceptions of participants, and the value of outputs in a given context (Read, 2003).

The "Teamworker" GSS Process

"Teamworker" GSS is employed to facilitate a given group, providing a semistructured environment, allowing both focussed discussion and structured, individual responses to issues, in a face-to-face setting. The low-impact technology guides participants through sessions where a series of questions are presented, to which they respond (individually and anonymously) via the GSS. The process mimics the nominal group

Figure 1. GSS group meeting components (Gear, Read, & Minkes, 1996)

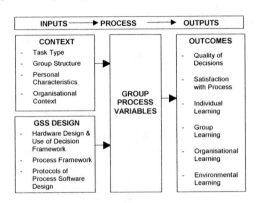

technique in that participants are able to discuss differences of opinions based on anonymous inputs. The following diagram (Figure 2) illustrates the stages of the GSS group process.

A question is presented to the group via the GSS, providing several options for participants to choose from. Each member is required to select the option that reflects their judgement via their individual handsets. The GSS displays the range and distribution of responses in histogram form (barchart) via a large, group screen. This stimulates a discussion that is focussed on the reasons for differences of opinion. During this group discussion, the participants are able to explore the various points of view, and assess their decision, in light of this interactive session. The question may be repeated via the GSS screen, and participants are shown the new histogram.

In the consensus-based decision environment, a face-to-face group discussion enables the exchange of important information, such as a review of relevant literature, presentations from experts, and the sharing of personal concerns. The use of this kind of "low-

Figure 2. Protocol of a typical "low-impact" GSS group process

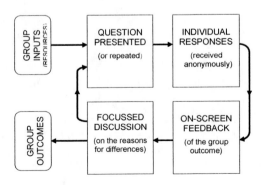

impact" GSS enables individual judgements to be made anonymously, in order to reduce personal anxieties that may affect a participant's ability to express their opinion in a group setting. It is proposed here that, by providing anonymous judgement conditions within a face-to-face group environment, participants can absorb and reflect on the information available, whilst feeling less anxious, and therefore, more able, to develop and express their personal judgements.

Social Influences

"Social influence" focuses on the idea that interpersonal processes can lead to changes in the beliefs, feelings, or behaviours of another person (Forsyth, 1995). However, these social influences can sometimes cause changes that may be detrimental to an individual's judgements. Whilst the main aims of forming workgroups may be to increase the number of ideas and perspectives that are brought to bear on the task, and to improve on the pool of knowledge used to provide background and weight to the judgements made, the group situation itself, and the idea of expressing oneself in public, may cause obstacles or distortions in the overall outcomes they produce.

The main aims of the GSS process, however, are to facilitate constructive, focussed discussion (the communication of expert knowledge, ideas, opinions, etc.); provide time for individual reflection; and reduce the biasing or destructive anxieties of working with others. Participating in a group can be a daunting experience, as various perspectives and levels of expertise, status, and power are present that may provoke a kind of "performance" or "judgement" anxiety in other members. When a person is required to communicate and express him/herself in a group situation, they may feel that their knowledge, opinions, ideas, and even their personal characteristics, are at risk of being brought into question or possibly undermined.

During a GSS process, there are periods of group discussion, interspersed with anonymous voting rounds, where individuals can express their view privately. Once a round of voting has taken place, and the range of opinions has been displayed, a discussion on the reasons for differences of opinion may bring some clarity to any conflict that may arise. However, if the discussion fails to reconcile these differences of opinion, each individual must make their decision based on their assessment of the information exchanged, and the rationalisation of their own views, during personal reflection.

In any face-to-face group situation where new or different ideas are presented that are contrary to the view held by one or more participants, the group outcome requires that each individual resolves this conflict, whilst in the confines of the group environment, when forming their final judgement. The apprehension of actively participating in this kind of environment may cause a distortion or biasing effect on the process of individual reflection.

Adverse social influences that can sway a person's judgement *toward change* may include being inhibited by an opposing expert or dominant opinion, or the persuasive power of a large opposing majority. Majority influence could be "adversely" influential to an anxious individual in a minority position. Moscovici (1980) argued that, whilst minority influence leads to true opinion change (conversion), majority influence produces agreement in public, but possible disagreement in private (compliance). Conversely, adverse influences *not to change* one's judgement may include a reluctance to change from a majority (popular) to a minority (unpopular) position; or a reluctance to express a change in one's opinion as it could be seen as a sign of weakness, no matter how well-founded the opposition's case may be. These outcomes are undesirable, and will *not* help to improve the quality of consensus decisions.

The danger is that a participant's decision could be influenced more by the fear of having their status/knowledge/personal characteristics undermined (e.g., selfpreservation), and less on what is best for the task at hand. The perception of risk to a person's standing in the group may lead to a voting position that is based on more subjective, less objective or altruistic, reasons. This could result in a reluctance to give up one's own opinion (leading to *no change* in judgement), or a reluctance to express a minority view (leading to either *staying with* or *moving to* the *majority*).

The framework developed below aims to explain how the GSS environment can assist in overcoming the anxieties of expressing individual opinions in a group situation.

Towards a Conceptual Framework for Individual and Collective Learning In a GSS Environment

The conceptual framework in this chapter is based on the interrelationships between anonymity, participation, anxiety, and learning in groups, focussing on the role of conversation, and surfacing differences of opinion as an aid to learning. This framework is developed in order to gain insights into the role and value of "low-profile" group support technology of the form described in this chapter. It may be useful to potential users of this type of technological intervention to share our experience of linking practice to a theoretical framework. This framework is based on three assumptions which are central to "conversational learning" (see Baker et al., 2002):

1. **Social learning:** Individual learning can occur as an outcome of a social rather than solely personal process.

2. **Learning and anxiety in groups:** Individual learning processes are mediated at critical moments by the level of unease, or perhaps anxiety, that is experienced by an individual in a group setting.

3. **Exploring differences in conversation:** Opportunities for individual learning can emerge naturally when groups of individuals are able to explore their reasons for differences of view related to an issue or task.

The overall statement that emerges from the above is that a group of individuals working on a task can learn with each other by exploring their reasons for differences of judgement in conversation, provided that the process is designed to limit the level of anxiety that such a process may invoke in each participant. This has been put, most eloquently, by Jensen and Kolb (2002): "If truth is to 'do its work' we need to create space that is hospitable and not filled with fear."

Social Learning

Our thinking is based on the proposition, put forward by Vygotsky (1978), that psychological processes (e.g., of thinking and learning) have to be explained as part of active collaboration and participation with the social environment. Vygotsky argued that states of consciousness cannot be explained by consciousness itself, but in the interaction between thinking people. That is, consciousness "arises, functions, and develops in the process of peoples' interaction with reality (Spirkin, 1983, p. 153). The interaction is with physical objects and tools, as well as with what has been termed "psychological tools" (Vygotsky 1978; Wertsch, 1985). These include a wide variety of metaphors and models, but most importantly, language, which serves to stimulate and mediate mental activity. Individual learning, from this perspective, concerns a personal process of working with, and internalising, the interactions of a public process, during which there has been an exchange of thoughts, ideas, and beliefs.

A detailed presentation of this theoretical perspective in relation to second-language learning, has been provided by Lantalf and Appel (1998). These ideas closely parallel that of the social psychologist George Herbert Mead, who stated from a pragmatic viewpoint "that mind can never find expression, and could never have come in to existence at all, except in terms of a social environment" (1972, p. 242).

"Learning and Anxiety" in Groups

Inevitably, individual learning implies a degree of unease, if not anxiety, with one's current condition. Learning involves the acquisition of knowledge, revised ways of thinking, and of learning how to learn. It may also involve relaxing, or rejecting, attachments to prior beliefs, knowledge, and ideas that have served well enough before.

The approach to learning proposed in this chapter is based on anonymised feedback of opinions and judgements, and reflection on them, which goes beyond a personalised process to a social perspective. This philosophy has been presented for example by Reynolds (1998), who has used the term "critical reflection" with key characteristics concerned with a questioning of existing assumptions, a focus on the group rather than on the individual, and a view that learning is facilitated by a democratically organised forum.

Each person in a learning group is likely to experience some degree of unease, if not anxiety, at key stages of the process. The material may be new, or it may be difficult to make a personal contribution to the conversation. In this situation, there are two basic courses of action open to each participant: towards learning, or towards an avoidance of learning. (see Vince and Martin, 1993, who develop this proposal in relation to organisational learning). Individual behaviours will be conditioned by personality traits, but the design of the learning opportunity has the potential to stimulate or stifle learning.

Exploring Differences in Conversation

In the last two sections, we presented a viewpoint that communication is material, and is central to our being and knowing. We assume that we are a species motivated towards learning, which is enacted through conversation. Our third assumption is that the emergence of "difference" is essential to learning (Wyss-Flamm, 2002, pp. 150-151). Exposure to difference(s) can stimulate the need to try to enter each other's minds, something for which conversation is crucial (Argyris & Schon, 1978). An awareness of "difference" has the potential to generate a conversation focused on the reasons for them. This awareness can lead to intrapersonal, as well as interpersonal processes, interacting with each other as the conversation progresses. However, returning to our earlier proposition concerned with "learning and anxiety," the quality of the conversational flow, in terms of its potential for learning, is likely to be strongly affected by feelings of anxiety. As Wyss-Flamm has put it "we would expect the level of psychological safety in the conversational space to set strong tone for conversational learning in a team."

The level of "personal safety" is likely to effect whether "the difference" is treated as an opportunity for learning or a flight from it. The design and process for the use of technology in support of learning, which we describe in this chapter, is aimed at the creation of a conversational space that is safe enough for risk taking behaviours to emerge so that differences can be worked with. An aim of our approach is to encourage the emergence of "dialogue" (Isaacs, 1993, p. 25). This form of conversation differs from "debate" (with perhaps an adversarial tendency), but instead encourages a collective and collaborative communication process, during which people can identify and explore their individual and collective assumptions, views, and beliefs, and probe into the reasons for them, as part of a mutual "learning and deciding" activity. Groves, Gear, and Read (2002) have reported an analysis of the quality of conversation in groups of health professionals utilising the teamworker design of GSS.

The GSS technology, in design as well as in mode of operation, has the potential to provide a "safe container" in which differences can be exposed and worked with, in an environment of reduced threat to each person (see also Rogers, 1970; Schein, 1993). The GSS that we describe in this chapter is designed to reduce the dialectical tensions that will be present.

The model shown in Figure 3 is an attempt to represent, visually, the complex relationships between anonymity, participation, and learning in groups supported by a "low-impact" GSS. Whilst the nature of GSS inputs provide a democratic platform (i.e., one person or one subgroup — one vote) it is important that individuals can share information effectively, so that each member can understand the issues, and the group can be more confident in the equal sharing of responsibility for the quality of process and, hence, the final outcome. The figure implies an environment provided by the GSS which is not static, but changing as a group session develops, and as the participants come to understand the nature of the process, and how to make effective use of it.

By providing judgemental phases in the group process that are anonymous, it is argued here that the personal risk of having one's judgement undermined (i.e., open to some degree of ridicule or "loss of face") is reduced. Figure 3 outlines the expected changes

Figure 3. Anonymity, participation and learning in GSS process

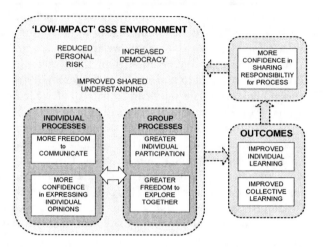

to the group process, as compared with more "normal" group processes, under these conditions.

As each member moves through the group process, the anonymity provided by the design can facilitate a less stressful environment for individuals to communicate within. When the results of an initial round of inputs have been displayed, discussion can focus on the reasons for differences of opinion. Without having to reveal individual judgements, a participant can experience *more freedom to communicate* with others, without jeopardising their personal standing in the group. This enables *greater participation* from individuals in the group discussions, encouraging greater *confidence in expressing individual opinions*, and aiding the group as a whole to *explore* the reasons for differences of opinion together.

The perceived improvements in the communication between participants during the anonymous GSS process should enhance the opportunities for *individual* and *group learning* and, ultimately, should improve the quality of the judgements made.

As the GSS process employs a democratic system of gathering judgements, the responsibility for the effectiveness of the process, and its outcomes, is divided equally between individual members at each stage of a group session. Advancements in individual and collective learning should improve the group's *confidence in sharing this responsibility* and, hence, for producing the most beneficial, or appropriate, group judgement. These help to improve the perceptions of democracy (or social equality), and the perceptions of a "safe" (less risky) environment for individual expression and communication as they move through subsequent issues.

A number of trials of this type of GSS have been carried out in classroom contexts (Gear and Read, 1993; Irving & Hunt, 1994; Jones, Connolly, Gear, & Read, 2001). The following section presents, briefly, an application of this approach with a group of postgraduate students as they explore and debate business cases. (A detailed description and analysis of this case study can be found in Jones, Connolly, Gear, & Read et al., 2005.)

Case Study: An Application in Postgraduate Education

Background

The focus of these trials has been to explore ways in which a "low-profile" GSS, used in conjunction with business cases, has the potential to improve the learning experience within a tutorial setting with postgraduate management students. The trials consisted of several classroom tutorial sessions, each of about 2 hours. The students were given the case material to study and analyse individually, and were asked to identify the strengths and weaknesses in the case. The trial sessions formed a part of the "normal" teaching programme. The aim was to produce a practical assessment of the use of the GSS in the classroom.

The "Teamworker" handsets were allocated either to individual students, or to small groups of about four students sitting around tables (one group, one handset). A set of questions was prepared for each session and exported into the software of the GSS. These "Likert" type statements, multiple-choice, and open ended "ad hoc" questions, were sometimes generated during the sessions. Sometimes, questions were repeated following discussion of differences. A set of 10 to 20 questions was found suitable for a 1- to 2-hour period.

One of the researchers was also the teacher, using the technology in order to guide the analysis and discussion of the case. The teacher, and the students themselves, were part of an "action research" activity in which the introduction of the technology represents an intervention into "normal" practice (McNiff, 1993). The sessions were evaluated in a number of ways in order to assess the process and its benefits/problems. These ways included nonparticipant observation, lecturer field notes, informal discussions with students, and a set of evaluation questions presented to the students at the end of each session.

Teacher Perceptions

From the teacher's point of view, the sessions were more positive and beneficial than sessions run in a more "conventional" way. The students were able to participate, and focussed discussion was generated easily in every trial. The feedback screen display of differences of opinion provided a focus for stimulating discussion. The "individual" and the "subgroup use" handset sessions produced high levels of conversation and involvement, and were far more dynamic than normal non-GSS supported tutorials. The allocation of handsets to subgroups was especially encouraging, as there was a high level of "within subgroup" as well as "plenary" level discussions of the reasons for differences of opinion, as well as discussion within subgroups regarding their choice of response to a question. A feature of the sessions was the extent to which the students "took over" and controlled the sessions for themselves. At times, the teacher needed to move things on in order to cover the material.

Student Perceptions

The students were asked to answer some reflective questions on their experience of the tutorial, and of the use of the new technology. The handsets were used for this purpose to encourage honesty of response, due to the anonymity. The questions covered a range of issues from general reactions to the tutorial to future use of the technology. All the students were positive about the sessions. They all reported finding the technology easy to use, and most students reported that they found it easier than usual to contribute to the conversations. All students agreed that the influence of dominant personalities was reduced, and felt that it would be useful to use the technology for other sessions involving the analysis of business cases.

Discussion of Case

This case description has presented the key themes that have emerged from using a GSS with postgraduate student groups. There was wider and more even student involvement, and a more focussed conversation than experienced at more traditionally run sessions. The anonymity provided by the technology appeared to lower the risk of exposure, and encourage conversation.

The trials show that interactive sessions of this type can be useful as a means of analysing business cases. Some students even suggested how the GSS could be used in their own work organisations. These included: feedback to management (e.g., suggestions for improvement to organisation), staff appraisal, analysing decisions, role-play for training, skills development, attitude surveys, and market research. The following section summarises some other areas where we have trialed applications of this type of GSS.

Other Applications in the Field

A number of other field-based applications and trials of a low-impact GSS are summarised here, in order to give some indication of the wide range of situations where a "low-impact" GSS may be able to augment the normal, meeting process (Gear, 1993; Read, 2003). All of these applications involve processes of "learning and deciding" in groups.

a.   **University-based education and training:** This concerned undergraduate teaching in a university-based Department of Pharmacy. The need was to ensure the development of professional skills when dealing with patients, and in accurate prescribing of appropriate drugs or medication for a given condition. This involved the relationship with the patient, in order to make a proper diagnosis and prescription decision.

b.   **Values and priorities in health care:** The organisation is a Primary Care group (PCG) in the London area. The PCG held a stakeholders' conference involving about 80 people, selected in order to represent a cross section of the local community. The conference was designed to achieve two objectives. Firstly, to establish a number of high-priority areas concerned with healthcare. Secondly, to agree on preferred approaches to how the local community could work with the PCG in order to implement solutions.

c.   **Group interactive learning:** The applications have taken place in the Business School at the University of Glamorgan. The online support has been trialed as an aid to the tutorial sessions where undergraduates and graduate students are analysing and discussing business case studies. The aim has been to produce a practical assessment of the use of "teamworking" in classroom sessions. In particular, the trials were aimed at assessing the degree to which the technology can assist teachers to overcome some of the problems that are commonly experienced in this situation. Typically, these are ensuring that all students become involved in the debate of issues surrounding a case, surfacing opinions, and facilitating debate that focuses on key aspects.

d.   **Development of consistency of professional judgement:** The application is concerned with the use of "Teamworker" for group, interactive learning for public-sector professionals, in order to develop greater consistency of application of a client assessment model. The organisations involved over 100 municipalities in Norway and Denmark. The assessment model judges each of 17 criteria of assessment, on a 4-point scale, where "1" represents complete independence of needing help, and "4" corresponds to complete dependence on help from others. A crucial aim of the approach is to develop consistency of use of the model in order to provide appropriate care on an equable basis in all regions.

e.   **Portfolio selection in commercial R&D:** The organisation is a multinational pharmaceutical group, with R&D laboratories collaborating with each other across sites in Europe and North America. The decision area is concerned with the selection of a preferred portfolio of projects to which to allocate scarce resources, especially manpower. A number of factors are taken into account in this process, including market potential, competition, stage in development, chances of technical success, therapeutic area balance, long- and short-term returns, resource constraints, and key resource availabilities. A series of meetings is held each year to decide the portfolio, and other review meetings are called at other times to decide changes.

f.   **Research proposal selection in a public body:** The organisation is a British Research Council. Committee-based decisions concerning the selection for funding of research proposals submitted by researchers in universities and polytechnics are considered by peer review. Committees of 15-25 members consider long lists of proposals in each of a number of scientific areas. The overall budget is predefined, but the precise apportionment of this figure between the scientific areas is deliberately left open when the committees meet.

g.   **Perceptions in retail marketing:** The organisation is a medium-sized retail chain selling a wide range of audio, video, and TV equipment, with a significant regional presence and image. In particular, it had achieved a pre-eminent position in terms of certain upmarket brands. It was thought by some store managers that prospective customers viewed the company as expensive and upmarket because the expensive brands were stocked and associated strongly with the chain. The management group were in disagreement as to how their other lower priced, mainly Japanese, brands were perceived by their customers, and how closely the chain's image related to these other brands.

h. **Option selection in defence:** The organisation is a research establishment within the UK Ministry of Defence. A set of seven options had been identified for a military system to meet a well-defined threat. A considerable amount of experimental- and simulation-based data was available. The criteria by which to judge the options were predefined.

i. **Analysis of key competencies and performance:** This application is located in the brewing industry. The chief executive had formulated a clear, vision statement for the business, and also established a set of 13, associated, key, task performance factors. These were the set of task abilities he expected in his key team of operational managers in order to achieve the vision. It was considered essential to assess the strengths and weaknesses of the key team of mangers, both individually, and as a whole.

j. **Long range planning:** The organisation is a large multinational manufacturing company in a high-technology business. Concern was expressed to ensure that the company was making wise, strategic decisions regarding technologies intended for commercial introduction and exploitation on 10-30 year future time frames.

k. **General practitioner workshops:** A series of studies are currently underway, involving groups of GPs, and other health professionals, in workshops that explore the diagnosis and treatment of a number of medical conditions. Topic areas include hypertension, depression, teenage pregnancy, and childhood asthma, with forthcoming sessions on the diagnosis and treatment of cancer. Comparisons are noted between established and *ad hoc* groups of varying sizes.

l. **Panel testing and tasting:** The organisation is a major brewer with a large range of beers and lagers at a number of dispersed sites. Production is tasted and tested by panels of experts on a daily basis. The objective is to identify, for each branded product, deviations in either direction from a defined product profile. The profile is based on 35 dimensions related to identifiable aspects of taste, appearance, and smell.

m. **Child protection conferences:** These child protection conferences bring together family members, the child where appropriate, a chairperson, and those professionals most closely involved with the child and family, which can include a social worker, youth worker, police representative, school or play-group representative, school nurse, and so forth. Two principal questions are considered: Is the child at continuing risk of significant harm? If so, does safeguarding the child require the intervention delivered through a formal child protection plan? If the conference decides that both of these criteria are satisfied, the child's name is placed on the register, and a child protection plan is agreed.

Conclusions

The low-impact, handset-based type of support is designed to provide an additional channel of communication for a group. Validation of this type of GSS has to be concerned with developing an understanding of the social processes that are taking place. The mode of operation of the technology, and the design of the group process used in conjunction with the technology, has been designed to minimise defensive reactions among individuals and within a group. In support of this statement, it is important to note that the individual always maintains control over what he or she communicates, whether verbally or through input from a handset.

The response to each question screen is input as an anonymous (nonattributed) judgement, appearing as a contribution to an aggregated display. The ensuing conversation is then focussed on the reasons, and reasoning, that may underlie the range of opinion that is fed back to the group. The reasons behind displayed differences of opinion can be explored and discussed in a personalised or nonpersonalised way. Any declaration of a personally held view is entirely a matter for the individual participant to decide, and is not a process requirement. Each person always remains in control of there own actions. A feature of the listed applications was the ease with which discussions, aided by the technology, included the expression of reasons underlying displayed differences. It appears that the process design can provide a level of safety that enables each participant to make and receive contributions more easily.

The technology and accompanying protocol addresses two aspects of communication that are often in conflict. On the one hand, the technology is helping to reduce the risks associated with personal communication, while on the other hand, it is seeking to increase the outputs of collective communication, all taking place in a learning environment. This suggestion has been made by Gear et al. (2003) in the context of using the technology as an aid to organisational learning in employee groups. Indeed, in a sense, the classroom may be regarded as a micro-organisation, and the ensuing process, a form of organisational learning.

The trials with postgraduates described in this chapter have presented an example of one approach to social learning, by creating a temporary, and relatively safe, classroom environment. The students are encouraged to learn by exploring their opinions in relation to others in a relatively safe situation, with reduced barriers. This form of temporary "suspension" has been proposed as key to a process of "dialogue" (Isaacs, 1993).

We remain cautious about what can be claimed, although our conclusions are encouraging. Group processes are not only extensions of processes appropriated to individuals when engaged with a task. A new entity is created with its own dynamics, with complex, social processes involving position modification and learning between participants. It does appear that "low-impact" group-support systems can aid social processes by means of appropriately designed software. This can incorporate selected features from, for example, multiple-criteria decision-making, nominal group technique, and other managerial models and methods, developed to aid "learning and deciding" type activities. There are various ways in which this can be done, depending on the particular context, as demonstrated in the wide-ranging nature of the applications listed in this chapter. We hope that the results of field trials presented in this chapter will stimulate further developments of practice and theory for this type of group support in a variety of contexts.

References

Argyris, C., & Schon, D. A. (1978). *Organisational learning: A theory in action perspective*. Reading, MA: Adddison-Wesley.

Baker, A. C., Jensen, P. J., & Kolb, D. A. (2002). *Conversational learning: An experiential approach to knowledge creation*. London.

Dalkey, N. (1969). *The Delphi Method: An experimental study of group opinion*. CA: Rand Corporation.

Finlay, P. (1998). On evaluating the performance of GSS: Furthering the debate. *European Journal of Operational Research, 107*, 193-201.

Forsyth, D. R. (1995). *Our social world*. CA: Brooks/Cole.

Gear, A. E., & Read, M. J. (1993). On-line group process support, *Omega, 21*(3), 261-274.

Gear, T., Read, M. J., & Minkes, A. L. (1996). Towards validation of a group decision support system. *Proceedings of the Annual Conference of The International Association of Management*, Toronto.

Gear, T., Vince, R., Read, M., & Minkes, L. (2003). Group enquiry for collective learning in organisations. *Journal of Management Development, 22*(2), 88-102.

Groves, S., Gear, T., & Read, M. J. (2002, June). *Dialogue in practice: The quality of conversation in professional groups with on-line support*. Presented at Developing Philosophy of Management – Crossing Frontiers': Reason in Practice Conference, St Anne's College, Oxford.

Irving, A., & Hunt, A. J. (1994). Does immediate feedback of a students performance improve their learning experience? In H. C. Foot, C. J. Howe, A. Anderson, & A. K. Tolmie (Eds.), *Group and interactive learning*. Southampton: Computational Mechanics.

Isaacs, W. (1993). Taking flight: Dialogue, collective thinking and organisational learning. *Organisational Dynamics, 22*, 24-39.

Jensen, P. J., & Kolb, D. A. (2002). Conversation as communion: Spiritual, feminist, moral and natural perspectives. In A. C. Baker, P. J. Jensen, & D. A. Kolb (Eds.), *Conversational learning: An experiential approach to knowledge creation* (p. 19). London: Quorum Books.

Jones, C., Connolly, M., Gear, A., & Read, M. (2001). A case for group interactive learning with group process support. *British Journal of Educational Technology, 32*(5), 571-586.

Jones, C., Connolly, M., Gear, A. E., & Read, M. J. (2005). Collaborative learning with group interactive technology: A case study with post-graduate students. Accepted for *Management Learning*.

Lantolf, J. P., & Gabriela, A. (Eds.). (1998). *Vygotskian approaches to second language research*. NJ: Ablex.

Mead, G. H. (1972). In A. Strauss (Ed.), *George Herbert Mead on social psychology*. Chicago: University of Chicago Press.

Mcniff, J. (1993). *Teaching as learning: An action research approach*. London: Routledge.

Moscovici, S. (1980). Towards a theory of conversion behaviour. In L. Berkowitz (Ed.), *Advances in experimental social psychology* (Vol. 13, pp. 209-239). New York: Academic Press.

Nunamaker, J. F. Jr. (1997). Future research in group support systems: Needs, some questions and possible answers. *International Journal of Human Computer Studies, 47*(3), 357-385

Nunamaker, J. F., Dennis, A. R., Valacich, J. S., Vogel, D. R., & George, J. F. (1991). Electronic meeting systems to support group work. *Communications of the ACM, 34*, 40-61.

Palmer, I., & Hardy, C. (2000). *Thinking about management*. London: Sage.

Read, M. J. (2003). *Development and evaluation of a group process support system in organisational settings*. PhD Thesis, University of Glamorgan, UK.

Reagan-Cirincione, P. (1994). Improving the accuracy of group judgement: A process intervention combining group facilitation, social judgement analysis and information technology. *Organisational Behaviour and Human Decision Processes, 58*, 246-270.

Reynolds, M. (1998). Reflection and critical reflection in management learning. *Management Learning, 29*(2), 183-200.

Rogers, C. (1970). *Carl Rogers on encounter groups*. New York: Harper and Row.

Rohrbaugh, J. (1989). Demonstration experiments in field settings: Assessing the process, not the outcome, of group decision support. *Harvard Business School Research Colloquium*, Boston.

Schein, E. (1993). On dialogue, culture and organisational learning. *Organisation Dynamics, 22*(2), 40.

Spirkin, A. (1983). *Dialectical materialism*. Moscow: Progress.

Van de Ven, A. H., & Delbecq, A. L. (1971). Nominal versus interacting group processes for committee decision making. *Academy Management Journal, 17*, 605-621.

Vince, R., & Martin, L. (1993). Inside action learning: The politics and the psychology of the action learning model. *Management Education and Development, 24*(3), 205-215.

Vygotsky, L. S. (1978). *Mind in society: The development of higher psychological processes*. Cambridge, MA: Harvard University Press.

Weingart, L. R. (1997). How did they do that ?: The ways and means of studying group processes. In L. L. Cummings & B. M. Staw (Eds.), *Research in organizational behavior* (Vol. 19, pp. 189-239). Greenwich, CT: JAI.

Wertsch, J. V. (1985). *Vygotsky and the social formulations of mind.* Cambridge, MA: Harvard University Press.

Wyss-Flamm, E. D. (2002). Conversational learning in multicultural teams. In A. C. Baker, P. J. Jensen, & D. A. Kolb (Eds.), *Conversational learning: An experiential approach to knowledge creation.* London: Euorum Books.

Chapter XVII

The Trial of an Audience Response System to Facilitate Problem-Based Learning in Legal Education

Kelley Burton, Queensland University of Technology, Australia

Abstract

This chapter provides a case study of how a lecturer in the School of Law at the Queensland University of Technology (QUT) used an audience response system (ARS) in a lecture for a second-year, core, undergraduate law subject to facilitate problem-based learning. It identifies the positive student response to the use of an ARS, and explores the main benefits, for example, active engagement of students in the learning process, facilitation of formative assessment where the students develop initiative and peer relationships, and the provision of timely and worthwhile feedback. The chapter also identifies some of the problems that the author faced in the trial, and provides some suggested solutions and recommendations. The author hopes to encourage other lecturers to take advantage of an ARS to enhance student learning, and identifies some future ARS research opportunities.

Introduction

The QUT prides itself on being a university for the real world, and takes advantage of technology that enhances student learning. The ARS was used in a law lecture at the QUT to develop not only what students need to know, but also what they need to do in the real world (real-world learning). The ARS aided this by facilitating problem-based learning and developing the problem-solving skills of the law students.

Christensen and Kift (2000) claim that employer and student groups have strenuously driven the need for law schools to plan the curriculum to develop what lawyers need to do, rather than what they need to know. Further, the Australian Law Reform Commission (1997), in its issues paper entitled, "Rethinking the legal education and training," has supported the notion that legal education should facilitate the development of generic and transferable skills so that law graduates can cope with the dynamic legal profession, and the fact that law graduates may frequently move across to other disciplines during their careers. According to Le Brun and Johnstone (1994), problem-solving skills are generic or transferable skills because they are relevant to graduates from all disciplines, and are not restricted to law graduates.

The author has previously published a refereed, scholarly journal article on this topic (Burton, 2004), and hopes to inspire lecturers in law schools, and in other disciplines, to use an ARS to facilitate the development of problem-solving skills in their lectures. In particular, this chapter:

1.   Provides a case study on how an ARS was used in a law lecture in a core, second-year law undergraduate subject to facilitate problem-based learning, and to develop the problem solving skills of law students. It also recognizes the positive response from the law students involved in the trial.

2.   Identifies some of the problems that the author faced when they trialled an ARS in their law lectures, and provides suggested solutions and recommendations.

3.   Identifies some future ARS research opportunities.

Background

Problem-solving skills are entrenched in the law degree across all four-year levels at the QUT. The QUT Law School strives to use authentic problems, that is, problems that replicate real world scenarios, in its problem-based learning to reinforce its position as a university for the real world, and to better equip students for the transition from university to the workplace.

In early 2004, the author became aware that the QUT had purchased the necessary technology for an ARS, and attended a training session conducted at the QUT on how to use it. The author was aware that other faculties at the QUT had taken advantage of an ARS, and decided to trial it in a law lecture, on the basis that it embraces student-centered learning.

Previously, the lecturer had taught the same topic in the second-year, undergraduate core law subject by explaining the legal authorities using a series of PowerPoint™ slides to set out the content. She then asked the students to apply their knowledge of the law to factual scenarios similar to the ones used in the ARS trial. She asked the students to think about their answers to the problems and discuss them with the person sitting next to them. One student from the lecture group would volunteer their answer, and the lecturer would indicate whether it was right or wrong. The benefit of using the ARS was that it enabled all students present at the lecture to respond to the problem, whereas the traditional learning approach only enabled the lecturer to hear the answer of one student, or a couple of students, if the first student had the wrong answer. This means that the ARS facilitated active learning because it actively engaged all students present in the lecture in the learning process, and encouraged them to participate and be proactive in the lecture.

The other main benefits, perceived by the author, of using an ARS, over the previous method of teaching were, for example, facilitating formative assessment tasks that developed student initiative and peer relationships (collaborative learning), and providing students with timely and worthwhile feedback. This approach is supported by the QUT's Teaching Capabilities Framework, which was approved by the University Academic Board in 2003.

A literature review, conducted at the time of this trial in 2004, indicated that even though other disciplines throughout the world had taken advantage of an ARS, there were no publications to suggest that one had been previously trialled in legal education.

Case Study: Use of ARS In Undergraduate Core Law Subject

The author of this chapter trialled an ARS in a second-year, undergraduate core law subject (Real Property A) at the QUT. Each week, the internal students, those that attend the campus each week, had a 2-hour lecture and a 1-hour tutorial over a 13-week semester. During the week 5 lecture, the author trialled an ARS to facilitate problem-based learning. An ARS was used on a one-off basis in a lecture, and was not integrated into subsequent lectures or tutorials.

Even though the second-year law students had attended many lectures during their undergraduate education, they had not previously encountered an ARS in lectures. The second-year, undergraduate law students had been exposed to PowerPoint™ presentations, and these were considered to be normal service, as many first- and second-year lecturers used them during their lectures. However, the students were beginning to tire from this type of technological integration. Williams (2003), from the QUT Brisbane Graduate School of Business, identified that the student attraction to PowerPoint™ slides "waned to the point where, faced with a torrent of multi-colored, animated slides, students began to describe the experience as being akin to 'death by PowerPoint™'' (p. 740). This comment signifies the importance of not overusing technological innovations in lectures, because overuse leads to ineffectiveness. The ARS is a novel and innovative approach to learning and teaching, and if it is overused, its fate is likely to be the same as PowerPoint™ slides.

One hundred and forty full-time students and 40 part-time students participated in the trial of the ARS. The trial was conducted in week 5 of the first semester in 2004 on the Gardens Point campus at the QUT. All students participating in the trial were internal students, that is, students that attend the campus during the semester for lectures and tutorials. These are different from external students, who usually attend the campus once a semester for the External Attendance School, and who listen to the weekly lectures and tutorials online or on compact discs. This is commonly referred to as distance learning. One of the objectives of the week 5 lecture was to require the students to know the time limits within which someone must recover land from an adverse possessor. The lecturer introduced this topic by discussing the relevant case law and statutory provisions. She then used an ARS to facilitate problem-based learning, so the students had the chance to apply their knowledge of the law to factual problems.

In order to develop the problem solving skills of the undergraduate law students, the lecturer presented the students with four, authentic factual problems. Each problem was presented on a PowerPoint™ slide. On the next PowerPoint™ slide, the lecturer provided a multiple-choice question requiring students to determine when the right of action to recover the land would accrue or expire. The lecturer did not need to flip between the PowerPoint™ slides showing the factual problem and the multiple-choice question because the students had printed the PowerPoint™ slides out before the lecture. Each multiple-choice question had four possible answers, one of which was correct. After the lecturer read the factual problem, and the multiple-choice question and answers to the students, the students were given a few minutes to reread the factual problem, and to select an answer on their keypad. The lecturer could have provided as many possible answers as there were keys on the keypad, but decided to provide four possible answers, as this is a common number of answers in multiple questions, and was more manageable for the students in the lecture time frame. Examples of the PowerPoint™ slides using the TurningPoint software in the trial are shown in Figures 1 and 2.

Figure 1. Factual problem

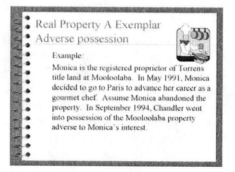

Figure 2. Response screen

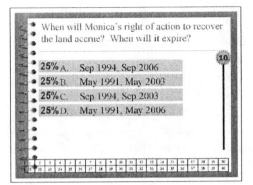

Another example of an issue to explore was:

"Samuel is the registered proprietor of Torrens title land at Stanthorpe. He leaves the property in 1993 to establish a vineyard in Italy. In 1994 Zack takes possession of the property adverse to Samuel's interest. In 1997, a severe drought hits Stanthorpe and Zack leaves the property. In 1999, Slater takes adverse possession of the property". The associated response screen reads "When will Samuel's right of action to recover the property expire?", with options of 2005, 2006, 2009, and 2011 available for response.

This formative assessment task, that is, one that does not contribute to the final mark for a student for the subject, provided students with timely and worthwhile feedback during the lecture. These PowerPoint™ slides were available on the online teaching site for the remainder of the semester, which meant that the students could study these problems and multiple-choice questions after the lecture, but before they were summatively assessed during the final exam.

A lecturer is not limited to multiple-choice questions when using an ARS. The lecturer could use a range of questions or statements, on the PowerPoint™ slides, for example, yes or no questions, true or false questions, or fill in the blank questions. From a law perspective, law lecturers could ask questions about the content of the law, and the relevant cases and legislation.

An example of a true or false, or yes or no question on the adverse possession area of the law would be: "In Queensland, a registered proprietor must recover the land from an adverse possessor within 12 years." The answer is true or yes.

An example of the same content in a fill in the blank question is: "In Queensland, a registered proprietor must recover the land from an adverse possessor within _____ years."

Lecturers may prefer to use questions where the topic is numerical, or able to be answered by short answers. Where the topic is open-ended, the lecturer may prefer to use statements whereby students select agree, neutral, or disagree. These statements would be designed to encourage debate. For example, law lecturers may ask the students for their opinion on whether the law should be reformed.

An example of a statement on the adverse possession area of the law would be: "The 12 year statutory time period for the registered proprietor to recover land from the adverse possessor should be longer."

As indicated above, an ARS provides the lecturer with the flexibility to create a range of questions or statements, and it is difficult to imagine a topic where an ARS could not be used.

The lecturer in this trial posed statements using the ARS to obtain feedback from the undergraduate law students. The lecturer created three statements about the ARS and put them to the students in the full-time lecture and the part-time lecture. The lecturer limited the feedback statements to three because this was more manageable, given the two-hour lecture timeframe and the remaining content that had to be covered in the lecture. Statements or multiple-choice questions offer a wider range of answers, and therefore, more meaningful feedback than yes or no questions, or true or false questions. The three statements were:

1.   The Audience Response System helped me to learn the lecture materials;

2.   It was useful to compare my responses with the responses of other students; and

3.   The Audience Response System should be used in more Law lectures.

For each statement, a five-statement Likert scale (from Strongly Agree through to Strongly Disagree) response was elicited.

The student feedback is indicated in Table 1, with numbers representing percentages. The lecturer did not keep a record of which student had which keypad, so anonymous feedback was collected from students who participated in the trial. More students are likely to respond if they know that their responses are confidential.

There was not a huge disparity between the feedback from the full-time and part-time students. Overall, 90.5% of students strongly agreed, agreed, or were neutral to the ARS being helpful to learn the lecture materials. Overall, 86.5% of students strongly agreed, agreed, or were neutral to it being useful to compare their responses with the responses of the other students. Overall, 88% of students strongly agreed, agreed, or were neutral to the ARS being used in more lectures. The students responded positively to the use of an ARS in lectures, and the anonymous feedback from the students supported the continued use of ARS. However, the author believes that this positive response was largely due to the fact that an ARS was a novel learning approach, and it actively engaged the students in the lecture materials.

Table 1. Feedback from the undergraduate law students

Statement posed to students on the ARS	Strongly Agree		Agree		Neutral		Disagree		Strongly Disagree	
Full Time (FT) or Part Time (PT)	FT	PT	FT	PT	FT	PT	FT	PT	FT	PT
ARS helped me to learn the lecture materials	45	53	39	26	7	11	3	8	5	3
It was useful to compare my responses with other students	44	32	30	30	18	19	2	8	6	11
ARS should be used in more lectures	50	53	27	21	7	18	6	3	10	5

Problems, Solutions, and Recommendations

Despite the successful trial of the ARS in the second-year, undergraduate law subject, the lecturer encountered some problems. Lecturers intending to use an ARS should be conscious of the following problems, and should be guided by the recommended solutions. These problems, solutions, and recommendations are generic, and are relevant to all lecturers, irrespective of discipline.

One of the problems with ARS for lecturers is that it takes extra time to prepare for lectures. Lecturers generating special PowerPoint™ slides using the TurningPoint software should receive hands-on training on how to design the PowerPoint™ slides. The author spent 2 hours at such a technology training session. This training should provide lecturers with knowledge of the various ways in which the ARS can be used, for example, the ability to ask multiple-choice questions, yes or no questions, true or false questions, fill in the blank questions, and statements. Lecturers need to reflect on the topic they are canvassing, and create appropriate questions or statements about the topic. They then need to generate special PowerPoint™ slides that use the TurningPoint software. The author spent a couple of hours generating the PowerPoint™ slides using the TurningPoint software, and forwarded a copy of them to the trainer for peer review. Lecturers will find that the initial workload is higher than a usual PowerPoint™ presentation, but the workload in subsequent years is minimal, if the questions or statements only need minor changes. Further, the benefits to the students in the form of actively engaging students in the learning process, facilitating formative assessment where the students develop initiative and peer relationships, and providing timely and worthwhile feedback, outweighs the extra time and effort. However, to maintain student interest and the impact, an ARS should be used at discerning points in time in a lecture or subject, rather than continuously.

Another problem is that if the ARS is not permanently installed in the lecture theatre, the lecturer will need to know how to install the equipment. This is very time consuming for the lecturer because they would need to attend the lecture theatre for about 30 minutes before the lecture started, and remain in the lecture theatre after the lecture to collect the keypads, in numerical order from the students, and pack the ARS away. The lecturer should plan ahead and make enquiries as to who is using the lecture theatre directly before and after the lecture. To assist the lecturer, training on installation should be given. However, to overcome this problem from the lecturer's perspective, support staff may be able to install the equipment in the lecture theatre. A better alternative is to have a dedicated lecture theatre permanently set up with an ARS, where the keypads could be permanently affixed to the tables in the lecture theatre. This would minimize the lecturer's stress associated with setting up and dismantling an ARS, and cope better with a busy campus timetable, with back-to-back lectures in a lecture theatre. Unfortunately, the author was unable to trial an ARS in the Real Property A week 5 lecture in 2005, because the lecture theatre timetable was full with back to back lectures, and an ARS had not been permanently set up in the lecture theatre.

Where the ARS is not permanently installed in the lecture theatre, a low-risk theft problem may arise with respect to the keypads. This would be the case where the lecturer has decided to use the ARS anonymously, and has not kept a record of which student is holding which keypad. The lecturer should advise students that the keypads cannot be used to operate other electrical devices, and encourage the students to act honestly. There is also a low risk that the students might steal the batteries in the keypad. However, the batteries are usually screwed into the keypads to prevent this from occurring.

Problem-based learning using an ARS in lectures takes up valuable lecture time, and its impact is increased if it is used sporadically throughout lecturing the content, as opposed to using it constantly. A lecturer may need to restructure the content to be canvassed in the lecture if they intend to introduce problem-based learning using an ARS. Lecturers should also ask questions that are of a reasonable degree of difficulty, and limit the number of responses given to students so that they can quickly select the correct answer. Also, lecturers should take advantage of the counter, which is an inbuilt feature of most ARS software that limits the time within which the students must respond.

Another problem with large cohorts of students is that they want to establish whether the ARS has received their response. To overcome this, the lecturer should take advantage of a rotating grid, which is a feature of some ARS software. The rotating grid appears at the bottom of the PowerPoint™ slide, and shows the number of the keypads. The numbers are highlighted once the ARS has received the response from the student keypad.

A further problem experienced by the author with ARS was that it was only available to internal students, that is, those students who were physically present in the lecture theatre. It is possible that some external students (involved in distance learning) attended the lecture within which the ARS was trailed, as a roll was not taken of the students present in the lecture. However, most (if not all) external students would have obtained the PowerPoint™ slides using the TurningPoint software via online teaching sites, and listened to the lecture on the online teaching site using audio streaming. The author perceives that the best way of replicating the learning experience for external students is to use an ARS during the external attendance school, that is, when the external students come to the university campus during the semester.

Future Research Opportunities

Despite the positive student response to the use of an ARS in undergraduate law lectures, future research should be conducted to confirm the pedagogical soundness of this learning and teaching approach. Researchers in this area may wish to build upon the existing research and fill the following gaps.

In particular, to substantiate the first feedback statement, research should be conducted to determine whether there was a direct correlation between the use of ARS and an increased understanding of the lecture materials. Perhaps this could be achieved by comparing the results of students in one year who did not use the ARS, with the results of students in the next year who did use the ARS. One flaw with this research is that it assumes that the ability and knowledge of the cohort of students in two, consecutive years are initially the same. Alternatively, the retention rates of students could be examined.

To support the second feedback statement, research should be conducted to determine how useful it is for the students to see the responses of the other students. Arguably, a student who selected the wrong answer may be inspired to work harder if they could see that the majority of the other students selected the correct answer. Perhaps this could be achieved by conducting face-to-face feedback sessions with students or student surveys.

Further feedback needs to be obtained from the students with regard to the third feedback statement. In particular, lecturers need to ask their students about the extent to which an ARS should be used in their subject. Perhaps the lecturer could ask the students whether an ARS should be used in all lectures, in half of the lectures, or a couple of the lectures. Perhaps the lecturer could ask the students how often an ARS should be used in one lecture to facilitate problem-based learning.

To validate the third feedback statement, research should be conducted to establish whether the popularity of ARS continues over time. Using ARS in lectures is a novel learning and teaching approach. The students in the trial supported the notion that it be used in more lectures, and it would be interesting to ascertain whether this trend would continue after the ARS has been used frequently for many years. It is suspected that students will tire from the overuse of ARS, it will have a similar fate to PowerPoint™ slides, and students will expect lecturers to utilize a future learning and teaching approach. Lecturers may be willing to test this conclusion.

A future trial could be conducted whereby the students are summatively assessed on a topic by multiple-choice, true or false, yes or no, or fill in the blank questions. To do this, a lecturer would need to link the number on the keypad to the student name. One of the problems with this electronic type of exam would be that students could not refer back to previous questions if they wanted to change their answer. Robust procedures would need to be in place to ensure that cheating or collusion did not occur. However, the prime motivation for using an ARS would be for facilitating formative assessment, which provides the students with progressive and worthwhile feedback before they are summatively assessed on a topic.

It is a logical argument that if a lecturer keeps a record of which student holds a particular keypad, the student may be less likely to respond, for fear of ridicule or embarrassment if they select the wrong answer. Qualitative feedback from the students in a future trial could confirm whether the students were hesitant about selecting answers, or whether they were more careful about selecting an answer. Quantitative feedback in the form of response rates could be obtained from the students to determine whether it took them more time to select an answer. Another study could be conducted to conclusively prove that the concentration levels of students in higher education are improved during lectures when an ARS is used.

Further qualitative feedback could be collected from the students about the usefulness of multicolored responses, for example, the correct response could be in green, and the incorrect responses could be in red.

The use of an ARS in higher-education law lectures is a novel concept, and is worthy of further investigation.

Conclusions

The chapter illustrated how a lecturer trialled an ARS in a second-year law, undergraduate subject at QUT. This trial involved a student-centered approach to learning, because it used an innovative resource to facilitate the development of problem-solving skills, engaged students in the lecture materials by compelling them to be proactive, rather than passive in lectures, and encouraged students to develop relationships with their peers. The ARS facilitated formative, problem-based assessment, and provided the students with worthwhile feedback before they were summatively assessed on the topic.

The lecturer who trialled an ARS in a second-year law, undergraduate subject at the QUT encountered some problems, and has suggested some possible solutions in this chapter. From the lecturer's perspective, the main problem is the time it takes to design special PowerPoint™ slides posing questions or statements using the TurningPoint software, and the time it takes to set up the ARS before the lecture, if it is not permanently affixed in the lecture theatre. To overcome these two problems, lecturers should obtain hands-on training on how to design the PowerPoint™ slides, training on how to efficiently and effectively set up an ARS, have support staff responsible for setting up the ARS before the lecture, or have the ARS permanently affixed in the lecture theatre.

ARSs are innovative pedagogical tools, and this chapter has identified some future areas of research, and opportunities to seek feedback from students. Some of the recommended themes for future research include confirming whether ARS helps students to learn and apply the lecture materials, whether students are more cautious about selecting responses when the lecturer has kept a record of which student is holding which keypad, whether the study patterns of students are influenced by witnessing the responses of other students in the lecture, whether ARS is suitable for summative assessment, whether ARS improves the concentration levels of students, whether color schemes make it easier to learn with ARS, and whether the popularity of ARS continues over time.

When conducting this future research, lecturers should be aware that they can use the ARS itself to seek feedback from students. To do this, lecturers merely need to compose a multiple-choice, true or false, yes or no, or fill in the blank questions or statements, and put them to the students during the lecture. The students provide the feedback by responding to the question or statement, and the ARS collects the responses, that is, the feedback.

With the benefit of the ARS technology, and the ability to generate multiple-choice, true or false, yes or no, or fill in the blank questions or statements (on PowerPoint™ slides using the TurningPoint software) that relate to the lecture materials, lecturers could transfer this conducive learning experience to other law schools and disciplines.

References

Australian Law Reform Commission. (1997). *Rethinking the legal education and training* (Issue Paper No. 21). Canberra: Australian Government Publishing Service.

Burton, K. (2004). Interactive PowerPoints™: Is there any point in giving power to law students in lectures? *E Law – Murdoch University Electronic Journal of Law, 11*(4). Retrieved from http://www.murdoch.edu.au/elaw/issues/v11n4/burton114.html

Christensen, C., & Kift, S. (2000). Graduate attributes and legal skills: Integration or disintegration? *Legal Education Review, 11*, 212.

Le Brun, M., & Johnstone, R. (1994). *The quiet revolution.* Sydney: Law Book Company.

Williams, J. (2003). *Learning by remote control: Exploring the use of an audience response system as a vehicle for content delivery.* Adelaide: Australasian Society for Computers in Learning in Tertiary Education (ASCILITE).

Chapter XVIII

Live Assessment by Questioning in an Interactive Classroom

Michael McCabe, University of Portsmouth, UK

Abstract

This chapter presents an overview of audience response systems as tools for promoting learning in an interactive classroom. The comparison with a popular TV programme is used to introduce the role of questioning in face-to-face teaching, before examining the intrinsic pedagogical benefits of questions. Technical aspects of different systems are summarised, and pedagogical issues discussed, based on the author's personal teaching experience. Appropriate ways of using audience response systems in the classroom, and guidelines for question delivery are presented. New technology will continue to open up opportunities, but the challenge for the future remains to use the technology effectively and in pedagogically sound ways.

From TV Quizzes to Interactive Classrooms

The learning benefits of questions in face-to-face teaching have been exploited since the time of Socrates. Audience response systems have enabled the benefits of questioning learners to be extended to the modern world of mass education. Mass entertainment has also taken advantage of audience response systems, and consideration of a popular application helps reveal the role of questioning for more serious educational purposes.

TV quiz programmes are a trivial form of assessment. In the UK, there used to be a quiz show called "Double Your Money" that had a simple format. Contestants simply answered a set of progressively harder questions, and doubled their winnings at each stage, up to £1000. Today, that format has been given a new lease of life in "Who Wants to be a Millionaire?" Why?

The main difference is that the programme has become more interactive and lively. Contestants can seek help by "Asking the Audience," "Going 50:50," or "Phoning a Friend" before giving an answer. Despite an extremely simple, multiple-choice question, these three lifelines, supported by technology, make all the difference. The quizmaster, the audience, and friend become actively engaged with the contestants in helping them to maximise their prize money. It is not that questions can be made harder, or that gaps in a weak contestant's knowledge can be overcome, that revives the quiz format. Interactive engagement helps a contestant converge gradually towards the correct answer to a difficult question, and gives the programme its appeal. An audience response system, a computer to eliminate choices, and a phone are the necessary tools that help to make the lifelines work, and promote the human interaction.

A secondary difference is the thousandfold increase in prize money, which is significant even allowing for inflation. The reward alone is unlikely to account for the popular appeal.

With interactive classrooms, defined here as learning technology used to support human communication and questioning during face-to-face teaching, the techniques used to enliven a simple quiz programme have developed considerably in the delivery of live, face-to-face assessment. In simple terms, developing the quiz analogy:

Ask the Audience = collection of class responses to questions via handsets or computers, and subsequent display of results for peer discussion, during which students can explain to others the reasoning behind their choice.

Go 50:50 = provision of additional help, hints, advice, or feedback by lecturer or computer.

Phone a Friend = computer-controlled conscription, or volunteering of an individual student's question response and explanation of their individual answer, for class-wide discussion (using a microphone in a large class).

Fastest Finger = identification of students who give the quickest (correct) answers.

contestant = individual student

quizmaster = lecturer

audience = other students

question without lifeline = assessment without feedback

question with lifeline = assessment with feedback

increasing prize money = weighting of assessment as low- or high-stakes

intermediate prizes (£1K, £32K and £1M) = intermediate learning objectives

cheque handover = module/course completion

The game-show contestant is motivated by prize money (and the opportunity to appear on TV). In educational terms, the prize money is analogous to the stakes or weighting attached to an assessment. The catchphrase "assessment drives learning" might, therefore, be interpreted to mean that higher-stakes assessment motivates students to learn better than lower-stakes assessment. However, any high-stakes assessment is likely to motivate students to complete it, however poorly designed and limited in its educational value. The prize money may make the quiz programme more exciting, but it is the lifeline interactivity that gives it extra appeal, and helps contestants to progress in their quest for £1M. Similarly, the live, formative assessment in an interactive classroom can help students make progress in their learning. The fact that students are already familiar with audience response systems from TV programmes encourages them to engage with this new approach in the classroom.

Although interactive classroom technology is still in its infancy, and the underlying pedagogy is still very much the subject of active research (Abrahamson, 1998; Beatty, 2004), it is emerging as a powerful method for delivering formative, normally no-stakes assessment. Its primary purpose is, therefore, to improve student learning, rather than to be used as a grading tool.

Student Learning and Questioning

Lecturers naturally ask questions to promote dialogue with a class, although this gets progressively more difficult as a class size increases. Why are questions so important for learning? Even without the reward of marks, grades, or prizes, the extrinsic value of asking questions is in motivating students to learn. Ultimately, students should become sufficiently selfmotivated themselves to ask their own questions, but the lecturer is the initial poser of questions. Thalheimer (2003) attempts to quantify the intrinsic, as opposed to the extrinsic, learning benefits of questions that arise from

a.   **Focusing on key concepts:**

Interactive classroom questions take up significantly more time than straight content delivery.

Personal experience of encouraging other lecturers to use audience response systems shows that resistance to their use can arise from an unwillingness to reduce the "completeness" of course coverage. Time has to be spent introducing questions, collecting responses, discussing answers, giving hints, providing feedback, and explaining solutions. It is therefore necessary to focus on key concepts, rather than expanding on the subject with interesting sidelines. UK and

U.S. research groups have used interactive classrooms to improve the conceptual understanding and reasoning of science students (Dufresne, Leonard, Mestre, & Wenk, 1996; Mazur, 1997; Nicol & Boyle, 2003) by developing thought-provoking questions. Conceptual questions are more likely to promote high-level learning than simple knowledge-based questions, especially when they are combined with suitable methods for promoting discussion. For example, students might be asked to choose between trajectories for a spacecraft, in order to explore the underlying physical laws.

b.   **Providing retrieval practice:**

Retrieval practice often involves applying familiar ideas or existing knowledge in new situations. Learning is reinforced by having to seek solutions to new problems, based upon current understanding. For example, students familiar with Kepler's Laws and the motion of planets around the sun may be asked to consider the motion of stars around the centre of our galaxy.

c.   **Encouraging repetition:**

Questions promote the review of learning resources from a new angle, and different questions on the same topic can provide extra reinforcement. In an interactive classroom, there is a new dimension to repetition. For example, a question may be posed for an initial attempt at an answer. Group responses are then presented for peer discussion, during which individuals are invited to convince their neighbours that their response is correct. The question is repeated, and further responses gathered. Convergence towards a correct or agreed solution to a problem is an ideal objective.

d.   **Giving feedback:**

Without the aid of technology, it is extremely difficult to give timely feedback to questions, especially for a large group of students. One way of dealing with this problem is to use computer-based or computer-assisted assessment (CAA), which provides immediate marking and feedback, has greater accessibility, and encourages repetition. Multiple-choice questions (MCQ), despite their obvious limitations, provide a starting point for CAA, not just because of their simplicity, but because they allow straightforward diagnosis of incorrect responses and targeted feedback. Although dozens of other CAA question types exist, it is generally harder to automate feedback for incorrect answers. Despite its common use and well-recognised value, the lack of direct, human involvement in CAA can make its use an impersonal, solitary activity, and it is not guaranteed to engage students, unless there are moderate stakes involved. An interactive classroom provides the opportunity for immediate, live feedback from the lecturer, and from the rest of the class, through use of technology. Interactive classrooms often use MCQs for much the same reason as CAA, the ability to give targeted feedback. The difference in an interactive classroom is that question feedback is not only computer generated, for example, by a histogram showing frequency of MCQ choices, but also by other students and the lecturer. While it can be extremely difficult to automate computer feedback for questions that are not multiple-choice, human feedback can be given in an interactive classroom.

Technicalities

Computer-assisted assessment may be viewed as the forerunner of the interactive classroom. Over 25 years ago, there were "first generation" Optical Mark (Character) Readers that, although they still have their place, are not designed for rapid results and feedback. Around 15 years ago, the move from stand-alone to networked PCs made "second generation" CAA more attractive, because of its ability to give immediate results and feedback. Within the past 10 years, "third generation" online CAA has become possible, and it has become increasingly valuable as a tool in the assessment workshop. Dozens of different, objective, question types can be delivered with automatic marking and feedback. The role of the lecturer is to prepare questions for authoring, and occasionally to look over shoulders in the computer laboratory as a "guide on the side." The primary goal of CAA is not to support learning, but rather to automate the assessment process for the lecturer. Learning benefits undoubtedly arise from the effective and regular use of CAA, but these could be regarded as an afterthought. On the other hand, the primary goal of an interactive classroom is to support teaching and learning with face-to-face assessment.

Early "first generation" interactive classroom systems, such as Classtalk (Dufresne et al., 1996) and Teamworker, were expensive, and did not achieve widespread use. Since 1999, cheaper and easier-to-use "second generation" products have become widely available in universities and some schools, especially in the US. The PRS Personal Response System and eInstruction CPS Classroom Performance System use small handsets or keypads, often referred to as "clickers" or "zappers," to send infrared signals to classroom receivers connected to a PC that has special software installed. Other products, with varying costs and facilities, include RxShow, Interactive Presenter, Qwizdom, H-ITT, and IML Question Wizard. There is no consensus over the terminology used to describe interactive classroom systems. Commonly used terms are

- **Electronic voting system:** appropriate when question types are multiple-choice only
- **Group decision support system:** appropriate for meetings rather than classes
- **Personal response system:** although this is the name of a specific commercial product
- **Audience response system:** although this name implies a passive involvement
- **Group response system:** appropriate for describing the generic use of one-way handsets
- **Classroom communication system:** better reserved for two-way systems to be described.

"Third generation" interactive classrooms use wired or wirelessly networked PCs (desktop, laptop, tablet, PDA) as input devices, and allow two-way communication between student and lecturer, typically via a Web browser. Discourse (McCabe and Lucas, 2003b) is a good example that enables a wide range of open and closed (objective)

Figure 1. Question, status boxes, results and feedback on a single screen

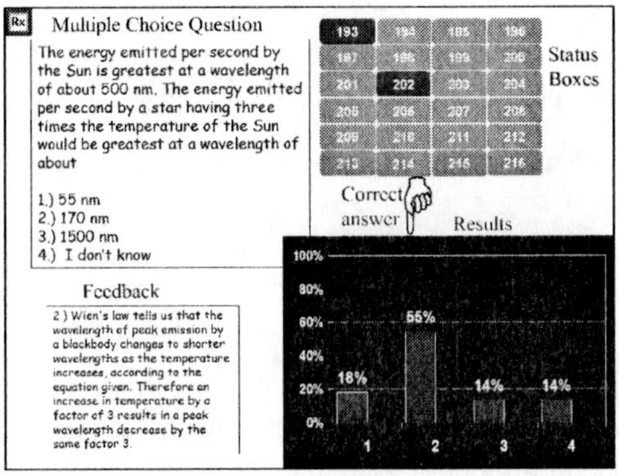

question types to be asked interactively. For example, text or mathematical answers can be collected, viewed, and analysed with far more controlled delivery of results and feedback than is possible with one-way handsets. In the future, it is likely that similar systems will appear as integral components within virtual/managed learning environments, and may even become possible by using mobile phones. The fact that nearly every student already has a mobile phone, while handsets have to be purchased, makes them an excellent candidate for increasing the uptake of audience response systems. For the present, attempts to use mobile phones as audience response systems have been very limited.

Some of the more expensive handsets, such as IML and Qwizdom, operate using radio rather than infrared signals. One advantage is limited two-way communication back to a small screen on each handset. The most basic feedback required by the user of a handset is confirmation that their signal has been received and accepted as valid. One-way communication usually provides this confirmation via status boxes on a common audience screen that may need to be projected separately from the questions (Figure 1).

The drawback is that not all rooms have the facility for twin-screen projection. In a two-way system, individuals can receive this confirmation by an indicator or display on their own handset, but the drawback here is that the speed and proportion of the responses are no longer apparent to the group if status boxes are no longer used. In particular, the lecturer still needs to see polling levels and validity of answers. The two-way handsets and keypads can be thought of as bridging the gap between cheap handsets with limited capabilities, and more sophisticated PC-based systems allowing a wide range of re-sponses.

Practicalities

Live question responses from large numbers of students can be collected, analysed, and discussed without resorting to technology. Raised hands and fingers, numbered cards, coloured cubes, and other aids are effective ways of eliciting answers to simple questions, but they have several drawbacks. Such basic methods are:

- limited in response types,
- slow in response analysis and feedback,
- poor on anonymity,
- open to copying of responses.

Although the underlying pedagogical approach may be the same, technology allows the delivery of group questions to become more dynamic, varied, and interactive. Beatty (2004) suggests that: "Technology doesn't inherently improve learning; it merely makes possible more effective pedagogy ...."

The motivation of lecturers wanting to use audience response systems and interactive classrooms D'Inverno, 2004; McCabe, 2003a, 2004c; Wit, 2003 commonly includes desires to:

- increase interaction with students during face-to-face teaching, enlivening classes by reducing the boredom ("Death by 1000 PowerPoint Bullets") and increasing the stimulation of lectures;
- move away from traditional lectures to other forms of learning;
- improve learning and assessment results by engaging students;
- increase discussion amongst the students, by encouraging peer support when answering questions; and
- provide immediate feedback, especially for individuals failing to answer questions correctly.

Less often quoted, but nevertheless extremely useful, is the review of class results at the end a session. The focus of a subsequent class, or next year's class, may be changed according to those questions that were answered well or badly. Questions with similar splits in responses tend to provoke better discussion.

The anonymity of students in answering questions may be regarded as a benefit of using handsets, allowing the involvement in class delivery to be informal and relaxed. If, on the other hand, students are allocated a uniquely numbered handset known to the lecturer, there are other benefits. A lecturer can now:

- monitor individual attendance, register students, and chase up absentees;
- checkup on the participation of an individual student during interactive lectures;

- track the performance of individuals, identifying those not making acceptable progress; and
- offer personal advice or remedial support to improve retention.

Whether one-way infrared handsets, two-way radio devices, or classroom communication systems with networked computers, there are common pedagogical principles, which can be applied. They can all be used for preclass, midclass or postclass tests, to break up and even replace the content delivery in a routine lecture. They can all be used for collecting subjective data or answering objective questions, to stimulate group discussion or individual responses/reflection, and more specifically to:

- break up delivery of content during lectures (self-assessment);
- give a test at the start of a lecture (diagnostic);
- give a test at the end of a lecture (formative);
- deliver a revision test at the end of a module (summative);
- evaluate a course module;
- poll student understanding/interest/opinions;
- conduct experiments, for example, gather personal/subjective data;
- deliver response-dependent classes, for example, contingent teaching (Draper & Brown, 2004);
- promote interactive engagement and discussion (Nicol & Boyle, 2003);
- play games, for example, prisoner's dilemma; and
- make group decision making more dynamic and democratic.

By adopting approaches such as peer instruction (Crouch & Mazur, 2001; Mazur, 1997), Socratic questioning can even become the exclusive method for delivering content and key concepts. Typically, a lecturer presents a question, students input answers, class results are presented graphically, student groups discuss results, and students input their answers again, possibly converging towards a common response. The cycle is usually concluded by the lecturer and may have many variants, according to the extent of lecturer and student involvement. The lecturer may offer intermediate hints, information, guidance, and feedback, in response to class results, before a further round of polling. Individual students may be encouraged to justify and explain their answers to the rest of the class in order to provoke class-wide or group discussion, before proceeding to another poll.

Dynamic, peer-supported learning (McCabe, Horowitz, & Beakes, 2004a) extends peer instruction by combining the collection and display of results with class discussion and lecturer feedback. When results are presented statically after each poll, each of these stages is sequential, and therefore necessarily time-consuming. The time required to deliver and discuss questions is often given as a reason for sticking with content-driven lectures. When numerical or graphical results are presented dynamically, that is, changing immediately in response to revised answers, the stages of questioning, answering, and discussing operate simultaneously. The result is a higher level of interaction and engagement with more effective use of class time.

Many of the principles and guidelines for the setting of objective CAA questions, such as MCQs, can be applied equally well to interactive classroom questions. There are, nevertheless, some differences and additional factors which need to be taken into account.

A selection of useful guidelines for question delivery with audience response systems is identified from practical experience.

- Questions for live delivery are often better if they are simpler than in conventional (formative or summative) tests. Besides requiring more time and reducing the pace of a session, hard questions are less likely to split the class and provoke discussion. Harder questions are often better if they are structured or staged.

- Questions are often effective when they are linked logically together, with the solution to the previous question given at the start of the next question. This helps to promote continuity and dialogue with the class.

- Interactive classes can be structured by dividing them into sections, for example, diagnostic, preliminary questions followed by formative, content questions followed by summative, concluding questions, and finally evaluation questions.

- There is less need for rigour when questions are low stakes. Questions may include deliberate (or accidental) mistakes, be ill-posed, invalid, or ambiguous. For example, a multiple-choice question, for which only one selection is required, may have more than one correct choice, no correct choices, or choices that are only partially correct. These "unsound" questions may provoke discussion and support learning far better than a formally valid question.

- Questions may be better delivered in "hidden" mode, in which choices are revealed in a delayed sequence, or all together after the question has been attempted. For example, if a student can verify the correct choice by working backwards, it is appropriate to hide the choices until an answer has been worked out on paper.

- Good questions should encourage group discussion (peer-supported learning), involving repetition of the same question after the class results. Normally, this means a split, but not equally weighted, response distribution.

- Good questions should encourage class-wide discussion involving repetition of the same question after individuals have explained their choice to the whole class. The individual student can be randomly selected by the lecturer or, less threateningly, by computer.

- Reuse of choices with different question stems is a useful technique for helping to reinforce learning and generate questions quickly.

- "I don't know," "I used to know," "None of these," and "All of these" are useful options that can be used to reveal levels of understanding or ignorance. For example, students may be either encouraged to make an educated guess or reveal their ignorance by the addition of an "I don't know" option.

- Mal-rules, logically generated but incorrect answers, for example, in mathematics $(a+b)^2 = a^2 + b^2$, are especially important for the design of distractors. They help to draw out common misunderstandings, and provoke group or class discussion. The skill is in being able to predict or gather common mal-rules in advance of the class. The most popular mal-rules may be identified by analysis of responses recorded in previous classes.

Classroom Issues

The design of question-based classes using audience response systems tends to be more time consuming than traditional, content-based delivery. In a recent trial involving a group of lecturers, an attempt was made to replace the content of some basic mathematics with a series of interactive questions (McCabe, Horowitz, & Beakes, 2004b). The aim was still to achieve full coverage of the topic. The final result was both time-consuming to prepare, and would have been equally time-consuming to deliver. That leaves several possibilities:

- Interactive classroom sessions can be used intensively for occasional teaching sessions, for example, a revision class. When the setting up of equipment, and issuance of handsets is a major exercise, this may well be the preferred option.

- Attempts to provide full content coverage can be dropped and question sessions used to cover key topics or concepts, as in Peer Instruction (Mazur, 1997) or Just-In-Time teaching. If content coverage is not an issue, and students are coming to classes well prepared, 100% question delivery makes sense.

- Interactive questions can be used to punctuate, rather than replace other teaching methods. Recent evaluation (McCabe et al., 2004a) has suggested that students like content-driven lectures that are punctuated by short, self-assessment questions. This may be regarded as the compromise between lecturers who regard interactive questions as seriously restricting the time available for "content delivery," and those who would like to see greater use of interactive questioning. The question of how to balance interactive questions and content delivery remains open to debate, but is undoubtedly dependent upon the subject matter and circumstances.

The unpredictability of student responses makes it difficult to prepare good feedback in advance. Although this is an issue for conventional CAA, as well as interactive classroom questions, there is a significant difference. For an individual attempting a computer marked MCQ, feedback can be given according to their personal selection. In a group, and especially in a large class, there can be a two-way, three-way, or greater split in responses. It may seem appropriate to respond to the majority vote, but minority votes are important, especially when they reveal a common misunderstanding. Deciding between revoting and "closing off" a question by giving the correct answer or apt feedback is an important skill for a lecturer to develop.

The preparation of questions and consideration of all possible scenarios in advance is a long and arduous task. Branching to different questions according to responses, referred to as "contingent teaching" (Draper & Brown, 2004), is a valuable technique, but it is generally impossible to prepare for all possible contingencies in advance. It may be practical to plan for two different alternatives, but even then, it is discouraging that some carefully prepared resources have become redundant. The problem is compounded if there is a need to update content regularly.

The experiment, mentioned earlier in this chapter, was conducted at a working conference for UK undergraduate mathematics (McCabe et al., 2004b). Six university lecturers, led by myself, worked together for many hours to prepare a fully interactive class on a limited topic. Questions alone were prepared for delivery using an audience response system. The result was extremely lengthy, and required many times more pages than the original text to print out. It would also have taken considerably longer to deliver to students. Even then there was discussion about whether all possible contingencies had been covered.

Although carefully prepared interactive classes are important, a willingness to stray from the script and deliver questions "on-the-fly" according to student needs is also advantageous. This aspect of interactive classroom teaching is, perhaps, the greatest skill required by a lecturer.

The extra time spent in preparing fully interactive classes can be justified, if they deliver improved learning. Experience and evaluation of interactive classrooms show that they can help achieve this goal. In practice, the time required both for comprehensive preparation and effective delivery of all classes in a fully interactive, contingent mode would be prohibitive. Audience response systems are, nevertheless, recommended for all "interactive lecturers." The question of how the balance between use of audience response systems and other teaching methods can be achieved remains open to further exploration and research.

Questions on Questions

Many questions remain about the use of audience (group) response systems in teaching. How does class-wide discussion compare with peer-supported learning? How can classes be best structured? How much lecture time should be devoted to interactive questioning, as opposed to straight content delivery? Do interactive classes really improve student learning? Do some types of students benefit more than others? How can pedagogy drive developments in the technology, rather than the other way round?

It may be naïve to pose this final question, but this should not stop the pedagogical questions being addressed. There is an increasing use of audience response systems in UK higher education and beyond. They should be used, not just as gimmicks, but also as tools to promote learning.

It is likely that developments in information technology, communications, business, and even entertainment will govern the future trends. Better integration of audience response system software with PowerPoint™ and other presentation packages may encourage uptake and improve delivery. Online learning systems may make live, audience response at-a-distance easy to manage. Expensive radio systems with many question types may become more affordable. Mobile phones may become a practical alternative to custom handsets. Widespread use in business decision-making, or even the next generation of game show, might pave the way for more effective use of audience response systems in education.

References

Abrahamson, A. L., (1998). *An overview of teaching and learning research with classroom communication systems*. Retrieved from http://www.bedu.com/Publications/Samos.html

Beatty, I., (2004). Transforming student learning with classroom communication systems. *EDUCAUSE Research Bulletin, 2004*(3). Retrieved from http://www.educause.edu/ecar

Crouch, C. H., & Mazur, E. (2001). Peer instruction: Ten years of experience and results. *Am. J. Phys., 69*, 970-977. Retrieved from http://ojps.aip.org/journals/doc/AJPIAS-ft/vol_69/iss_9/970_1.html

D'Inverno, R. (2004). Making lectures interactive. *MSOR Connections, 3*(1). Retrieved from http://ltsn.mathstore.ac.uk/newsletter/feb2003

Draper, S. (2005). *Interactive lectures interest group*. Retrieved from http://www.psy.gla.ac.uk/~steve/ilig

Draper, S. W., & Brown, M. I. (2004). Increasing interactivity in lectures using an electronic voting system. *Journal of Computer Assisted Learning, 20*, 81-94

Dufresne, R. J., Leonard, W. J., Mestre, J. P., & Wenk, L. (1996). Classtalk: A classroom communication system for active learning. *Journal of Computing in Higher Education, 7*(2), 3-47.

Mazur, E. (1997*) Peer instruction: A user's manual*. NJ: Prentice Hall.

McCabe, E. M. (2003a). Do mathematics interactive classrooms help academics engage learners, MICHAEL? *MSOR Connections, 3*(4), 21-24. Retrieved from http://ltsn.mathstore.ac.uk/newsletter/nov2003/pdf/mathinteractive.pdf

McCabe, E. M. (2004c). Taking the MICK: What is a mathematics interactive classroom kit? *MSOR Connections, 4*(1), 25-27. Retrieved from http://ltsn.mathstore.ac.uk/newsletter/feb2004/pdf/mick.pdf

McCabe, E. M., Horowitz, H., & Beakes, C. (2004a). CAA and peer supported learning in interactive classrooms. *Proceedings of the 8th International Conference on CAA*. Retrieved from http://www.caaconference.co.uk

McCabe, E. M., Horowitz, H., & Beakes, C. (2004b). Teaching mathematics in an interactive classroom. *Proceedings of the 2004 UK Undergraduate Mathematics Teaching Conference.* Retrieved from http://www.umtc.ac.uk/index.html

McCabe, E. M., & Lucas, I. (2003b). *Teaching with CAA in an interactive classroom: Death by PowerPoint – Life by discourse.* The 6th International Conference on Technology in Mathematics Teaching. Retrieved from http://www.tech.port.ac.uk/staffweb/mccabem/umtc04/ICTMT6paper.doc

Nicol, D. J., & Boyle, J. T. (2003). Peer instruction versus class-wide discussion in large classes: A comparison of two interaction methods in the wired classroom. *Studies in Higher Education, 28*(4), 458-73.

Thalheimer, W. (2003). *The learning benefits of questions.* Retrieved from http://www.work-learning/mall/PP_WP003.asp

Wit, E. (2003, May). Who wants to be ... The use of a personal response system in statistics teaching. *MSOR Connections, 3*(4). Retrieved from http://ltsn.mathstore.ac.uk/newsletter/may2003/

Chapter XIX

Eight Years
of Asking Questions

Jim Boyle, University of Strathclyde, Scotland

Abstract

Eight years ago, the Department decided to embark upon a radical change to its first-year teaching. A core feature of that change was the introduction of "classroom feedback systems" in large, engineering science classes, starting with ClassTalk and then moving on to the Personal Response System. This chapter gives a brief history of the reasons for this change, which involved other, complimentary, teaching, and learning strategies, our experiences, current developments, and a look to the future, in particular, the way we would like to see the technology developing.

A Brief History

The University of Strathclyde was founded in 1964 from the Royal College of Science and Technology, one of the three big "technological" universities in the UK (along with Imperial College of Science & Technology in London, and the University of Manchester Institute of Science & Technology). The Royal College was originally Anderson's University, founded in 1796, later the Glasgow Mechanics' Institute, and arguably, the original from which the Mechanics' Institute Movement (and the world's great technological universities) grew worldwide (Mechanics' Worldwide, 2004). To this day,

Strathclyde still has the premier reputation for engineering education in Scotland, and attracts the best students. The Department of Mechanical Engineering has avoided the national UK trend of falling admissions to engineering and science, and further, the quality of the student intake is the highest in the UK. In the Scottish educational system (which is different from that of England — university courses last one year longer since students enter at a younger age) entry is based on the "Higher" Examinations, which are graded at A, B, C and so on. Minimum entry requirements to mechanical engineering are AABB, with a minimum of B in both mathematics and in physics: however, the majority of our students enter with AAAA. The Highers are taken in the fifth year of a six-year high school program, so it is possible for students to enter university directly from fifth year. In our case, around 20% do this, while the rest continue to sixth year and take "Advanced Highers" — again, most of our students will have two Advanced Highers at A or B grade, usually mathematics, physics, or technological studies. In general, the incoming student cohort each year (around 140) is, therefore, amongst the best qualified in the UK, and very motivated to succeed. Nevertheless, during the early 1990s, a worrying trend developed: over the first two years on a five-year MEng program, nearly 25% left. Further, attendance at class became poor after the first few weeks. Retention and motivation were clearly an issue and the Department decided that something had to be done.

In making this change, the Department could do so from a position of some strength. Unusually for a large, research-oriented department, there had long been a history of good pastoral care for students (a counselling scheme and a long-standing open-door policy) and an interest in innovations in teaching and learning. Various strategies, such as Keller Methods, PSI, Peer Marking, and many others (including extensive team-building exercises, Outward Bound, European & U.S. exchange programs, support for various UK engineering student team competitions, and so on) had been adopted, as appropriate, over a period of 25 years. Many of these initiatives had been led by successive Heads of Department, and there was a culture that aimed to enhance the student learning experience. Yet the retention problem remained. It became clear that most of the innovations had been introduced in later years, and that the unconscious decision had been made to just let the incoming students "settle down" and get accustomed to the University and get to know each other first. A study of the literature on student retention clearly demonstrated that this strategy was fatal. Subsequently, the decision was made to develop a strategy that tried to give the students that essential "sense of belonging," but which also improved the learning experience.

This decision, by good fortune, coincided with an initiative from senior management in 1996 to fund a few projects in teaching and learning with technology. The writer, and colleagues, had been examining closely the educational literature to look for learning models that would both enhance the student experience, and also improve the "sense of belonging" in the difficult transition from school to university. The early use of "classroom feedback systems," as they were known at the time, had come to our attention through the use of ClassTalk (http://www.bedu.com/) in the U.S., so a proposal was put to management to purchase a system, and further, to make extensive visits to innovative educators in the U.S. Since the other proposals across the university mostly focussed on producing CD-ROMs or building prototype course management systems for the WWW, this one caught management's attention, and was funded.

So, in 1996/97 the New Approaches to Teaching and Learning in Engineering (NATALIE) project began, with an aim to redesign the first-year course, and to improve retention. The literature, at the time, did not point to any real innovations in engineering education that could help to address these problems, but the movement in the U.S. to improve freshman science teaching, and in particular physics, was showing considerable promise. The NATALIE team identified the notion of active and collaborative learning (or interactive engagement) as a core philosophy to improve the student experience, and one that was in line with our beliefs in what should constitute an "engineering" education, since engineers have to be trained to "do things" and work in teams. The Department's previous experience with students working actively in small teams in later years was very positive. However, it was not felt, for various reasons, that this could be readily done in the first year, mostly due to resource problems, and contracting staff numbers. Classes that were essential to an introductory engineering degree program, such as basic engineering sciences and mathematics, still had to be undertaken in a large class format. The challenge was to find some approach that allowed active, collaborative learning in the large class. At this point, the use of "classroom feedback systems," ClassTalk, at Harvard University and University of Massachusetts, Amherst, and the emergence of "Workshop Physics" and "Studio Teaching" at Rensselaer Polytechnic Institute became of focus, and the team decided to visit educators at these institutions:

During the 1990s, Eric Mazur at Harvard and the Physics Education Research Group (PERG) at UMass, Amherst had, among others, been researching the use of ClassTalk in large, freshman physics classes. ClassTalk had been developed by Louis Abrahamson at Better Education Inc. as a wired system using TI graphics calculators to enable Socratic dialogue in the large class setting. Mazur had introduced the idea of asking simple "ConcepTests" during traditional first year physics lectures before ClassTalk had been developed, using scanning forms (or show of hands) to poll the class. ConcepTests are, of course, simple, conceptual questions that test understanding of key concepts, and that require no calculation. He eventually devised a means of asking the questions that allowed the students to discuss the ideas in their own terms with their peers — a technique which he came to call Peer Instruction (Mazur, 1997). It was Mazur's book, and Peer Instruction that motivated the NATALIE team to adopt ClassTalk. The Physics Education Research Group at UMass, Amherst have, of course, been very well known in the development and research of "teaching by questioning" using feedback systems (Dufresne, Gerace, Leonard, Mestre, & Wenk, 1996); the visit here was particularly inspiring, especially their enthusiasm, and deep belief in constructivism in science teaching. They motivated the NATALIE team to look much closer and more deeply at the pedagogical research: this remains a strong theme in our work with students, and a core part of our philosophy. In fact, as a result of these visits, we now always strongly advise anyone thinking of adopting classroom voting systems to do the same — visit real classes and teachers, talk to the students and spend a lot of time with educators who have been using for some time (our experience is that all are very helpful, and we never turn down requests from teachers to visit our classrooms) — and, read the literature on research-based teaching and learning!

The advice we obtained from these initial visits also helped us in several different, and unexpected, ways. Funding was available in the NATALIE project to rebuild a large classroom (120 seats) to install ClassTalk (and ultimately PRS) and to include fixed PCs and data projectors. However, observation of the classes at Harvard and Amherst convinced us that we could include strong elements of group-work, especially if using Peer Instruction as a question and discussion technique. So it was decided to have the classroom rebuilt with group seating for four students: the room was promoted as the "InterActive ClassRoom." Since we were rebuilding the classroom for our use (not exclusively, since Strathclyde operates a central-pool teaching room resource) we also had some flexibility with class times, and decided to make each of the lectures (which we now call "Sessions") 2-hours long (this had been suggested by the team at Amherst to allow a more relaxed start and end to class, and to allow longer discussions, if required). PERG at Amherst also warned us that in-class discussion of physics concepts with first-year students required some skill, partly because the students had little experience of this — they had problems explaining what they were thinking — and to go slowly. This was probably the best advice we had — we have experienced this and observed student discussions over the past 8 years with wonderment. (Subsequent seminars with high school physics teachers, and numerous visits to high school classes, have reinforced this. certainly, in Scotland, the emphasis at school in later years is elementary problem solving in order to "pass the exam" with limited active discussion of key physics concepts).

Although the official launch of the InterActive ClassRoom was the start of the 1997 academic year, several of the NATALIE team had spent the previous 18 months preparing, not only with the visits to U.S. institutions, but also with the use of ConcepTests (decided by a show of hands) and observing student group discussions in each year. The Force Concept Inventory (Hestenes, 1992) and Mechanics Baseline Test (Hestenes, & Wells, 1992) were also used with first-year students (interestingly, our highly qualified Scottish students seem to perform well above "average" on the first attempt at these tests, compared to studies in the literature (Hake, 1998). This appears to be a consistent result, but we have never had the time, or inclination, to investigate further.

October 1998 marked the start of the use of the InterActive ClassRoom in three core subjects — mechanics, thermo-fluids, and mathematics — initially with ClassTalk, but moving over in the last two to PRS after a few months. We decided we needed to concentrate on question/discussion technique and question-sets, rather than the technology. However, the mechanics class (which the writer teaches) also used the ClassTalk TI-86 graphics calculators for dynamics and motion simulation, so the use of ClassTalk continued. Students were placed in groups of four for all these classes, and they remained in their group for the whole academic year, sitting in the same designated seat in each class. Group formation was based on a simple questionnaire that assessed their physics background (some had come from fifth year in high school, some had taken the Advanced Higher Exam in physics), computing experience (since they were also obliged to produce presentations), whether they were staying at home or in university halls, gender, and (by way of a short interview while choosing "elective," nonengineering classes) social skills. For some years, incoming students to our Department had taken part in a full day's introduction to team building skills (through games) on the first day at University. This was adapted to allow the new groups to work and meet with each other before classes in the InterActive ClassRoom started. Within a few weeks (although the lecturer's rediscovered "classroom pressure" with all the in-class activity and talking), it became apparent that this would be an unqualified success — attendance at class was over 90% (and has remained so since), and the class discussions and renewed interest in the subject (as something which was not just "hard sums") very apparent.

This renewed student interest was not only down to the use of ClassTalk & PRS: rather, unconsciously, a serious attempt had been made to "redesign" the whole presentation of the material. To take one class as an example — Mechanics-1, a basic first-year introduction to mechanics which (in the Scottish system) covers a reassessment of Newton's Laws, work, energy and momentum, static equilibrium (with Framework calculations as an example), stress and strain, motion in a circle, and dynamics of rotation. Each two-hour session is designed to contain frequent changes of pace with minilectures, videos (we use the Annenberg Foundation's *Mechanical Universe* (http://www.learner.org/resources/series42.html) reconstructions of the history of mechanics and lectures from CalTech, lectures from the UK Open University, and many other from the History Channel and Discovery), in-class demonstrations, group exercises on structured problem solving, and so on. A lot of the questions come from the *Video Encyclopaedia of Physics* demonstrations (http://www.physicsdemos.com/). We play music (and music videos), and intentionally try and make the class a relaxed and (hopefully) humorous occasion. When the project started, we decided to have two lecturers in class, with one looking after the technology. Although this is not necessary now, we have continued with this, since it significantly helps the classroom dynamics of questioning and discussion. (Since we have combined lectures, tutorials, and demonstrations into the one session, analysis, in fact, shows that this uses less total staff time, and is considerably more effective in terms of student learning.) During class, we discuss what is happening when the responses come in from PRS, and decide what to do next, which questions to ask next, and occasionally, thinking up questions on the spot. Both of us can move through the class while the class are discussing a question, and we frequently have open discussions (even disputes) with each other about the topic at hand. This shows the students that we are also thinking about the subject during class, and that we do also make mistakes and have problems explaining what we are thinking — there has been no loss of authority, and we find this prompts the students to be much more open themselves and willing to speak up in class.

In the first year, ClassTalk or PRS was introduced into the two, basic engineering science classes, and mathematics (which is taught by the maths department). All the lecturers who used it, and the students, thought it was an unqualified success, and fundamentally changed the quality of the "lecture." We were aware that we still had a lot to learn and, in mechanics at least, not happy with the textbook we were using, since it emphasised problem solving much more than conceptual understanding, decided to change. In the second year of the project, the next major change to our first-year classes was put in place. Traditionally in UK, engineering education design was not introduced until later years. We decided (looking at the success of the U.S. ABET2000 projects) to introduce a major component of design in the first year, and base this on a version of Problem-based Learning known as Mechanical Dissection (http://www-adl.stanford.edu/). This accounted for one-third of the first-year time: the students worked in the same groups as in the engineering science classes. One year later, we arranged for them to work in the same groups in all classes, with the exception of student electives. Now, with more than 30 groups each year, over a period of 6 years we have only had one or two wholly dysfunctional groups. We ask at the end of the first semester if they would like to reform groups, or sit in different seating configurations, but every year the students decline this offer.

Finally, during the third year of the project, Strathclyde decided to embark upon a major program of teaching room refurbishment. Since the InterActive ClassRoom had been successful, the architects developed the concept of a managed teaching cluster (adjacent lecture and seminar rooms, all with multimedia and PRS, with the technology managed by a resident technician) with classrooms based on the InterActive ClassRoom, but with better group seating, and two Teaching Studios based on the Rensselaer Polytechnic Institute model, but with PRS installed. With this facility, some of the first-year classes, notably engineering analysis (computing) and parts of maths and mechanics, moved into the Studios, in particular one with shared computers, so that students could also carry out simulations and investigations — some Web-based — in preparation for question and discussion sessions.

It should be clear to the reader that the changes made to our first-year classes have been substantial, and not just the introduction of a voting system. There is considerable group work, specially designed classrooms, various teaching models (Peer Instruction, problem-based learning, and studio teaching), and a revised curriculum that is much more sensitive to what the students have studied at school (of which, more in the next section.) Nevertheless, we can see that use of a voting system does significantly change classroom dynamics and student engagement: in simple terms, they come to class and are very active and involved in discussing the subject matter. Since the NATALIE Project started (it is now finished and all of the above is mainstream), attendance has been consistently high, and retention is no longer an issue (We typically lose between 6 and 10 students from an intake of about 140, most deciding that engineering is not for them). The following section summarises some of the important lessons we have learned in relation to the use of feedback systems (voting systems, response systems and so on).

A Few Lessons Learned

The way that we developed our use of response systems has been closely related to the other aspects of our redesign of first year. Essentially, we use PRS to stimulate discussion of key concepts, based on a constructivist viewpoint. Mazur's Peer Instruction forms the basis of what we do, but there is also class-wide discussion, with students explaining their viewpoints, or quizzing the lecturers. Much of what we do has also developed from problems that have arisen with the school/university transition, and the fact that we are teaching introductory *engineering* sciences to *engineering* students, and we need a slightly different perspective on the content than if just teaching "physics." Nevertheless, some basic issues, problems, and solutions can be extracted; these are summarised below in no particular order:

- We have found it important to explain why we teach in this way, and show evidence that it is worthwhile for the students to put thought, preparation, and effort into what happens in class. By and large, this is all new to them, and we need to help them with the transition. In the Scottish system (and probably in most other places), the students have entered university having been successful at passing exams: their problem solving skills are not particularly well developed, and they have not spent much time "talking," or even thinking, about physics out of the context of written exam questions, especially in later years of high school. We therefore have to "front load" at the start of the academic year with the new students, and show them the research-based evidence, videos of other classes, and so on. In addition, we start with a lot of questions on concepts they should be familiar with, in order to show them how the class works, and what is expected of them — "practice" sessions, in one sense. Further, we need to continually remind the students about this, in particular, when we start a new topic.

- Responses to questions, and the outcome of peer discussion, do change from year to year. We have developed the questions from Mazur's book, and Epstein's *Thinking Physics* (Epstein, 2002), and just about any other source! The first-year mechanics class is taught in two sections (140 mechanical engineers in one classroom, and 120 others from across the engineering faculty in another), so four academic staff are involved. We have spent a lot of time over the past 8 years reviewing and revising the questions, adding more and, more importantly, devising question sets. To us, a "question set" is a set of related questions that allow us to ask "starter" questions, supplementary follow-up questions, and so on, depending on how a particular question session proceeds. Sometimes we also go back to previous, related, topics and questions to get the class to think about them in a different way or in a new context. Quite complicated, but good fun, and it keeps the lecturers' minds alert.

- To us, question wording is also very important. Students in our classes usually try to overcomplicate the question and read more into it than intended. However, early attempts to rewrite questions brought another issue to the fore. We realised we are trying to teach student engineers and an important feature of this is related to what *assumptions* are made. In the mechanics class, we decided to adopt a very structured approach to problem solving, based on multiple representations (Dufresne, Gerace, & Leonard, 1997) and Thomas Moore's problem-solving frameworks (Moore, 2003) (we use of lot of ideas from Moore's book). Problem solving is based on three, basic, problem representations: pictorial, conceptual, and mathematical. An essential feature, to us, of the conceptual representation, is a clear statement of the "engineering" assumptions that are being made. These assumptions are now also highlighted in the questions we ask in class, and often drive the discussion. Some questions we have now made intentionally ambiguous to emphasise the need for assumptions. An example follows.

One of the fascinating questions from Mazur's book relates to students' understanding of the concept of change in momentum:

Think fast! You've just driven around a curve in a narrow, one-way street at 25 mph when you notice a car, identical to yours, coming straight toward you at 25 mph. You

have only two options: hitting the other car head on, or swerving into a massive
concrete wall, also head on. In the split second before the impact, you decide to

1. *Hit the other car*

2. *Hit the wall*

3. *Hit either one it makes no difference*

4. *Consult your lecture notes*

The correct answer is 3. We usually pose this question (and we tend to call them "situations") just after a short lecture and demonstrations on *impulse* (the change in momentum for linear motion). Students have usually only studied momentum at school in the context of collision problems (and used conservation of momentum). We try to make the point that change in momentum of an object (impulse) is often more important for a mechanical engineer, and ask this question to begin making that point. (The collision in the question only really matters to you (in terms of survivability): in both cases, your change in momentum is the same — mass times initial velocity down to zero-so your impulse is the same). Typically, after a Peer Instruction session, the students will be split amongst the first three answers. We then explain our "analysis of the situation," as in the above, and ask for comments. Without fail there is considerable dispute in the class, all of which usually comes down to what assumptions the students are making involving elastic bumpers, the cars changing direction, and many others. This allows us to spell out the importance of making, and clearly stating, assumptions in a rather powerful way (and probably not the way Mazur intended)!

- Keep up to date with the research literature on teaching and learning (which seems obvious). We are continually finding new ideas and adapting them to the way we work. For example, we have also introduced "ranking task exercises" (O'Kuma, Maloney, & Hieggelke, 2000) and started to use features of Just-In-Time Teaching (Novak, Patterson, Garvin, & Christian, 1999): more of this later. Share experiences with other users, even in different subject areas.

- If using classroom discussion and teaching by questioning with first-year students, find out what they have understood, and what they can do, from school. (Of course this would be generally true anyway). Certainly in Scotland, there have been recent changes to the high school curriculum. For example, it took us a year or so to realise that the concept of "centre of mass" had disappeared from the syllabus; and surprisingly to us the students have difficulty with the concept. It is not what is *in* the school syllabus that matters, but what is *not*, and how the content is linked up. As another example, we find every year, students who have had Newton's First Law of Motion misquoted with the "moving in a straight line" aspect omitted. (When we asked their teachers, we were told it was not felt necessary since "they were only studying straight line motion anyway"!)Since we are trying to convince the students that one of the skills they have to learn as a mechanical engineer is recognising situations where objects are not moving in a straight line, and trying to find the forces that are causing accelerated motion, this can be problematic, to say the least. Student misconceptions are well known, but usually not intentional. In mechanics, since the students have studied physics already for several years at school, keeping up with developments at school is relatively easy — we read their notes and textbooks, try the exams, speak to teachers, and visit schools.

- Be prepared to continue the discussions out of class, and stay behind in class, if feasible. This may again seem rather obvious advice, but since we spend hours in class getting the students to discuss and make mistakes, it makes a poor impression if a student (more usually a group of students) come up after class to ask for an explanation of something they did not "get" and you have to make apologies and run away.

- If you can spare the resource (and certainly for large classes), make each session 2-hours long with a break, and have two lecturers in class: we have found this to be a key component to our success. We felt that to support students' "sense of belonging" in their first year at university, we could justify extra resources (and, of course, it should be noted that since the writer is Head of Department, this was perhaps easier than in many cases!).

- Evaluate what you are doing. We continually use Minute Papers or "Muddiest Part" surveys (now mostly done online in WebCT). Do an extensive evaluation, but not too soon after adopting the technology. We carried out an evaluation after 3 years, but it was done by a facilitator from our Centre for Academic Practice. The evaluation (Boyle, & Nicol, 2003; Nicol, & Boyle, 2003) showed clear, student support and enthusiasm for the use of response systems, and helped us to convince others, including university management, that continued support was worthwhile.

One of the more significant outcomes of our experience over the past 8 years has been the importance of careful course redesign. The introduction of response systems required us to think about such issues as assessment, support materials, timetabling, and use of course management systems (WebCT in our case), and so on. The next section tries to rationalise some of this (using a lot of hindsight).

Course Redesign

When we embarked on the NATALIE project, our aim was not only to improve teaching in the large lecture room, but also to improve the student's experience of their first year at university. We mixed together different teaching styles (Peer Instruction, problem-based learning, and studio teaching) with group-work and experienced, sympathetic academics. Most of this was unplanned from the beginning. We just adapted, as we found new ideas that we thought could fit in to what we were trying to do: introduce active, collaborative learning. This fairly ad hoc approach is also found in individual classes (in Strathclyde, a "course" is a degree program while a "class" is a "course," say, Mechanics-1), as explained previously. However, we are being continually asked to try and advise others on how to go about a similar change. As a consequence, we have tried to "rationalise" our experience to try to explain what made it a success. Fortunately, the recent work of L Dee Fink (2003) on "significant learning" has allowed us to put much of what we have done in context as a rational approach to course redesign:

Dee Fink has posed the fundamental question: How can I create courses that will provide significant learning experiences for my students? He has described what he believes are the characteristics of a "significant" learning experience:

- **Process**

    ➢ *Engaged*: Students are engaged in their learning.

    ➢ *High energy*: Class has a high energy level.

- **Results, impact, outcomes**

    ➢ *Significant and lasting change*: Course results in significant changes in the students, changes that continue after the course is over, and even after the students have graduated.

    ➢ *Value in life*: What the students learn has a high potential for being of value in their lives after the course is over, by enhancing their individual lives, preparing them to participate in multiple communities, or preparing them for the world of work.

In our experience, the NATALIE Project has created a significant learning experience. During class, the students are actively engaged, and there certainly is a high, energy level. Much of this is enabled by the creative use of a response system. The first-year classes also certainly lead to a significant and lasting change in the students. They are confident that they can discuss the subject in their own terms, without fear of looking ignorant or uncertain; they are willing to talk about the subject, and grow to ask as many questions as the tutors do. When they move into classes in later years that are based on more traditional lecture formats, they complain: conversely, the academic staff in these classes complain that the students ask questions! They are, overall, more reflective about what they are studying, which, of course, goes to the very core of a higher education. The use of group discussions and Peer Instruction is of enormous value in this. The students have practised the defence of their ideas, sometimes in public; they have had many opportunities to explain the "correct" answer to other students, and help them in their understanding, in their own words.

Dee Fink goes further and develops a "taxonomy of significant learning" in response to the more traditional taxonomy of Benjamin Bloom and his associates (Bloom, 1956), pointing out that most users refer to the cognitive domain, and that now there is a need to go well beyond this, and even cognitive learning itself. So Fink has devised a new and broader taxonomy that is based on a simple idea: For learning to occur, there has to be some kind of change in the learner. "No change, no learning." The complete taxonomy is shown in Figure 1, reproduced from Fink's book.

Figure 1. The taxonomy of significant learning (Fink, 2003)

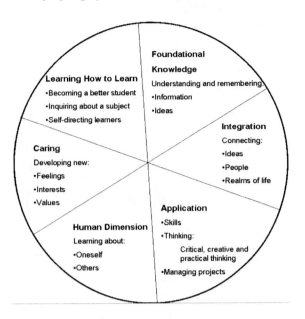

Each of the categories shown in Figure 1 relate to features of our first-year redesign, and of individual classes. The use of ConcepTests and Peer Instruction reinforces foundational knowledge and critical thinking. In class, reflection on the learning process additionally helps the students "Learn How to Learn." Discussion and group-work is a strong component of the human dimension, and so on. We believe our own analysis of how we have transformed the teaching and learning experience for our students and staff, reveals features of most, if not all, of Fink's taxonomy of significant learning. It provides a good case study for Fink's approaches to course redesign in an integrated fashion: even if we undertook the redesign without the benefit of Fink's more systematic approach, our experience included these features as good educational "common sense." But, without the use of response systems, it would have been difficult to do much in the large class setting.

Where Next?

Like many of the earlier adopters of response systems, we have been looking for other technologies to enhance the classroom experience, and to make better use of active learning time in class. We mentioned earlier that we have adopted Just-In-Time Teaching (JiTT). This uses feedback from preclass Web assignments to adjust classroom activities, and lessons to emphasise what students need help with. Warm-up questions and puzzles are placed online (in our case in WebCT) a few days before class, and students are encouraged to participate. (We have not yet built in "grade prizes" for doing this, since at the time of writing we are assessing what the students will do unprompted.) The warm-ups and puzzles are related to planned in-class activities, and often are based on ConcepTests we will use in class, but posed in the form of a "short paragraph." Some warm-ups and most puzzles make use of Physlets (Christian, & Belloni, 2004), small interactive Java applets that demonstrate physics principles. The puzzles are usually explorations of concepts and situations to be discussed in class. So far, about 30% of the class have participated, and the results are so far surprising to us — we cannot guess what the students will have difficulty with, and suspect that it is those students who are not thinking quickly enough during class, or perhaps struggling with some of the material, who are trying the warm-ups. We will need to study this further, but the initial results have been useful in preparing us for class, and we are convinced that JiTT will be a very useful supplement to Peer Instruction.

Obviously, the use of a Course Management System like WebCT opens up other possibilities to enhance the learning experience. PowerPoint™ is used (reluctantly) for presentations in class, although the PRS questions are usually placed on an overhead projector. All are made available as handouts in WebCT, and accessed quite frequently by the students. A textbook is used in each PRS class, so the PowerPoint™ presentation usually contains summary material and related ideas not in the text. For example, when we introduce the notion of forces in bars, and stress and strain, we take the opportunity to show videos of the Hyatt Regency - Kansas City walkway collapse, and explain the cause (with the students voting on likely candidates); this is contained in the presentation. Of course, it also adds to the caring, human dimension and integration of Fink's taxonomy in our attempts to remind the students we are training professional engineers, and not just "teaching physics!" Discussion forums are also set up in WebCT for each topic, although, as may be expected, a lot of the talk centres around homework (which is handed out every other week, and counts towards the student's final assessment, although marking is not so onerous, since we use Tom Moore's problem-solving frameworks, and his two-pass grading system). The most powerful example of the discussion forum was seen during the students' preparation for a class test. The mechanics class is assessed by two, class tests and homework. Each class test is divided into two parts: a compulsory part that accounts for half the marks, and is based around ConcepTests and conceptual understanding, and a problem-solving part, usually with two questions from three. First-year students are quite wary of the questions on conceptual understanding: although they have classroom experience of discussing the concepts with their peers, they have no experience of writing this down (something which will need to be addressed when we get a 9-day week). During the day before the first class test, there were over 200 postings to the WebCT discussion forum, with students comparing answers to conceptual questions from previous and sample class tests. The tutors (the writer included) tried not to intervene too much, but in most cases, other students could resolve issues, which were then confirmed by others. One particular thread involved a question from Mazur's book on balancing and the location of the centre of mass. Despite this being covered in-depth in class, there remained some fundamental misconceptions, which surprised us (the students again made the problem too complicated). We think this discussion should be published in full somewhere for someone to analyse! In class a few weeks after the test, we talked with students who had been particularly active in the discussions, and asked their views: all said they had never had an experience like it, being able to discuss exam questions with other students, and the tutors, the night before the test. This experience has had a powerful effect on us, and will influence changes that we plan to make to assessment in the near future (and which will be discussed in the following).

Course management systems like WebCT have certainly enhanced our use of response systems to the benefit of both student and tutor. However, there remain three issues that we feel should be developed further:

- Although we use PRS when teaching, we also have CPS and H-ITT systems, and have tried most others on the market. As our use of the systems has matured, like many, we now feel that we have outgrown simple multiple-choice questions. At the very least, we would like matching questions and ranking questions. While we understand the desire of the system developers to keep the software simple (perhaps to promote wider adoption amongst the less technically skilled) we also believe, since these are educational products that have the potential to be used in many different ways (academics can be very creative), that the availability of an SDK (software developer's kit) would be a major improvement. A few years ago, we borrowed a set of the RF-based XTOL Series 8 (http://www.xtol.co.uk/) keypads to try in-class testing. The XTOL software does come with a very powerful SDK, and we were very reluctant to hand the system back.

- A common issue with the students is the difficulty with keeping a record of the discussions in class. In the past, we have tried to encourage them to keep notes, but we realise that discussions tend to happen quite fast. We have resisted putting our explanations of the "correct" answers to ConcepTests online (mostly for future security), but do have samples of the more difficult questions as quizzes in WebCT. Many possible video solutions to this have been tried by response system users, but we do not believe that this solves the problem (again in terms of future security of questions). If we were to follow this route, we would probably try to recreate something like Jason Brotherton's eClass (Brotherton, & Abowd, 2004). In any case, we are not wholly convinced that this is a major issue.

- One of the reasons for having more flexible and adaptable software is the potential for in-class testing as part of assessment. Although most systems on the market do allow in-class quizzes, we have found that these are quite restrictive for large classes. As mentioned in the preceding, the first year mechanics class is assessed by regular homework, and two class tests that are half conceptual and half structured problem solving. The students remain focussed on "passing" the class tests, and we have not yet devised a suitable assessment strategy that breaks them free from this habit. (Of course this is risky in itself, since the students have learned to be successful at school with written exams and conventional studying). Yet we are convinced that a suitable balance of in-class testing with response systems, online quizzes, and discussions (recalling the experience we had with WebCT the night before the first class test — a lot of learning and self-assessment was taking place), online homework systems, and short, final written tests should be sufficient.

We would now like to move the student's focus away from "the exam," and use the active-learning sessions and homework to provide formative and self-assessment. Research shows that if the students do realise the advantages of this as a form of assessment — and treat it seriously — then the final summative assessment can be straightforward. Fortunately, Strathclyde has recently been successful at attracting a significant amount of government funding (the Scottish Higher Education Funding Council, SHEFC) to carry out a "transformational change" in assessment. Our mechanical engineering first-year classes will be used as a pilot. The intention is to make use of our fairly unique experience to follow closely the suggestions of the UK Learning & Teaching Support Network (LTSN) Generic Centre's suggestions for assessing large classes (Rust, 2001), in particular "do it in class" and "self-assessment." It is proposed that two fundamental changes are made. Firstly, since current software is not well structured for large in-class assessment through quizzes, the intention is to use the experience of one of the partners in the project, Glasgow University, who have developed their own software support for PRS, to construct an improved quizzing capability more suitable for large classes. Secondly, it is intended to introduce an intelligent, online, homework system for problem solving in engineering sciences. Such systems are in use in many institutions in the U.S., and by U.S. publishers, but their content is not immediately suitable for the Scottish first year (In fact, it should be noted this is a particular issue due to the unique nature of the Scottish educational system). The *Mastering Physics* (http://www.masteringphysics.com/) homework system is the leader in the field, being highly interactive. We feel this system is particularly suitable since the "hints," which can be included in the problems, can be based on ConcepTests. (However, the content would need to be highly modified, and it is likely that an approach would have to be made to the original developers, Effective Educational Technologies (http://www.effedtech.com/index.html), who also provide the *MyCyberTutor* system, for further development).

Conclusions

Audience response systems have changed the classroom. Those of us who use them could not return to the conventional lecture — you get "hooked" on interpreting the feedback and finding out what is going on in students' minds–and it is different every year. We can see more and more educators adopting them as the word spreads, and as publishers (Duncan, 2005) recognise their worth in class, alongside online support. But those of us who have been using for some time are now looking to the future. In Strathclyde, together with the SHEFC initiative on assessment mentioned previously, a new initiative — Teaching and Learning Through Technology (TLTT) — has been launched. The writer has taken on the lead role of being the institution's "Academic Champion" for this project. While the project was initially envisaged by senior management as an "e-learning strategy," the strategy has been widened to include all learning technologies, partly to capitalise on Strathclyde's reputation for early adoption of response systems and studio teaching, amongst others (we also have a successful

Laptop Initiative for the students). Part of the strategy has been to look a few years into the future. It is fairly clear that the convergence of PDAs and mobile smart-phones will have an impact. Strathclyde already has its Microsoft Exchange Servers linked into a mobile phone company (Orange in the UK) GPRS network: several hundred staff use this with Mobile Windows or Pocket PC smart-phones — the writer uses an *i-mate* PDA2K Pocket PC with GPRS and WiFi–and this will be rolled out to students very soon. We are very close to ubiquitous computing, and we are certain this will have an effect on the nature of future response systems. The free ClassInHand (http://classinhand.wfu.edu/) software, developed for WiFi enabled Pocket PCs at Wake Forest University in North Carolina, probably points the way to the future. ClassInHand features a portable Web server, presentation software, quizzing with feedback capability, and a feedback meter. It is expected that all Windows Mobile smart-phones will have WiFi built in, so the next generation of audience response systems, using something like ClassInHand, may have already been defined:

" ... *technology revolutions come in two flavours: jarringly fast and imperceptibly slow .... the slower upheavals grind away over the course of decades, subtly transforming the way we live and work. The emergence of mobile phones around the world has been slow but overwhelmingly momentous ... as our phones get smarter, smaller and faster and enable users to connect at high speeds to the Internet, an obvious question arises: is the mobile handset turning into the next computer? ... " Brad Stone:* Newsweek, *June 14, 2004.*

Perhaps the really big revolution in teaching and learning in higher education will not come with students sitting at screens tapping into Google on keyboards, but with ubiquitous smart-handsets that will emerge from the convergence of mobile phones, WiFi Pocket PCs, and audience response systems.

Acknowledgments

All of the above was not achieved without a team effort. The help over the years from Bobby Hamilton, Bill Dempster, Tom Gray, and David Carus, in particular, and numerous other ARS users in the Department and across the University, is gratefully acknowledged.

References

Bloom, B. (Ed.). (1956). Taxonomy of educational objectives. The classification of educational goals. In *Handbook I: Cognitive domain.* San Francisco: Addison-Wesley.

Boyle, J. T., & Nicol, D. J. (2003). Using classroom communication systems to support interaction and discussion in large class settings. *ALT-J, 11*(3), 116-125.

Braxton, K. (2000). *Reworking the student departure puzzle.* Nashville, TN: Vanderbilt University Press.

Brotherton, J. A., & Abowd, G. D. (2004). Lessons learned from eClass: Assessing automated capture and access in the classroom. *ACM Transactions on Computer-Human Interaction, 11*(2), 121-155.

Christian, W., & Belloni, W. (2004). *Physlet physics.* Upper Saddle River, NJ: Pearson.

Dufresne, R. J, Gerace, W. J., & Leonard, W. J. (1997). Solving physics problems with multiple representations. *The Physics Teacher, 35*(5), 270-275.

Dufresne, R. J., Gerace, W. J., Leonard W. J., Mestre, J. P., & Wenk, L. (1996). ClassTalk: A classroom communication system for active learning. *Journal of Computing in Higher Education, 7*(2), 3-47.

Duncan, D. (2005). *Clickers in the Classroom.* Upper Saddle River, NJ: Pearson.

Epstein, L. C. (2002). *Thinking physics.* San Francisco: Insight Press.

Fink, L. D. (2003). *Creating significant learning experiences.* San Francisco: Jossey-Bass.

Hake, R. R. (1998). Interactive engagement versus traditional methods: A 6,000 survey of mechanics test data for introductory physics course. *American Journal of Physics, 66*(1), 64-74.

Hestenes, D., & Wells, M. (1992). A mechanics baseline test. *The Physics Teacher, 30*(3), 159-165.

Hestenes, D., Wells, M., & Swackhamer, G. (1992). Force concept inventory. *The Physics Teacher, 30*(3), 141-158.

Mazur, E. (1997). *Peer instruction: A user's manual.* Upper Saddle River, NJ: Prentice Hall.

Mechanics' Worldwide (2004). *1st International Conference on Mechanics' Worldwide 2004: Buildings, books and beyond.* Swinburne University of Technology, Prahan, Melbourne.

Moore, T. A. (2003). *Six ideas that changed physics* (2nd ed.). New York: McGraw-Hill.

Nicol, D. J., & Boyle, J. T. (2003). Peer instruction versus class-wide discussion in large classes: A comparison of two interaction methods in the wired classroom. *Studies in Higher Education, 28*(4), 457-473.

Novak, G. M., Patterson, E. T., Garvin, A. D., & Christian, W. (1999). *Just-in-Time teaching: Blending active learning with Web technology.* Upper Saddle River, NJ: Prentice-Hall.

O'Kuma, T. L., Maloney, D. P., & Hieggelke, C. J. (2000). *Ranking task exercises in physics.* Upper Saddle River, NJ: Prentice-Hall.

Rust, C. (2001). *A briefing on assessment of large groups* (LTSN Generic Centre Assessment Series, No.12). York: LTSN.

Chapter XX

Interactive Response Systems in Higher Education

Mick Wood, University of Central Lancashire, UK

Abstract

The University of Central Lancashire (UCLAN) undertook an "interactive response system" (IRS) pilot scheme using IML Question Wizard (IML), complete with 100 handsets, during semester one of the 2004/2005 academic year. This case study will explain the scheme rationale and methodology of implementation. A number of example applications will be explored and evaluated, including IRS use by academic and support staff, as well as utilising the system at a number of conferences. The case study will conclude with a look at UCLAN's future plans to expand the system.

Introduction

The University of Central Lancashire, the sixth largest university in the UK with approximately 36,000 students and 2,500 staff located on four campuses, has a mission-led commitment to widening participation with the aim "to provide the widest possible access to those individuals who seek to benefit from its educational activities and to remove barriers to those with special needs."[1]

UCLAN has a diverse student population, and exceeds Higher Education Funding Council for England (HEFCE)[2] derived benchmarks[3] against a range of factors including disability, students from the socio-economic classes 4, 5, 6, and 7[4], and low participation neighbourhoods. UCLAN also has the third highest number of part-time students across the sector.[5]

Senior management at UCLAN recognised that the diversity of the student population could lead to a higher than average number of students dropping out of their degree programmes. "In many cases it is institutions taking risks in student recruitment by admitting mature students and those without traditional. 'A-Level' qualifications or "highers" that inevitably have the highest drop out rates." (MacLeod, 2002). It is also worth pointing out that behind the statistics lie real people, each one with hopes, dreams, and ambitions, and that "students who discontinue their studies could be damaging their self-confidence and self-esteem" (McGivney, 1996).

An institutional research project (as yet unpublished) — The Student Experience Project (SEP) — began in 2001. The aim was to gain a greater insight into the student experience by tracking a cohort of 750 students, from pre-enrollment through to the completion of their degree in June 2004, in order to gain an overall picture of their student experience.

The SEP discovered that, although many students were extremely satisfied with their time at UCLAN, others were finding the University experience much more challenging. For example, students enrolled in classes with a large cohort often felt isolated and had little or no connection with other students. This was particularly prevalent for those students who had come from relatively small sixth form colleges where they were more likely to have known their peers well. These findings are consistent with the results of the Institute for Access Studies at Staffordshire University which state that "loneliness is the most likely cause of students dropping out of university ... the feeling of belonging was central to the decision to stay or go" (Times Higher, 2002).

Academically, the SEP revealed that many students were used to the highly-structured learning environment of preuniversity education. Although many students enjoyed the challenge of independent learning, others found it difficult to cope with the greater personal freedom of degree-level studies. Some students admitted that they had little idea of what was actually required of them at University, or of how well they were progressing. One solution to this problem is the greater use of active learning in the classroom, that is, "involving students in doing things and thinking about the things they are doing" (Bonwell & Eison, 1991, p. 2).

According to Boyle and Nicol (2003), "there is now a considerable body of research that shows deep and lasting learning is fostered when students actively engage with the concepts they are learning..." An IRS system could encourage active and group/ collaborative learning, thereby drawing the more isolated students into the mainstream; be used for both summative and formative testing; and be used in revision classes to help students gauge their own performance.

IRS Procurement[6]

Professor Patrick McGhee, Pro Vice-Chancellor (Academic) is responsible for identifying new technologies that may have a beneficial impact on learning and teaching. Following consultation with representatives of the Learning Development Unit (LDU) and Information Systems Services (ISS), Professor McGhee authorised the purchase of an IRS to evaluate its suitability in dealing with the issues raised as a result of the SEP.

The IRS selection process began in March 2003. UCLAN required a flexible and scaleable system with many features, and which was modern, robust, and easy to set up and use. In addition, the system had to fit in with the existing IT systems and infrastructure. IML visited UCLAN to demonstrate Question Wizard and the decision was taken to proceed with IML. The initial investment, equating to approximately $50,000 for a one hundred handset system, places IML at the high end of the IRS financial spectrum.

"The IML IRS provides diverse functionality that allows us to integrate the system with a wide range of teaching and discussion activities. Students and staff immediately recognise the positive benefits of the technology and, unlike so many other classroom devices, the impact is neither superficial, nor short-lasting. Having used the system personally there is no doubt that it provides an immediacy that other technologies do not offer. In particular it allows the less confident audience members to participate as equals alongside the more vocal constituencies, ensuring that sessions are genuinely inclusive." Professor Patrick McGhee, Pro Vice-Chancellor (Academic).

IML Overview

IML Question Wizard is Microsoft Windows based software, and requires an IBM-compatible PC running Microsoft Windows XP, 2000, ME, 98, 95, or NT4 with Service Pack 4. In effect, Question Wizard is a Microsoft PowerPoint™ plug-in, although it is also compatible with Lotus Freelance Graphics and SPC Harvard Graphics.

Presenters can create new or use pre-existing presentations with Question Wizard; question "objects" are simply added as additional slides that the presenter then displays during a presentation. Each element of the question object can be formatted to match the existing slides, ensuring uniformity of presentation. Audience responses, which are stored in a relational database for future reference, are instantly displayed on screen in chart form.

IML "communicator" radio handsets are self-powered input devices that allow users to respond to questions. Each handset consists of a keypad with an LCD display window and in-built microphone to facilitate two-way communication. One particularly useful feature of the LCD is the word "valid" or "invalid" that is displayed when users have voted. This has the benefit of informing participants whether their vote has been received and counted.

The handsets communicate via a "base station" that is connected by a data cable to a serial port on the PC, or via an USB-serial converter. Each base station can simultaneously support up to 1,500 handsets. The handsets themselves can also be used as a base station, although this is only useful for relatively short periods of time as the handset operates on battery power in this scenario.

Question Wizard requires a licensing "dongle" that is plugged in to the parallel port on the computer. Question Wizard can also be run in simulation mode to generate test data. This is useful for both evaluating the system, and creating and testing questions prior to a "live" presentation.

IML Technical Issues

The installation of the Question Wizard software on the UCLAN network coincided with the rollout of a new Windows XP image. Although initial network testing was satisfactory, a number of technical issues were discovered, some of which took several weeks to resolve.

For example, Question Wizard 6 was not compatible with Microsoft PowerPoint™ 2003. IML updated the software to Question Wizard 7, which necessitated an update of the BIOS on the communicator handsets and base station. The default file directories (which store the presentations, results, databases, etc.) were changed to overcome network "write" permission constraints, and various "ini" files were reconfigured.

To run the system, a stand-alone computer is required with a serial port to connect the base station. A serial port to USB converter was used to enable the system to work with laptop computers that did not have a serial port. This also required the reconfiguration of the "com" port, and the installation of driver and dll updates.

A number of other minor issues were easily resolved. For example, the standard IRS dongle is PS2, but many new laptops lack a PS2 input. IML quickly supplied a USB dongle.

Question Wizard Features

Question Wizard supports a variety of question types including single digit responses to multiple-choice questions, 127 character free-text responses, multiple-digit responses (including decimal points), ranking questions, multistage questions, and cost-benefit analysis. A variety of queries can also be performed and displayed in real time, based on previous responses. Ad hoc questions can easily be added "live" to a presentation at any time in response to audience feedback. Questions can also be timed so that a vote automatically closes after a predetermined period. UCLAN has obtained permission from a UK national TV company, Channel 4, to use their famous "Countdown" clock music, something that UK students really relate to and enjoy.

Responses can be displayed in a variety of ways. If questions are sensitive in nature, the presenter can opt not to display responses at all, although the data is still captured. Responses can also be stored within the handsets, and downloaded by the presenter at a later stage. This feature is useful for summative testing, perhaps used in conjunction with smart cards.

Users particularly enjoyed the free-text questions. A Macromedia Flash based executable file selects the text responses from the database and displays them dynamically on screen. IML gave the LDU access to the source Flash file, which we then modified to optionally play mp3 files as the text responses are displayed. It should be noted that responses are not vetted before being displayed: malicious users could potentially text obscene or offensive messages although this has not happened in practice.

Over time, a bank of questions are created and stored within IML. It is easy to browse and select such questions if required, saving users the time and effort of retyping.

Data is stored independently for each IRS session, meaning that the same presentation can be given to multiple audiences or classes. Data derived from multisessions can be combined and queried to produce "global" results.

The IRS database can also be used to create a variety of queries. For example, answers to one question (e.g., What is your gender?) can be cross-referenced by the answers to another question (e.g., Do you like the IRS system?) and immediately displayed on screen and saved within the presentation. This, in effect, is how the quiz /scoreboard/team functionality works. An initial question can be used to assign users to teams. The software then tracks responses, based on the initial answers, and will display scoreboards based on individual and/or team responses. Presenters can assign marks for both correct answers and near misses.

Individual responses can be tracked using smart cards. User information is "burned" on to the smart card so that when the card is inserted into the slot on the handset, the IRS automatically associates inputs from the specific handset with the user. In this situation, users can vote anonymously by simply removing the card. Smart card technology lends itself to both summative and formative assessment although, at present, UCLAN has not used this feature, preferring instead to allow anonymous responses.

Post presentation users can print the PowerPoint™ slides, including charts, data, scoreboards, and so forth, as normal. A variety of reports can also be produced.

Training

I undertook a two-day training course with IML to gain familiarity with the IRS. I also visited a number of other institutions, both academic and nonacademic, to evaluate their use of the system.

I produced a 30-page "Getting Started" guide, and an accompanying Web site[7], drawing upon the material used at the initial training. The guide concentrated on the basic functionality of IML, but did not include sections on the more advanced IRS features such as two-way audio, or the ability to store responses for future recovery. I felt that these features should be introduced at a later date, rather than confuse potential users with too much information.

I publicised a training course based upon the guide in a twice-weekly global email sent out to all members of staff at UCLAN. Initial response to the publicity was encouraging, with more than 30 replies from academic staff across a range of subject disciplines including law, biology, languages, physiology, and psychology.

This led to the facilitation of a number of training courses, including one specifically for UCLAN technicians who would provide technical support, if required, for staff wishing to use the system.

Each academic member of staff who undertook a training course was invited to take part in the pilot scheme, and several accepted the invitation. Time pressure, and a (perceived) increase in workload, were the main reasons for declining the invitation, although each person indicated that they would adopt the system at some future date.

I was keen to ensure that the pilot scheme was successful, so I "volunteered" to prepare and format questions and presentations on the users' behalf. I transported and set up the equipment at the various venues, and "drove" the presentation to ensure that there were no technical hitches. Unfortunately, this seems to have become a "job for life," although the process has reinforced my skills and expertise in using the IRS.

IRS "In Action"

Planning Your Career, a level two elective module[8] drawing second- and final-year undergraduate students from across the university, used the IRS to test students individually and in teams, using multiple-choice questions (MCQ). E-Marketing involved approximately 150 students in two cohorts. One cohort used the IRS for summative testing, the other cohort considered the IRS as a possible marketing tool, and also had a team quiz. However, the most extensive pilot of the IRS involved a cohort of approximately 200 students enrolled on three "level-one" physiology modules.

Lectures form the core material for the physiology modules, that are, in turn, compulsory to nine different degree programmes. The lectures are supported by additional tutorial and laboratory classes for various groups. The modules aim to introduce the student to some essential physiological, neurological, endocrinological, immunological, and biochemical principles. The modules are a core prerequisite for second-year physiology modules, and are perceived by students to be difficult. There is a wide age range and gender balance across the modules and courses.

The diversity of the group has, for a number of years, presented a challenge for teaching staff. Many students are mature, with no formal study, whilst others do not have a science background. Increasing student numbers has made communication between the lecturer and students difficult, as individuals are generally reluctant to ask questions or interact with the lecturer, even if encouraged to do so. Feedback about how the course material is being received and understood by students is, therefore, hard to obtain.

A quiz was held using the IRS every third lecture. Students were given a calendar showing when the quizzes would occur, as well as being reminded the week before they were held. Handsets were provided to groups of two or three students and used to register the group by identifying the course they were studying. Approximately 10 multiple-choice questions were asked per session, based on the material from previous weeks' lectures. The groups discussed the options before submitting their vote. Competition was encouraged as each response counted towards an "end-of-semester" team score.

The first time that the IRS was used, the students were briefed on the use of the handsets and the purpose of the system. It was contextualised as part of a series of in-class tests that would assess student knowledge and revision of a number of biological topics. This process took less than 5 minutes. Distribution of the handsets required that one student from each of the groups had to collect (and eventually return) a handset on behalf of their colleagues. I did not receive any negative comments from the students about this process. In subsequent sessions, the students automatically collected handsets en route to their seats.

A typical IRS session was observed by Ros Healy (Senior Lecturer, Centre for Employability), who then produced a report. In her report, Ros wrote:

Michael led the interactive process whilst Darrell Brooks (Senior Lecturer, Department of Biological Sciences) explained and elaborated upon the responses. This seemed to work particularly well as it freed the lecturer to concentrate on the content whilst the technical aspect was managed by the expert.

Students responded very positively to the experience and they had no difficulty in understanding the process or in using the equipment. The questions posed evoked discussion in the small groups and some disagreement about the correct response. It was clear the groups were thinking carefully about the problems that had been posed.

It was a good technique to reveal the answers after the lecturer had explained the varying options as more detailed discussion took place in the groups before the correct answer was revealed. Once answers to the questions were displayed students became very animated and were pleased to see visual confirmation of (correct) responses, again this led to engagement and enthusiasm.

By the time team scores were displayed students were exceptionally engaged and animated; concentration on responses seemed to be improved and there were spontaneous rounds of applause when students correctly answered a question. I would say the system is an excellent tool for team building and team development.

My overall impression was that students greatly enjoyed the interactivity offered by the system. It exploits the natural competitiveness between groups though I do think this has to be sensitively handled. It is a very useful learning tool for a group dealing with a difficult academic topic as it makes learning fun.

IRS Evaluation

"Planning Your Career" students were informally asked at the end of IRS sessions whether they had found them useful and enjoyable. The result was unanimously positive. Several students explicitly mentioned the IRS in their module evaluation questionnaire (MEQ),[9] commenting how much they enjoyed using the IRS technology in lectures.

The "E-Marketing" MEQ explicitly asked students three IRS related questions. When asked whether using the technology was useful and an aid to concentration, 81.8% (N=66) agreed, whilst 18.2% found the technology distracting. When asked whether the IRS had been useful for testing prior knowledge (N=70) 28.6% responded "Very Useful," 61.4% responded "Useful," whilst 10% responded "Not Useful." Finally, when asked if the IRS was a useful method of introducing new concepts (N=71) 21.1% responded "Very Useful," 67.6% responded "Useful," whilst 11.3% responded "Not Useful."

A more formal evaluation took place of the *physiology* module using a combination of online questionnaires, peer observation, a small focus group of three students, and a direct comparison of examination results between 2003 and 2004. It should be noted that the results of this evaluation should be considered as preliminary; a more detailed and structured evaluation will be undertaken when the IRS system is fully implemented across UCLAN.

Online Questionnaire

A total of 95 students completed the online questionnaire (almost 50% of the class), with the results input into SPSS[10] for statistical analysis. The questionnaire consisted of 11 statements with 5 possible responses ranging from "strongly disagree" to "strongly agree."

The results of the questionnaire were overwhelmingly positive. For example, of those students who completed the questionnaire, 99% liked using the system, 99% preferred "IRS lectures" to the more traditional type, 97% liked the timed questions, 90% thought that the IRS made them pay more attention than they would normally have done, 93% thought that the IRS enabled them to evaluate their progress in relation to the rest of the class, and 96% thought that more lecturers should use the technology. In summary, more than 90% of the students were positive about **every** aspect of the IRS.

Peer Observation

As part of a Teaching Peer Observation System[11] at UCLAN, other academic staff attended the IML quiz sessions, and provided feedback.

It was pointed out that at one of the early sessions, it took over 10 minutes for the system to be set up. This raised the concern that the benefit of using the system was outweighed by the time to produce the quizzes and set up the IRS at the start of each lecture.

Another member of staff sat amongst the students and noticed that, while some groups were actively engaged in the quiz, discussing the questions, others were not. In the latter case, the students were going with a "gut" feeling about the answer, without the benefit of discussion. Strategies to improve the dialogue between group members will need to be considered in the future.

Focus Group

The physiology students were invited to participate in a focus group, and approximately 12 students volunteered. Unfortunately, the focus group had to be scaled down due to unforeseen circumstances. It is recognised that the three students who did take part were all females, in their early twenties, and not truly representative of the student cohort. However, when questioned, the responses from the three students were consistent with the results of the online questionnaire.

The students did not feel that the novelty of using the IRS would wear off, "...doing a quiz like that is fun anyway"; they all felt that using the IRS was an improvement over traditional lectures, "... I found I was actually reading back over the work so that when a quiz came I knew more of the answers;" and class attendance improved, "... when there was a quiz coming up there was more people in the lecture theatre ... if there wasn't going to be a quiz, then you tend to think 'oh well I can get the notes off Web CT'[12]."

The students felt that the IRS helped them honestly gauge their own progress, "... you were listening more so that you could find out exactly where you'd gone wrong ... in a normal lecture the lecturer would give out the answer and you could say 'yeah I was going to say that' but with the handsets you know that you were wrong so it highlights your weaknesses."

When used in group work, the students were very positive, "... everyone was discussing the answer, so it got us working together ... it's like we're teaching each other ... one person would say 'I think it's this answer because ...' and the others will say 'no you're wrong because ...'"

Finally, the students felt that the IRS was particularly good for revision purposes, "... I thought it was really useful. It really showed us what we needed to know for the exam."

Examination Results Comparison

The physiology module assessment includes a variety of tests, quizzes, and written work. It includes two "end of semester" examinations consisting of 40 MCQs, each with four possible answers. The "end-of-semester" examination questions were in exactly the same format as those used in the IRS lectures. Students need to score an average of 40% over the different assessment methods to pass the module.

Fundamentally, the only difference between the teaching methods of the two cohorts was the use of the IRS. In other words, the same lectures were delivered by the same lecturer, in the same location, with the same assessment criteria required to pass the module.

In order to usefully compare results, the students were divided into three main groups, depending on their main degree course. There was a quite large spread of results across each group. It is important to note that this was the students' first experience of examination pressures, and that they nearly always improve when the second "end-of-semester" examination is taken.

The following statistical analysis compares semester-1 examination results between the 2003 and 2004 student cohorts. Differences were tested using a one-tailed t-test.

- **Group 1** consists of mainstream physiology students studying biology/biomedical sciences. Their career path would lead them into work in hospital laboratories. These students are highly motivated academically, being fresh out of college with recent experience of learning. The difference between the results for this group was highly significant ($p = 0.001$), with the average scores increasing from 41.5% (N=58) to 54.9% (N=76), an increase of 13.4% in absolute terms. This group won the end of year prize.

- **Group 2** consists of complementary medicine students. They were mainly mature students with no recent formal education or qualifications. They are considered to be highly motivated, and committed to studying well anyway. They were already working hard, and the IRS helped to alleviate any anxiety they may have felt about their academic performance. The average scores for students in this group increased from 49.7% (N=43) to 55.9% (N=41), an increase of 6.2% in absolute terms.

- **Group 3** students are sports scientists and therapists. These students required excellent "A" level results to get on the course, but they tend to be more interested in the actual sport itself, rather than academic study. The average scores for students in this group increased from 33.5% (N=63) to 34.8% (N=72), an increase of just 1.3% in absolute terms. These students, as mentioned in the peer observation comments, appeared to treat the IRS as a bit of fun, and did not really engage in the process.

All groups showed some improvement, although there was quite a large standard deviation across each group. It is difficult to wholly attribute the improvement in performance to the use of the IRS, and there may well be unrelated "non-IRS" factors to take into account. However, as previously mentioned (Boyle, & Nicol, 2003), increased engagement with learning is likely to improve learning. The IRS promoted student discussion about the course material; made lectures more entertaining; improved attention and attendance; improved confidence about what students should expect in the examination; and increased student motivation to research, review, and learn the course material. Ultimately, the results and student feedback concerning the use of the IRS are very encouraging.

Additional Benefits of IRS

Although the IRS was purchased to deal with issues raised by the SEP, it has also been used for a variety of other purposes, perhaps helping to justify the expenditure incurred in purchasing the system. For example:

Service Departments

- Information Systems Services (ISS) have used the system to ascertain staff thoughts on a number of department "away days."

- Library and Learning Resources (LLRS) use the system to test the effectiveness of their student induction training.

- Human Resources (HR) regularly use the system when training staff to serve on recruitment panels to clarify how much information the delegate had taken in and understood.

"The IRS is extremely successful. Every opportunity we've had to use it the feedback has been excellent. Some of the delegates themselves are extremely interested in using the IRS in their own remit." Wilma Butterworth, Staff Development Advisor, Human Resources.

Conferences

The IRS was used at the fourth annual LDU conference, which was held at UCLAN in the summer of 2004. The theme of the "Accessibility in Practice" conference was the practical implications of implementing the UK's Special Education Needs and Disability Act 2001 (SENDA), particularly in relation to the accessibility of Web sites.

The IRS enabled presenters to ask conference delegates their opinions about a variety of Web accessibility issues. Bob Regan, the Senior Product Manager of Macromedia, used the system to ascertain the technical knowledge of the audience **before** delivering his presentation, thus enabling him to "pitch" his presentation at the right level — I have termed this "contingent presenting."[13]

"There are a few things I think that are interesting about the using of IRS. It provides everyone with a chance to share their opinion. If there is no wrong answer, then there is no reason to be concerned about sharing your thoughts. One technique I love using with these types of systems is to call on individuals students to ask how they voted, and explain why. It is better than the old 'paper chase' model of call and answer but students must still stay engaged at a deeper level than passive listening. If done properly, it can be a powerful tool for discussion." Bob Regan, Macromedia

The IRS was also used at the annual "Heads" conference, attended by approximately 70 of UCLAN's senior management. UCLAN's commitment to the IRS was reinforced by the Vice-Chancellor, Malcolm McVicar, who used the system to obtain the views of senior management, across a range of issues. At the end of the conference, the "Heads" were asked two specific IRS questions. There were 71 responses to both questions.

Q1 — Did the voting system add value to the conference?

Yes — A lot — 80%

Yes — A bit — 8%

Not really — 8%

Sell it on EBay — 4%

Q2 — Do you intend to encourage use of the voting system with your staff and students?

Yes — For teaching — 17%

Yes — For general meetings — 37%

Yes — For both — 25%

Can't see an application for the system — 19%

No — 2%

As a result of the conference, three "Heads" volunteered to pilot the IRS within their own academic departments.

Future Plans

The evaluation of the IRS indicates a successful pilot scheme. Informal discussions between IRS stakeholders at UCLAN have confirmed their overall satisfaction with the IRS. The next phase requires that the IRS be integrated into mainstream student and academic life at UCLAN. This raises a number of issues that must be considered as the integration process proceeds over time.

Managing the IRS itself requires that the equipment be in a certain place at a certain time; that handsets are fully charged up, and so forth. Whilst implementing the pilot scheme I have been undertaking these duties personally, but it is impractical to expect this situation to continue indefinitely. Therefore, plans are being formulated to install IRS into the main lecture theatres, enabling staff to access the system on demand. This would help to resolve the (perceived) time issue, raised previously. A centrally-located repository of handsets may be created to issue handsets as required.

A number of portable systems would also need to be available for staff lecturing in smaller teaching rooms. The responsibility for managing the IRS still needs to be formalised, but it is hoped that university technicians will agree to this additional role.

Requests to use the IRS have been increasing on a regular basis. I have been creating questions on behalf of IRS users, but this is impractical on a long-term basis. Training materials have already been written, tested, and used, but the responsibility for the long-term training and development needs of staff wishing to use the IRS needs to be established.

Conclusions

"The IML IRS is a powerful demonstration of how technology can add real value to the contemporary learning experience. We have used the system in a variety of fora, from small seminar teaching to large conferences, at UCLAN and in each application the system offered staff and students immediate audience response and the opportunity to analyse the data in more detail post event." Malcolm McVicar, Vice Chancellor, UCLAN

There has been a very positive response from the vast majority of IRS participants, both presenters and delegates. The implementation has been achieved without any real problems of substance, with the participants keen to make the pilot scheme successful.

Staff at UCLAN, at all levels, recognise that the diversity of the student population could lead to a higher-than-average number of students dropping out of their degree programmes. They also recognise the contribution that technology can make in engaging those students in their own learning process. However, in order that technology can contribute to the academic enterprise, it must be accepted by both academics and learning technologists.

Successful implementation of any change process requires leadership from all levels of any organisation, but initially, the commitment and resources must come from senior management. Recognition and celebration of UCLAN's diverse student population, and the contribution that this specific technology can make to student engagement, was supported by senior management. The responsibility for implementing the pilot scheme was the politically neutral Learning Development Unit. This Unit promotes the integration of traditional teaching approaches with new technologies, and is respected across academic, functional, and financial boundaries of the institution. This is essential for the introduction of any new technology.

Many of the issues raised by students during the SEP have been addressed, at least in part, through the introduction of the IRS, although it is too early to say whether the actual retention figures have improved.

"Research has shown that the vast majority of students enjoy using the IRS system. The system addresses a number of the key SEP issues and is a valuable addition to the academic teaching toolkit." Diane Richardson, Student Experience Project Leader.

References

Bonwell, C. C., & Eison, J. A. (1991). Active learning: Creating excitement in the classroom (Report 1). *ASHE-ERIC Higher Education Reports*.

Boyle, J. T., & Nicol, D. J. (2003). Using classroom communication systems to support interaction and discussion in large class settings. *Association for Learning Technology Journal (ALT-J), 11*(3), 43-57.

Lonely students quit as hard-up students hang on. (2002, September 13). *The Times Higher*, Based on research by Liz Thomas, Director of the Institute for Access Studies, Staffordshire University, UK.

MacLeod, D. (2002, December 18). Loss and retention. *The Guardian*.

McGivney, V. (1996). Staying or leaving the course. NonCompletion and retention of mature students in further and higher education. *NIACE*

Endnotes

[1]   UCLAN, Widening Participation Strategy (Section 1.1) available online at http://www.uclan.ac.uk/other/sds/local/documents/corporate/strategies/widepartstrat.doc

[2]   Further information about HEFCE can be found at http://www.hefce.ac.uk/

[3]   The benchmarks are performance indicators, a range of statistical indicators intended to offer an objective measure of how a higher education institution (HEI) is performing - http://www.hefce.ac.uk/Learning/PerfInd/2003/guide/what.asp

[4]   For a tabular description of the socio-economic classes see http://www.statistics.gov.uk/methods_quality/ns_sec/class_collapse.asp

[5]   Statistics from Higher Education Statistics Agency (HESA) - http://www.hesa.ac.uk/

[6]   Please note that the author had no input in the purchase decision, and is unaware of whether other IRS were considered or evaluated before deciding to proceed with IML. The author has no financial interest in IML.

[7]   http://www.uclan.ac.uk/ldu/irs/

[8]   For an overview of modules, levels, electives, and so forth, see http://www.uclan.ac.uk/ldu/resources/toolkit/modcats/

[9]   The Module Evaluation Questionnaire (MEQ) is used by UCLAN to gather student feedback. Its purpose is twofold in that the student feedback provided will enhance the students' experience of learning and teaching, and it will contribute to the monitoring and review of quality and standards. http://www.uclan.ac.uk/quality/meq/index.htm

[10]   SPSS is a statistical software package developed for use in the social sciences. http://www.spss.com/

[11]   Peer Support for Learning and Teaching Through Observation http://www.uclan.ac.uk/quality/peerobs/app_01.htm

[12]   Web Course Tools (WebCT) is the online virtual learning environment (VLE) used by academic staff at UCLAN to enhance their teaching. See http://www.webct.com/

[13]   For a discussion of contingent teaching as it applies to IRS, see "Degrees of contingency," by Steve Draper, Department of Psychology, University of Glasgow. http://www.psy.gla.ac.uk/~steve/ilig/contingent.html

Section III

Chapter XXI

CommuniCubes:
Intermediate Technology for Interaction with Student Groups

Stephen J. Bostock, Keele University, UK

Julie A. Hulme, Keele University, UK

Mark A. Davys, Keele University, UK

Abstract

This chapter describes an innovation supporting interaction between a teacher, and a student group. It argues that there are five modes of engagement for students in groups. The mode of group interaction with a teacher can benefit from mediation by a voting, or response, technology. An exploratory pilot study of a novel, nonelectronic technology to support this mode is described. CommuniCubes enable every student in a group to vote individually on options presented to them. They were used by a large group in a stepped, lecture theatre, and by smaller groups in seminar rooms. The evaluation found the overall student response to be positive. The reasons students gave for CommuniCubes being both helpful and unhelpful to their learning are summarized. The costs and benefits of this technology and electronic voting devices are compared, and the issues for further research are discussed.

Modes of Engagement

There is a continuing dilemma in higher education. The didactic lecture continues to be widely used with large groups, yet the evidence is that it is ineffective for student learning (Bligh, 1998). It is used for reasons of tradition, efficient use of faculty time, and existing infrastructure. "For the individual learner, the lecture is a grossly inefficient way of engaging with academic knowledge. For the institution it is very convenient, and so it survives" (Laurillard, 1993, p. 109). If lectures are only verbal information transmission, then student activity is restricted to listening and note-making. In contrast, we know that understanding requires "active learning" (Biggs, 2002): learning activities and interactions with other learners. In most universities, face-to-face interaction between a student and a teacher is seen as essential to the quality of the learning experience. Theories of student learning stress the necessity of interaction such as dialogue or discussion (Laurillard, 1993; Mayes, 2001), but as a class size grows, so the amount and quality of interaction with individuals is diluted.

There have been numerous responses to the problem of organizing learning activity and interactivity in large groups (Davies, 2003; Gedalof, 1998; Smith, 1997). One is to improve the lecture's efficiency of information transmission through improved performance and display technologies (Andreson, 1990). Another is to reduce the information being transmitted, and include individual or small group activities (e.g., Bligh, 1998, chapter 19; Brown & Manogue, 2001; Davies, 2003; Race, 2000, chapter 2). Another is to use technology to facilitate responses to structured questions from all the students in a group, typically through electronic voting handsets. These personal response systems (PRS) vary in sophistication from those supporting simple, anonymous voting, to those providing individual feedback (e.g., d'Inverno, 2003; Draper, 2005; Draper & Brown, 2004; McCabe, 2004; McCabe & Lucas, 2003; Wit, 2003).

There are numerous lists or classifications of teaching/learning activities (e.g., Biggs, 2002; Conole & Oliver, 1998; Hegarty, Bostock, & Collins, 2000; Laurillard, 1993; Shuell, 1992), some fine-grained and others broader. The following list seems especially appropriate for face-to-face teaching. Concentrating on student engagement in the teaching/learning situation, we suggest there are generally five types of teaching/ learning activities (Brown & Manogu, 2001), *five modes of student engagement in groups.*

1. **Transmission/reception:** A didactic transmission of information involves the teacher talking, and possibly writing notes (chalk and talk), or displaying a transcript. This places the students in a passive role, with their cognitive activities limited to listening and taking notes, which, for most students, is unlikely to result in understanding at the time.

2. **Multimedia transmission/reception:** Enhanced presentations use additional media to bring impact and realism to the information transmission. This might take the form of integrated, digital, multimedia presentations, but not necessarily: for example, demonstrations, images, sounds, video, and debates between tutors. Students see and hear more realistic or more applied situations, in more memorable

forms. It may present the content of learning, rather than talk about the content in mode 1.

3. **Individual activity:** Individual, student learning activities can be prompted, for example, by a teacher asking students to solve a problem, answer a question, ask a question, write a "one-minute essay" (Draper 2005), or complete a gapped handout. Such learning activities are an opportunity for students to rehearse and apply new information, or practice skills.

4. **Student interactivity:** Interactions between students in small groups can be organized within large groups even in the most restrictive of circumstances, such as a tiered lecture hall. Students can be asked to work in small groups to solve problems, write questions, or debate disagreements.

5. **Student/teacher interactivity:** Teacher/student interactions, in real time, with a face-to-face group, gives the teacher immediate feedback on student performance or opinion, and gives students immediate feedback on their own performance. It requires a mediating technology, generically termed a personal response system (PRS) or "keypad." Without a PRS, we must rely on shows of hands and volunteering, but both have limitations, especially for weak students.

In mode 2, technology may be used to facilitate transmission of information. While modes 3 and 4 do not necessarily require technology, problem a occurs in large groups when we want to consolidate the results of these individual or small group activities: we can select possibly representative students, or ask for volunteers, but we cannot get a poll, or representative sample of results, easily and quickly. We can ask for the results on paper and compile them for the next session, but we then delay the discovery of student performance, and lose an opportunity to give immediate feedback to students, which reduces its value. While student activities and interactivities (modes 3 and 4) may not involve technology, only in mode 5 are the advantages of immediate, two-way feedback possible for student groups. A PRS can demand interactivity from all students, who then get feedback on their individual conceptions and skills. Student voting gives feedback to a teacher on student learning, so that teaching can be immediately adapted to respond to the students' current needs. A PRS can demand participation, and thus attention, from all students, avoiding the need for volunteering.

No single mode is best, and each may be valuable in some circumstances. There is a general educational argument for a variety of teaching methods in lectures (Bligh, 1998), so effective lectures will often use a mix of some or all modes. Different sequences of these modes, in other terms, have been developed (Agnew, 2005; Boyle & Nicol, 2003; Saroyan & Snell, 1997). Students rate lectures with student or teacher interactivity high, and rate didactic, formal lectures very low (Sander, Stevenson, King, & Coates, 2000; Saroyan & Snell, 1997).

While the previous discussion was made in terms of "large groups," how large is large? Gedalof (1998) considers 50 as the threshold for a large group, on the grounds of the possibility of individual contact with students in the time available, and of being able to remember their names. Therefore, a class of, say, 15 might not seem to qualify as a "large group." It is not large if problems of one-way *transmission* (modes 1, 2) are being considered. However, we are now concerned with the impact of group size on the quality of the *interaction with a teacher* (mode 5), and this might be assumed to be in proportion to group size. Reducing the quality or frequency of a one-to-one interaction to one fifteenth of that is a very significant reduction, even if it is less severe than reducing it to one fiftieth. It is this reduction in the interaction possible with individual students that makes the mediation of the communication by a voting technology potentially advantageous in groups of any size.

Personal Response Systems

The thoughtful use of a PRS has delivered educational benefits in a range of subjects (D'Inverno, 2003; Elliott, 2003; Purchase, Mitchell, & Oinis, 2004; Stuart, Brown, & Draper, 2004; Uhari, Renko, & Sioni, 2003; Young, 2001). The snags with mode 5 are the reliance on complex technology, and its cost. The costs of a basic electronic PRS will no doubt continue to fall but, for the time being, the cost is significant, especially for large groups. It is not easy to demonstrate to an institution that this is a wise investment in student learning. In North America, it seems possible to shift the cost of handsets to students, in institutions where the detection and display equipment is widely used. In the UK, this is unlikely. Another cost is training faculty to use the equipment, and educating them to design new lectures to make best use of it. As with any new technology, there will be a minority of staff prepared to take a risk, spend their own time, and try it. However, for students to encounter engagement mode 5 as frequently as other modes, most faculty must use it. For many faculty, the time costs and the risks of dependency on the technology are significant disincentives. A lecture designed to use a PRS will struggle if it fails, with damage to learning and to faculty prestige.

Manual methods of attempting student/teacher interaction in medium-sized and large groups are well established: a show of hands to vote on a question, or asking for volunteer answers or questions. There is no technology and so no risk of it failing but, unfortunately, for most students it is not effective. Volunteers are unrepresentative. A dependence on volunteering means that participation is not required of all students but is optional, for a minority, and the weaker students do not participate.

Between these two ways of mediating student/teacher interaction, electronic and manual, is the possibility of "intermediate technology": "a *different* kind of technology, a technology with a human face, which instead of making human hands and brains redundant, helps them to become far more productive than they have ever been before" (Schumacher, 1974, p. 128). Innovative teachers in the past have used coloured cards or similar devices with which every student can/must vote (Cavanaugh, 1996; Harden et al., 1968 and Dunn, 1969 are cited in Elliott, 2003). How effective can such mechanical devices be? Can we gain most of the educational benefits without the electronics? The remainder of this chapter considers an exploratory pilot study of one such device, and an initial evaluation of its use with medium-sized and large student groups.

CommuniCubes

The desirable properties of a voting device include permitting individuals to indicate a choice of four or five options, quickly, easily, and reliably; counting the votes quickly; and displaying them, if the teacher so desires. Simple mechanical aids such as coloured cards have some disadvantages over an electronic PRS: an element of volunteering is still present if students must hold them up, students may make errors in the process of translating their choice into a colour to be shown to the tutor, there are only a small number of options, and there is no automatic counting. The CommuniCube was designed to minimise these difficulties, without incurring the risks and costs of electronic devices.

CommuniCubes are lightweight, 10-cm cubes, small enough to be handheld and large enough to be visible in a lecture hall seating 400. Five of the cube faces have contrasting, bright colours designed to be distinguished in poor lighting. The sixth (top) face has a design that maps a number (1 to 5) to each of the five coloured faces (Figure 1).

CommuniCubes work most easily when they can rest on a surface in front of each student. When a student rotates their cube to read the number of their selection, a particular coloured face is thus presented to the teacher. Students need not be concerned with the colour to display, removing possible errors in displaying their choice. If only four choices are needed, the cube is simply rotated with the map face on top. If the choice made is number 5, the cube is flipped so the map faces the student and the fifth face is presented to the teacher.

It takes 1 or 2 minutes to train students to use it. Blind students can just as easily use a Braille version, or one with numbers as "bumps." Training faculty in its use involves learning a script to instruct students, and practice in counting or estimating the numbers of different colours being displayed. The manual counting or estimation of colours is not a difficulty, as accuracy is usually not needed. The colours were checked for use with red-green colour blindness in the teacher; students do not use the colours, only the map face, so visual impairment is not an issue for them.

While no automatic record of individual voting can be made, a mechanical system makes additional information available to the teacher. The pattern of voting across a lecture theatre is immediately clear. For example, frequently, those sitting at the back, vote differently from those at the front. Also, voting in a lecture theatre is semianonymous

Figure 1. CommuniCubes

between students, as they cannot see many other students' cubes, but it is not anonymous to the teacher, who will probably recognise particular students and their voting selection. This is additional useful information in understanding the range of student performance or opinions.

The types of questions that can be asked are the same for CommuniCubes as with an electronic PRS: about factual content, answers to problems, personal views or experience, preferences for future topics, and so on. The result of voting is measured by the teacher or an assistant, by counting the cube faces of different colours in smaller groups, and estimating their proportions in larger groups. After voting and counting, the third stage is giving feedback to students on the result. Often, a verbal report is all that is needed. Where there are more options and the students will benefit from seeing more accurate results, two types of pie chart displays have been used. Where a computer display is being used, a spreadsheet with a pie chart for each of the number of options (2 to 5) displays the result as numbers are entered. A second display option is a mechanical pie chart, large enough to be visible in a lecture hall, where each sector is revealed by sliding its handle around the graduated circumference. This is even quicker.

An Initial Evaluation

The CommuniCubes were evaluated in 2003-2004 in two types of student groups: lectures with 120 first-year psychology students (taught by JH, Figure 2), and seminars with 15 to 25 law students in their second or third year (taught by MD). Every student had a CommuniCube. They were used in the second semester, so the groups had experienced similar teaching situations without any voting technology, and therefore had a basis for comparison. Teaching periods were one hour.

The teaching methods were different to those in the lecture theatre, as were the uses made of the CommuniCubes. In the lecture theatre, voting was used for "concept checking": after a short exposition of a concept (mode 1), a multiple-choice question checked understanding (mode 5) before proceeding to the next concept. The lectures proceeded as an alternation of engagement modes 1 and 5. In the smaller seminar groups, voting was

Figure 2. CommuniCubes in action

used for revision, and for answering a case problem prior to students being divided into working groups on the basis of their answer, that is, to launch peer discussion (Draper & Brown, 2004). This used modes 1, 3, 4, and 5.

To minimize the effect of novelty, a questionnaire was administered after three or four weekly sessions (Figure 3).

The total numbers of students responding to the questionnaire were small (41); all of the law students, and a small proportion of the psychology students (who probably suffered from questionnaire fatigue). The "litmus test" question of whether students would recommend further use of the cubes was answered positively by 73%, with a similar pattern in psychology and in law (Figure 4).

Responses to the question about the net advantage of the cubes to their learning were overwhelmingly positive (Figure 5). The modal value overall was "a significant advantage," although for the psychology students, it was between that point and neutral (4 on the scale).

Figure 3. The questionnaire (compressed)

Question A. How do you think use of the cubes has been helpful to your learning? (up to three reasons)
    1. The most important reason is ...
    2. The next most important is ...
    3. The next most important is ...
Question B. How do you think use of the cubes has been unhelpful to your learning? (up to three reasons)
    1. The most important reason is ...
    2. The next most important is ...
    3. The next most important is ...
Question C. On balance, how do you rate the net advantage/disadvantage to your learning experiences of using the cubes? (put a cross against one number on the scale)
From my experience of using the cubes, on balance I think there is :
(a horizontal line with the scale marks left to right)
    1 an overwhelming advantage
    2
    3 a significant advantage
    4
    5 no overall advantage or disadvantage
    6
    7 a significant disadvantage
    8
    9   an overwhelming disadvantage
    10

Question D. Would you recommend we use the cubes in this course next year?
    (please circle an option)   yes/ no/ maybe

Figure 4. Would you recommend we use the cubes in this course next year?

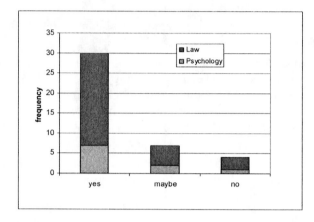

Figure 5. The net advantage to your learning

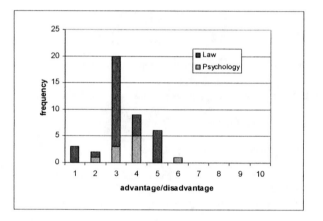

To gain some insight into why students thought the use of the CommuniCubes helpful or unhelpful, the questionnaire asked students to give up to three reasons why they were advantageous to learning, and up to three why they were not. The answers to these open questions were categorized and scored by how frequent a type of answer was given, and how important it was said to be: a score of three for the most important, two for the second and one for the third. Here, the two groups gave somewhat different answers (Figure 6), no doubt reflecting how they were used, and the physical arrangement of the students in the rooms. In the lectures, the most important reasons for the cubes being helpful were getting feedback on understanding and being fun. In the seminars, there was little anonymity in making responses with the cubes, and the most important advantages given were about everyone being forced to participate. No doubt, students' perceptions of the usefulness of the technology were related to how they were asked to use it.

Figure 6. Reasons for the CommuniCubes being helpful and unhelpful to learning

Scores for the different reasons given	Psychology students in lectures	Law students in seminars
Number of students responding	10	32
Reasons helpful to my learning (scores)		
Gave me feedback on my understanding	12	4
It was fun, interesting, variety	12	6
Participation, made me think, contribute, be involved, express an opinion	8	69
Preparation for the sessions improved	-	5
Can express an opinion without embarrassment	-	16
Can see other's opinions and work with them	-	12
Reasons unhelpful to my learning (scores)		
Can get the answer from seeing others' votes	12	13
A distraction, irrelevant	9	-
Slowed things down, wastes time	7	15
Had to make a decision too quickly or when undecided	-	8
Limits the options to respond or discuss	-	11

Higher scores are more frequent or more important answers. The answers to open questions were categorized and scored by how frequent a type of answer was given, and how important it was said to be: a score of three for the most important, two for the second and one for the third. Scores for each category were then totalled.

The disadvantages to learning given in the lectures were worries about the lack of anonymity in voting, the time taken to vote, and to collect and replace the cubes at the start and end of the lecture. In the seminars, these reasons were also given, plus a few worries about multiple-choice questions limiting the responses that could be made about the more discursive content. It is interesting that both groups gave the lack of complete anonymity as their main worry. This may reflect an unnecessary concern about displaying the right answer (given that this was formative assessment and not recorded or graded), rather than displaying their own understanding. It may be that more emphatic guidance on the purpose of using the cubes could overcome this, or it may be that our students are just too easily embarrassed. However, as Figure 5 and the lower scores in Figure 6 demonstrate, students volunteered far fewer disadvantages than advantages.

There is no intention to make comparisons based on the academic level of students or their subjects, as these were confounded with the group size and style of teaching. There was no control group in this data, nor could a valid control be arranged. (How could students who had not used a voting technology offer an informed opinion about one?) The students who used the cubes, and responded to the questionnaire about their use, were comparing their experiences with the cubes to previous teaching/learning situations without them. Furthermore, the data only attempt to measure immediate reaction to the technology, rather than the impact on course learning outcomes or longer-term effects (Kirkpatrick, 1994). This would need a larger study. While the data only represent student perceptions, these are an important contributor to learning outcomes.

Discussion

Learning for understanding requires students to engage with the subject through intellectual activities (Biggs, 2002). Many university students and faculty continue to value the dialogue possible in face-to-face teaching, and many courses continue to schedule seminars and lectures. However, increasing student numbers, in many places, erode their effectiveness by diluting the dialogue. Without thoughtful design, classes easily degenerate into mere transmission of information (mode 1), which is known to be ineffective for student learning (Bligh, 1998; Laurillard, 2001). While interactivities within small student groups are valuable, they fail to make full use of the discipline and pedagogical expertise of the teacher. This interaction needs to be mediated by a technology by which all students make a response; interaction between a teacher and a group by traditional methods (volunteering, shows of hands) is ineffective for many students.

Electronic personal response systems have been found to be effective when used by innovative teachers (Draper, 2005), but they are expensive, and they make the teacher dependent on complex equipment. CommuniCubes are designed to fill this gap: an

Figure 7. Cost effectiveness

	CommuniCubes	**Electronic PRS**
Weaknesses and risks		
Apparent risks of equipment failure	Nil	Significant for novice users
Price per handset	$1 - 20	$120
Staff training	10 minutes	1 hour
Student training	1 minute	1 minute
Time to set up detection and display equipment	nil unless a pie chart display is wanted	10-15 minutes unless permanently installed
Distribution and collection of handsets	5 minutes depending on numbers and room	5 minutes depending on numbers and room
Strengths and opportunities		
Number of possible responses	5	8 or 10
Response time	Under 1 minute	Under 1 minute depending on the system
Counting	Done by teacher	Automatic
Display of data	Done by teacher optionally	Automatic
Storage of individual results	Not possible	Possible
Topological patterns	Automatic	Difficult

intermediate technology that is cheap and simple, cannot break down, and is good enough for the purpose of requiring multiple-choice responses from all students in a group. This initial evaluation suggests that they can be effective both in lectures and seminars.

Every technology has its strengths and weaknesses (Figure 7).

Electronic PRS are improving and becoming gradually cheaper. Their software can store question banks and individual student responses, although this is not, necessarily, welcomed by students (Elliott, 2003). Some advanced versions can give automatic, individual feedback (McCabe, 2004), but these special capabilities require staff effort to design, and come at yet higher cost. Their use as mainstream practice is unlikely for some years to come, even in developed countries. It seems likely that they will remain the expensive research tool of e-learning enthusiasts for the time being.

CommuniCubes, on the other hand, are designed to have just enough functionality to support multiple-choice questions, and thus still stimulate student engagement. The initial evaluation has justified this hope. Their cost depends on the exact construction. Those used in these first experiments were cut from high-density foam and spray painted. They suffered from the experiments of all prototypes, and eventually cost $20 each. However, the construction is flexible. CommuniCubes that are assembled from a printed card are available at a much lower cost, and are thus effectively disposable.

CommuniCubes will be further evaluated in a wider range of disciplines and situations. This study indicates that issues worth investigating in future include the importance of anonymity of voting (to fellow students and to the teacher); the compulsion to vote rather than merely the ability to do so; the impact of the prior knowledge that a voting device will be used on student's preparation and performance in class; and more detailed comparisons with an electronic PRS in terms of pedagogical flexibility and cost-effectiveness.

Even if electronic PRS become more widely available, CommuniCubes may prove to be a useful way to introduce faculty to designing more interactive sessions for student groups. They can experiment with pedagogical designs that mix the five modes of engagement without the equipment and training needed with an electronic system, and its perceived risks. They require no complex equipment or even electricity. They may thus prove particularly useful in developing countries.

CommuniCubes are the intellectual property of Stephen John Bostock and copyright University of Keele.

References

Agnew, C. (n.d.). How do I encourage active learning? *The resource database: Geography, Earth and Environmental Sciences.* Retrieved April 19, 2005, from http://www2.glos.ac.uk/gdn/abstracts/a116.htm

Andreson, L. (1990). Lecturing to large groups. In C. Rust (Ed.), *Teaching in higher education* (SCED Paper 57). Birmingham, UK: SCED Publications.

Biggs, J.B. (2003). *Teaching for quality learning at university* (2nd ed.). Buckingham: Society for Research in Higher Education & Open University Press.

Bligh, D. (1998). *What's the use of lectures* (5th ed.). Exeter: Intellect.

Boyle, J. T., & Nicol, D. J. (2003). Using classroom communication systems to support interaction and discussion in large class settings. *Association for Learning Technology Journal (ALT-J)*, *11*(3), 43-57. Retrieved April 19, 2005, from http://www.psy.gla.ac.uk/~steve/ilig/papers/nicol1.pdf

Brown, G., & Manogue, M. (2001). AMME medical education guide no.22: Refreshing lecturing: A guide for lecturers. *Medical Teacher, 23*(3), 231-244.

Cavanagh, R. A., Heward, W. L., & Donelson, F. (1996). Effects of response cards during lesson closure on the academic performance of secondary students in an earth science course. *Journal of Applied Behavioural Analysis, 29*(3), 403-406.

Davies, P. (2003). *Practical ideas for enhancing lectures* (SEDA Special 13). Birmingham, UK: Staff and Educational Development Association. Retrieved from http://www.seda.ac.uk/

D'Inverno, R. (2003). Making lectures interactive. *MSOR Connections, 3*(1), 18-19.

D'Inverno, R., Davis, H., & White, S. (2003). Using a personal response system for promoting student interaction. *Teaching Mathematics and its Applications, 22*(4), 163-169. Retrieved April 19, 2005, from http://eprints.ecs.soton.ac.uk/9202/

Draper, S. (2005). *Interactive lectures*. Retrieved April 19, 2005, from http://www.psy.gla.ac.uk/~steve/ilig/il.html

Draper, S. W., & Brown, M. I. (2004). Increasing interactivity in lectures using an electronic voting system. *Journal of Computer Assisted Learning, 20*(2), 81. Retrieved April 19, 2005, from http://www.blackwell-synergy.com/links/doi/10.1111/j.1365-2729.2004.00074.x/abs/

Elliott, C. (2003). Using a personal response system in economics teaching. *International Review of Economics Education, 1*(1), 80-86.

Gedalof, A. J. (1998). *Teaching large classes* (STLHE Green Guide Number 1). Halifax, Canada: Society for Teaching and Learning in Higher Education.

Hegarty, J. R., Bostock, S J., & Collins, D. (2000). Staff development in information technology for special needs: A new, distance-learning course at Keele University. *British Journal of Educational Technology, 31*(3), 199-212.

Kirkpatrick, D. L. (1994). *Evaluating training programs: The four levels*. San Francisco: Berrett-Koehler.

Laurillard, D. (1993). *Rethinking university teaching: A framework for the effective use of educational technology*. London: Routledge.

Mayes, J. T. (2001) Quality in an e-University. *Assessment and Evaluation in Higher Education, 26*(5), 465-473.

McCabe, M., & Lucas, I. (2003). *Teaching with CAA in an interactive classroom*. Retrieved April 19, 2005, from http://www.psy.gla.ac.uk/~steve/ilig/papers/mccabe2.pdf

McCabe, M. (2004) Talking the MICK: What is a mathematics interactive classroom kit? *MSOR Connections, 4*(1), 21-27.

Purchase, H. C., Mitchell, C., & Ounis, I. (2004, July 7-9). Gauging students' understanding through interactive lectures. Key Technologies for Data Management. In H. Williams & L. MacKinnon (Eds.), *Proceedings of the 21st British National Conference on Databases, BNCOD 21*, Edinburgh, UK. Retrieved April 19, 2005, from http://staff.psy.gla.ac.uk/~steve/ilig/papers/hcp1.pdf

Sander, P., Stevenson, K., King, M., & Coates, D. (2000). University students' expectations of teaching. *Studies in Higher Education, 25*, 309-323.

Saroyan, A., & Snell, L. S. (1997). Variations in lecturing styles. *Higher Education, 33*, 85-104.

Schumacher, E. F. (1974). *Small is beautiful*. London: Abacus.

Shuell, T. (1992). Designing instructional computing systems for meaningful learning. In P. Winne & M. Jones (Eds.), *Adaptive learning environments: Foundations and frontiers*. New York: Springer-Verlag.

Smith, B. (1997). *Lecturing to large groups* (SEDA Special 1). Birmingham, UK: Staff and Educational Development Association.

Stuart, S. A., Brown, M. I., & Draper, S. W. (2004). Using an electronic voting system in logic lectures: One practitioner's application. *Journal of Computer Assisted Learning, 20*(2), 95.

Uhari, M., Renko, M., & Sioni, H. (2003). Experiences of using an interactive audience response system in lectures. *BMC Medical Education, 3*(12). Retrieved April 19, 2005, from http://www.biomedcentral.com/

Wit, E. (2003). Who wants to be … The use of a personal response system in statistics teaching. *MSOR Connections, 3*(2), 14-20.

Young, P. (2001). *Why use interactive lectures?* Social Policy and Social Work Subject Centre, UK. Higher Education Academy. Retrieved April 19, 2005, from http://www.swap.ac.uk/learning/Interactive2.asp

Chapter XXII

Creating a Constructed Response System to Support Active Learning

Tim Pelton, University of Victoria, Canada

Leslee Francis Pelton, University of Victoria, Canada

Abstract

This chapter describes the design and development of a constructed response system. The classroom interaction system (CIS) is a retro-hybrid technology that recovers most of the benefits of traditional slates while overcoming many of their limitations. Using "neo-slates" (handheld computers), students create responses to instructor prompts and submit them wirelessly to the teacher. The teacher may then, anonymously, present enlarged versions of exemplary, alternative, or erroneous student-generated representations to the class to illuminate concepts, enhance discussions and support student learning. The teacher can also review the database of student responses to support assessment, reflection, and follow-up intervention. Continuing development plans are discussed.

Introduction

Evolution and Renewal of Classroom Technologies

It seems that almost as soon as a new technology emerges, its application and utility in education is explored. Likely technologies are typically applied tentatively at first, and then either gain acceptance, as teachers and students find them to be useful, easy to incorporate, and cost effective, or are rejected because they are ineffective, cumbersome (Cuban, 1986), or too expensive, relative to the benefits derived. Looking back at older, discarded, teaching technologies — both the ones that were successful but later replaced and those that were less successful and never embraced — and considering their potential for revival or repurposing in the context of modern computer technologies may provide us with new ideas to support learning in classrooms today.

Slates

Handheld slates were a common and useful technology in traditional classrooms in the 18th, 19th, and early 20th centuries. By having students hold up their work, teachers could quickly scan the room, and determine the level of student participation and understanding, and either adjust their lesson to meet class needs, identify and help students needing extra assistance, or motivate those who were not getting their work done. It is noteworthy that slates are still in common use in third world countries where the cost of paper is too high relative to the communities' means (Government of Tamil Nadu, 2005).

Although it is likely teachers lamented the loss of handheld slates, the transition to paper and pencil represented a practical advance in technology. The benefits of paper and pencil over slates included increased drawing accuracy (i.e., resolution), expanded work area for more complex representations, and improved readability (i.e., contrast). Paper and pencil use also allowed teachers to improve assessment by supporting retention of student class work for parent review, student completion of homework and teacher review outside of class time, and the introduction of written tests.

Modern whiteboard materials, in concert with an increased interest in constructivism, have supported a resurgence of the use of handheld "slates" in classrooms. Newer handheld dry erase whiteboards are larger, less fragile, and support increased drawing accuracy and readability. From grade school to large university physics classes (Crouch & Mazur, 2001), handheld whiteboards are used as a tool to support students in creating graphical representations, to share their conceptual understandings, or demonstrate their problem-solving processes. Using this revived technology increases the proportion of students who are actively engaged in learning in the classroom, and enhances the quality of discussions.

Yet, representations created by students on handheld whiteboards are still fleeting, and modern sensibilities mean that the discomfort or angst experienced by some students associated with the public sharing and critical analysis of their personal work samples cannot simply be dismissed. Computer technology may be key to supporting and extending the application of handheld "slates" in the classroom.

Audience Response Systems

Over the past decade, multiple-choice based audience response systems (ARS) have matured and become very useful tools in supporting student engagement and participation in the classroom (eInstruction, 2005; Roschelle, Abrahamson, & Penuel, 2004; Pelton, & Francis-Pelton, 2005). With these systems, students select a response from a list of choices, and then transmit their selection, wirelessly, to the teacher's computer where results are displayed as a frequency chart or a bar graph. The apparent pedagogical value of these selected response systems suggests that a constructed response system may also be useful in supporting student learning.

Recent developments in handheld computers and wireless technology have made it possible to construct a retro-hybrid slate technology that combines the pedagogy of slates or whiteboards with the enhanced functionality of wireless equipped handheld computers. With a program of research and development, we are creating a classroom interaction system to support an examination of the viability of such a classroom technology.

In the remainder of this chapter, we describe our vision of a CIS, along with an overview of some of the potentials and limitations that such emerging technologies might have in the classroom. Next, we describe the development process undertaken to achieve a workable prototype CIS, including the functionality of the various components, and the adjustments and accommodations made to improve the pedagogical value and practical operation of the CIS. Finally, we describe our intentions for future enhancements and research, and our interest in finding other researchers who may wish to collaborate with us on this project.

What is a CIS?

An Example

The teacher describes a problem scenario in which the students are challenged to find the surface area of a parallelogram that measures 6 m along the longer edge with the parallel edge being 4 m away. Using their individual handheld computers, students throughout the room construct and annotate a diagram identifying the relevant features of a parallelogram and showing their calculations of its area. As they complete their task, the students press a hot key on their handheld computer to capture an image of their screen and wirelessly transmit that image to the teacher's laptop. The teacher reviews the images as they arrive, and selects some examples to share anonymously with the class through a data-projector (both single images and small comparative sets of images). The class discussion continues, with the shared images supporting and augmenting the traditional verbal communication. After class, the teacher reviews some of the student responses, and sends emails to several students to arrange tutoring sessions.

The CIS System Elements

We have developed a prototype CIS to achieve the communication described above. It consists of two components. The first component is a transparent utility program running on the students' handheld computers, and the second component is the management software running on the teacher's laptop. The utility program, Neoslate, waits patiently for the student to work on their solution. When the student presses a specified hot key, the Neoslate utility then simply captures an image of the current screen, and sends it to the teacher's laptop, using the built in wireless transmission system. Students can create their responses using whatever software applications they need. They may use the handheld computers to:

- construct an image or edit an existing graphic using a drawing or painting program;
- annotate or modify an existing text sample provided by the teacher, using a word processor;
- collect and enter data, or open an existing data file and manipulate that data, within a spreadsheet program, to create a graph or statistical summary;
- capture a photographic image of a shared document, a physical construction, or a group activity, zooming in on, highlighting, and annotating important details; or
- relate a list of words using concept mapping software.

The CIS manager software helps the teacher to manage the student responses. After the teacher sets up a new question and description, the program waits for the student submissions to arrive and stores them in a database. As images arrive, the software provides the teacher with tools to review and select exemplars, and then present enlargements of these images (either individually or as a collage with between one and eight other images) to the class via a data-projector. The projected images are presented to the class anonymously, in order to minimize the potential student discomfort (e.g., embarrassment, sensitivity to criticism, etc.), and to limit distracting submissions (e.g., clowning, etc.).

Figure 1 shows two different handheld computers upon which two students have created their responses to the prompt in the example above. Once a student presses the Neo-slate hot key, the current contents of the handheld computer screen are captured and transmitted to the teacher's station. Figure 2 contains a screen image of the CIS manager software taken after receiving several student responses.

Although it is expected that the anonymous sharing of authentic student representations or work products using the CIS may have some benefits beyond those attainable through handheld whiteboards, selected response systems, or other hybrid response systems, each of these systems has a different set of features, costs, and benefits.

Comparing the CIS to Handheld Whiteboards

The observed or anticipated advantages of the CIS over handheld whiteboards include

- enlarged images presented through a data projector make it much easier for all of the students to clearly see the examples being shared;

- handheld computers do not generate dust or noxious fumes;

Figure 1. Two handheld computers showing two student responses

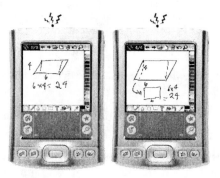

Figure 2. The CIS manager interface

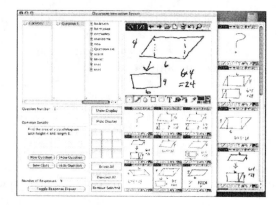

- opportunities to provide templates and base images may reduce the time students will require to construct their responses;

- anonymous presentation of student responses;

- access to advanced applications that are particularly relevant to individual courses; and

- an enduring database that allows the teacher to review responses outside of class time to assess student achievement and needs, support instructional planning and support teacher reflection on instructional efficacy.

Of course, the traditional handheld whiteboards have some advantages over the CIS. These advantages include:

- a per student equipment cost that is two orders of magnitude lower for whiteboards ($2-$10) than handheld computers ($200-$500);

- ruggedness (handheld computers are much more fragile);

- lower threshold and friction (i.e., requiring far less time and effort for student training and ongoing use); and

- a larger drawing space.

Comparing the CIS to other Response Systems

As mentioned earlier and elsewhere in this book, the CIS is not the only type of audience response system capable of supporting classroom discussion and interaction. While the CIS does have the relatively unique capacity to support the sharing of constructed graphical responses, it will not be the best tool to apply in all circumstances.

Selected response systems have some obvious advantages over the CIS including:

- a substantially lower cost per student ($50-$100);

- ruggedness ("clickers" can withstand multiple drops and bumps, and have no screen to break);

- support for medium and large classes (i.e., 25-500+ students compared to 25-100 students for the CIS);

- automated data analysis and presentation mechanisms that lower the cognitive and administrative load on the instructor; and

- lower threshold and friction (i.e., everyone already knows how to answer multiple choice questions and how to use a remote control).

Some hybrid response systems also allow students to construct and submit text or numeric response strings (e.g., Quizdom, 2005). It is anticipated that these systems may find their niche in supporting in-class testing.

Texas Instruments (2004) has created a system whereby their graphing calculators can be used both to support selected response questions, and to transmit graphs or other calculations. This tool shares many functions with the CIS, and appears to work well in a classroom where each student is expected to have and use a graphing calculator. However, because graphing calculators are special purpose computers, the expected utility of this tool outside of mathematics and physics classes may be limited.

Finally, there are other systems that make use of full-size computers (desktop or laptop). While they too have their purposes and advantages, the per student costs are typically an order of magnitude higher than the CIS, and the required computer hardware tends to dominate the classroom landscape in an unhelpful way.

Creating a Classroom Interaction System Prototype

Needs Analysis

During the initial needs analysis for the CIS concept, feedback and suggestions were solicited from experienced teachers, administrators, faculty, and preservice teachers (Pelton, & Francis Pelton, 1996a, 1996b). From this feedback, the requirements and functionality of the two main components of the CIS — a laptop running the CIS manager software and handheld computers running the Neoslate software — were identified.

Although the CIS concept was well articulated in 1996, it was not until 2003 that handheld computer and laptop computer technology climbed over the economic and practical thresholds that would make an initial attempt to construct a prototype viable. Specifically, the electronic "slates" needed to:

- fit within existing classroom contexts (i.e., small, rugged, easy to use);

- have screens of sufficient size and resolution to support effective representation and communication (current handheld computers are minimally viable with 3" diagonal screens and 320x320 pixel resolution);

- include an efficient wireless communication mechanism (radio or infrared) within a practical range; and

- have a reasonable per student cost (ideally less than $200).

Although the cost of the first suitable handheld computers (e.g., the Sony Clie TG50) was approximately $500 per unit in 2003, the price for suitable devices has already fallen to approximately $200 per unit, and is expected to fall to about $100 per unit in the near future.

Time was an important ally in this process. The mellowing effect of leaving an idea "on the back burner" over several years helped to clarify our understanding of how the system would need to function in order for it to be manageable by teachers in the classroom. Also, the availability of general-purpose handheld computers for use as the student slate, instead of a purpose-built electronic slate, expanded the envisioned uses of the system (Pelton, & Francis Pelton, 2003).

A clear understanding of the potentials and functionality of this new hardware facilitated the second round of needs analysis and design. The initial prototype CIS consists of two software programs (Neoslate and CIS manager) that were designed and developed by the authors, along with three talented student programmers over a period of 26 months.

Defining and Refining the Neoslate Software Functionality

The Neoslate utility program was created for Bluetooth-enabled (Bluetooth SIG, 2005) Palm OS 5 based handheld computers. The Neoslate program includes functions that:

- enable, disable, and set the NeoSlate hot key (i.e., the hardware button on the handheld computer used by the student to initiate the send feature);
- manage the login process in which the student may enter a unique ID;
- capture and compress an image of the current screen;
- create a wireless connection with the teacher's laptop; and
- transmit the captured image.

As each student finishes creating a response, he/she simply presses the designated hot key on the handheld device to begin the transmission process. When the hot key is pressed, a pop-up window opens, and the student selects his/her ID. The utility then uses this ID, and the current time and date, to label the image and send it on its way to the teacher's laptop. The last three student IDs entered into the Neoslate software are retained in a list of current users to reduce the number of times a student needs to enter this information. This feature was designed to allow up to three students to efficiently share each handheld computer when (a) the number of available handheld computers is small relative to the class size, or (b) the units are being used by more than one group (class) of students. If a student's login ID is not currently displayed, the student is able to enter it (via pop-up keyboard), and then submit his/her response.

Defining and Refining the CIS Manager Functionality

The CIS manager software runs on Mac OS X based computers equipped with an internal Bluetooth transceiver and having a monitor spanning capability (the second display is used for the data projector allowing the main CIS screen on the laptop to remain private). This software provides

- automatic receipt and storage of student response images;
- access to student response images as they arrive,
- an opportunity to magnify and inspect images;
- a staging matrix that can be loaded with examples from the current set of responses;
- a mechanism to present images from the staging matrix either singly or in small comparative groups; and
- flexible access to the complete database of response images (by student question, time and date).

During the rapid prototyping process, features were adjusted to improve the usability of the system and reduce cognitive load on the teacher during the lesson. The review of all student responses is accomplished by manipulation of a sliding bar on the response "tray" (see the right hand side of Figure 2). If the teacher wishes to inspect an image more carefully, a single click within the image in the response tray will select the image and present it, enlarged 2x, in the main viewing window (top center of Figure 2). If the teacher wishes to include a student response in the staging matrix, a double click on an image in the response tray loads the image in the next available slot (lower center of Figure 2). Alternatively, the teacher can drag an image from the response tray into any cell of the staging matrix. Finally, to present one or more of the images in the staging matrix, the teacher highlights between one and nine of the display flags (the smaller 3x3 matrix directly below the "Hide Display" button in Figure 2) and selects the "Show Display" button. The "Show Display" function presents the image(s) identified by the highlighted display flags to the students through the data projector.

The student response database is a simple tree structure containing a response folder for each question asked during each class, held each day, of each month, of each year. This simple database allows others to create their own utilities to manage or access the database, if they wish. Each response directory will contain a small text file (containing the question text entered by the teacher into the question details field) and a set of GIF and JPG formatted image files (one for each of the student responses).

Observations of a CIS in the Classroom

Some of the expected and observed benefits associated with the introduction of a CIS into the classroom include

- active participation of all students as they generate representations of their understandings, and submit these to the teacher, simultaneously;

- the reduction of student apprehension, as student responses are displayed anonymously; and

- increased feedback to the teacher, supporting timely accommodation of student needs and responsive adaptation of lessons.

Observations on using this initial prototype CIS have illuminated many potentials, and some limitations. University level students, who had the opportunity to use the CIS to support a problem-solving class, responded very positively toward it. The training time required for students to learn the Neoslate utility, and the basic paint and memo programs (used to generate responses) was minimal. As the students became familiar with the applications on the handheld computers, the images they produced became more sophisticated (adding color, using predefined shapes, and applying a variety of tools to create their responses), and more accurate.

The anonymous presentation of student-created responses provided by the CIS was comforting to many students, and yet, when images were presented, students often claimed their creations. A more complete discussion of some of the observations made during the piloting of the CIS is in the chapter titled *Selected and Constructed Response Systems in the Mathematics Classroom* in this book.

Future Enhancements for the CIS

The CIS is evolving, and the next iteration will include incremental improvements in the user interface and function set along with substantial additional features that will extend the utility of the system. Anticipated additional features include

- "over the shoulder" observation of student progress;

- random polling of student screens to support the use of handheld computers in exams;

- efficient delivery of templates, images, and data files to students for use in their construction of responses;

- selected, text, and numeric response capabilities;

- *in situ* private interviewing and polling of students to support research; and

- support for 16-bit images from integrated cameras.

When the "over the shoulder" observation feature is implemented, teachers and researchers will be able to observe the processes students are using to create their responses, and monitor student activity and participation levels.

It is hoped that a random polling and recording feature tool will support the use of handheld computers in examinations. Although some students regularly use their handheld computers for classwork and homework, they are typically not permitted in examinations, because of their potential to support cheating. But, the debarment of handheld computers from examinations is contrary to the ideal of allowing students to use authentic and familiar "tools" to support their accomplishment of performance tasks. With the ability to randomly observe and record images from the handheld computer screens, the concerns about the inappropriate use of resources during exams should be reduced.

Observations of student use of the prototype system have demonstrated that the generation of complex representations is often time consuming. By broadcasting templates, images, or data files, the time required for students to generate the common and mundane elements of their responses will be reduced, and they will be able to more effectively focus their efforts on communicating their understanding. Complex images of biological, physical, logical, or conceptual systems might be presented with instructions to the students to select, identify, annotate, correct, and so forth. Content files to be opened in a spreadsheet program or in other applications might be presented with instructions to modify, highlight, or annotate the content, to convey their understanding.

The simplicity and benefits of using selected response questions to support discussions is obvious: they require no training, and introduce little tangential cognitive load to use. Including a selected, text, or numerical response system as part of a broader CIS will enhance the utility of the tool in the classroom. This is an example of the flexibility associated with general-purpose handheld computers. Ultimately, many educational technologies that are found to be useful with respect to supporting learning or research in the classroom can be duplicated and included as tools on the handheld computers (e.g., graphing calculators are already commonly available).

The CIS could also become very useful as a minimally disruptive, bidirectional, communication mechanism. This feature will permit a researcher to send questions electronically to any subset of students in the room. While this *in situ* interview system might interfere with the observed classroom process, to a small degree, it will provide a unique opportunity to dynamically collect prospective data efficiently and inexpensively.

Finally, newer handheld computers often include an integrated camera. Although the existing CIS functionality already supports the collection of GIF images from the student, the Neoslate software does not yet fully support the capture and submission of 16-bit color images. As the Neoslate software is enhanced to manage 16-bit color images, students will be able to capture, annotate, and share images from other classroom activities (e.g., constructions created with manipulatives) or share something that they have observed outside of the classroom as part of a homework assignment. Future accommodation of video clips, using a tool to support the transformation of short, video sequences into animated GIFs, and a modified submission protocol, may also be possible.

Conclusions and Invitation

In many classroom settings, teachers promote, direct, and mediate discussions to develop students' understandings of the lesson topics. Often however, discussions in classrooms are dominated by a few outgoing students, while many other students, who may, or may not, understand the underlying concepts associated with the discussion, remain silent (Dickman, 1993; Reynolds & Nunn, 1997). Because students who do participate in classroom discussions are more likely to be forming opinions or questions, and constructing understanding, it seems obvious that there is some pedagogical value in utilizing methods or technologies that support the engagement and active participation of all students.

Having students create and anonymously share graphical representations of their conceptual understandings, or of the processes followed when solving a problem, appears to be the next logical advancement in audience response systems. The assessment of the efficacy of the CIS, with respect to encouraging participation and supporting learning, will be the focus in the next phase of this research.

The CIS prototype presented here is noncommercial, and was designed to support learning and research in the classroom. The authors encourage others who are interested in participating in the ongoing development and evaluation of the CIS prototype to contact them.

References

Bluetooth SIG (2005). *Bluetooth: The official Bluetooth website.* Bluetooth SIG, Inc. Retrieved February 25, 2005, from http://www.bluetooth.com

Crouch, C. H., & Mazur, E. (2001). Peer instruction: Ten years of experience and results. *American Journal of Physics, 69*(9), 970-977.

Cuban, L. (1986). *Teachers and machines.* New York: Teachers College Press.

Dickman, C. B. (1993). Gender differences and instructional discrimination in the classroom. *Journal of Invitational Theory and Practice, 2*(1).

eInstruction's Classroom Performance System (2005). Retrieved February 25, 2005, from http://www.einstruction.com/

Government of Tamil Nadu (2005). *Backward classes, most backward classes and minorities welfare department.* Retrieved February 12, 2005, from http://www.tn.gov.in/policynotes/bcmbc2004-05-1.htm

Pelton, T. W., & Francis Pelton, L. (1996a). The electronic slate: Including pre-service teachers in research and development. In B. Robin, J. Price, J. Willis, & D. Willis (Eds.), *Technology and teacher education annual* (pp. 519-523). Charlottesville, VA: Association for the Advancement of Computing in Education.

Pelton, T. W., & Francis Pelton, L. (1996b). *The classroom interaction system: Using electronic slates to enhance communication during the lesson process.* Paper presented at the Thirteenth International Conference on Technology and Education, New Orleans. ICTE.

Pelton, T., & Francis Pelton, L. (2003, May). *The classroom interaction system (CIS): Neo-slates for the classroom.* Connections '03. Victoria, BC.

Pelton, T. W., & Francis Pelton, L. (2005, March). *Helping students learn with classroom response systems.* Paper presented at the Sixteenth International Conference of the Society for Information Technology and Teacher Education. Phoenix, AZ.

Quizdom. (2005). Quizdom audience response systems. Retrieved November 15, 2005, from www.quizdom.com

Reynolds, K. C., & Nunn, C. E. (1997). *Engaging classrooms: Student participation and the instructional factors that shape it.* Paper presented at the annual meeting of the Association for the Study of Higher Education, Albuquerque, NM.

Roschelle, J., Abrahamson, L. A., & Penuel, W. R. (2004, April 16). *Integrating classroom network technology and learning theory to improve classroom science learning: A literature synthesis.* Paper presented at the Annual Meeting of the American Educational Research Association, San Diego, CA.

Texas Instruments (2004). TI Navigator learning system website. Retrieved January 10, 2005, from http://education.ti.com/us/product/tech/navigator/features/features.html

Chapter XXIII

Instructor Mobile Audience Response System

Jay Dominick, Wake Forest University, USA

Anne Bishop, Wake Forest University, USA

Abstract

This chapter describes a new class of audience response systems: an instructor mobile audience response system, or IMARS. While the typical ARS features mobile data entry devices in the hands of students and a desktop console for the instructor, the IMARS features a mobile device for the instructor and almost any device with a browser for students. The ClassInHand™ software, developed at Wake Forest University, is an example of a prototype IMARS system. It has the principal benefit that the system frees the instructor from being tethered to a desk during class, by turning a wirelessly connected PocketPC into a mobile teacher console. This chapter describes the basic components of an IMARS system, and discusses how it has been used in an educational setting.

Introduction

The instructor mobile audience response system is a new concept that is based upon the standard features of an automated response system. Existing literature deals with either the ARS aspect or the mobility aspect, but not both. Our adoption of the ARS model is based on the teaching methods of Dr. Eric Mazur at Harvard, in which he describes the "ConcepTest" (Mazur, 1997), a multiple-choice question designed to uncover misunderstandings of a particular concept. As stated in the newsletter of the Vanderbilt University Center for Teaching (Fall, 2002): "One reason Professor Mazur's teaching model receives so much attention is that he focuses not on 'coverage,' but on 'uncoverage.' The term 'coverage' refers to the familiar process of covering the contents of a course. 'Uncoverage,' by contrast, refers to the process of surfacing common misconceptions, and enabling students to see how complex ideas in a discipline or course fit together." Audience response systems facilitate the concept test, and this teaching methodology.

What's new about IMARS and ClassInHand™ is the focus on mobility for the instructor, a factor that is important to many faculty members who use the classroom as a theatre for student engagement. Most response systems require the instructor to be anchored to a console or display station in order to execute and analyze the response activity. Simply using a "mobile" laptop computer, rather than a desktop computer, does not free the instructor from the necessity to return, at regular intervals, to the teacher station to manage the system. While the laptop promised mobility for instructors and students, in the context of the classroom, it resembles a fixed computing solution. Others (Cain, 2003) have described the laptop as "luggable" rather than portable, and it certainly is not portable when acting as a response system that requires connectivity to a projector, network, or to special-purpose response systems. The IMARS moves the instructor interaction and control to a wireless PocketPC, a truly mobile device.

McLaughlin (2001), at West Virginia University, predicted: "Over the next couple of years, we should see a convergence of the PDA, wireless networking, and a broad array of useful PDA software. With this convergence the PDA will likely become a general-purpose information appliance, smaller and more portable but otherwise filling the same function as the PC. It will probably become an indispensable tool for students, faculty, and administrators in higher education." This convergence began on the Wake Forest University campus in 2001, and accelerated with major improvements to the campus wireless infrastructure in 2004 (Dominick, & Bishop, 2003; Fulp, & Fulp, 2003). In addition, improvements in the PDAs themselves, particularly with the inclusion of embedded Wi-Fi and improved battery life, opened new possibilities to instructors for in-class experiments. With the increased acceptance of laptop computers as a standard student technology asset, general-purpose response systems that are Web-enabled become more important. In a ubiquitous computing environment, such as was available for the researchers at Wake Forest University, any classroom becomes an IMARS classroom instantly, with the simple addition of wireless networking and a PocketPC for the instructor.

Architecture

A typical ARS consists of at least three major elements:

1. A question presentation system that includes the primary interface for the respondent. Respondent interfaces may range from simple mechanical button-press systems to computer-driven touch-sensitive displays.

2. A results reporting system that provides the data to the instructor. The display may be in terms of unfiltered data, or may be displayed as graphs, or time-series data. More advanced software-based response systems will include an interface for the instructor to manage the response interaction. In particular, such a system will make it simple for the instructor to add, modify, delete, store, and retrieve both questions and results. Other tools may be included in the ARS that approximate online testing and quizzing systems. These features may include extraneous features such as user authentication to enable student-by-student assessment over time and randomized question presentation.

3. A processing system to deliver the questions, capture the responses, and perform any necessary storage or calculation.

The IMARS has all of these major components. In the implementation of ClassInHand™, the primary component providing question presentation and response collection is a custom designed Web server, developed especially for a mobile device based on the PocketPC platform. In this case, the respondent uses a Web browser on any Internet connected device. This eliminates the need for students to install and learn to use special client software or devices. In addition, students can submit free-form text, at any time, through the browser, as well as numeric input appropriate for a rating or opinion-based class activity. The index page for this mobile Web server presents links to all these types of activities, for easy access by students.

The storage system is comprised of files organized into folders within the My Documents folder of the PocketPC's file system. There are only three stored html pages: the index page mentioned previously, and the pages required for free-form and numeric input. Question text for concept tests and responses for all types of input supported by the application are contained in dynamically generated files organized into subfolders within the main application folder.

The results reporting system utilizes a custom-developed lightweight scripting language, and a custom CGI engine to process the scripting. This combination of scripting language and CGI engine controls the resources within the application, and manages presentation of dynamic html pages. Figure 1 illustrates the distribution of responses for the *quiz* feature in histogram form on the PocketPC screen, including both counts and percentages for each response. Responses for the *text feedback* and *numeric feedback* features are shown individually on the instructor's PocketPC screen immediately, upon submission.

Quiz results displayed on the instructor's PocketPC can also be shared with the class through a computer connected to the classroom projection system. This is accomplished by utilizing the classroom's wireless network to establish a communication link between the instructor's PocketPC, and a ClassInHand™ software component on the computer. This communication link also enables the instructor to browse the hard drive of the computer from his PocketPC, locate and start a PowerPoint presentation on that computer, and manage the slides by tapping on the PocketPC screen. This combination of controlling the lecture presentation, and receiving student input from the same mobile device, allows instructors to move freely about the room during the lecture and feedback activities, rather than being tethered to their desks to manage a console, and enables blending lecture and feedback based on pedagogy, rather than separating them into discrete activities based on the technology required for each. This sets the IMARS apart from typical Audience Response Systems.

The user interface for the instructor is comprised of four main screens easily accessible by tapping the appropriate tabs along the bottom of the PocketPC screen. The default screen is the Web Server (Figure 2), and contains buttons the instructor can tap to instantly start or stop the presentation and response system. Next is the Agent screen

Figure 1. Response display

Figure 2. Web server

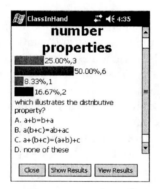

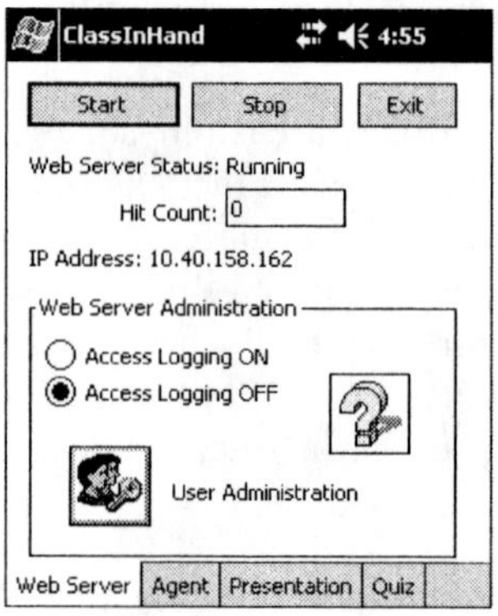

Figure 3. Agent

Figure 4. Presentation (text feedback)

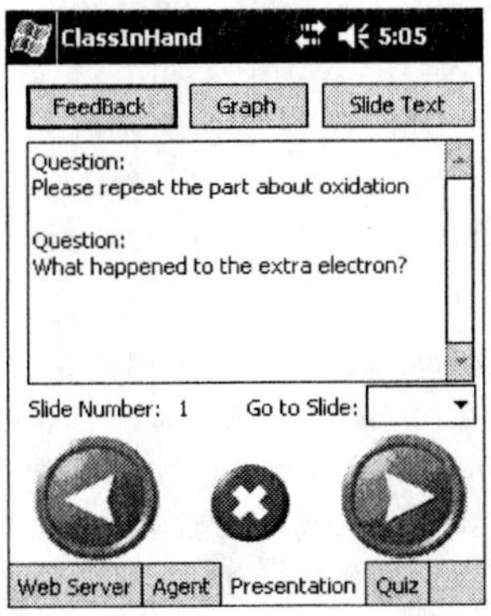

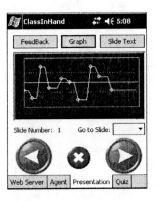

Figure 5. Numeric feedback

Figure 6. Quiz

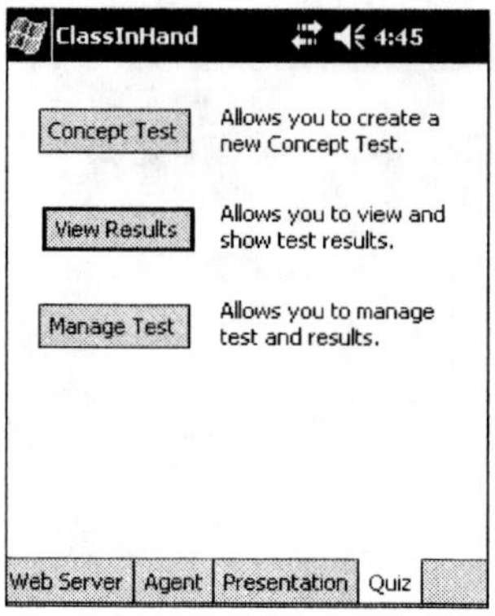

(Figure 3), used for establishing the communication link between the PocketPC and the computer used for external display as described above.

Next is the Presentation screen. It contains thumb-sized buttons for managing the PowerPoint™ presentation and viewing its slide text and notes in the display area. By tapping on the Feedback or Graph buttons, respectively, the display area shows text feedback from students immediately upon submission (Figure 4), or numeric feedback in a continuous graph display format (Figure 5).

The Quiz screen (Figure 6) enables the instructor to drill down to subsequent screens to create and manage quizzes, either prior to class or on the fly during class. In the case of on-the-fly questions, it may be more appropriate for the instructor to reference an externally displayed set of questions, such as from a textbook, handout, or written on a chalk board, or simply a question spoken aloud. In these cases, the instructor may use the default (or blank) question. The quiz screen also has buttons for quickly managing which quizzes appear in the student's browser, editing test questions, showing results to the instructor, exporting results to a file, resetting results' totals to zeroes, and for displaying results to the class.

Challenges

Developing software for the PocketPC platform presents challenges, among them processing power, memory, storage, and limited screen size for the user interface. Managing each of these challenges was critical to the development of a usable system.

We expected the processing power of the PocketPC to be a major limitation. Adapting a Web server to the mobile environment required selective implementation of customary Web server features. The Web server supports a specific subset of HTTP commands in a manner that is designed to enhance both speed and security. By taking advantage of the PocketPC operating system's architecture, which supports multiple processes, each containing multiple threads, we were able to create a very powerful application that was both robust and secure.

Another challenge when writing applications for these small devices is the limited memory available. Unlike most Web servers, the ClassInHand™ Web server does not cache html or images, mainly because of memory constraints. We also created several of our own custom internal data structures when we found that those available as a standard part of the programming environment used too much memory.

Storage on the PocketPC is comprised of volatile memory, rather than hard drive space, as we are accustomed to. If the battery fully discharges, files are lost. To manage this potential problem, ClassInHand™ makes it easy for instructors to save quiz results for later analysis, anonymous text submissions for discussion or reflection, and signed text submissions for graded assessments. These files can then be synchronized or beamed to a desktop computer for permanent storage.

Developing a functional and convenient user interface with the limited real estate on the screen posed another potential challenge. Considering the advantages of a touch screen, we created buttons large enough to tap with either stylus or finger, and tabs to move among the four major screens. The instructor can quickly switch among functions within the application by simply tapping on the screen.

Pilot Projects

In order to evaluate the software, we engaged in triangulated studies in several classes. The study methodologies employed consisted of periodic surveys for students, class observations, and follow-up interviews with students and instructors. The subject classes were all undergraduate classes of between 15 and 100 students, in a variety of academic disciplines. The study periods lasted for an entire semester, and included training for both faculty and students. There was no compensation provided for study participants. A discussion of the classes involved in the project follows.

Physics

Our first pilot project was in an introductory level physics course of 100 students, held in a traditional, tiered, lecture-style class. The instructor had previously used the concept test approach to determine the level of student understanding in his classes, but he had done so by requiring students to record responses on index cards. When students held up their cards, the size of the class and the dynamic of the interaction prevented the instructor from seeing more than the responses for the first, two or three rows of students. He had neither an accurate count, nor a record of the responses, to help him determine the effectiveness of his presentation of the lecture material. Using the ClassInHand™ software, the instructor was able to get quantitative, digital feedback that he could use immediately. Additionally, the instructor could save the responses for later reference. His students also used the text feedback feature of the software to pose questions during the lecture.

Chemistry

In this class of 40 students, the instructor tightly integrated concept-test quizzes with his lecture slides, and used ClassInHand™ on a regular basis in every class meeting. He typically started the class with a one- or two-question quiz using the text feedback feature. He gave students 2 minutes to complete the questions, and managed this by simply tapping on the screen to stop the Web server when time was up. Students signed their names to these submissions, and the instructor graded the submissions later. Most classes included two or three concept tests at logical points in the lecture. At the end of each class period, students submitted additional text feedback, anonymous this time, summarizing the most important point from the day's lecture, and indicating any points of difficulty. The instructor took this feedback very seriously, and found it valuable in directing the next lecture's starting point.

Educational Technology, Nutrition

In both of these classes, each with approximately 20 students, the instructor used the quiz feature of the software, but less often than in the sciences, due to the nature of the material. In addition, both of these instructors required students to do PowerPoint™ presentations on assigned topics. During each presentation, students rated their classmates' presentations using ClassInHand™.

Sociology

The instructor used primarily the Text Feedback feature of ClassInHand™ in this class of 26 students. At the beginning of each class period, she asked a question about the assigned reading, and had students submit signed text responses. She could read the responses as they were submitted, and immediately address any misconceptions that were evident in the students' responses.

Mathematics

In two sections of calculus, each with approximately 35 students, the instructor used methods that required minimal setup on his part to assess student understanding of calculus concepts. He had only two questions built into his ClassInHand™ Web server: Do you understand? (with "Yes" and "No" as possible answers), and a blank question with A, B, C, and D as possible answers. After explaining a concept, he used the Yes/No question to determine what percentage of students felt that they understood the concept. If most of the class responded affirmatively, he followed up by quickly drawing four illustrations on the chalkboard, labeling them A-B-C-D, and asking a question about the drawings that required students to apply the concept just discussed. Students used the A-B-C-D question to submit their answers. The distribution of responses either confirmed that the students did in fact understand the concept, or showed that they only thought they understood. In the latter case, or if students had answered "No" to the "Yes/No" question, the instructor could offer additional explanation.

Discussion

The experiment with the IMARS system at Wake Forest provided several interesting insights that relate to the pedagogical and technical aspects of mobile device utilization. Within the pedagogical realm, instructors utilizing automatic response technology must be able to, and prepared to, take action on the feedback that they are receiving. Technical issues are perhaps the most obvious factors related to any AR system, but in a mobile environment, the complexities of the technology assume a critical importance. The following sections will discuss these issues in turn.

Pedagogical Aspects

The particular IMARS system developed at Wake Forest was designed primarily to provide the instructor with a flexible, mobile control tool for the classroom. A key component was the ability of the instructor to receive instantaneous response on his/her handheld. As noted before, this response could be through the numeric feedback, a quiz, or through text response. The key advantage of a mobile AR system is that the feedback system is more naturally a part of the instructor's environment. Instead of having the information display located at a fixed teacher station, the feedback follows the instructor, who can see the feedback privately on his device while teaching the class. Further, as the device is used for classroom control activities such as controlling a PowerPoint™ presentation on a projector-connected PC, feedback presented on the device is more likely to be seen by the instructor throughout the class. As such, it makes it more likely and more natural for the active instructor to engage feedback. The feedback activity that we observed in our experiments highlights several points worthy of discussion.

In all of the classes that we observed, the primary method of feedback for instructors was through the quiz feature, in the spirit of Mazur's concept test. This form of feedback was immediate and focused. The purpose was to assess student knowledge of a particular issue. It provided an electronic parallel to paper quizzes or hand-raising, but with the benefit of fast response and anonymity. As such, it fit well within the paradigm of faculty expectation, and was relatively well received by faculty and students alike. The potential benefit of an electronic recording of "ad hoc" quizzes was described by one of the instructors in the following manner:

I think by institutionalizing this, by incorporating it in a formal way into the course and saying, before you leave class you must do this, I think that will do much to improve the course in two ways: (1) it will allow me to immediately address in the next class deficiencies in the way I communicate to the class; and (2) once again it will improve my course from semester to semester. I will see these are what the responses were and this was good, that was bad. And so the things that worked, I'll keep, the things that didn't work, I'll trash and find another way to approach it.

The important element was that the automatic response allowed the instructor to obtain immediate and actionable feedback that could be used to improve the teaching of the class. It was useful for addressing particular issues, but in addition, the process of *experiment, evaluate, and correct* is facilitated via the electronic technology because it is easier to record, store, and manipulate the data. These are aspects that would apply equally to mobile response systems and fixed response systems.

More challenging to the faculty was the ad hoc text based feedback. Because the feedback display system is carried by the instructor, he or she is more likely to interact with text feedback in unplanned situations. When presented with ad hoc feedback, or by a response such as "I don't understand", an instructor is faced with the necessity of making multiple decisions very rapidly. First, for a single piece of text feedback (the typical case in our study), the instructor must quickly assess whether this is a widespread feeling, or whether it is an isolated experience. Second, the instructor must decide what action, if any, to take. Third, the instructor must balance the time spent on addressing the question, with the objectives of the syllabus. Finally, instructors wishing to encourage response and feedback in the classroom feel reluctant to simply ignore difficult feedback, for fear of providing negative reinforcement.

In our study, we found that unsolicited text feedback produced difficulties for instructors who were not prepared for such events. As opposed to the structured responses from quizzes, as noted prior, which have finite possibilities, informal feedback is an event that has no defined response set. The instructor has to make snap judgments about what to do. This can be uncomfortable for an instructor even if he/she is prepared for it. One thing an instructor can do to manage freetext feedback is to set expectations correctly at the beginning of class, informing students as to whether feedback will be viewed and acted upon immediately, or reviewed after class.

It is important to note that in all cases where feedback is sought, the instructor must carefully consider the impact of that feedback. In courses which are linked to a tight time frame, such as many introductory courses with common syllabi, the instructor faces a difficult choice. If he/she acts on the feedback, the risk is that some other topic in the class will suffer in its time presentation, and that the students will be at a disadvantage in their later courses or on a common examination. If he/she ignores the feedback from the student, the entire purpose of the feedback system is compromised. These are issues that apply to all classroom response systems.

In all of our pilot classes, the instructors felt that the anonymity of the responses was an important feature of the software. Students were able to respond honestly without fear of exposing their uncertainty or lack of knowledge to either the professor or their classmates, and thus were not hesitant to participate. They viewed this as a self-test where they could determine their level of knowledge without affecting their grades. For occasions when nonanonymous feedback was important, instructors had students use ClassInHand™'s text feedback feature, and simply sign their names to the submissions. One of the instructors who used both signed and unsigned feedback remarked that he received more communications from students through ClassInHand™ than email, because students were sometimes hesitant to reveal their identities when asking a question. In no case was submission of inappropriate material a problem.

Technical Issues

In our studies, we found that there were several technical challenges presented with an IMARS device. Because the device is battery powered, power consumption becomes a critical factor influencing the utility of the device. It is possible to plug the devices into a charging station, but this decreases the mobility, and hence the spontaneity of its use. The built-in power management features of PocketPC proved to be a hindrance, rather than a help, in using ClassInHand™. As can be expected, battery life dropped significantly with extensive display and wireless network use. We learned in early testing that the power saving features must be turned off prior to use in class: otherwise, when the instructor's PocketPC Web server went into power-save mode, students lost their connectivity to the response system. Because use of wireless connectivity drained the battery at a relatively fast rate, early PocketPC models ran dangerously low on power during one 50-minute class period of continuous use of ClassInHand™ for both ARS functions and controlling PowerPoint™ slides. In virtually every course, on at least one occasion, the instructor was unable to use the device because the batteries had been depleted. Instructors in our pilots learned quickly that to be successful, they must not only disable the power-saving features of the device, but also make sure they started classes with a fully-charged battery. As with any classroom-based system, repeated technical problems lead to perceptions of unreliability, and eventual rejection of the device. While there were periodic technical problems in each of the classes studied, none were severe enough to cause complete rejection. Battery technology has improved greatly since our first pilot in 2001, and a fully-charged PocketPC with power-save features turned off can now easily be used for an entire lecture period with power to spare.

We had anticipated that there would be performance problems with the device during intensive feedback sessions. However, careful planning and attention to programming details mitigated this potential problem. Test results have shown that in one minute, the ClassInHand™ Web server can take as many as 15,015 hits using 25 threads with no socket errors. We did not see any limitation in processing power in any of the pilot classes.

Also, there were no major problems presented by the limited screen space available on the devices. Initial concerns about using a small-form factor device were that the controls and feedback would be too small to read by instructors. The ClassInHand™ software was designed to provide an easily navigable interface, with large icons to facilitate quick orientation on the screen (Figure 5). Quick orientation is important because the device is typically carried by the instructor in whatever manner is comfortable, and brought up into view when demanded by the situation. Being able to rapidly find the necessary function on the device is a key component in making the use of the device effective in the class.

The unique capability of the instructor mobile audience response system is that the entire experience is mobile, depending only on the presence of a WiFi network, rather than desktop computers or wired keypads. Because students connect to the instructor's mobile Web site to provide responses, it is even conceivable that the software could be used in a distance-learning environment, where the students at remote locations are participating synchronously to provide feedback to the instructor.

Conclusions

ARS systems can be valuable to an instructor who wishes to inform his practice, and is willing to make the adjustments that such a teaching style requires. The key aspect of the IMARS system is that the response system is mobile, and part of the instructor's personal space. Unlike fixed systems, an IMARS implementation, as demonstrated by ClassInHand™, allows the instructor to gather response from the class without compromising her classroom technique. As with all response systems, the instructor must be both prepared to, and capable of, acting upon the data that is received. The relative immaturity of handheld computing technology provides some implementation challenges, but the problems are likely to be short term rather than endemic. With the increasing availability of super, small, mobile computing devices — from laptops to Web-equipped cellphones — instructors will be able to engage students in both ad hoc and planned feedback activities without the need for large-scale investment in fixed response systems. This will particularly be the case as the classroom experience itself evolves from the traditional fixed-seating environment to an environment that is dynamic in its space.

References

Cain, M. (2003). PDA: Paradigm-disrupting appliance? *Journal of Academic Librarianship, 29*(1).

Dominick, J., & Bishop, A. (2003). A pedagogical characterization of handheld computing use in a university setting. *Proceedings of EdMedia.*

Fulp, C. D., & Fulp, E. W. (2002). A wireless hand-held system for interactive multimedia-enhanced instruction. *Proceedings of the ASEE/IEEE Frontiers in Education.*

Mazur, E. (1997). *Peer instruction: A user's manual.* Upper Saddle River, NJ: Prentice Hall.

McLaughlin, D. (2001). Information technology user devices in higher education. *New Directions in Higher Education, 33.*

Vanderbilt University Center for Teaching (2002, Fall). Highlights from a conversation with Eric Mazur. *The Teaching Forum, 5*(1).

Chapter XXIV

Using Mobile Phones and PDAs in Ad Hoc Audience Response Systems

Matt Jones, University of Waikato, New Zealand

Gary Marsden, University of Cape Town, South Africa

Dominic Gruijters, University of Cape Town, South Africa

Abstract

This chapter investigates how to create ad hoc audience response systems using nonspecialist devices. The chapter revolves around two case studies: one involving the use of mobile phones, and the other based on PDAs. Both case studies are carried out in tertiary education institutions, showing how these devices can be used to facilitate audience participation using devices that students might, themselves, bring to lectures. Both are evaluated from the perspective of the student and the educator, using a mixture of observational and interview-based techniques.

Introduction

Anyone who has given a talk or lecture to a large audience will be well acquainted with the uncomfortable silences, embarrassed glances, and nervous shuffling that greet requests for audience participation. This anecdotal evidence is supported by survey findings presented by Draper and Brown (2004), indicating that if a lecture class is asked for a verbal response, 0% to 3.7% of students are likely to respond: even for the less exposing, "hands-up" response style, the participation rate might also be a low 0.5%-7.8%.

Not all audiences are so shy, though. In the late 1990s, the television game show, "Who Wants to Be a Millionaire?" attracted large, viewing numbers throughout the world. As part of the game format, the contestant could "ask the audience," getting each member to answer the multichoice question using a handset.

Draper and Brown have taken similar handsets out of the TV studio and into the classroom. In Draper and Brown (2004), and an earlier paper (Draper, Cargill, 2002), they present pedagogic motivations for their work, which we share, and will not elaborate on here, beyond noting the value of interactivity and engagement between the learners (students) and the learning-leader (lecturer).

In a long-term, extensive study, summarized in Draper and Brown (2004), the personal response system they used for multiple-choice questions (MCQs) was seen as being of benefit: for example, 60% of 138 first-year computer students rated the system "extremely" or "very" useful; and, similar responses were seen in other disciplines as varied as medicine and philosophy. Handsets are also likely to increase the participation levels: when asked whether they would work out an answer if asked to vote using the system, between 32%-40% agreed.

Of course, specialized handsets have many advantages such as providing simple, direct ways for students to respond (they just press a button): however, there are some drawbacks, including large costs involved in providing handsets ubiquitously, for every student and every lecture; organizational-overheads (e.g., handing out and collecting handsets); and, the impoverished range of responses possible (a single selection for MCQ use).

Inspired by Draper and Brown's experiences, we sought to address these sorts of drawbacks by using a technology that most students now carry with them to every lecture — the mobile telephone. We were interested in whether the pervasiveness and easy familiarity students have with this technology would allow it to serve as a replacement for the purpose-built handsets. Furthermore, we wanted to explore the possibilities beyond MCQs such as students sending free-text questions or, perhaps suggestions and comments to the lecturer. Although other researchers have considered the use of mobile phones in a university setting, for example (Cheverst et al., 2003), we believe this to be a novel application.

Mobile phones are becoming increasingly sophisticated, with a number of current models, sometimes termed "smartphones," providing the sorts of functionality, such as web browsing and document editing, and wireless connectivity, like Wi-Fi and Bluetooth, as well as conventional mobile telecom networking, seen on the handheld personal digital assistants (PDAs). In light of these technological advances, we developed MISPE — the mobile information sharing in the presentation environment, to explore future interaction possibilities for audiences.

The use of personal technologies, like advanced mobile phones and PDAs, has the potential to help all students play a more active role in their education experiences. For people in developing countries though, for example those in South Africa or India, the mobile is a "bridging technology" that can span the digital divide (Marsden, 2003). In these contexts, access to traditional information technology is limited: meanwhile, in South Africa, for instance, over 40% of the population owns a cell phone (rising to 70% for Europe). Staggeringly, over one billion people worldwide own a GSM handset!

In this chapter, we present our experiences in terms of two case studies: the first involves the use of mobile phones to enable the audience to give real-time feedback and responses; the second considers the role of an ad hoc network consisting of the audience's personal technologies, and the lecturer's computer, using MISPE. We discuss both technology issues such as infrastructure requirements and limitations, as well as others relating to the users' experience.

Case Study: Text Messaging

While the specialized handset studies provided us with a very useful set of functional and nonfunctional possibilities, we decided to also run some sessions bringing together a group of eight experts in both human-computer interaction and education (all of which were also lecturers), to brainstorm requirements. In the process, we developed scenarios such as this one:

Dr. Monday begins her lecture on advanced linguistic analysis to 300 first-year students. "Before we go any further, are there any questions about last week's topic? Send me a text now from your mobile phone to 444." After a minute, Dr. Monday checks the computer display and sees there are 25 questions, listed in the order they arrived: she can reorder the list alphabetically and by size of message as well. She selects one of the questions to answer.

Later in the lecture, Dr. Monday wants to test the students' understanding of "focus." "Here's a quick quiz," she says. "If you think focus is related to the subject, text 1 to 444; if you think it is related to the topic, text 2; and if you think it is related to the verb, text 3 to 444." Moments later, Dr. Monday can display a bar chart showing the students what the most popular choice was. "Most of you are wrong," she says, wryly, "The correct answer is 2 — the topic."

Several times in the lecture, Monday asks the students to text their current "happiness level": "send a text message to 444 now to show how well you understand the lecture so far," she says, "enter H followed by a number from 0 to 9, where 0 is the worst." She can view the changing level of "happiness" over time as a line graph.

After the lecture, Monday returns to her office, and can access all the questions sent by students: she can also review the bar charts for each multiple-choice question, and see the "worm" trace plotted over time. All this information helps her review the lecture content, and plan for next week's session.

Such discussions clarified some of the additional forms of interactivity mobiles might provide over specialised handsets:

- allowing multiple responses to an MCQ, for example, "choose 2 of the 5 features listed below";

- parameterised responses, for example, "text your answer (1-5) and how confident you are in your answer (0-100%)";

- open-ended "conversations" between the lecturer and audience; and

- as an active, lecture-experience feedback device.

Pilot-Study System

Before building a full-scale system tailored specifically to the lecture-context, we decided to acquire a third-party, commercial text-polling system to first explore the issues and feasibility of our ideas. The software chosen was the SMS PollCenter by Code Segment. (For information and a demonstration, see http//www.codesegment.com/) The system runs on a PC (we ran it on a laptop in the field studies), and also requires a mobile phone to be connected to the computer via a serial cable, so that sent text messages can be gathered. MCQ results can be displayed in a range of forms such as bar chart and a pie chart. The "SMS Chat" facility displays incoming texts in a scrolling whiteboard format. Software such as this has been used commercially to provide audience response facilities in a range of situations, including television programmes and conferences. Figure 1 illustrates the system in use.

Figure 1. Pilot system use

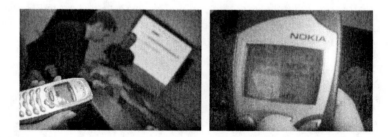

Left-hand image shows a mobile phone being used to send user's response to the lecturer-posed MCQ: background shows lecturer and live results chart summarizing audience's overall response. Right-hand image shows free-form question: "How do I write a function in C++?" being entered on mobile phone: when sent, it is displayed in the system's "SMS Chat" window (which can be displayed to just the lecturer or the entire audience).

Field Studies

Initial Experience Gathering

In the first deployment of the system, we studied its use over six, 1-hour sessions spread over 2 months. Our aim was to gather impressions in a range of contexts, so we chose situations with different characteristics, and used the system in a variety of ways (Jones & Marsden, 2004). Three courses were involved:

- A: first-year programming class run in New Zealand (NZ);

- B: first-year programming class run in South Africa (SA); and

- C: a fourth-year human-computer interaction class in South Africa.

For courses B and $C,$ we carried several trials, each separated by around a week. During each session, researchers set up and operated the system for the lecturer: they also observed the class interaction, and were involved in interviewing students at its end. In classes A and $C,$ the authors were the lecturers — we wanted to experience the system from the front, as it were: two other lecturers were involved in presenting class B. Figure 2 shows the system in use in the first-year programming class in Cape Town.

Figure 2. The pilot system in action at the University of Cape Town. Lecturer is discussing results of an MCQ poll (shown on the RHS display; the poll question is displayed on the LHS screen).

Table 1. Summary of sessions and system use

Session/ system use	Course	Question type	Response elicited	Visibility	# people in class	#unique respondents (% of total)	
1	A	factual	MCQ	Full	155	35	(23%)
2.1	B	factual	MCQ	Full	180	32	(18%)
2.2	B	personal	chat	Full	180	16	(9%)
3.1	B	personal	MCQ	Partial	150	17	(11%)
3.2	B	factual	MCQ	Partial	150	10	(7%)
4.1	C	personal	MCQ	Full	40	15	(38%)
4.2	C	personal	chat	Full	40	3	(1%)
5.1	C	factual	MCQ	Full	40	6	(15%)
5.2	C	personal	chat	Hidden	40	3	(1%)
6.1	C	personal	MCQ	Full	33	10	(30%)
Mean					**101**	**15**	**(15%)**

In each session (e.g. session 2), there was one or more uses of the system (e.g., 2.1, 2.2). Questions were either factual (based on lecture content), or personal (eliciting subjective opinion). Text messages sent were either single selections relating to an MCQ, or free text (chat style). Messages/poll results were either fully visible (results shown during polling and dynamically updated), partially visible (final results shown at end of polling), or hidden (only the lecturer saw the messages).

A summary of each session, and use of the system within them, is shown in Table 1, along with data on the number of text messages received during each use. While this table gives some raw indications of interactivity, it is worth highlighting some of the specific behaviours and effects we noticed. First, 19% of all logged responses to MCQ style questions were in a form that was not recognized by our answer matching filters: for example, in Session 2.1, the students were asked to enter a single integer, but one sent "Turn 72 degqees" (sic). Second, on average, 10% of respondents sent more than one message in response to a question (either resending their initial response, or changing their vote). Third, in SA, 6% of all messages were spam (e.g., "Let the universe decide SMS "oracle" to 34009"); no spam was received in NZ. Fourth, in most of the MCQ cases, as the lecturer discussed the results of the poll chart, additional messages would arrive — sometimes this was a mobile telephone network effect (5%-10% of messages were delayed), but there was also evidence of a "playfulness" as students attempted to "disrupt" the lecturer by altering the results.

At the end of each session, we asked for volunteers to remain behind and give feedback on the system. Overall, we spoke to around 50 people in this way. Views were consistent, in that students liked the idea of the approach (it gave them more of a role in the lecture, changed the pace of the session, etc.); strongly preferred the MCQ style of interaction over the chat scheme (as texting a freeform question could take too long, and the display of comments to the whole class could be distracting); but, they had concerns over the cost of sending messages (over and over again we were told "if sending a message was at a reduced rate, or free, I'd use it a lot more").

We also discussed the experience with the class *B* lecturers. They were less enthusiastic and more cautious about the scheme than the students. Their main concerns were the potential negative impacts of the technology on the "natural" flow of the lecture, and the need for more flexibility in the software to respond dynamically.

Longitudinal Study

Following this probing set of sessions, we carried out a more focused, longer trial during another course, using the most successful of the methods: multiple-choice questions where results are visible to all.

Over the first 5 weeks of a first-year programming course, one of us used the system to support lecture materials. The course included two lectures every week, and during one of the lectures, students were presented with an MCQ that they could answer using their mobile phone. On average, the number of people attending the lecture was 112 (which represented around 50% of those enrolled in the course). Table 2 presents the data for each weekly session.

During the sessions, we further observed the impact of the system on the lecture experience. Even though the numbers of people responding to the MCQ were low, there was a noticeable effect on the entire audience. The approach helped to strengthen the rapport between the lecturer and the students.

To gain a further perspective on the relative usefulness of the new system, we also deployed two other methods of gathering audience feedback during weeks two to five of the course. Each week, in the lecture that did not include the mobile MCQ system, we distributed post-it notes to each student, and asked them to write an anonymous, short comment, question, or suggestion to the lecturer. These were then collected up after the lecture when the students had left the room.

In addition, we used a Web-based polling system accessible to all the students in the course via their own or university computer. The same MCQ that had been asked in the class lecture via the mobile system was presented. Students could answer the question, and then the current results (showing the frequency of people selecting each choice) were then displayed. We recorded the number of unique respondents one week after each question was posed.

Both of these more conventional methods achieved higher participation rates than our new approach: on average, both achieved around 27% of the total number of possible respondents, where the total number in the post-it note case was the number of attendees in the lecture, and in the Web poll context, the total number of enrolled students.

Table 2. Week-by-week response rates to MCQ used in first-year programming class

Week	# people in class	#unique respondents	response rate
1	110	16	15%
2	105	5	5%
3	110	19	17%
4	110	12	10%
5	126	8	6%
Mean	**112**	**12**	**11%**

Discussion

The results suggest that using the handsets to SMS responses to MCQs could improve the level of participation: in the initial study we saw a response rate of 7%-38% (much higher than that predicted by Draper and Brown for "hands-up"). The system was most successful when the results were always on display to the students (from the start to the end of the poll): we discovered that students liked watching their messaging change the display dynamically.

Even when the messaging rate was low, the technique appeared to have a positive impact on the lecture experience: the sessions became more participative, with the lecturer engaging the students in a discussion of the poll results, for instance.

While a novelty effect might well have been in play, in the initial study the response rate seen in 6.1 (30%) compares favorably with that of the earlier session for that class (4.1 (38%)), even though the second session took place approximately 1 month after the earlier one. In the second study, as the weeks went by, there were fluctuations in response rate, but we did not detect a steadily decreasing pattern of enthusiasm. Given Draper and Brown's experience, we predict the enthusiasm for the approach will grow, particularly if charging issues can be resolved (e.g., by providing free texting for students).

The "chat" form of interaction was disappointingly received in the initial study (and we did not proceed with it in the second study). However, we intend to explore this form further with a tailored system, as its potential was undermined by the constraints of the pilot system (e.g., lack of filtering or censoring facilities for the lecturer). Another area for potential was discovered in the form of interesting emergent "community" behaviour when the chat screen was visible to all students: as well as communicating with the lecturer, students posed questions to *each other,* and received replies from within the audience. While there is much exciting work on mobile communities for noncollocated people, this experience suggests there is some useful work to be done on supporting *immobile* mobile communities, such as crowds in football stadia.

Unlike when using specialized handsets in closed networks, designers of mobile phone-based response systems will have to accommodate "invalid" input, both from the users and spammers. In setting up software to process student MCQ responses, for instance, the aim should be to accommodate the variety of answer messages likely to be sent (e.g., "1," "one," "the first choice").

While the more conventional feedback methods used in the second study led to greater participation, they did not, however, foster higher in-class interaction.

Case Study: PDAs

One of our motivations for using mobile phones as the basis of an audience response system, rather than the purpose-built handsets seen elsewhere, was to consider the richer forms of interaction they might facilitate. The previous case study, for instance, illustrated some potential roles of text messaging.

The study also showed, though, that entering responses, particularly free text questions or selections, can be problematic due to the impoverished text-entry facilities of conventional handsets. PDAs and advanced phones provide more sophisticated input and output facilities to the user — stylus-based handwriting recognition and larger, higher resolution displays, for example.

To consider the potential for these emergent, more advanced sorts of personal technology, we built the mobile information sharing in the presentation environment that connects students and their PDAs to the lecturer, with their laptop machine, in a lecture setting. In the sections that follow, we focus on describing the usage scenario and evaluation of the approach: a detailed discussion of the architecture and implementation can be found in Fry, Gruijters et al. (2004).

Usage Scenario

Students arrive at a lecture with their PDA or smartphone — these devices are the "clients" of the system. The lecturer turns on his or her laptop, and uses it to run the "server" application. Students then connect to this local, lecture server, wirelessly, the system supporting both Wi-Fi, and the shorter-range Bluetooth protocol.

The class begins, and as the lecturer presents the materials to the students in the form of a slide presentation, their devices receive the slides. Once the slide has arrived on a student's PDA, they may annotate it with pertinent information in much the same manner as they would usually annotate hard-copies of slides. At any point, the student can also write a question that is directly displayed on the lecturer's laptop.

As the lecture proceeds, the lecturer presents questions — eliciting free-form text answers — and MCQ polls for the audience to respond to, watching the results appear in his/her slideshow in real time (see Figure 3 for an example).

Once the class is over, the lecturer can save all information created during the class (student answers, student questions, and voting results) enabling them to reflect on the impact of the presentation on its audience.

The image on the left shows the display on the student PDA. This screen is generated automatically, without the lecturer having to explicitly place controls on the screen.

Figure 3. MISPE client (PDA) and server (laptop) example views

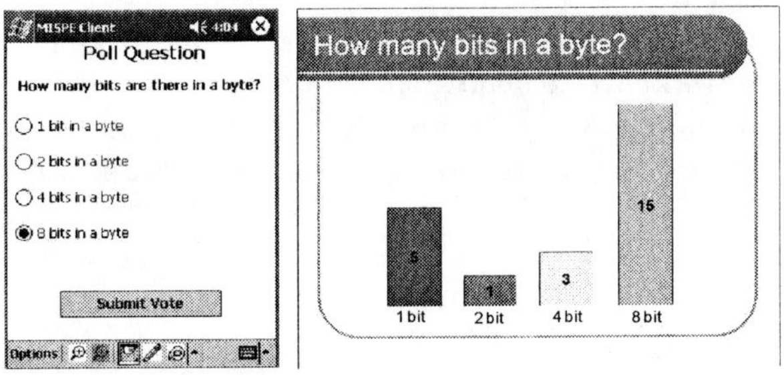

Instead, the lecturer works through a dialog box configuring the type of question they require. The software then renders the question in the most appropriate way for the handheld device. The image on the right shows the results received from the PDAs. The lecturer's software is a shell wrapped around PowerPoint™, with audience response slides being created automatically.

Related Work

The Pebbles project has done a substantial amount of work in the areas of collaborative environments involving handheld computers and other devices (Myers, 2001). Among the Pebbles applications is the Slideshow Commander, which allows educators to run a PowerPoint™ presentation from his/her laptop while controlling the presentation from a PDA connected via a wireless link to the laptop. The PDA provides thumbnails of the slides available, and allows the educator to move freely between slides using their PDA.

A system that allows multiple people to share an interactive whiteboard using PDAs is described in Myers, Stiel et al. (1998). This system allows multiple contributors to take turns to use a pen or drawing device on a virtual whiteboard, using PDAs to wirelessly access this single whiteboard display. PebblesDraw, as the system is named, allows users to take turns drawing on their PDAs, and having their contribution appear on a single, central whiteboard or display.

While these systems are useful in an educational context, they supplement a very small proportion of the educator's overall workflow. MISPE differs from the systems developed by Pebbles by designing and evaluating a system that addresses more of an educator's workflow than just presenting information.

In terms of authoring presentation material, Hexel, Johnson, (2004) describe a tool that allows presenters to create materials that can be customised for specific members of an audience. This tool provides a server that delivers customised presentation data, based on the specifics of the audience members, with relation to language, culture, or disabilities. The tool provides no authoring capabilities in terms of questions or voting. In addition, the system provides only one-way communication from lecturer to audience member.

The work by Hexel et al. (2004), and that reported in Webster and Ho (1997), provides evidence that the sorts of features seen in MISPE may enhance the educational experience. This work suggests that learners experience higher engagement in multimedia presentations which (1) are more challenging, (2) provide more opportunities for feedback, (3) allow more presentation control, and (4) vary in multimedia features.

MISPE uses ad hoc networking. Ad hoc networks are networks that are able to exist without a specific network infrastructure, and without a fixed network topology (Buszco et al., 2001; Doshi, Bhandare, 2002). They also do not require a central, authoritative body. This makes them suited to a highly mobile environment where network nodes may come and go as they please.

Evaluation

An initial, small-scale, user-centred evaluation of MISPE has been carried out to assess its usefulness and usability in real lecture settings.

Method

Two lecturers volunteered to use the system during a lecture. The class size for both lectures was small: five in the first lecture and six in the second. The mean age of the student participants was 18, and all reported having moderate levels of computer experience (the course they were participating in was computer-related).

Researchers attended both sessions to carry out naturalistic observations: that is, to record impressions of how the system impacted on both the lecturer and students during the lecture itself. The observers recorded any unusual uses of the systems, as well as common trends of normal use. They were asked to collect data on the features most used, comments made, and overall user reactions to the system. They were also asked to note how the students' interaction with the technology affected their participation in the lecture: were they able to effectively make annotations, and ask and answer questions, while still listening to the lecturer, or did they fall behind, losing the flow of the content?

Observations of the educators specifically noted the normal teaching style and actions of the educator, as well as when and how the educators interacted with the system.

At the end of both sessions, the lecturer and participants were questioned about the usefulness and usability of the system.

Impressions and Feedback

Lecturers' Perspective

Overall, the response of the two lecturers was enthusiastic: they were keen to use the technology again. In terms of the audience response features provided, they rated the facilities that allowed them to pose questions, and to carry out in-class votes, as the most useful.

In terms of student submitted comments and questions during the lecture, however, the usefulness of the system was hampered by the limited way the system accommodated the dynamic, "performance" nature of lectures. The technology, then, was seen to disrupt the natural flow of the lecture: lecturers would stop interacting with the class for periods of between 10-15 seconds, as they focused on their computer in an attempt to select a comment to discuss, or a student's answer to display to the rest of the class.

The immobile nature of laptop also caused problems: the lecturers often moved around the lecture room during the class. While they stood next to the computer when they wished to control the slideshow, they would often move away from the system to talk about the new slide displayed. This made it difficult for them to view any audience feedback — spontaneous comments or questions — that occurred as they were speaking.

Students' Perspective

The students felt the system led to them being more engaged during the lecture. Being able to ask and answer questions, and to receive feedback using their own device, made them feel more personally involved. Most students used the system to submit many comments and questions during the lecture: they were uninhibited as, in contrast to conventional verbal question asking, they felt their comments would be less disruptive.

There were, though, two usage trends that may lead to a negative impact on the lecture experience. First, students "played" a lot with the system when the lecturer talked for a long while about a slide's content. When they became bored, that is, the system became a distraction. Second, despite the more flexible, easier to use text input methods seen on the PDA, compared to those of the mobile phones in the first case study, the authoring of slide annotations and questions still took too long, causing students to fall behind, and to lose the context of what the lecturer was discussing.

Discussion

As in the texting case study, the use of MISPE provides some evidence that personal technologies can enhance the audience's participation. From the lecturer's point-of-view, though, we need to design a better way for them to control and interact with the system when they are in full-flow of a lecture performance. Specifically, the system should accommodate the lecturer's mobility: as in the SlideShow commander (Myers, 2001), it would seem important that the lecturer has a handheld device that they can use to orchestrate the slideshow and audience participation. Simple interactions with this control device, for example, one-handed button presses, need to provide them with direct access to, say, incoming student comments.

The frustration observed by students as they wrote or answered free-text questions could be overcome by providing a much more lightweight way of authoring. In the present version of the system, submissions have to be entered as textual strings, either by the student tapping on the letters of an onscreen keyboard, or by using the handwriting recognition facilities of the device. A faster approach would be to allow users to use sketching facilities: a scrawled note or comment can be created with the image being sent the lecturer without any preprocessing.

Conclusions

Personal technologies — mobile phones, both conventional ones, and the increasingly sophisticated smartphones, along with wireless-capable handheld computers — offer the potential for increasing audience participation in lecture settings.

Unlike the special-purpose handsets used in other trials, these devices offer practical benefits (such as lower cost set-ups, flexibility in deployment, and richer forms of audience response) as well as less tangible impacts on the audience experience arising from the personal nature of the device itself. People relate to these technologies they own and carry everywhere in engaging ways.

In the text-messaging studies, we saw higher participation rates than might be experienced using traditional verbal or hand-show methods. While the response rate was not overwhelming, with, on average, 15% of the audience directly taking part, the impact on the overall lecture experience was significant. In our studies, students had to pay the cost of every message sent, and they indicated that if the service was free, they would more readily respond using it.

In the PDA trial, where all student messages were free, we saw a much higher level of question answering and comment giving. In the next several years, most mobile phones will be equipped with Wi-Fi and Bluetooth capabilities, so that messaging sending costs can be eliminated.

Lectures are often dynamic, lively performances with their own rhythms and flow. Lecturers and audiences will want to use a range of participation methods, both technologically-based and traditional: one moment, the lecturer will ask for a show of hands; the next for questions to be sent to a shared, digital whiteboard.

There is a need, then, for any audience response system to fit within this ecology of resources. Too often, technology fails to accommodate the context, fails to fit in: instead of playing its part in the ecology, it devours, in the process destroying the user experience. In our case studies, we saw some examples of the impact of suboptimal contextual design, but also suggested ways of improving later prototypes.

Acknowledgments

Thanks to Hussein Suleman and Donald Cook, who set aside time in their lectures. Dave Nichols and Mike Mayo helped with the NZ observations, and the Waikato HCI group worked on scenarios.

References

Buszko, D., Lee, W., & Helal, A. (2001). Decentralized ad hoc groupware API and framework for mobile collaboration. *Proceedings of the 2001 International ACM SIGGROUP Conference on Supporting Groupwork* (pp. 5-14). ACM Press.

Cheverst, K., Dix, A., Fitton, D., & Rouncefield, M. (2003). Exploring the utility of remote messaging and situated office displays. *Proceedings of Mobile HCI 2003* (pp. 336-341). Springer.

Doshi, S., Bhandare, S., & Brown, T. X. (2002). An on-demand minimum energy routing protocol for a wireless ad hoc network. *Mobile Computing and Communications Review, 6*(3), 50-66.

Draper, S. W., & Brown, M.I. (2004). Increasing interactivity in lectures using an electronic voting system. *Journal of Computer Assisted Learning, 20*, 81-94.

Draper, S. W., Cargill, J., & Cutts, Q. (2002). Electronically enhanced classroom interaction. *Australian Journal of Educational Technology, 18*(1), 13-23.

Fry, B., Gruijters, D., & Reid, S. (2004). *MISPE - Mobile Information Sharing in the Presentation Environment*. Technical report CS04-22-00. Cape Town: University of Cape Town, Department of Computer Science.

Hexel, R., Johnson, C., Kummerfeld, B., & Quigley, A. (2004). PowerPoint™ to the people: Suiting the word to the audience. *Proceedings of the Fifth Conference on Australasian User Interface* (pp. 40-56). Dunedin, NZ: ACM Press.

Jones, M., & Marsden, G. (2004). Please Turn ON your mobile phone: First impressions of text-messaging in lectures. *Proceedings of the 6th International Symposium on Mobile Human-Computer Interaction (Mobile HCI '04)* (pp. 436-440). Glasgow, UK: Springer.

Marsden, G. (2003). Using HCI to leverage communications technology. *Interactions, 10*(2), 48-55.

Myers, B. (2001). Using hand-held devices and PCs together. *Communications of the ACM, 44*(11), 34-41.

Myers, B., Stiel, H., & Gargiulo, R. (1998). Collaboration using multiple PDAs connected to a PC. *Proceedings of the 1998 ACM Conference on Computer Supported Cooperative Work (CSCW)* (pp. 285-294). Seattle: ACM Press.

Webster, J., & Ho, H. (1997). Audience engagement in multimedia presentations. *ACM SIGMIS Database, 28*(2), 63-77.

Chapter XXV

Reflections on the Use of ARS with Small Groups

David A. Banks, University of South Australia, Australia

Abstract

Audience response systems are typically used with large groups of students, often in lecture theatre settings. This chapter reflects on 10 years of the author's use of these systems, and provides examples illustrating the way that a variety of ARS, including a wired system and two infrared systems, have been used with small groups. In the examples outlined here, the data from the ARS was used to trigger discussion, rather than being used for multiple-choice "right or wrong" purposes. In the context of this chapter, groups of between 5 and 50 students are considered as "small" to differentiate from "large" lectures with possibly hundreds of students. Given the likely convergence of numeric keypad technology and text entry systems such as PDAs and mobile phones, the use of a larger, text-entry system is also outlined, to show how such systems can be utilized to explore course evaluation issues.

Using an ARS with Small Groups

The ARS has an obvious attraction, when used with large groups as a tool to help overcome the reluctance of some students to participate in discussion, or even to ask a question. In some cases, cultural backgrounds will lead to a need to avoid "loss of face," and this is a significant problem as some parts of the world substantially increase their numbers of overseas students. This same problem of fear of involvement can also apply to small group working. Two examples are given here of the use of an ARS with small groups, both using the system to support peer feedback. In the first example, the system was used with a small group (less than 10 participants) to help students identify issues in their presentation skills, the second example being that of a more general peer review process in group work, again with small groups.

Using an ARS to Examine Student Presentation

Students studying a Higher National Diploma (HND) data communications course taught by the author, raised concerns about their ability to perform well in a presentation that formed part of the assessment. They had carried out similar presentations in other subjects, but felt that a simple mark for the previous presentations had not allowed them to learn from the process, and consequently, improve their presentation skills. The concerns of the students were such that an extra formative presentation session was built in to the course, so that they could undertake a practice presentation, and receive feedback on their performance.

The ARS used in this case was a fairly early cabled system provided by OptionFinder in the UK in 1995. (See Figure 1 for an illustration of the way that the keypads were connected.)

The ARS was familiar to the HND group, as it had previously been used as a focus for discussing some aspects of communication systems. It was therefore offered to them as

Figure 1. Four keypads daisy-chained

Table 1. Presentation criteria developed by students

1.	Intro and summary: Did the presentation have a good introduction and summary?
2.	Up-to-date: Did the presentation seem to be based upon up-to-date information?
3.	Accuracy: Did the material seem to be accurate?
4.	Comprehensive: Did the material seem to be comprehensive, or too shallow/deep?
5.	Structure: Did the structure (flow, logic) seem to be correct?
6.	Clarity: Was the presentation clear-were keywords explained?
7.	Timing: Did the presentation make good use of the recommended time allocation?
8.	Pace: Did the speaker present at a reasonable pace?
9.	Audiovisual aids: Did the speaker make good use of OHP or other audio-visual aids?
10.	Interest: Was the presentation interesting?

an opportunity to use it to allow students to anonymously rate the presentation performance of their peers. The judgment criteria were developed by the students in an informal meeting. Fifteen criteria were developed by the group as a general list. This was then reduced, using the ARS, to the 10 that they felt to be most important (Table 1).

At a later point in the course, the ARS was set up and each student gave a short presentation on a subject, similar to the one that would form their final assignment topic. After each presentation, each member of the "audience" scored each item, and the results were presented on a public screen for discussion. Each presenter was first invited to comment on the process and the outcome, after which all students and the academic discussed ways in which that individual might improve the areas of perceived weakness. The students found the process to be useful, fun, and surprisingly nonthreatening. It was observed that students tended to talk about the data, rather than the individual that the data related to, and this effect has been noted on a number of occasions when the ARS has been used.

It has to be noted that these were all UK born students, and the idea of discussion about their performance was not felt by them to be as stressful as the videotaped mock interviews and de-brief sessions that were also part of their program of studies. This meant that there were few cultural inhibitions likely to impede face-to-face discussion, and that the students were used to, at least some degree of reflection and personal criticism, unlike the following example.

Small Group Peer Review with an ARS

A second, more recent, example of an ARS being used to support small groups is that of peer review sessions held as part of a Masters course currently taught by the author. The course title is Collaborative Information Systems, and it is a process-based course,

Table 2.

a.	Attended all meetings they were required to
b.	Contributed significantly to the groups work
c.	Carried out all required work
d.	Worked to promote cooperation within the group
e.	Appreciated the efforts of others and supported them
f.	Acted in a socially responsible way
g.	Displayed good communication skills
h	Offered innovative insights
i.	Welcomed the inputs and ideas of others
j.	Acted as a group member rather than as an individual

with a very significant and intensive group-work element. (Banks, 2003b) The cohorts have a majority of overseas students, many from cultures where willingness to openly critique other people is problematic. The cohort of 50 students operates as 10 groups each of five students working on the production of conference-style papers with both inter- and intragroup reviews of the developing paper taking place several times in the overall process. A summative peer review was used on the original course, based on anonymous spreadsheets sent to the lecturer. The individual spreadsheets were used to generate a mark for each individual member of the group on the basis of the marks generated by their peers. The group-work assessment criteria were developed by the whole student group the first time the course was run, and are shown in Table 2.

During the end of one early course, student feedback suggested it would have been useful to have an extra peer review early in the course, so that individuals could see how they were being perceived by others, and could make appropriate changes in their approach before the final assessment (Banks, 2003a). This was introduced in subsequent courses as a "diagnostic" session using initially an ARS from IML UK with Question Wizard software, and more recently, with an ARS from KEEpad in Brisbane with TurningPoint software. It was felt, based on the experiences with the HND group, that a similar "talking to the data rather than the person" effect could occur, and that this would be a useful approach with the Collaborative Information Systems students, particularly given the typical cultural mix.

The diagnostic peer reviews occupy a full 3-hour session in which each group member uses the ARS to score their peers (Figure 2), in turn, against criteria in Table 1. For each item, a score between zero and five is entered, and this is averaged by the system to produce a composite peer score.

Each student's score is then examined in turn by their group and the member of staff, and possible explanations for the pattern of scores are discussed. A typical pattern of scores is shown in Figure 3.

Figure 2. Small group peer review

Figure 3. Typical profile for an individualistic student (letters refer to criteria in Table 2)

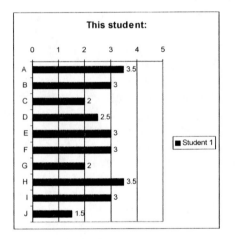

In cases where the "Displayed good communication skills" score was low, it was not unusual for a student to volunteer that their English language skills are not very good. At this point, the member of staff will probably suggest that the student should avail themselves of the services of appropriate, student support groups, but will also ask how the group is going to manage this weakness in terms of the overall project that they are engaged in. Balance of work within the group can thus be explored, and students are referred to the lecture material that covers individual and team problem-solving styles, group development stages, group roles, and other relevant material. In effect, this becomes a minicounselling session that has been found to help groups identify and deal with the later pressures of the course. For example, the chart in Figure 3 suggests a student who has good ideas, but is probably a "loner" who enjoys the initial idea-generating parts of a project, but loses interest once that phase has passed. Once similar patterns are identified for all group members, both the group and the individual are better able to accommodate their differences, and structure group work around the various strengths and weaknesses within a group. The session is kept reasonably short to fit within the 3-hour time slot (there are typically 10 groups to work through this process), and after each group has completed their review session, they see another member of staff for a more detailed debrief. (The data from the peer review session is printed out during the initial debrief session, so that they can work on the data with the other tutor in the extended debrief).

At informal discussions with students later in the course discussion, one (Australian) student commented that they felt uncomfortable with some perceived negative feedback that was obtained, but this was countered by the majority of students who expressed the view that only by becoming honestly aware of the way that they were being perceived, could they modify their behaviour to either better perform, or at least give the impression to others that they could perform better (Banks, 2003b).

It would be possible to develop this diagnostic session further by using a stronger counseling-based approach, such as those the author has used with external groups he has worked with as a consultant (Banks, 2001a; Banks & Wheeler, 2003c), but this does raise a number of potential problem areas, and would probably not be viewed as being appropriate within a nonbusiness or nonsocial work educational setting.

Recent sharp increases in student numbers (student numbers on this course are now more than 120), combined with reducing staff resources also mean that such time-hungry practices are no longer viable. In an effort to still retain the diagnostic mechanism with just one member of staff, an approach was adopted where the ARS was used to collect the scores prior to the group discussion. Each student was provided with a keypad and the first task was to enter their group number (i.e., 1 to 10) to provide the demographic data required to organize the subsequent data into group sets. Every student was issued with a list of their group members, each member of the group being allocated a number from 1 to 5. The students then rated student number 1 in their specific group according to each of the criteria, then the process was repeated for student number 2 in their group, and so on. This reduced the time needed for gathering the data that the discussion was based on, but some students did find the process complicated, and failed to follow the instructions. The approach was abandoned in later courses for the very practical reason that as group numbers grew, a point was reached where there were more groups than buttons on the keypad! (Perhaps there is an opportunity for manufacturers to provide the equivalent of a keyboard "Shift" function to double the number of available buttons?)

"Lost in the Desert"

One issue explored within the Collaborative Information Systems course is that of the situation where an individual member of the group may have an ideal solution to a problem, but the group processes are such that this optimum solution is not adopted. The reasons for this may include the individual with the "right" answer not being able to communicate their rationale to the other members of the group, shyness acting as an inhibitor; cultural issues; established group norms; and so on. To help students to better appreciate this difficulty, an ARS-based "Lost in the Desert" exercise was introduced (Banks, & Bateman, 2004). In this scenario, an aircraft has crashed in the desert, and the passengers have to recover items that will help them survive until rescue services arrive. There are 15 recoverable items, and these have to be prioritized in order of retrieval from the wreckage. The first step is for each individual to make a prioritized list, on paper, which is then captured via the ARS when all students have completed this first task. A useful practical tip here is to display a screen that is captioned "Press 'A' when you have completed your list." This enables the facilitators and participants to see the progress of the exercise, and when, say, 95% of participants have indicated that they have completed the task, the facilitator can prompt the remainder to finish the task. In practice, students glance at the screen as they work, and will tend to speed up as the completion percentage rises. Once the individual data has been captured, the students form groups (typically five students) and negotiate a group list, which is also captured, this time from just one nominated member of each group. (The same "Press button 'A'" screen is also used here to manage the time.)

Once all data is captured, the individual and group rankings of the items are compared with a list prepared by a desert survival expert, and scores are allocated for matches with the expert order of items. High-scoring individuals can be identified by keypad number, and the scores of groups can also be displayed. The resulting data usually indicates that is not unusual for a group to obtain a low score for the group list, even when one or more members of the group may have an almost perfect match with the expert ranking. The exercise is the trigger for discussion of what went on in the groups, issues of trust and perceived authority, what process they observed, how they felt as they tried to make their cases, what actions they could take in the future to help reduce the barriers, and so on.

This exercise revealed some of the limitations of the eight-button keypads that were in use when the exercise was first conducted. To accommodate the eight-button keypads, the list of 15 items had to be split over two display screens. Students were asked to identify their highest priority item from the list spread across the first two screens (i.e., the first eight items on the list displayed on one screen, then the remaining seven items displayed on a second screen). The process was then repeated for the next highest ranked item over two screens again, and so on. If all 15 items had been ranked, this would have required 30 screens to be worked through for the capture of individual rankings, and then the same again for the group items. If participants are required to enter very large amounts of data over a short time, there is the possibility of "button fatigue' in which some participants will randomly press buttons simply to bring the process to an end. The splitting of the list over two screens also confused a number of students who had Non-English speaking backgrounds, and examination of the data after the session indicated multiple data entries for a number of students, thus invalidating their scores. In a modified version of the exercise, only the top five items from both individuals and groups were captured, in an effort to reduce button fatigue simplify the process.

The 8-button keypads were replaced with 10-button keypads provided by KEEpad, but this still acts as a limitation for this type of exercise, unless the original process is modified. This is not to criticize the simpler keypads at all, but simply to point out that some systems are perfect for some tasks, but may not be appropriate for others. For example, there are situations where it may be desired to administer learning-style or decision-style inventories, where a preferred ranking of four possible responses for a test

Figure 4. Multiple-digit transmission from a keypad (The small disc below the logo is a microphone that can link the keypad to a public address system for question and answer sessions. This is an older keypad, and the more recent IML product retains the microphone capability, but also has a backlit monochrome graphics LCD and a range of other features.)

item has to be generated by each participant for each test item. This would require that, typically, four digits would need to be transmitted for each test item, and the IML system, for example, with its LCD screen and ability to be deal with multiple digit transmission, would clearly be better suited to this type of task than a simpler input device (Figure 4). However, the cost of the more sophisticated system is considerably higher than a basic keypad. The PDAs, mobile phone, and hand-held systems developed in earlier chapters would be ideal for such situations.

Other uses for the ARS in this course include a version of Prisoner's Dilemma, and a competition/collaboration "game." The system is also used in the "voting before discussing"[1] mode, where a question is asked, the students vote, and then the data is explored. The example in Figure 5 shows the discussion taking place after the question "In the context of this course, do you consider yourself to be (a) an individual, (b) a member of a team, or (c) a member of a group?" The question was introduced before the lectures had discussed the group/team area, and the students asked to explain what they felt the difference between these terms to be. The 'Individual' category (around 5%) raised further discussion as this course is designed around intensive group work. Observation of previous cohorts suggests that the individuals are more likely to be Australian students, and this observation could be tested by the introduction of a demographics question to elicit nationality with this data, later cross-tabbed with the individual/team/group response data.

What is interesting and encouraging about the use of an ARS in this course is that many students comment on how it helps them to understand, in a very practical way, the problems inherent in collaboration and group-work, and the overall feedback on the use of the ARS has been very positive.

Figure 5. Exploring interpretations of terms

ARS and Course Evaluation: Moving Beyond Numeric Scores

End-of-course student evaluations are clearly important in providing feedback that can suggest directions for course improvement. My own institution has used both paper-based and Web-based versions of the course evaluation questionnaire (CEQ). Each has its own problem. In the case of Web-based versions of the CEQ, the response rate is frequently so low that the resulting data offers little insight. In the case of paper-based approaches, a higher completion rate is assured, but there is a cost involved in using an administrator to distribute and collect the forms, and there is a loss of time in form completion, usually at a time when students are seeking exam preparation input. An ARS can be used as a rapid data collection device to overcome many of these problems, given that the captured data can be exported as a spreadsheet or database file. This automates the process and provides some benefits, but there is an even more useful benefit to be obtained if, instead of just using the ARS for simple data capture, some time is spent exploring the meaning of the data with the students.

In 1995, the author used the OptionFinder ARS to work with nine engineering students as part of a quality audit for the course. (Banks, 2001b) All items on the standard CEQ were administered using the ARS instead of pencil and paper. After the data had been collected, the results were shown to the students, and they were asked for any comments. It became clear that as they had answered the questions on the CEQ, each of them had

Figure 6. First and second response pattern to "Clarity of assessment methods" criterion (1=Very satisfied, 6=Very dissatisfied)

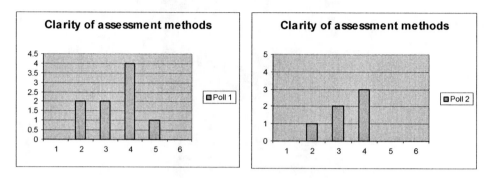

used different criteria to determine their rating of the items. Sometimes the course was the focus for the decision, sometimes the lecturer, sometimes the support services, and sometimes the unavailability of the drinks vending machine. After some discussion between staff and students about the issues, a more common, shared understanding of the CEQ was developed, and the process using the ARS was repeated. This produced changes in the shape of the responses that suggested a more common approach (i.e., shared meaning) was being taken towards the assessment of the CEQ items (Figure 6).

This exercise occupied more than 1 hour, and the students felt that the session had been extremely valuable, but it was never repeated on future courses, as it was felt by senior management that it occupied too much time that could have been better spent on teaching, and also that the process could be used to manipulate the views of the students. (An external observer had been invited to act as nonparticipant observer, and was able to verify that no sinister manipulations were taking place.) This process does require considerable, extra, nonteaching time, and therefore, may not be applicable to all courses, but perhaps may be worthy of consideration in courses where there may be concerns about quality, or where decisions about the possible viability of a course are based on CEQ data. Relying on raw numbers gathered by an ARS or paper-based approach to make judgments about the quality of a course, without making an effort to understand the shape of the data or what triggered the student responses, clearly runs the risk of producing an uninformed decision making process.

Text-Entry Face-to-Face Systems

As ARS move towards text and graphical entry input, the possibility for deeper group exploration of issues becomes possible. Powerful, keyboard-based group support systems, or electronic meeting systems, have existed for a considerable time,[2] and the author has used one such system at the University of South Australia. The system was housed in the Enterprise Process Improvement Centre (EPICentre, Figure 7), a facility

Figure 7. Electronic meeting room

established at the School of Information Systems around 1995 to support research, consultancy, and teaching. The system used GroupSystems software, and was used by the author a number of times to support work with local businesses, and with student groups. The major use with student groups was, essentially, demonstrating to them how such systems could be used in the context of policy development as part of an undergraduate Information Systems Policy course, but it was also used as a vehicle to explore CEQ scores on a number of courses (Banks, 2001b).

Students completed a paper-based version of the CEQ, and were then asked to indicate what had been in their minds when they allocated a score to a specific item. Each item had a series of folders attached to it so that students could select an item and open a subfolder labeled with the score they had allocated, and enter text into that folder. The resulting data revealed similar results to that found on the earlier work with the engineering group, with misunderstandings, choice of inappropriate reference points for judgment, and so on. There was also evidence of reversals of scores, reinforcing the view of the author that decisions made on the basis of the raw numbers, without deeper consideration of what that data may actually mean, would be inadvisable.

What was more interesting than the numbers and text generated was the process. It produced much useful information with very little "flaming," and a number of debates (or threads) between students could be seen taking place as they argued about the appropriateness of criteria or, in some cases, defending the member of staff against the more provocative statements. It has to be said that standing in front of a public screen and inviting students to make anonymous text comments about ones performance is a slightly daunting situation, particularly the first time it is experienced. Having the students as the major participants, and taking cues from them, would appear to be problematic for some staff. It is not unusual to see academics walk away from ARS demonstrations at conference stands, or after an ARS demonstration, shaking their heads and muttering in a disparaging tone of voice "Infotainment", or "Edutainment." Others have been heard to comment that they would not like their students to be "running the show — after all, who is in charge?" Clearly, we need to dispel the idea that contingent approaches to teaching and learning, using keypad technology, provides students with the ability to pause, rewind, fast forward, or maybe even change channel if they are bored.

(Although this would be an intriguing approach to experiment with.) Equally, we need to carry out some long-term research to establish the effect of novelty-value in the use of these systems, and the potential dangers of overuse or inappropriate application.

Where Do We Go From Here?

PowerPoint™ is deceptively easy to use, and ARS software typically provides standard slide outlines that allow swift development of multiple-choice questions. However, the literature relating to "response set," sometimes referred to as *response style* and *response bias,* has to be taken into account at the design stage. Response set is the "tendency of some people to answer a large number of items in the same way (usually agreeing) out of laziness or a psychological predisposition" (Neuman, 2003). Similarly, the design of multiple-choice questions has to be sufficiently rigorous to avoid the possibility that the wording reveals the answer without the need for genuine deliberation on the part of the student. Barrow and Blake (2004) explore multiple-choice question design from the perspective of "guessing or assessing," and provide some useful practical insights. Haladyna (1990) comments that "we place more emphasis on analyzing responses than we do on how we obtain them." There are some interesting recursive opportunities here to use ARS to support research into the design of multiple-choice questions for use with ARS.

The chapters in this book suggest that the adoption of an ARS leads academics to consider different ways of producing a richer, innovative, contingent, and constructivist learning environment. Once an ARS has been used, it seems to trigger new lines of thought in terms of pedagogical design. For example, a paper examining the adoption of active learning in a lecture-based engineering class by Hall, Waiz, Brodeur, Soderholm and Nasr (2002), discusses the idea of "muddiest point in the lecture" developed by Mosteller. Anyone familiar with using an ARS would immediately see how this approach could be combined with an ARS to produce some very interesting blended approaches.

Audience response systems are just one more tool in the armoury of the educator. As we move forward in an educational world increasingly populated by "customers," we may have to learn to adopt multimedia approaches to deliver the requirements of those customers at their time and place of choice, and in line with their changing expectations. Perhaps we can see the future exemplified in Mark Kubinec's Digital Chemistry course at UC Berkeley. Kubinec combines online and in-class instruction using Webcasting, streamed video, PowerPoint™, peer instruction, ChemQuiz questions, and personal response systems[3].

Conclusions

One factor that shines through in much of the literature relating to ARS is the high level of enthusiasm expressed by staff, and (many) students using these systems. For staff, the enthusiasm appears to come not from the technology, as such, but from the opportunity it engenders for critical self-evaluation of the processes that we sometimes take for granted. Lectures could become dull or mechanical, with an endless procession of PowerPoint™ slides after they have been delivered a large number of times. Sometimes we ask a question, then move on to answer it ourselves, without really engaging the students. Student enthusiasm may be predicated on novelty, fun, richer learning environments, or a clearer sense of being a member of a learning community, particularly in city-centre campuses.

One of the most powerful effects of introducing an ARS is that it encourages academics to reflect on how and why they currently act. Marc Dickstein[4], having introduced an ARS into medical education at Columbia University, notes that the whole organisation of a lecture will change as its purpose is re-evaluated in readiness for the introduction of an ARS. Paschal (2002), discussing the use of an ARS in the area of systems physiology, control systems, and neurophysiology, concludes that the use of instant feedback in lectures can negate the need for homework, saving time for both students and staff. Many contributors to this book have made similar observations about the impact of such technology upon the way we think about pedagogy. It may be that the greatest impact that these systems have is to make us all re-examine what we do, how we do it, why we do it in a particular way, and how we can do it better.

Audience response systems are a powerful agent that can promote and enable change. The current signs are that such changes are positive, but in common with the introduction of all technologies, the ARS must be introduced in a way that ensures it is used appropriately, rather than force everything we do to fit the technology. They are just one of a range of developing technologies, and we must ensure that the driver is always about building a learning environment that is socially oriented, inclusive, and responsive to the changing needs of the teaching and learning community.

Acknowledgments

The work outlined above could not have been carried out without the generous support of the following people and organisations: Jeff Earl and Christine Eldred of OptionFinder UK; Peter Knowles of IML UK; and Richard Neal of KEEpad, Brisbane, Australia. The author wishes to point out that he has no commercial affiliations with any of these organizations.

References

Banks, D. A. (2001a). *The role of counseling-related strategies in the facilitation of electronic meetings.* The 6th International Conference of the International Society for Decision Support Systems, Brunel University, UK.

Banks, D. A. (2001b). *A critical reflection on the value of course evaluation question-naires: Using group support tools to explore student evaluations.* Information Resources Management Association Conference, Toronto.

Banks, D. A. (2003a). *Using keypad-based group process support systems to facilitate student reflection.* Australasian Society for Computers in Learning in Tertiary Education (ASCILITE) Conference Proceedings, Adelaide.

Banks, D. A. (2003b). *Collaborative learning as a vehicle for learning about collabo-ration.* Informing Science + IT Education Conference (InSITE), Pori, Finland.

Banks, D. A., & Bateman, S. (2004). *Audience response aystems in education: Support-ing a "Lost in the Desert" learning scenario.* International Conference on Computers in Education (ICCE2004): Acquiring and Constructing Knowledge Through Human-Computer Interaction: Creating New Visions for the Future of Learning, Melbourne.

Banks, D. A., & Wheeler, S. (2003c). *Ethically assessing a complex IS dilemma.* 7th World Multiconference on Systemics, Cybernetics and Informatics (SCI 2003), Orlando.

Barrow, G., & Blake, R. (2004). *Guessing or assessing? Multiple-choice and the false pass problem.* Hempstead, UK: G R Business Solutions. (See http://www.grbps.com/bkmini.pdf for an outline of the book.)

Haladyna, T. (1990). Advances in item design. *Rasch Measurement Transactions, 4*(2), 103-104. Retrieved July 27, 2005, from http://www.rasch.org/rmt/rmt42b.htm

Hall, S. R., Waitz, I., Brodeur, D. R., Soderholm, D. H., & Nasr, R. (2002, November 6-9). Adoption of active learning in a lecture-based engineering class. *The 32nd ASEE/IEEE Frontiers in Education Conference,* Boston (T2A-9 to T2A-15).

Neuman, W. L. (2003). *Social research methods: Qualitative and quantitative ap-proaches* (5th ed.). Allyn and Bacon.

Paschal, C. B. (2002). Formative assessment in physiology teaching using a wireless classroom communication system. *Advances in Physiology Education, 26,* 299-308.

Endnotes

[1]   An interesting discussion of the use of voting before discussing (VBD) titled "Voting before discussing: Computer voting and social communication" by Brian Whitworth and Robert J. McQueen of Manukau Institute of Technology (New Zealand) can be found at http://www.cis.njit.edu/~bwhitworth/case.html (Accessed 25/7/2005).

[2]   For useful insights to these systems, see "Lessons from a dozen years of group support systems research: A discussion of lab and field findings" by Nunamaker, Briggs, Mittleman, and Vogel, http://mies.cs.depaul.edu/research/JMIS.html

[3]   See http://socrates.berkeley.edu/~kubinec/

[4]   See http://cumc.columbia.edu/news/journal/journal-o/fall-2004/students.html

About the Authors

The first part of **David A. Banks** career was spent with a large, UK, telecommunications company, dealing with data, broadcast television, and video-conferencing systems. Upon gaining a Master of Philosophy, he moved into higher education. He spent one year in New Zealand as a visiting research fellow. He has used ARS in educational settings since 1995, and has also designed and managed electronic meetings for a number of organisations in the UK and Australia, using both keypad and full text-entry systems. He was nominated by the UniSA Students Association for a 2003 Postgraduate Teaching Excellence Award in the category of Lecturer of the Year.

*   *   *

Louis Abrahamson earned a BSc in applied mathematics & physics from Rhodes University (1964), and a BSc (Honors) in physics (1965). In England, he worked for six years at the British Aircraft Corporation on Concorde flyover noise and sonic fatigue, earning a PhD from the University of Southampton engineering and applied science (1973). In the U.S., he was employed by a NASA contractor for seven years before starting his own research and technology company. In 1986, he received a NASA award for work in support of the Presidential Commission investigating the Space Shuttle Challenger disaster. In 1990, he was a principal founder of Better Education Foundation, USA, a company to research and develop networked classroom technology and pedagogy. Abrahamson is the inventor of *Classtalk*.

Ian D. Beatty is a postdoctoral research associate. He earned a PhD in physics education research from the University of Massachusetts, USA, in 2000. His primary focus is on innovative applications of technology to science instruction, and on the pedagogy that accompanies them. When not working or traveling, he teaches wilderness survival and leadership skills to high school students, and does volunteer work for the Appalachian Mountain Club.

Peter Bertok is a senior lecturer at the School of Computer Science and Information Technology, Royal Melbourne Institute of Technology, Australia. He earned his PhD from the University of Tokyo, Japan, and his master's degree from the Technical University of Budapest, Hungary. He has been teaching undergraduate and postgraduate students for many years. He has authored more than 80 refereed publications.

Anne Bishop joined the Information Systems Department at Wake Forest University, USA, in 1981, and led the implementation of many of its business software systems. After the introduction of ubiquitous computing on the Wake Forest campus in 1996, Bishop originated the idea for the university's portal, and managed its development, launch, and ongoing enhancements. She has published extensively, including authored chapters in a number of books, and she has co-authored an article titled "Programming Handheld Devices to Enhance Learning" for the *Educause Quarterly*. Bishop is currently the director of research and development in information systems at Wake Forest University, where her focus is developing software for, and using mobile technologies in academics and student life.

Stephen J. Bostock started academic life as an environmental scientist, became an adult educator, and then a computer scientist, and finally a staff and educational developer, and a fellow of the UK Staff and Educational Development Association. Throughout these careers, he has been concerned with using technology to support teaching and learning. His own experience with students includes statistical analysis software, the early use of the Web for large courses, Web-based, anonymous, peer assessment, and computer-based assessment. As advisor for Technology and Learning at Keele University, UK, he runs both short and sustained staff development programmes for using technologies, both online with a VLE, and for face-to-face teaching. His recent interests include integrating online and face-to-face technologies.

Jim Boyle started his academic career as an applied mathematician before taking a doctorate in mechanical engineering, later followed by a DSc for innovative research contributions in high temperature design. For the past seven years, considerable effort has been applied to bring about a major change in engineering education through a re-emphasis on teaching and learning. Boyle is the developer of the *New Approaches to Teaching and Learning in Engineering* project, which aims to introduce active, inquiry-led learning into the curriculum through Socratic dialogue and peer instruction in large classes, a version of problem-based learning, applied to design teaching, and the use of studio teaching.

Ray A. Burnstein is currently a research professor and professor *emeritus* of physics at the Illinois Institute of Technology, Chicago. He earned his PhD in physics at the University of Michigan under Donald A. Glaser, who received the Nobel Prize in physics in 1960. Burnstein is a high-energy physicist, and has directed an active, particle physics research program at IIT for more than 30 years. He was awarded fellowship in the American Physical Society for his neutrino physics experiments. In the field of under-graduate science education, he was an early advocate for undergraduate research programs at four-year colleges. He pioneered the use of wireless keypads systems in the classroom to produce a more interactive classroom environment, a technique that is now widely accepted.

Kelley Burton is a full-time associate lecturer in the School of Law at the Queensland University of Technology (QUT), Australia, and has approximately five years of univer-sity teaching experience. She has taught 10 undergraduate core law subjects, spanning across all year levels of the law degree, including skills-based subjects. She has received the following awards for her outstanding teaching and learning performance, and her ongoing efforts in supporting new ways of learning: 2001 QUT Faculty of Law Achieve-ment in Teaching (Casual Academics) Award, 2003 QUT Compassionate Pioneer Award and 2003 QUT Faculty of Law Excellence in Teaching Commendation Award.

Michael Connolly is head of the School of Humanities, Law and Social Sciences at the University of Glamorgan, UK. His research interests lie in public policy and management, including the nature of change and its management, as well as the nature of new public management. Professor Connolly has published widely, and recently has looked at some of the organizational implications of e-learning.

Quintin Cutts is a lecturer in the Department of Computing Science at the University of Glasgow, Scotland, with a research background in programming language design and implementation. His more recent research principally concerns the improvement of face-to-face teaching and learning. In this context, he has jointly led, at Glasgow, the largest take up of ARS technology in any UK university, and explored the design, deployment, pedagogical rationale, and evaluation of ARSs with researchers in Australia and the U.S. He is also research active in the areas of computer science education, particularly the learning of programming, public understanding of computer science, and in peer assisted learning.

Mark A. Davys is a teaching fellow in the School of Law at Keele University (UK), where he specialises in teaching property law to undergraduates. He is also a qualified (but no longer practicing) solicitor, and an ordained minister in the Church of England.

As Chief Information Officer, **Jay Dominick** is responsible for strategy, planning, and operations for Wake Forest University's, USA, highly regarded information technology efforts. Dominick was responsible for the implementation and support of the ubiquitous laptop-computing project at Wake Forest, which established a new model for technology deployment in higher education. He is active in state-wide networking as member of the North Carolina Research and Education Network (NCREN) advisory board, and is a co-founder of WinstonNet — a community fiber-optic network in Winston Salem. Research interests include the study of mobile/pervasive computing in educational environments, and the use of electronic textbooks and the implications of their use from cognitive, physical, and social perspectives.

Stephen W. Draper has a PhD in artificial intelligence and worked as a post-doc with Don Norman, where he entered the field of human computer interaction, and co-authored the book, *User Centered System Design*. He is currently at the University of Glasgow, UK, where he has worked on evaluation of applications of learning technology, and developed the method of integrative evaluation. The practical teaching innovations he has recently been concerned with include the use of EVS in lectures, and setting up a peer assisted learning scheme.

Anita Duff has more than 35 years experience within the state educational system. She has been a classroom teacher and has led teams of teachers. She has a commitment to new areas of learning practice, especially with regard to literacy and understanding the learner. Currently, she is exploring the benefits of providing mentoring to novice classroom teachers.

Robert J. Dufresne received a doctorate in theoretical nuclear physics from the University of Massachusetts, USA, (1987). Recently, he has focused on building a theoretical understanding of "transfer of learning." He has a parallel interest in literacy, and runs a family business producing curriculum materials for reading recovery.

Kristi A. Durbin teaches educational research and career development theory in the Department of Education, University of Canterbury, Christchurch, New Zealand. She earned BS and MS degrees in education from Purdue University, West Lafayette, Indiana, and the EdSpec and EdD degrees in higher education from Florida State University, Tallahassee, Florida. She is a member of Phi Beta Kappa, Golden Key, and Phi Kappa Phi honour societies, and the National Career Development Association.

Steven M. Durbin teaches introductory circuit analysis, electronics, solid-state devices, and electromagnetic field theory in the Department of Electrical and Computer Engineering, University of Canterbury, Christchurch, New Zealand. He earned his BS, ME, and PhD degrees in electrical engineering from Purdue University, West Lafayette, Indiana, and previously taught at Florida State University and Florida A&M University. His research interests are in the area of novel electronic materials. He is the co-author of more than 100 publications, including an undergraduate circuits text. Durbin is a senior member of the Institute of Electrical and Electronics Engineers and member of the Royal Society of New Zealand.

Tony Gear holds the chair of management and decision making at the University of Glamorganm UK. Gear is director of the Group Process research unit. His research is concerned with the development of theory and application of various forms of technology in support of room-based groups engaged on a wide variety of tasks. He has published papers that describe the use of online support for groups in decision conferencing, child protection conferences, focus groups, client assessment in social services, and assessment of research proposals for funding.

William J. Gerace is a professor of physics and director of SRRI. He earned a PhD in theoretical nuclear physics from Princeton University in 1967. In the 1970s, he branched out into physics education research (PER), founding UMPERG. He is a Fulbright senior specialist in science education, traveling extensively. In the first half of 2005, he taught physics or physics pedagogy on every continent but Antarctica, and he has long-term collaborations ongoing with South Africa, Argentina, and Cyprus.

Michele Groves graduated from Melbourne University with a BSc in biochemistry and microbiology, and subsequently spent many years as a hospital scientist in the public and private health care sectors. Her academic career began when she was employed to teach undergraduate students at a newly established medical school in Kuala Lumpur, Malaysia, which offered an integrated, problem-based learning (PBL) curriculum. On arriving in Queensland, Australia, Groves was employed by the Biochemistry Department of the University of Queensland to write, review, and tutor PBL cases, primarily in the University's newly introduced graduate entry, PBL Medical Program, but also in undergraduate science courses.

Sam Groves is a research assistant at the University of Glamorgan, currently completing an MPhil/PhD in the analysis of group-based judgment processes in the field of care sciences. Her work is focused on the use of a technological group support system (GSS) in the decision-making environment, specifically in the medical field. She achieved a BSc (Honors) in psychology with criminology, which has led to her current occupation as a PhD student for the University of Glamorgan Business School, and a PhD researcher for the University's School of Care Sciences. Her current research concerns the approach to analysing GSS group processes, and the effect of technological support systems in field settings.

Dominic Gruijters was born in the northern suburbs of Cape Town in 1982. He successfully completed high school in 2000 and enrolled for a BSc degree in Information Technology at the University of Cape Town the following year. He graduated in 2003 and obtained a place on the dean's merit list. In 2004 he went on to complete his BSc Honours degree in Computer Science with a first class pass. Dominic is currently working on his Masters degree in computer science. His fields of research are education and implementing computing technologies in developing nations. He enjoys hiking, camping, reading and wine-tasting.

Margaret Hamilton is a senior lecturer in the School of Computer Science and Information Technology, RMIT University, Melbourne. Her research interests extend to many aspects of computer science education and online technologies, as well as the area of bioinformatics and molecular modelling. In the area of teaching and learning in computer science, her interests include the planning, designing, and writing of programs; the concepts of problem-based learning; issues in the detection and management of plagiarism; and the implementation of wireless-based technologies, such as keypad voting devices and tablet computers for mobile computing.

Kevin Hinde is senior teaching fellow in strategy and economics at Durham Business School, UK. He has been actively involved in teaching and learning innovations within higher education. Until recently, he was a programme director for e-Learning and a learning and teaching coordinator at Northumbria University. In 2001, he won the Economics Centre of the Higher Education Academy prize for an "Outstanding Electronic Resource."

Harold M. Horowitz is president of Socratec, Inc., USA, a company dedicated to the design, development, and marketing of interactive, PowerPoint™ presentation systems. Dr. Horowitz retired from IBM after many years of service as a systems engineer, project manager, and in various executive management positions. His last project at IBM was as program director of the educational technology area, where he was responsible for developing instructional automation to improve the learning process. He served as an adjunct professor at the University of Maryland and the University of Connecticut. Currently living in Florida, he volunteers his time to instruct teachers in interactive instructional design with the hope that the ARS technology could make a difference in the "No student left behind" initiative in the U.S.

Jiankun Hu is a senior lecturer at the School of Computer Science and Information Technology, RMIT University, Australia. He has obtained a master's by research degree in computer science and software engineering, Monash University, Australia, and a PhD in the field of electrical and electronic engineering from the Harbin Institute of Technology, P.R. China. He was awarded the prestigious research fellowship from the Alexander von Humboldt Foundation, Germany. He has been awarded two ARC (Australia Research Council) Linkage Grants. His current research interest is in the field of networking and security. He has more than 60 publications in refereed, international journals, and conferences.

Julie A. Hulme is a senior lecturer in psychology at Staffordshire University, and a member of the Higher Education Academy and the British Neuroscience Association. She has experience of teaching biology and neuroscience (in which she has a PhD), as well as psychology, and has also worked in education. Her teaching experience has been gained in a variety of institutions, including Further Education, as well as several universities (Manchester Metropolitan, Keele and Staffordshire), and this has led her to a strong interest in student learning styles, and effective teaching. Her most recent research interests include widening participation, student support, adult basic skills learning, and cognitive neuropsychology.

Andrew Hunt is a research associate at Durham Business School, UK. Until recently, he was a senior lecturer in economics at Northumbria University.

Cath Jones is a principal lecturer and undergraduate coordinator in the School of Humanities, Law and Social Sciences, University of Glamorgan, UK. She has used group support systems (GSS) for teaching undergraduates, postgraduates, and professional groups. Her research focuses on two areas: issues surrounding collaboration, and applications of technology in educational settings. She has published on the use of GSS in interprofessional situations and higher education. Currently, she focuses on online learning, and a critical evaluation of the student experience. She is part of an evaluation team undertaking a longitudinal study of an online learning project in higher education. From this, she has presented papers on collaboration in online learning.

Matt Jones has recently moved from New Zealand to Wales (UK), where he is helping to set up the Future Interaction Technology Lab at Swansea University. He has worked on mobile interaction issues for the past 10 years and has published a large number of articles in this area. He has had many collaborations and interactions with major handset and service developers, including Orange, Reuters, BT Cellnet, Nokia, and Adaptive Info; he has one mobile patent pending. He is an editor of the *International Journal of Personal and Ubiquitous Computing*, and on the steering committee for the Mobile HCI conference series. Along with Gary, he has recently completed a book for John Wiley & Sons titled *Mobile interaction design* (published late 2005).

Eugene Judson began his career in education teaching science to seventh- and eighth-grade students. He was the director of evaluation for the Arizona Collaborative for Excellence in the Preparation of Teachers. He has held the position of director of academic and instructional support at the Arizona Department of Education, and is currently a research scientist at Arizona State University, USA, for CRESMET — a research center that focuses on the applications of educational technology, science, and mathematics in grades K through 20. Dr. Judson earned his master's degree in educational media and computers, and completed his doctorate in curriculum and instruction. Dr. Judson's dissertation examined the relationship between teachers' beliefs about learning processes and how teachers use technology in classrooms.

Gregor E. Kennedy is a senior lecturer and head of the Biomedical Multimedia Unit, an educational technology research and development unit within the Faculty of Medicine, Dentistry and Health Sciences at the University of Melbourne, Australia. The Unit supports the faculty with the design, development, implementation, and evaluation of technology for teaching and learning. Dr. Kennedy has been researching in the educational technology field for many years and is principally interested in multimedia interactivity and cognitive engagement, the use of audit trails to investigate learning processes and outcomes, and student-centred evaluation.

Sally Kift is an associate professor at Queensland University of Technology, Australia, and is the assistant dean, teaching and learning in the QUT Faculty of Law. Her particular research interests are in legal education and criminal law, and she has published widely in both. Kift has received national recognition for her excellence in teaching, and was short listed as a finalist in the Australian Awards for University teaching (AAUT) in 2001 (*Law and Legal studies category*). In 2003, she was one of eight national Teaching Award winners (winning the AAUT *Economics, Business, Law and Related Studies* category) who each received a $40,000 federal government grant. Among other things, this award acknowledged Kift's work in first-year curriculum development, support for casual teaching staff, the improvement of the first-year student experience, and the development of graduate capabilities in core curriculum.

Leon M. Lederman, internationally renowned specialist in high-energy physics, is director *emeritus* of the Fermi National Accelerator Laboratory in Batavia, Illinois. Since 1998, he holds the position of resident scholar at the Illinois Mathematics and Science Academy (IMSA), and since 1993, Pritzker professor of science at the Illinois Institute of Technology in Chicago. Lederman is a member of the National Academy of Sciences, and has received numerous awards, including the National Medal of Science (1965) and the Nobel Prize in Physics (1988). He was instrumental in founding IMSA, a residential high school for the gifted, and the Teachers Academy for Math and Science, which provides professional development for primary school teachers in Chicago.

William J. Leonard led development of the successful NSF-funded Minds•On Physics curriculum (ESI-9255713) for inquiry-based high school physics. He has, of late, been developing innovative assessment tools, studying methods for detecting and quantifying students' active mental "engagement" in learning activities, and teaching for the UMass Department of Electrical and Computer Engineering. He also works at the considerably more challenging task of raising two young children.

Gary Marsden is currently an associate professor in the Department of Computer Science at the University of Cape Town, South Africa. Formerly, he was part of the Interaction Design Centre at Middlesex University, London, and he holds a PhD in HCI from Stirling University, Scotland. He has been working in the field of mobile interaction for the last 10 years. In particular, he is excited at the potential mobile computing has to make a significant impact in developing countries.

Michael McCabe is a principal lecturer in the Department of Mathematics at the University of Portsmouth on the south coast of England. He has considerable experience of using different types of audience response system in his teaching of mathematics and astronomy. He has a general interest in the use of learning technology, including computer-assisted assessment, online learning, and simulation software. In 2001, he was awarded a UK National Teaching Fellowship to support his work on "Live and OnLine Assessment" project (LOLA).

Sandy Minck gained her medical degree in 1989, and completed the Fellowship of the Royal Australian College of General Practitioners (RACGP) in 1996. Minck has more than 10 years experience in medical education, specialising in interactive educational methodologies. She was the manager of the Quality Assurance and Continuing Education Unit of the RACGP Queensland Faculty from 1996-2001, where she was responsible for implementing the RACGP's continuing development program for GPs, designing and developing educational programs, and supporting and educating providers of medical education. In 2001, Minck travelled to London, where she designed and implemented the online continuing medical education program for Doctor's.net.uk, the UK's largest internet portal for doctors.

Vivienne O'Connor is an associate professor at the University of Queensland, Australia, and Bond University involved with the MBBS Programs. She established a Standardised Patient Program for Queensland, and is co-editor of the textbook *Obstetrics, Gynaecoloy and Women's Health* (Cambridge University Press).

Tim Pelton is an assistant professor in the Department of Curriculum and Instruction, University of Victoria, Canada, where he teaches courses in mathematics education and technology in education. His research interests include numeracy, measurement, and the application of technology to enhance learning. He has co-developed the enhanced instructional presentation model (EIP) and the classroom interaction system (CIS). Other areas of current research include the creation of meaningful measurement scales of learning and growth, the examination of learning theories and instructional practice in mathematics, problem based learning (PBL), gambling and numeracy, and computer adaptive testing (CAT).

Leslee Francis Pelton is an associate professor in the Department of Curriculum and Instruction at the University of Victoria, Canada, where she teaches courses in mathematics education and technology in education. Her areas of interest include numeracy, problem solving, assessment, and technology applications to enhance learning. She has codeveloped the enhanced instructional presentation model (EIP) and the classroom interaction system (CIS). Other areas of current research include mathematics curriculum analysis, computer-mediated learning, and gambling and numeracy.

William R. Penuel is senior researcher at the Center for Technology in Learning, SRI International, USA. His research focuses on technology supports for inquiry learning, and assessment in science and technology education. He brings more than 10 years experience in conducting evaluations of programs in schools, youth development organizations, and community centers. His current research interests center around new methodologies for studying the effectiveness of designs for learning with technology in school and community settings.

Martin Read is head of Department of Business Information Systems in the Business School at the University of Portsmouth, UK. He is a member of the School's Centre for Enterprise Research and Innovation. He has published widely on applications of "group decision support systems," and is an expert on "groupware programming" and associated software for the support of groups engaged on a variety of tasks, including training in groups, classroom support, project selection, marginal economic analysis, and multiple criteria decision making. He is very experienced in database design and maintenance.

Jeremy Roschelle is co-director of the Center for Technology in Learning at SRI International, USA. His research examines the design and classroom use of innovations that offer the possibility of enabling many more people to learn complex and conceptually difficult ideas in mathematics and science. Through cognitive science-based research on the "Envisioning Machine" and later "SimCalc," he has explored how computer-based representations can make the mathematics of change, and the related physics of motion, more accessible to students. Two themes in his work are the study of collaboration in learning, and the appropriate use of advanced or emerging technologies (such as component software and wireless handhelds) in education.

Daiyo Sawada is an *emeritus* professor of education at the University of Alberta, Canada, where for 35 years he worked in mathematics education, educational research methodology, and foundations of education. During that time, he published more than 100 journal papers, and participated in the supervision of more than 150 master's and PhD students in the areas of math education, science education, ESL, language arts, music education, educational administration, educational technology, educational psychology, curriculum studies, anthropology, and general systems theory. Since officially retiring from the University of Alberta in 1998, he served as the external evaluator for two major NSF-funded projects in math/science education, both headquartered at Arizona State University.

Felix Valenzuela earned his bachelor's degree in political science (*cum laude*) from the University of Texas at El Paso (2003). He is in his final year of Juris Doctorate study at Yale Law School, where he is an editor for the *Yale Journal of Law and the Humanities*.

Robert Webking is a professor of political science at the University of Texas at El Paso, USA. His work is in the area of political thought and philosophy, and he has taught extensively with and about innovative instructional technology.

Graeme White has been a full-time member of staff at RMIT University, Australia, since 1989, and is actively involved in undergraduate teaching of object oriented programming and data communication and networking, in the School of Computer Science and IT. He obtained a Bachelor of Science and Bachelor of Education from Monash University. His research interests include distributed systems, service oriented computing, grid computing.

Mick Wood has been building Web sites since 1995, and is an accredited university IT trainer. He currently works at University of Central Lancashire, in Preston, UK, as a multimedia development officer in the Learning Development Unit (LDU). He has a first class BA (Honors) in accounting and an MSc in multimedia computing, and has been researching Web accessibility and usability since 2000. He has presented at several UK Web accessibility conferences including the 2002, RNIB sponsored, Techshare Conference at the International Conference Centre in Birmingham, and has also organized four Web-accessibility conferences at UCLAN. He began working on the IRS system early in 2004.

Index